PEOPLE AND ORGANIZATIONS
Cases in Management and
Organizational Behavior

Consulting Editor in Management

JOHN M. IVANCEVICH
University of Houston

PEOPLE AND ORGANIZATIONS

Cases in Management and Organizational Behavior

JOHN E. DITTRICH

College of Business and Administration
University of Colorado

ROBERT A. ZAWACKI

College of Business and Administration
University of Colorado

1981

BUSINESS PUBLICATIONS, INC.
Plano, Texas   75075
IRWIN-DORSEY LIMITED
Georgetown, Ontario   L7G 4B3

ISBN 0-256-02423-5
Library of Congress Catalog Card No. 80–68032

Printed in the United States of America

1 2 3 4 5 6 7 8 9 0 ML 8 7 6 5 4 3 2 1

To a father, Mike Zawacki,
and a son, Jacob Dittrich,
who is braver than he knows.

Preface

This selection of cases is a compilation of the work of over 50 authors, practitioners and teachers who represent an extremely broad spectrum of backgrounds and interests (see "About the Contributing Authors"). In the book we hope to present to students of management and organizational behavior a variety of situations and settings in which a realistic and pragmatic analysis of specific organizational behavior topics can be conducted. Some of the shorter cases represent narrowly focused topics. The longer, more complex cases, however, as the real-life situations they report, reflect a multitude of topics—interrelating to provide a rich fabric of human forces and behaviors in work organizations.

The general design of the book is compatible with a wide range of popular books in organizational behavior and management. We have arranged the cases according to topic areas found in nearly all organizational behavior textbooks. The sections are arranged in groups which correspond to the appropriate level of analysis. The topics of perception, attitudes, personality, and motivation, for example, are found in a grouping best addressed at the level of the individual. Group dynamics, conflict, and communication are examined at the level of the group; and power, authority, formal organizations, and environmental influences at the level of the organization. A fourth grouping deals with specific forms of management intervention. In this grouping, MBO, behavior modification, and job design or redesign are examples of topics covered.

For students unfamiliar with the use of cases, a business case is a reporting—as accurately as possible—of a real-life situation. We have included below a brief section entitled "About Cases and the Case Method" which provides information about cases in general, and about the cases in this book.

ABOUT THE CASES AND THE CASE METHOD

There are three basic methodologies for teaching organizational behavior and management courses: lectures, cases and incidents, and experiential approaches. Each methodology has advantages and disadvantages.

For example, the lecture method offers the professor and students the advantages of: (1) conveying a lot of information in a short period of time, and (2) expert structuring of desired student learning outcomes. The advantages of the lecture method, however, may be more than offset by the disadvantages of: (1) students becoming bored and "turning off" the professor, (2) students using one or, at most, two of their senses (hearing and sight), and (3) the responsibility for learning outcomes resting on the shoulders of the professor. Thus, should students fail to learn the course material, they might say, "The professor didn't teach me anything."

The experiential approach reached its apex in the early 1970s. It is a teaching method that actively involves students in the learning process. Learning by doing involves many of the senses of the students who assume the major responsibility for learning. Disadvantages of experiential learning are: (1) it is a time-consuming approach—many exercises require two hours or more to complete; (2) it requires a professor who has the ability to summarize and bring closure on an exercise (otherwise, students may have fun, but not achieve course objectives); and (3) it is a method that assumes mature students who want to and are able to undertake the responsibility for their learning outcomes.

The third organizational behavior and management teaching methodology is the case and incident method. Cases as teaching tools originated from the early Harvard approach to teaching management which attempted to help the student close the "gap" between classroom theory and real-world practice by having students analyze real-world situations (cases) in the classroom. During the classroom discussion of a real-world case, the students will improve their diagnostic and problem-solving skills and also can learn by listening to numerous other students analyzing and presenting solutions to incidents and cases.

WHAT IS MEANT BY AN INCIDENT OR CASE?

This book consists of cases and incidents about organizational behavior and management. All the cases and incidents are based upon the description of real people in real organizations. None of the cases or incidents are contrived to make a point. The actual names of the participants and organizations have been changed to disguise or protect the real-world participants.

The thoughts and conversations found in this book reflect all of the strengths and inadequacies of the people found in these organizations, including their ability to communicate effectively. The transcribed conversations and comments of individuals, therefore, in some cases contain grammar, sentence structure, and syntax that could be improved upon. We believe, however, that despite these deficiencies, they provide, in their original form, a true sense of reality and immediacy, and have retained these sections without modification.

The incident, as a learning tool, is a short case that is based upon an actual situation. It is concise, and is written so that the student can easily identify a major issue. The typical manager in organizations is often confronted with decisions about "people problems" for which there are few or no precedents and very little factual data. The incident provides the student of organizational behavior and management with an immediate situation that must be diagnosed, analyzed, and resolved. In summary, it provides the student with challenges similar to those they will face on a daily basis in the "real world" of organizational behavior, on the job.

Incidents differ from cases not only in terms of depth of content but also in terms of the numbers of complex issues. The cases in this book were selected because they present the reader with the opportunity to focus on the application of organization behavior concepts and theories and by describing management problems in a wide range of work settings—both in the public and private sectors of our economy. Additionally, the incidents and cases in this book have been selected to demonstrate management problems in both decentralized and centralized organizations and small, medium, and large firms. An analysis of the incidents and cases in this book will reveal the following distribution.

Geographic Locations	*Percent*
Eastern United States	28.6
Midwestern United States	26.8
Western United States	19.6
Southern United States	17.9
Foreign	6.6

Sectors
Private

Manufacturing	33.9
Business	12.5
Other	23.2

Food service	Retail/wholesale
Insurance	Trade
Real estate	Data processing
Research	

Public

Hospital/medical	7.1
Government agency	12.6
University	3.6
Other	7.1

Airline
Library
Banking

Size

Large	21.4
Medium	35.7
Small	42.9

It is well to remember that there are no "right" or "wrong" answers to incidents or cases. Rather, each incident and case may have numerous solutions. The real learning outcome from incidents and cases is derived from a good exchange of information in the classroom by all the students.

Every student's opinion is to be valued and listened to, for out of diverse opinions comes an increased list of options for present and future managers. Student participation in classroom discussion is therefore an essential ingredient in learning, through this case approach, and cannot be over-emphasized.

STUDY SUGGESTIONS

After a quick reading of the case to determine its general content, students should carefully reread each case, considering any and all of the factors that may have a bearing on the attitudes expressed or behaviors demonstrated by persons described in the case. Once satisfied that at least *some* of the causal factors have been identified, students should attempt to relate the episode to their own experience in a similar setting, or where circumstances are similar. Finally, students may wish to attempt to project themselves into the role or roles of supervisors or managers in the case, and ask themselves what managerial actions would be appropriate in dealing with the situation. Notes taken through these three steps will be quite helpful in preparing for and participating in the discussion of the case in the classroom. Instructors may wish to assign study questions and assignments to assist students in focusing on a particular issue in the case.

We wish to express our deep appreciation to all the contributing authors whose work in case preparation and development is reflected in this collection. In addition, we wish to express our thanks to Randy Lang, Dennis Atkinson, Sandy Dittrich, and Lynn Munroe for their assistance in the preparation of the manuscript.

J. E. Dittrich
R. A. Zawacki

About the Contributing Authors

YOHANNAN T. ABRAHAM, Ph.D. (University of Oklahoma) is Associate Professor of Management at Southwest Missouri State University where he has been on the faculty since 1969. In addition to his teaching experience, he has held positions in several private firms both here and abroad. He is also engaged in providing management development programs and is a member of the Academy of Management and the American Society for Personnel Administration.

STEPHEN A. ALLEN, D.B.A. (Harvard Business School) is Professor of Management and Organizational Behavior at Babson College, Wellesley, Massachusetts. He has worked as a free-lance consultant in Europe and has held positions as Professor of Business Administration at IMEDE (Management Development Institute), Lausanne, Switzerland, and as assistant Professor at the Harvard Business School. His research, teaching and consulting activities center around organizational planning and executive role strategies.

FRANK C. BARNES, P.E., Ph.D. (Georgia State University) is an Associate Professor of Business Administration at the University of North Carolina at Charlotte. Prior to his doctoral work, he spent ten years in engineering and management with five companies, lastly as senior consultant in organizational problem solving with a major CPA firm. He has pursued an interest in the process of actual problem solving in complex organizational settings through research and case writing based on field experience. He is active in the Southern Case Research Association, AIIE, and the Academy of Management.

DAROLD T. BARNUM, Ph.D. (University of Pennsylvania) is Associate Professor of Labor and Industrial Relations at Indiana University Northwest. His work in the area of equal employment opportunity includes a book on racial practices in bituminous coal mining, and (with Gopal Pati) an article concerning the impact of Consent Decree I on the steel industry's human resource allocation system. Dr. Barnum has trained management and union representatives in collective bargaining, and has written cases, articles, and books on various aspects of labor relations.

HRACH BEDROSIAN, Ph.D. (Columbia University) is a Professor of Organizational Behavior and Management at the School of Business New York University. He is the author of numerous articles and a consultant to the American Bankers Association.

JAMES R. BRADSHAW, Ed.D. (Brigham Young University) is an Associate Professor of Business at Brigham Young University, Hawaii Campus. He has also been the business Division Chairman since December 1975 to the present. His previous experience has included teaching as a visiting full professor at Chaminade University, Honolulu, MBA program, and a student loan officer for the State Bank of Southern Utah. He is the author of a number of cases and articles and is a member of Delta Pi Epsilon, HBEA, WBEA, and NBEA.

EARL BURK, B.E.-Mech. (University of Missouri, Rolla) is a professional engineer and a graduate student in business administration at Southwest Missouri State University.

PAUL J. CHAMPAGNE, Ph.D. (University of Massachusetts) is Assistant Professor of Management at Michigan Technological University. His previous experience includes teaching at the University of Massachusetts and North Adams State College, plus several years as an insurance underwriter for the Travelers Insurance Company. He is the author of several cases and articles and is a member of the Academy of Management.

PATRICK E. CONNOR, Ph.D. (University of Washington) is Associate Professor of Management at Oregon State University. His major research interests concern the relationship of values to various organizational properties, and the management of long-term health care institutions. He has published numerous articles and three books on management and organizations.

GEORGE G. EDDY, Ph.D. (University of Texas) is a Lecturer of Management at the University of Texas at Austin. He is a consultant to small businesses, the author of numerous cases and articles, and is a member of the Southern Case Research Association and the Academy of Management.

GERALDINE B. ELLERBROCK, Ph.D. (Ohio State University) is a Professor of Management at California Polytechnic State University, San Luis Obispo. She is a member of the labor panel of the American Arbitration Association and an Accredited Personnel Specialist. She is a consultant for unions and management. Her cases have been published by the Harvard Intercollegiate Case Clearing House and in texts. She has written a casebook, *People Problems*.

BRUCE D. EVANS, M.B.A. (University of Michigan) is a resident faculty member at the Graduate School of Management, University of Dallas, where he has served since 1969. Consultant to numerous firms on management matters, he also draws upon his ten prior years in the non-life insurance industry, as a financial executive. He is the author of several cases and articles and was named an Outstanding Educator of America in 1974.

MARGARET FENN, Ph.D. (University of Washington) is a Professor of Business Administration at the University of Washington. She is a consultant to manufacturing, religious, banking, government (federal and state), and educational organizations. She is the author of numerous cases and articles.

HUGH L. FRENCH, JR., B.S.E. (Johns Hopkins University), M.B.A. (University of Dallas) is Manager of Career Development and College Relations at E-Systems, Inc., Garland Division. He is a registered Professional Engineer in the state of Texas.

JERRY L. GEISLER, Ph.D. (University of Missouri-Columbia) is an Associate Professor of Management at Southwest Missouri State University. His previous experience includes two years as Associate Professor of Management, Eastern

Illinois University. He has presented papers at Midwest AIDS and the Mountain-Plains Management Conference and is a member of the Academy of Management and the Southern Management Association.

VIRGINIA T. GEURIN, Ph.D. (University of Arkansas) is an Associate Professor of Business Administration at the University of North Carolina at Charlotte. She teaches in the organizational behavior area and is particularly interested in the area of male/female managerial styles and effectiveness.

MARK HAMMER, D.B.A. (Indiana University) is a Professor of Business Administration at Washington State University, where he specializes in management and organization development. He is the author of numerous articles in instructional technology, and is active as a trainer and consultant to a variety of business and government organizations. His experience includes service to IBM Corporation and Willamette University.

WILLIAM D. HEIER, Ph.D. (The American University) is a Professor of Management at Arizona State University. He has broad experience as a consultant to businesses and governmental agencies. He is very active in the business community, serving on several boards of directors. Currently, he is the chairman of the board of two consulting firms, in Florida and Arizona; the chairman of the board of an Arizona bank, and the chairman of the board of trustees of two national retirement and pension plans. He is the author of numerous articles and cases.

J. DAVID HUNGER, Ph.D. (Ohio State University) is an Associate Professor of Management and Organizational Behavior at the McIntire School of Commerce of the University of Virginia. He has conducted research and written articles on conflict management, management education, and organization climate for various journals. In addition, he has worked closely with the State of Virginia in conducting employee selection and performance appraisal seminars. He has written numerous cases and is a member of the Academy of Management, Southern Management Association, and American Psychological Association.

JAMES G. (JERRY) HUNT, Ph.D. (University of Illinois) is a Professor of Administrative Sciences at Southern Illinois University at Carbondale. He is the author of more than 60 articles and papers and has co-written or edited 6 books. He is past president of the Midwest Academy of Management and the Organizational Behavior Division of the Academy of Management.

BARBARA KARMEL, Ph.D. (Purdue University) is Associate Dean for Research and Professor of Organizational Behavior at the Atkinson Graduate School of Administration, Willamette University. She also serves as Director of the Center for Business-Government Studies. Her previous experience included three years as Associate Professor of Management, University of Wisconsin–Madison, and four years as Assistant/Associate Professor of Management, Oregon State University. She has published several articles and a book on leadership, job satisfaction, and managerial performance.

HERBERT S. KINDLER, Ph.D. (UCLA) is Assistant Professor of Management at Whittier College. His previous experience includes ten years as chief executive officer at the Instrument Society of America, a 20,000-member national engineering association. He is listed in *Who's Who in America*.

CHARLES R. KLASSON, D.B.A. (University of Indiana) is a Professor in the Department of Management Sciences at the University of Iowa, Iowa City.

ROBERT W. KNAPP, Ph.D. (University of Michigan) is a Professor of Business Administration at the University of Colorado, Colorado Springs. From 1972 to 1976 he was Associate Dean of the College of Business and Administration. His previous experience included two years as Assistant Professor of Business Economics at UCLA, and three years as staff economist at the General Motors Corporation. He is the co-author, with J. Daniel Couger, of *System Analysis Techniques.*

HAK-CHONG LEE, D.B.A. (Washington University) is a Professor of Management at State University of New York at Albany. He is currently Acting Director of International Management Institute in Seoul, Korea, on leave from SUNY at Albany. His previous experience includes visiting professorships at Yonsei University, University of Hawaii, and NSF research fellowship. He has written numerous cases and articles.

STEVEN A. LIPPMAN, Ph.D. (Stanford) is Professor of Management at UCLA, Graduate School of Management. He has written extensively on operations research, and the economics of risk and uncertainty with respect to investments and insurance.

CRAIG C. LUNDBERG, Ph.D. (Cornell University) is Dean and Professor of the School of Management, State University of New York (Binghamton). He has written over 65 professional articles and has consulted on organizational change to many private and public organizations. His previous experience included Oregon State University, Southern Methodist University, and the University of Pennsylvania. He is a member of the Academy of Management, the Organizational Behavior Teaching Society, and the American Sociological Association.

DAVID McGILL, B.S. (Southern Illinois University) is presently employed by a Fortune 500 company as a District Sales Manager.

GARY F. McKINNON, Ph.D. (University of Texas at Austin) is an Associate Professor of Business Management at Brigham Young University. He has taught at Southern Illinois University and the University of Texas, and has taught in graduate military programs for the University of Utah and the University of Montana. He is a member of the American Marketing Association, Association for Consumer research and is the author of numerous cases and articles.

LEON C. MEGGINSON, Ph.D. (Louisiana State University), Research Professor of Management at the University of South Alabama, has been president of the Case Research Association; Ford Foundation Resident Advisor for Management and Case Development in Pakistan; and Fulbright Research Scholar in Spain. He has written or co-written 9 books, and written over 100 cases.

EDWARD F. MILLS, B.S.B.A. (Philadelphia College of Textile and Science) is presently on the staff of the Collins and Aikman Corporation as Accounts Receivable Manager. He is enrolled in graduate studies at the University of North Carolina at Charlotte.

RONNIE L. MOSS, Ph.D. (University of Oklahoma) is a Professor of Management at Northwest Missouri State University. He has taught at various universities and has consulting experience with industry related to computer systems analysis. He has written many articles in management and data processing and has served in various offices in professional organizations.

JOHN A. MURTHA, B.A. (University of Washington) is a Foreign Service Officer in the U.S. Department of State. He has served in or inspected 29 missions in 21 countries. His previous experience includes seven years with the U.S. General Accounting Office in Seattle, Honolulu, and Washington, D.C.

NICK NYKODYM, Ph.D. (University of Toledo) completed his doctoral work in the fields of Organizational Behavior and Organization Development. He has had over ten years of experience in both line and staff management. He has had extensive experience as a consultant to various health care, service, retail, business, governmental, educational, and industrial organizations throughout the United States. He has published research in a wide variety of areas including consulting, organization development, and organizational communication.

GOPAL C. PATI, Ph.D. (Illinois Institute of Technology) is a Professor of Industrial Relations and Management at Indiana University Northwest. Besides teaching, he consults with numerous manufacturing and service organizations nationally in the area of management and organization development. He is the author of numerous cases and articles and is a member of the Academy of Management, Industrial Relations Association of Chicago, Human Resource Planning Society, and many other organizations.

DONALD J. PETERSEN, Ph.D. (Illinois Institute of Technology) is Professor of Management at Loyola University of Chicago. He has written numerous papers and has several cases published by Harvard University's Intercollegiate Case Clearing House. In addition, Dr. Petersen is a practicing labor arbitrator, listed on the panels of the American Arbitration Association and Federal Mediation and Conciliation Service. He is a member of the Academy of Management, Industrial Relations Research Association, and the American Society of Personnel Administrators.

DEWAYNE J. PIEHL, Ph.D. (University of Michigan) taught business policy at the University of Washington School of Business Administration. His previous experience included engineering and manufacturing management with a major electric motor firm.

TERRELL F. PIKE, Ph.D.(University of Mississippi) is Chairman of the Department of Management at the University of South Alabama. Dr. Pike has been a management consultant, a consultant in economic statistics, and is a Labor-Management Arbitrator listed on the Panel of Arbitrators of the American Arbitration Association. Her previous experience includes teaching Management and Economics at the University of West Florida, the University of Mississippi, and the University of Southern Mississippi. She is a member of the Academy of Management, American Association of University Administrators, and the American Economic Association.

W. DANIEL ROUNTREE, Ph.D. (Louisiana State University) is Professor of Marketing at Appalachian State University. His experience includes three years as Assistant Professor at Virginia Polytechnic Institute, seven years as merchandise manager with Thalheimer Department Stores, and three years with Sears. During academic year 1978 he served as Fulbright Lecturer in Istanbul, Turkey. He is the author of numerous cases and articles and is a member of American Marketing Association.

THOMAS J. RYBALTOWSKI, M.B.A. (State University of New York at Albany) is presently serving as Treasurer of the North Colonie Central School District,

Newtonville, New York. His previous experience includes management training specialist with the Peace Corps in 1976–77.

JERRY SAEGERT, J.D. (University of Texas) is a Lecturer on Personnel Management, Labor Relations, and Organizational Behavior at the University of Texas at Austin. He maintains a full-time law practice and lectures often for management development programs.

JACK L. SIMONETTI, D.B.A. (University of Toledo) is Department Chairman and Professor of Management, University of Toledo. Dr. Simonetti has published over 60 articles and presented over 45 papers in such journals and meetings as *The Academy of Management Journal, The Academy of Management Proceedings, Management International Review, Journal of Systems Management, The Journal of the Academy of Marketing Science,* and the *Personnel Journal.*

K. MARK WEAVER, Ph.D. (Louisiana State University) is Associate Professor of Business Administration at the University of Alabama. He previously taught at Bradley University. He is President of the Small Business Institute Directors Association. Dr. Weaver is author of numerous cases and articles.

THOMAS L. WHEELEN, D.B.A. (George Washington University) is a Professor of Management at McIntire School of Commerce at the University of Virginia. He has served as a Visiting Professor at the University of Arizona and Northeastern University. He is co-editor of *Development in Management Information Systems,* and *Collective Bargaining in Public Sector.* He is the author of numerous articles, cases and papers. He is serving on the Board of Directors of Southern Management Association.

GARY G. WHITNEY, Ph.D. (University of Washington) is an Assistant Professor of Management and Administrative Systems at Washington State University. He has been a consultant to many public and private organizations. He is a member of the Academy of Management and American Institute of Decision Sciences.

JOHN T. WHOLIHAN, Ph.D. (The American University) is Professor of Business Administration and Associate Dean at Bradley University. He is also Director of the M.B.A. program. He is active in the Midwest Case Writers Association and the Small Business Institute Program. He has written numerous cases. He is a member of the Academy of Management and the Academy of International Business.

RONALD M. ZIGLI, Ph.D. (Georgia State University) is Associate Professor of Management, and Assistant Dean of the College of Business at Appalachian State University in Boone, North Carolina. He has had more than eight years of experience in industry before coming back to academe. Particular areas of interest are the behavioral aspects of organizational management. He has conducted research in the areas of motivation, job satisfaction, job performance, small group behavior, and organization development. He has published in a variety of professional journals and periodicals and is an active member of the Academy of Management, American Institute for Decision Sciences, and a number of other professional organizations.

VIRGIL B. ZIMMERMAN, Ph.D. (Yale University) is Associate Professor at the School of Business, State University of New York at Albany. He has been a Professor in the University of California (Berkeley) technical assistance project and at the Scuola Superiore in Science Administration, Universita' de Bologna.

He is a consultant, guest lecturer, and training session leader for governments and countries.

Other Contributing Authors:

ANN MARIE CALACCI

CHARLES I. CASH

T. ROGER MANLEY

LEE NEELY

ROBERT E. QUINN

RICHARD RITTER

SUSAN M. SZYMANSKI

FRANK YEANDEL

Contents

Section 1

THE INDIVIDUAL

Factors, Forces, and Processes
Which Affect Behavior
in Organizations through the
Attitudes and Actions
of Individual Persons

The cases in this section cover a wide range of topics generally addressed at the level of the individual. All topics relate to personal attributes and processes, or responses of persons, in organizations. Readers will quickly observe that the cases found in each section and subsection contain several organizational issues for analysis and discussion. Thus, a case which has elements related to personality may also contain factors and issues relevant to attitudes or group dynamics, topics found in Section 2. Indeed, all of the cases in this book reflect the complexity of the characters, organizations, and industries found in real life, since they are, in fact, descriptions of real life situations and people. In this section we will direct our attention to the elements which relate most closely to the individual—the organizational participant whose perceptions, attitudes, and personality affect and are affected by the situation which the case describes.

Cases dealing with the personality characteristics or attributes of the individual portray situations which reflect such things as the apparent needs of participants (e.g., need for achievement, or the desire to dominate others), the extent of their neurotic characteristics or tendencies, extroversion, and the extent to which the individual is self-controlled, or tends to be controlled by others. Attitudes of participants are another set of characteristics which may have a bearing on the behaviors of persons in organizations. The components of attitudes, the behavior-attitude linkage, and the need for consistency or harmony in attitude patterns are important concepts reflected in the cases in this section.

The mechanisms or systems used by individuals in dealing with the task, the situation, and the environment include perceptual processes wherein we organize, categorize, and classify the information which we receive; and learning processes where we develop and acquire the knowledge and abilities needed to deal with information and to respond effec-

1

tively to new or changing situations. The critical role of reinforcers in aiding the development and internalization of these new behaviors is an important element in learning, and can serve as an important point for discussion. Problem solving, a third topic included in this set of processes, and learning are very closely linked.[1] Indeed, one might conceptualize each new element of knowledge or skill to be learned as a "problem" which must be solved. As problem solving becomes more complex, the process becomes more complicated, variables are less well defined, uncertainties more significant, and decisions more value laden. Cognitive skills and abilities are needed to deal with these complexities, and must be acquired in order to more effectively deal with the complications encountered. In addition, the ability to *implement* a chosen solution becomes more recognizably significant, since a solution unimplemented does not resolve the problem as presented, and the problem-solving process has not been completed.

Stress, one of several responses to situations, can take the form of anxiety, frustration, and one or more behavioral reactions to these internal states. While a variety of on-job responses to organizational stressors can be noted, organizational stress can be linked directly to the state of one's health.[2]

The last topical area found in the cases in this section deals with the complex link between employee motivation, productivity, and satisfaction. The direction of causal linkages between satisfaction and productivity has been the subject of extensive controversy.[3] Several motivation models have been suggested by theorists. They range from relatively simple operant conditioning models, through elemental drive and need theories, to more complex multifactor theories, such as the need hierarchy of Maslow, the need profiles of McClelland, and the two-factor theory of Herzberg, to much more complex contingency models, such as the Porter-Lawler expectancy-instrumentality model, the path-goal model of motivation, and other goal models.[4]

The cases in this section, which encompass the topic of motivation, offer an opportunity to examine the application of several of these conceptualizations and for the exploration of the likely consequence of several alternative management actions. Behavioral evidence of employee-need patterns may link to any of several concepts of motivational factors. The role of the supervisor in reinforcing desired behaviors, clarifying linkages between rewards and performance, and clarifying and structuring the talk situation, all elements in the motivation models mentioned above, can also be explored and discussed as the basis for action.

---

[1] J. R. Lang, J. E. Dittrich, and S. E. White, "Managerial Problem Solving Models: A Review and a Proposal," *Academy of Management Review* (October 1978).

[2] L. O. Ruch and T. H. Holmes, "Scaling of Life Change: Comparison of Direct and Indirect Methods," *Journal of Psychosomatic Research* 15 (1971), p. 224.

[3] C. N. Greene, "The Satisfaction-Performance Controversy," *Business Horizons* 15 (1972), pp. 31–41.

[4] See, for example, J. D. Wofford, "A Goal-Energy-Effort Requirement Model of Work Motivation," *Academy of Management Review* 4, no. 2, pp. 193–201; and J. E. Quick, "Dyadic Goal Setting within Organizations: Role-Making and Motivational Considerations," *Academy of Management Review* 4, no. 3, pp. 369–80.

ADDITIONAL SELECTED READINGS

Bem, D. J., and Allen, A.   "On Predicting Some of the People Some of the Time: The Search for Cross-Situational Consistencies in Behavior." *Psychological Review* 81 (1974), pp. 506–20.

Calder, B. J., and Ross, M.   *Attitudes and Behavior.* Morristown, N.J.: General Learning Press, 1973.

Elbing, A. O.   *Behavioral Decision in Organizations.* Glenview, Ill.: Scott-Foresman, 1970.

Gibson, James L.; Ivancevich, John M.; and Donnelly, James H., Jr.   *Organizations: Behavior, Structure, Processes.* Dallas: Business Publications, 1979, chap. 4, pp. 61–91.

Hackman, J. R., and Lawler, E. E.   "Employee Reactions to Job Characteristics." *Journal of Applied Psychology* 55 (1971), pp. 259–86.

Hall, Douglas T., and Fukami, Cynthia V.   "Organization Design and Adult Learning." In Barry M. Staw, ed., *Research in Organizational Behavior,* vol. 1. Greenwich, Conn.: JAI Press, 1979, pp. 125–67.

Hamner, W. C., and Organ, D. W.   *Organizational Behavior: An Applied Psychological Approach.* Dallas: Business Publications, 1978, chap. 9, pp. 193–214.

Himmelfarb, S., and Eagly, A. H.   *Readings in Attitude Change.* New York: Wiley, 1974.

Joe, V. C.   "Review of the Internal-External Control Construct as a Personality Variable." *Psychological Reports* 28 (1971), pp. 619–40.

Jones, E. E., et al., eds.   *Attribution: Perceiving the Causes of Behavior.* Morristown, N.J.: General Learning Press, 1972.

McClelland, D. C.   *The Achieving Society.* Princeton, N.J.: Van Nostrand, 1961.

MacCrimmon, K. R., and Taylor, R. N.   "Decision Making and Problem Solving." In M. D. Dunnette, ed., *Handbook of Industrial and Organizational Psychology.* Chicago: Rand McNally, 1976.

Matteson, Michael T., and Ivancevich, John M.   "Organizational Stressors and Heart Disease: A Research Model." *The Academy of Management Review* 4, no. 3 (July 1979), pp. 347–57.

Mitchell, Terence R.   *People in Organizations: Understanding Their Behavior.* New York: McGraw-Hill, 1978, chap. 5, pp. 91–117.

Organ, D. W.   "Extraversion, Locus of Control, and Individual Differences in Conditionability in Organizations." *Journal of Applied Psychology* 60 (1975), pp. 401–4.

Secord, P. F.; Backman, C. W.; and Slavitt, D. R.   "Impression Formation and Interaction" and "Describing and Typing People," in *Understanding Social Life: An Introduction to Social Psychology.* New York: McGraw-Hill, 1976.

Steers, R. M., and Porter, L. W., eds.   *Motivation and Work Behavior.* New York: McGraw-Hill, 1975.

Strauss, George, and Sayles, Leonard R.   *Personnel: The Human Problems of Management.* Englewood Cliffs, N.J.: Prentice-Hall, 1980, chap. 5, pp. 97–116.

Case 1–1 ───────────────────────────────────

Land Office Realty Company (A)

Ronnie L. Moss

BACKGROUND

The Land Office Realty Company was formed five years ago by two brokers, Janet Mason and Doug Smith. Janet had previously worked for three years for another real estate broker and had specialized in town properties. Doug had previous experience in commercial real estate. Both individuals saw the need to combine their specialties and formed a partnership company.

The new company had had quite a successful five years. In addition to the two brokers, there are now six associates, two full-time secretaries, and one part-time clerk. Three of the real estate associates specialize in town properties, two specialize in commercial properties, and one specializes in farm properties.

The office is open six days a week and provides private office space for each associate and the two brokers. The office also provides all materials needed for selling to the associates, such as business cards, secretarial help, and advertising. Each associate makes his/her own appointments to take prospects to view properties and provides the necessary transportation for the prospects. They also have the responsibility to pick up typed listing sheets from the secretary for new listings and place them in their listing manual. Properties that have been sold are also to be removed from the manual by the associate.

For the services provided by the office, the associates must split their commission with the office. The associates receive 65 percent of the commission made on a sale and the realty office receives 35 percent. Usually the commission is 7 percent of the selling price of the property but can vary depending on several factors, including the type of sale, selling price, and financial arrangements.

The brokers also split their commissions in the same manner as above, but at the end of the year any profit made by the realty office is divided equally between them.

COMPETITIVE SALES STRATEGIES

Each associate is responsible for obtaining prospects. Once a prospect is obtained by an associate, the associate becomes the prospect's exclusive representative in the office. No other associate can show the prospect properties unless requested to do so by the original representative. The

4

original representative will receive any commission made on property sold to the prospect through Land Office Realty Company.

All associates may sell any property listed with the company even if they are considered specialists in another area. Selling usually involves showing the property to the prospect, obtaining an offer to buy the property for a certain amount, and having the broker convey this offer to the owner or seller of the property. By law, only the brokers can convey offers to the seller and deal with the seller concerning the listed property. The associate must have the broker convey the offer of the prospect, and it must be done by the broker for which the associate is working.

Other realty offices in the area may be aware that an associate of a competitive office has shown a property and may try to find out the name of the prospect and how to contact him. If they do contact him, they will try to get him to purchase properties listed in their office that he has not seen with the other associate. Thus, a prospect may have two or more realty offices competing for the commission by showing him similar properties at various prices.

The associate who has the prospect "in tow" should, at that time, show him the best properties listed and in the price range that may interest the prospect and encourage the broker to try to close the deal in the shortest time, with the best terms possible for both seller and buyer. The associate must plan ahead and arrange appointments, one after the other, allowing plenty of time to view the property, yet, being able to see all the best ones in as quick a time span as possible. The word will soon be out and the other offices will be trying to contact the prospect, so the associate must move fast. Obtaining keys, answering questions or researching for answers, making appointments, and endless other arrangements are all part of the selling strategy.

CONVEYING THE OFFER

Mary, one of the associates with a specialty in residential property, has Bob Fuller as a prospect. Mr. Fuller has indicated an interest in a location for a branch office of the firm he represents. Mary has shown him six commercial locations for the past two days, and he has expressed a definite desire in two of them. Since the broker must convey the offer, Mary and Bob have gone to Janet's office, closed the door for privacy, and Janet has contacted the seller. The property was listed at $90,000, and Mr. Fuller begins making offers at $78,000 because of some problems he found with the property.

Two hours later, with both the buyer and seller changing their pricing positions, they are still $4,000 apart and have not completed the deal. At this point, Mr. Fuller decides to give up and try to purchase the second property he desired.

The second property desired by Mr. Fuller is a building formerly occupied by a grocery store and located on West Fifth Street. Janet places a call to the seller to convey the offer, but the phone is busy so they sit in her office discussing remodeling plans for the building.

Susan, another associate who has a specialty in commercial property, has been out of the office all morning with Tom Felton, who is looking for a location for a small automobile parts store. She has shown him two properties, and he likes one of them—the unoccupied grocery store building on West Fifth Street. They arrive at the realty office and, noticing Janet's door closed, she and her prospect go to Doug's office so the offer can be conveyed. Doug tries to phone the owner, but the line is busy. Mr. Felton, who has to leave town this evening, suggests that they drive over to visit the owner. Doug and Susan agree, and they prepare to leave the realty.

Doug opens Janet's door to tell her where he is going and on what property he is going to convey an offer. At that time, he finds out that Janet also has an associate and prospect trying to reach the seller of the same property. The Code of Ethics will not permit the brokers to allow their respective prospects to bid against each other; thus a decision must be made as to who will be allowed to proceed. Whatever the decision, the amount of commission to the partnerships will be the same, but the associate that is not allowed to proceed will lose several thousand dollars in a commission. This decision must be made immediately as each prospect desires the property.

Case 1–2 ————————————————————————————————————

The New Manager

James R. Bradshaw and Gary F. McKinnon

FRIDAY, JUNE 22, 1979

It was a hot, muggy Friday afternoon as William (Bill) Young walked in the front door of the main office of Columbia Federal Savings and Loan. In spite of the heat, Bill was fairly cool and calm considering he was to meet with M. B. Willard, vice president of personnel at Columbia Federal Savings.

"Hello," said Marie Webster, Mr. Willard's secretary and personal friend of Bill's. "You know that rumor I told you about from the grapevine that you would be named the new manager of one of the branches? Well, it may not be as rosy as you think." Before Bill could respond, Mr. Willard walked out and escorted him into his private office. After shaking hands and exchanging pleasantries about the weather, Mr. Willard came right to the point.

> Bill, when you joined us from Island Federal 11 months ago, we thought a lot of your abilities. As we told you at that time, we are one happy family here at Columbia Federal and we take care of each other. Once you prove yourself, we help you all we can in moving up in the organization. There is an opening at our Liberty Branch, and we would

like you to become our new branch manager there. You're a good man, Bill, and this is your first big step to the top of the organization.

Bill expressed his gratitude and accepted the position with enthusiasm. After a few more minutes of conversation, Bill rose to leave as Mr. Willard said:

Oh, yes, Bill, there is one more thing I should mention. There is kind of a touchy situation at the branch that the last manager just was incapable of handling. We need it finalized by September 15—but why don't we put the matter on a back burner until you get your feet on the ground and I get back from a trip?

Marie was away from her desk on an errand, so Bill didn't have a chance to pursue her comment.

MONDAY, JUNE 25, 1979

As Bill returned from a short lunch, he was pleased with the events of the past week; and although Liberty was not one of the largest of Columbia's branches, it did provide adequate opportunity for Bill to demonstrate his managerial capabilities. Bill's thoughts were interrupted as Janet Cole, the operations manager, appeared at his desk very upset. "Bernadette is using the women's room again, and we want it stopped!" *"What?"* was all that Bill could reply before being cut off. "We're all walking off the job if it continues!" she shouted as she stormed back to her desk.

Bill was puzzled. Bernadette was a fairly attractive teller, about 35 years old and stylishly attired in slacks with matching blouse. Her hair was a bit too bleached to suit Bill, and she wore a bit too much makeup, but she appeared to be an efficient teller. In fact, he noticed that one of the tellers went to her for help on a problem that very morning.

He reached into his desk for the personnel folders Marie had sent over that morning from the central office. Bernadette's file was on the top of the stack. As he read over Bernadette's file, he was immediately stunned— she wasn't Bernadette Peters—*he* was Bernard Peters. "Oh, no," muttered Bill, "what kind of a mess have I stepped into now?"

As he looked over the file, he found that Bernard had been at the bank for six years and was second in seniority only to the operations manager. His reputation as a teller was excellent and he had received very good evaluations until after returning from his vacation the previous year. The report noted that when Bernard returned from vacation, he appeared dressed as a woman, including the bleached hair and overdone makeup. In fact, someone penciled in the margin of the report that Bernard had returned as a fairly attractive female. The two evaluations the past year were both negative, but said nothing of inadequate work procedures or skills. They were just negative about his/her appearance.

Bill placed a call to Mr. Willard, only to learn that he was away for the week attending a banking convention. Bill had dated Marie a couple of times recently so he felt secure in asking her about the situation. She was almost laughing as she replied,

Oh, so you met Bernadette? I hope you don't throw me over for her. [A bit of a chuckle came over the phone, but Bill was not amused.] You know, she is the talk of the whole organization. Well, seriously, Mr. Willard wants him fired, but the last branch manager was too slow to act so was phased out last month. That's why you were advanced so soon.

The grapevine says the big news is that he has asked for a month's leave of absence after his vacation in September in order to have a sex-change operation. Bernard will return as Bernadette—all the way through.

By the way, Bill, you had better have some alternatives ready when Mr. Willard returns. The sooner you can solve this problem the better off you'll be.

FRIDAY, JUNE 29, 1979

Bill spent the week trying to get a better perspective about the "Bernadette" situation. The first thing he determined from the employee interviews he held was that the females rejected the idea that Bernard could use the women's lounge. In fact, all were committed to the idea that he would be excluded even after the sex-change operation. On the other hand, Bernard said that after the operation he had a legal right to use all facilities for women, and he would expect that the personnel files would be changed, indicating he was a female.

Bill noted that the leave of absence had not yet been granted for Bernard's operation, but Bernard wanted an answer within the next few weeks. It was evident from the conversation that Bernard was not going to resign from the bank and was willing to fight for his rights. It looked as though a standoff was coming sooner than he wanted. There were some signs that the employee morale in the bank was beginning to suffer, which affected customer service.

That evening Bill broke a date to work on a list of alternatives he could present to Mr. Willard. He felt there may be other alternatives, but five seemed the most feasible. He wasn't sure which of the five he would recommend to Mr. Willard, but knew he had to reach a decision before their meeting Monday morning.

1. Terminate Bernard Peters.
2. Refuse the leave of absence so he could not have the operation.
3. Transfer Bernard Peters to another branch after the operation and not tell the other employees she used to be a he.
4. Treat Bernard (Bernadette) as a female with all rights to facilities, etc.
5. Do away with the restroom and lounges as presently arranged and use unisex restrooms and lounges.

Case 1–3 ——

Ned Norman, Committee Chairman

W. D. Heier

Ned Norman tried to reconstruct, in his own mind, the series of events that had culminated in that most unusual committee meeting this morning.

For example, each of the committee members had suddenly seemed to be stubbornly resisting any suggestions that did not exactly coincide with their own ideas for implementing the program under consideration. This unwillingness to budge from some preconceived position was not like the normal behavior patterns of most of the committee participants. Of course, some of the comments made in one of last week's sessions about "old-fashioned, seat-of-the-pants decision making" had ruffled a few feathers but Ned did not really think this was the reason things had suddenly bogged down today. Still, Ned thought it might be worthwhile to review in his mind what had taken place in this morning's meeting to see if some clues existed to explain the problem.

First, Ned recalled starting the session by saying that the committee had discussed, in past meetings, several of the factors connected with the proposed expanded-services program and it now seemed about time to make a decision as to which way to go. Ned remembered that Robert Roman had protested that they had barely scratched the surface of the possibilities for implementing the program. Then, both Sherman Stith and Tod Tooley, who worked in the statistics branch of Division Baker, had sided with Roman and were most insistent that additional time was needed to research in depth some of the other avenues of approach to solving the problems associated with starting the new program.

Walt West had entered the fray by stating that this seemed a little uncalled for, since previous experience had clearly indicated that expansion programs, such as this one, should be implemented through selected area district offices. This had brought forth the statement by Sherman Stith that experience was more often than not a lousy teacher, which was followed by Tod Tooley repeating his unfortunate statement about old-fashioned decision-making! And, of course, Robert Roman had not helped matters at all by saying that it was obviously far better to go a little bit slower in such matters by trying any new program in one area first, rather than to have the committee members look "unprogressive" by just "trudging along on the same old cow paths!"

In fact, as Ned suddenly realized, if he hadn't almost intuitively exercised his prerogatives as chairman to stop the trend that was developing, he might have had a real melee on his hands right then! It was obvious that things were increasingly touchy among the members, so much so that despite his best efforts, everyone had simply refused either to participate or to support any of the ideas he (Ned) had offered to break the deadlock.

Feeling a little frustrated, early that same afternoon Ned had sought the counsel of his boss, who advised him to go talk to the division directors for whom the various committee members worked. In each area visited, Ned found that the division director was already aware of the committee problems and each one had his own ideas as to what should be done about them.

The director of Division Able stated that he was not much in sympathy with people who wanted to make a big deal out of every program that came along. He recalled the problem six years ago when the first computer had arrived in the agency and was hailed as the manager's replacement in decision making. He noted that, although the computer was still here, so was he, and that he had probably made better decisions, as a result of his broad background and knowledge, than the computer ever would! The Division Able director told Ned that he had been on several deadlocked committees but that, when he was chairman, he had simply made the decision for the committee and solved the problem. He suggested Ned do likewise.

The Division Baker director stated that he knew Ned was one of those guys who wanted to use the best information available in estimating a program's performance. He told Ned that Sherman and Tod, who worked in Division Baker, had briefed him on the problems the committee had encountered and that, in his opinion, their investigative approach was the proper one to take. After all, stated the director, it logically followed that a decision could be no better than the research effort put into it. He also told Ned that, although he realized research might cost a little money, he had told Sherman and Tod to go ahead and collect the data they needed to determine the best way to implement the expansion program. The director flatly stated, "These are my men and my division will be footing the bill for this research, so no one else has any gripe about the cost aspects." He expressed the opinion that almost any price would be cheap if it would awaken some of the company employees to the tremendous values of a scientific approach to decision making.

The Division Charlie director stated, quite bluntly, that he was not particularly interested in how the expansion program was decided. He said it looked to him like the easiest way to get the thing moving was to do it a piece at a time. That way, he noted, you can evaluate how it looks without committing the company to a full-scale expansion. He concluded by saying, "It doesn't take a lot of figuring to figure that one out!"

The Division Delta director stated that the aspect of "time" was against the committee's looking at all angles and that a decision should be made after looking at two or three possible solutions. He stated that he needed Quentin Quinn, his representative on Ned's committee, for another job and hoped the committee would be finished very quickly.

Ned now realized that he had more of a problem than he had suspected. In view of the approaches and opinions expressed by the division directors, it seemed highly unlikely that any of the committee members would move from their present position. Ergo, Ned is now chairman of a deadlocked committee!

In pondering his dilemma, Ned considered various ways to break the impasse. First, as chairman, he could simply exert his authority and try to force a solution. This was guaranteed to alienate most of the committee members and the division directors, who had representatives on the committee.

Second, Ned considered returning to his boss, who had formed the committee, with the recommendation that the committee be disbanded. While the reasons for this recommendation would be easy to explain, Ned's failure to prevent this problem might be much more difficult.

As a third possibility, the idea occurred to Ned that he might ask each committee member to bring to the next meeting, in writing, his recommended plan for implementing the program. Since these would surely represent the thinking of the four division directors, this information could then be presented by Ned to his boss with a request for guidance. If his boss could be persuaded to make a choice, Ned's problem would be solved. Of the three ideas he had considered, Ned liked the last one the best. Accordingly, he reached for the telephone preparatory to calling the first of his impossible committee members!

Case 1–4 ————————————————————————————————

The Military in Transition:
The Brown Shoe and VOLAR Armies*

David McGill

In 1971, the U.S. Army made a dramatic transition in training and disciplinary methods as one means of meeting its manpower needs. The transition came about as a result of the President's effort to have an all-volunteer army by 1973. The changes began in June 1971, and were still being carried out at the training centers and military installations throughout the country as of the time of this case, 1973.

The case observer was inducted on April 7, 1971, and took basic training under the "old-style" training. In June 1971 he was assigned to an Advanced Infantry Training company that was taking part in the new approach that was being called the "VOLAR concept," in which VOLAR was an abbreviation for volunteer army.

THE BROWN SHOE ARMY

The term *brown shoe army* comes from career NCO's as they refer to the older form or type of training used in building a combat-trained soldier.

---

* Adapted from a course assignment by David McGill for Professor J. G. Hunt, Southern Illinois University—Carbondale.

This term is very appropriate because the exercises a soldier was required to do had the effect of turning a soldier's boots brown. Long forced marches, crawling through sand and dirt, or running from place to place in sandy, rocky terrain were examples. Soldiers' boots would always show what they had been doing.

Under the old army training doctrine a recruit was nothing and should be treated as such. In many training centers recruits were required to wear a white tag (called a "maggot tag") above their name tag to denote them as a new trainee. The drill sergeants, or drill instructors, referred to individuals as maggots and treated them as such. They would only talk to maggots when the maggots did something wrong, and then only at the top of their lungs. Many recruits were afraid of their drill sergeants, as it was not uncommon to "fall down the stairs" if there was disfavor with a drill sergeant. To "fall down the stairs" refers to getting roughed up or beaten up. This once was a common occurrence in the army, but has been less frequently seen in recent years. Drill sergeants were not authorized to touch a soldier but the rule was seldom enforced by an officer even if the incident were reported. Fear or respect for authority and obedience was the desired effect of this threat of punishment. The sergeants wanted the recruit to do whatever they said, no matter how inconsequential it might seem at the time the order was given.

Life in the barracks, as in all of the military forces, was very structured. Everything had a place and everything must be in that place. Each locker had to be set up in the prescribed military manner, the standard operating procedure (SOP). The military had an SOP for everything (it seemed) that could ever possibly occur. The lockers were subject to inspection at all times. All socks, T-shirts, underwear, and handkerchiefs were to be an exact size and should occupy a certain portion of a locker. A recruit's clothes were to hang in a certain order and all field gear was to be arranged in a precise manner. All of this was subject to inspection. If a locker was found not in order, the unlucky recruit was usually assigned extra duty of some sort: kitchen police (working in the kitchen for one additional day over the required number of days), guard duty, or CQ runner (the Charge-of-Quarters runner who stayed up all night with the Charge-of-Quarters noncommissioned officer).

The meals were very good, or at least tasted good to the trainee. During the first eight weeks the trainee was allowed no snacks from home or the Post Exchange, or anything but army food. The discipline in the dining hall was very strict, with no idle conversation or smoking allowed after the meal. The theme was get in, eat, and get out as quickly as possible. Some companies had to stand at parade rest (a military position) while waiting in line, although this was the exception, not the rule.

The training received in the army was a type of programmed learning. The periods were broken down into blocks of instruction, each aimed at bringing the recruits to a certain level of achievement. As an example, in three hours, a recruit could be taught to disassemble and assemble an M-16 rifle in three minutes. Until the time of the class the recruit was unfamiliar with the rifle. One drawback was that there was no room for the individual to show creativity or excel above the class. Any behavior of this type resulted in punishment rather than reward. Many individuals resented this type of instruction because they were accustomed to learning at a faster rate and under a different system.

All learning was task-related and many people wondered whether they learned from the instruction or from the constant repetition. Again, pressures were extended by the drill instructors for the trainee to perform the tasks as required; nothing more and nothing less.

While the case observer was trained only in the use of infantry equipment, he learned that the training for any of the Army's Military Occupation Skills (MOS), from heavy equipment to dental assistant, was conducted in this manner.

Another facet of training was that of physical development. Wherever the company went, the soldiers walked, ran, or forced-marched. In addition, there were approximately two hours per day devoted to physical training. At the end of the eight-week cycle, all soldiers were in excellent physical condition.

There were many times during the training cycle when an individual was put to a stress test. Stress could come about in many ways. Stress was sometimes induced by keeping a troop up all night training and then continuing training the next day. The usual tension, coupled with the fatigue, would make people react abnormally. In addition, the troops were watched. If anyone made a mistake, that person was singled out, reprimanded, or pushed a bit. The instructors were looking for the soldier who relaxed and then couldn't react under stress. The purpose of inducing stress was to weed out people that were unable to cope with Army life or should not be assigned to a position of responsibility.

During the eight long weeks of basic training, the recruits were not allowed off the post. This was never explained to the soldiers, but was just an accepted fact. Recruits could only go to movies on post. Most trainees were not bothered by being restricted to the post, but some would try to sneak off, which frequently led them to serious trouble with military authorities.

Officers and noncommissioned officers (NCOs) in the Army had similar roles. Both were task-oriented but the methods used to achieve the task differed. The enlisted recruits had more contact with the NCOs than the officers, the pattern of the entire Army. Officers were there to see that the procedures were followed, but had little contact with the men.

NCOs had the major job of training the recruits. The mannerisms of the NCOs were very gruff and "hard-core." Many NCOs were not much older than the recruits but tried to throw their weight around. One example was a drill sergeant who held formations for the platoon at night to deliver his thoughts for the day. While most of the drill sergeants didn't abuse their position, there were always some who did. The similarity in ages is a problem that has plagued the Army for many years with little hope for a solution.

In short, the basic training in the "brown shoe army" was hard. When a soldier completed it, however, that soldier had a good knowledge of the

Army and its functions and was ready to proceed on to the next training assignment.

THE VOLAR ARMY

The phrase *VOLAR* comes from the new volunteer army program which the Army embarked upon in early 1971. Under this program, it was believed that a recruit should be treated as a soldier immediately upon entry into the Army. The trainee recruit and his rights were respected, and the maggot tags were done away with. The recruits, or trainees as they were now called, were still told to do things, but often there was an explanation offered.

The Army also instituted a new motivation program. In this program, a trainee's effort and performance was evaluated each day by his drill sergeant. A point system was used to reward the soldier for making his bed, going to training, and performing the assigned tasks. The maximum number of points for one week was 25 and various rewards were given for set point values. Twenty-three points, for example, would earn the trainee a weekend pass. If the trainee earned 19 points, there was a one-day pass. In the case observer's company, this reward program appeared to change the attitude of many. Before this change, soldiers did things because they were told directly to do them and were afraid of the consequences of not obeying. Now, under the new program, they performed the same tasks, but did so because of a new inward motivation and because the possibility of a reward. Much of the complaining and griping stopped and was replaced with talk about the weekends and what each person's weekend activities were to be. The instant respect of authority declined and discipline seemed to suffer under this approach. Morale, however, appeared higher. With the new system, soldiers no longer reacted because of orders from higher ranking individuals. Instead, they were primarily concerned with benefits in terms of points.

Life in the barracks under the VOLAR system was quite different from that under "brown shoe" basic training. The locker inspections and SOP's were replaced by the phrase, "must be clean and orderly." There were no locker inspections at all, the instruction really didn't matter. As a consequence, most lockers were pretty messy. The physical areas that were lived in still were to be kept clean. Since points could be earned by cleaning each living area, soldiers kept the areas clean. An addition to the barracks' dayroom was a beer machine. Called the VOLAR machine by most recruits, the beer dispenser was used quite heavily during the course of an evening. Coke and candy machines were also added. These additions appeared to increase morale but also seemed to decrease the physical condition of the users.

Meals were essentially the same under the VOLAR system, but the atmosphere in the dining hall was now relaxed. The rule of eating in military attire was dropped, as was the rule against smoking. Hamburgers and hotdogs were added to the noon meal, the Army's idea of giving the trainee what he wanted. This menu addition was warmly accepted by recruits.

The training methods for technical topics remained essentially the same, a consequence of having the actual training given by people other than the company personnel. One change was that more breaks were provided during the training sessions. Class would be held for one hour, and then a 15-minute break would be given. During the breaks, snack or "hoagie" trucks would come by selling drinks and sandwiches. The only other change was in the method of getting to and from the training site. Recruits were bussed or trucked to the training areas, areas that they had walked to in earlier days. Also, the rule of running from place to place was dropped. The whole atmosphere seemed to change from a rigid military setting to something like a rigorous Boy Scout encampment.

The individual soldier was still put to the stress test, but was subjected to much less stress in the process. The role of the drill sergeant changed from being an unapproachable figure of authority to that of a counselor who would talk to recruits and try to help them with their problems. With this change many people who were not able to cope with the stress were not detected.

In talking to many of the people who had gone through this new system of training, the case observer found that a number did not feel qualified as a combat soldier. This thought was echoed by career NCOs who the case observer worked with and talked to during his time in the Army. These people indicated that based on observation of both types of soldiers in combat in Vietnam, the soldier that was trained in an atmosphere as permissive as VOLAR didn't perform well in a combat situation. Their view was that this type of training is adequate for a loose, peacetime Army. For an Army to go to war, however, we need a highly trained, cohesive group of men who will obey orders and not question them. The problem of questioning orders came up quite often during the latter years of the Vietnam war. In a close situation, the lives of all the men might depend on one man carrying out a specific order.

In the opinion of the career NCOs and officers, the Army must revert to the former standards and training methods if it is going to be an effective deterrent to a foreign power.

Case 1–5

The Late Shift

Robert A. Zawacki

Mark A. Couger was one of three people interviewed for a job at a large eastern manufacturing firm that employed 600 people. Mark, 19, got the job. He started work the next day at the minimum hourly rate as a packer on the assembly line, working the 4:00 P.M. to midnight shift.

Recently there was a large increase in sales, and the company formed a second late shift to meet that demand. Mark was part of the buildup in the work force and was one of only three men on the late shift. An overwhelming majority of the workers were women, who wanted to be at home when their children left for and returned from school. They took this night work because their husbands could look after the children in the evening, and they could earn extra money for the family income. They also knew that they would be laid off if sales decreased because the company would return to one shift per day.

Mark started his job with high expectations even though the personnel director had warned him that working with women might be more difficult than he thought. Mark's supervisor, Maggie, was a 23-year-old woman who had been promoted rapidly because of the fast growth of the company. Although she was motivated to do well, she lacked self-confidence, and at times seemed threatened by the male employees.

During the first two or three weeks, Maggie observed that Mark was very productive, volunteered for new tasks, and generally appeared satisfied. She did notice that he took his breaks by himself or with only a few other employees. At the end of four weeks, Mark had learned how to fix all of the machines, was the only employee that could set up the machines, and always was asked to do the heavy lifting by the women. The other male employees just did their jobs and did not volunteer to set up the equipment.

At about the end of the fifth week, the employees had a three-day weekend and received one day paid vacation if they worked both the day preceding the holiday and the day after the holiday. Mark did not come to work the day after the holiday and, therefore, lost one day's pay. Maggie did not talk to him about his absence. Other than this one incident, Mark was always prompt and punctual.

Maggie saw that Mark had many informal supervisors because the women always would ask Mark to do the jobs that they didn't want to do or that were too heavy for them. Mark was fast becoming the "gopher" of the shift—he could do anything.

At the end of the 60-day probationary period, Maggie had a mandatory counseling session with Mark. She told Mark that she rated his performance as average, and was recommending him for a 30-cent-an-hour pay increase. Mark informed her that he was quitting work, effective Friday!

Case 1–6 ————————————————————————————————————

Progress Industries, Inc.

K. Mark Weaver and John T. Wholihan

Progress Industries, Inc., is a medium-sized manufacturing plant in a small town in central Illinois. Progress was established in 1922 and has since been producing products primarily made of sheet metal. These products are of two general types and result in two divisions in the company.

These divisions are the tank division and the funeral products division. The tank division is the larger of the two, having approximately 200 hourly or nonsalaried employees, while the funeral division employs approximately 100 people. The tank division produces truck tanks and trailers, which are made of mild steel, stainless steel, or aluminum, depending on their intended use, and also produces fertilizer tanks. The funeral division manufactures caskets made of copper, bronze, and steel and also does some burial vault work.

The factory is departmentalized based on the different processes which are necessary in the production of the tanks or caskets and also by type of tank. Each department has a separate function(s) to perform. Each of these departments is managed directly by a foreman, whose duties will be explained later.

Progress is located in a small farming community where it is the main industry and employs a large percentage of the labor force. Workers are drawn also from neighboring small towns within a 20-mile radius. Major competition for industrial workers comes from the surrounding large cities of Mattoon, Decatur, and Champaign, which are 25, 35, and 40 miles away, respectively.

The plant is a union shop represented by the International Union of Operating Engineers, AFL–CIO. There is presently a three-year contract in effect which expires June 10, 1976.

Wallace Dicks, vice president of operations, recognized that Progress has more than its share of problems. It has been constantly plagued by low productivity but always seems to make a profit. This profit has not necessarily been a result of good management, but of the low labor expenses incurred. "There is a trade-off between these wages and productivity," he said, "however the total expense per unit produced probably works out the same. That is, poor wages play a part in the poor productivity of workers; therefore, they will take longer to accomplish a task."

One of the other factors that must be considered is turnover. There is a cost that must be realized when new people must constantly be trained to replace people who quit. Progress management realizes that they must strive to make the quality worker stay with the company. The company must fill the workers' needs, and, hopefully as a result, get many years of service from them.

At Progress, for the fiscal year from October 1972, to September 1973, the rate of employee turnover was 57 percent. This is the figure for factory workers alone, many of which were high labor-grade (long-term and experienced) employees. In addition to this, Progress has lost the following key individuals during the last 20 months: two vice presidents; three division managers; three plant superintendents; three assistant plant superintendents; and seven foremen.

Also lost during this period were a sales manager, an engineer, data processing supervisor, personnel manager, invoice clerk, and two experienced truck drivers. Five of these positions had to be filled with inexperienced people from outside the firm. Some of these people felt their jobs with Progress were no longer fulfilling their needs. This concerned Mr.

Dicks, who stated, "The company wants their product to be of high quality, with few mistakes and with as little labor time to produce as possible. Therefore, the management must strive to show the worker how, if he produces in this manner, he will be provided with some type of goal or need satisfaction."

One of the production workers in the shop stated that the hourly employees felt that "the company really doesn't care about their welfare." This feeling was only evident in a department where the foreman was younger and did genuinely care about the workers. The workers felt this concern from their foreman and seemed to appreciate it, but still had a negative feeling about the "company," or upper level management. The job became a tiresome task and in many cases was just a source of income until a better job could be found. According to one employee, "It takes more than just a handshake from the president and a Christmas bonus to make someone feel appreciated, and this is the extent of the management's efforts at Progress."

Progress appears to use money as a primary motivational device. The company is not known for its high wage scale, and raises in pay of the average factory worker seldom exceeded 20 cents per hour at a given time. The illustration below shows the labor grade system used (as taken from the union agreement) and the accompanying rates of pay:

Tank Division

Labor Grade	Wage Effective June 9, 1974
15	$4.40–$4.73
12	4.23– 4.53
8	4.04– 4.36
7	3.87– 4.19
6	3.70– 4.02
5	3.53– 3.85
4	3.36– 3.68
3	3.19– 3.51
1	2.91– 3.14

Labor grades are offered upon request of the foreman. The offers are then posted on the bulletin board and workers are allowed to bid on the new labor grade. Final say on the matter of who receives the promotion rests with the plant superintendent. Several employees felt this was a mistake. Comments included:

I don't object to his having a voice in the matter, but I do feel that the major portion of this decision should be the foreman's. He knows what we can do.

I also feel that the changes in labor grades are too few and far between after an employee's first four or five years. These are the men who are most needed, since they are experienced, and should receive more recognition, not less.

One employee of the tank division stated, "I feel that the merit raise system employed by Progress is very vague and ineffective. No one really understands it."

The merit policy is explained in the following exerpt from the union contract.

ARTICLE XIX, Section 2.

Merit increases are figured as follows: Each foreman rates all of their people—the average rating in each department is then figured. We then take a department with a median average and add or deduct from each individual in other departments the difference in the average of this department and the others. This gives each individual the rating points we use in determining pay. Then we give the following merit increases if they can be given within their labor grade—if at the top of their labor grade they do not get a merit increase.

	Low ⅓ of L.G.	Mid ⅓ of L.G.	High ⅓ of L.G.
10 points or more below average	.06	.05	.05
1 to 9 points below average	.08	.06	.05
Average to 9 points above	.11	.09	.07
10 points or more above	.14	.12	.10

Furthermore, employees feel there is not enough money involved in these increases.

There have also been other incentives tried at Progress. One was aimed generally at rewarding departmental performance and was given as a monthly bonus. This did not seem to be very effective. According to a foreman, "I noticed that one of the most industrious and highly valued employees in my department flaunted his 'whopping' bonus of $1.74." Another incentive program which brought smirks to the faces of employees was the institution of a system, again on a departmental basis, that rewarded the departments having the fewest days lost per month from work injuries with S&H green stamps.

Another problem area which is related to low productivity is poor supervision. This is more serious on the foreman level than any other, as far as each individual worker is concerned. The foreman is the manager with whom he has the most direct contact. The foremen feel a need for more formal training, especially in the area of human relations.

Another problem at Progress, which also deals with cooperation, is communication between departments. "I personally have seen one department forced to expend much more time and effort to do a job which could be done more quickly and easily by another department with more facilities. The problem is not one of awareness, because people of authority to deal with this just haven't seemed to do anything about it," stated a foreman in the tank division.

There also seems to be a major problem that has just recently been brought to the surface. Some of the older, more experienced shop personnel possess a great deal of knowledge about certain facets of tank production that is not written down anywhere. If that person were to become unable to work, there would be no way of replacing all that necessary knowledge.

When management personnel were asked how to motivate their employees, several replies were received. One opinion was that the recent changes in supervisory personnel would help remedy the situation. Monetary policies of motivation were mentioned in different ways. Two respondents felt that the present system of monetary reward (the labor grade and merit system) is sufficient, while another respondent leaned towards a year-end bonus of $500 for meeting a set production schedule.

Most agree on the lack of a backup system for key employees and positions in the plant. On the whole, Mr. Dicks seems to be aware of some existing problems but no effective action has been taken. It seems as if there are plans being made to try and remedy some of the situations that exist, but as yet nothing positive seems to have resulted.

Case 1–7 ──

Lincoln Electric: Successful Employee Motivation Program

DeWayne Piehl

INTRODUCTION

A great variety of productivity incentive programs have been tried in various industries, ranging from industrial engineering-based incentive-pay programs of the 1920s to the more "humanistic" or "organization climate" programs of the 1960s and 1970s. Yet none of these programs has enjoyed a sufficiently long period of success to indicate that it might be the ultimate solution—or best solution—to the problem of employee motivation. The experience of Lincoln Electric stands out from the above experiences because of its continuous operation and success over the last 45 years. It is this long period of successful operations that indicates a study of the nature of the program; and its performance contains useful lessons for a manager. It also raises some interesting questions for the theorist because of the remarkably small amount of attention this program has received, despite its success. It is difficult to understand why no other firm has attempted to copy or otherwise employ a similar concept to the compensation, evaluation, and motivation of its employees. In this program Lincoln stands alone.

THE BASIC CONCEPT

From an economic point of view the program is based on maximizing output, minimizing inputs, and increasing efficiency. The inputs, in men's time, materials, and capital equipment are watched closely to reduce waste and achieve maximum output. The savings so generated are passed on to the customer (in this case an industrial customer who is probably quite price-elastic), which permits economies of scale to further the use of electric welding. The additional earnings so generated are apportioned between the customer in terms of lower prices and the employee in terms of an annual bonus. Both the customer and the employee share in the gains from the increased efficiency. Thus, the partnership between the employees and the customers is emphasized. Both are essential for the success of the enterprise and both share the gains from increased productivity.

Another factor, technological advance, was at work. The primary product of the company is electrical welding equipment. In addition, the company produces the welding rod that is consumed in the process of welding, and electric motors. The installation and growth of Lincoln's incentive program was concomitant with the introduction and development of electric welding.

The gradual decrease in the price of the welding equipment and the welding rods, permitted by the tremendous growth and productivity at Lincoln Electric, promoted the expansion of electric welding as a common industrial process. The growth of this process also added to the economies of scale. As electric welding received acceptance by industry as a common industrial process, this led to increased demand, which led to increased volume and, therefore, economies of scale. To a great extent the history of the success of the Lincoln Electric program is hand-in-hand with the growth and acceptance of electric welding by industry. As the cost of electric welding equipment and the operation of electric equipment decreased, new customers were encouraged to accept this process; and this led to growth and demand for the company's products. To a great extent, the history of the company and the history of the incentive program are also the history of electric welding. Indeed, the technological environment and the timing were favorable for the introduction of James Lincoln's concepts of worker and customer incentives. To the extent that the market is an industrial market and has a high price elasticity, this was also favorable for the development and success of Lincoln's philosophy. Other industries which did not enjoy such price elasticity, of course, would have great difficulty in adopting and implementing such a program.

In James Lincoln's philosophy: "The incentives that are most potent when properly offered and believed in by the worker" are the following: (1) money in proportion to production; (2) status as a reward for achievement; and (3) publicity of the worker's contribution and skill and imagination and the reward that is given for it. This results in added status.

From a behavioralist's point of view, this program appears to be based upon the assumption that economic motivation is the major factor. However, this is an oversimplification and ignores the third element in Mr. Lincoln's list of incentives. When a $7,000-a-year floor sweeper receives a $10,000 annual bonus at the end of the year and is then written up in an article in the *Cleveland Plain Dealer*, such recognition by his superiors and peers in so tangible a form has to be far more significant than the traditional paternalistic company gift of a turkey at Thanksgiving or Christmas.

Each employee is evaluated regularly by his immediate superior. In the case of the engineering department, the chief engineer showed this author the personnel records of his employees. He made annotations on their performance at least monthly and often more frequently when a particular event justified this. The importance of the evaluation of workers by their superiors, and direct connection between this evaluation and the dollar bonus paid at the end of the year, emphasizes the relationship between the employee, his superior, and the overall performance of the company. The better the performance of the company in economic terms, the larger dollar pool from which bonuses will be paid; and the higher the employee is rated by the supervisor, the greater his share of this pool will be. The combination of these two factors results in the annual bonus the employee receives. Thus the relationships among the employee, the supervisor, and the company as a whole are directly tied together; and this relationship is demonstrated in very tangible terms: a check at the end of the year. The recognition is further emphasized by in-house publications and also in newspaper and magazine articles released by the company's public relations department.

Another factor that behavioralists have failed to recognize is the scope of the program. All employees are included in this program: production employees, support employees (like floor sweepers), and management. The fact that the total group of employees are all included in the program and treated in a similar manner adds an element that is absent in most so-called incentive programs. It tends to emphasize the unity of purpose and the common objectives of all employees, regardless of status or function, as they work toward the success of the common enterprise.

The philosophy of James Lincoln is well expressed in the following statement:

> It is well to keep in mind in applying any incentive system, that money of itself is not as great an incentive to any of us as self-respect and status. We all will sacrifice money to keep our self-respect and to gain the respect and admiration of our contemporaries. This is shown by the enthusiasm of the amateur athlete in playing a game. The only reward he can have is self-respect and the respect of others whose good opinion he values. He will generally try harder than the professional who gets paid for his performance.

Exhibit 1 illustrates the relationships between the effectiveness of the compensation program and the pricing policies of the company. While worker compensation has grown dramatically over a period of 30 years compared to other industries, the prices of welders and welding rod have tended to remain the same, and during certain periods to decline. Thus, from the point of view of the customer, the cost of the welding rod and the welding process have declined relative to his other costs of production. This, in turn, has led to an increasing demand for welding and the products that it enables a firm to produce. From an economic point of view this program is quite successful.

EXHIBIT 1
Indexes of Lincoln Worker Compensation, Cost of Finished Steel and
Copper, and Selling Price of 300-Amp Welders, 1934–1964
(1934 = 100)

Year	Worker Compensation	Finished Steel	Copper	300-Amp Welder
1934	100.0	100.0	100.0	100.0
1935	111.6	100.8	106.3	88.4
1936	179.7	103.3	134.8	88.4
1937	170.7	123.6	134.8	88.4
1938	99.2	119.9	116.0	80.6
1939	142.7	112.7	126.8	71.3
1940	193.7	112.2	133.7	67.4
1941	294.8	116.8	134.8	64.3
1942	259.5	116.8	134.8	64.3
1943	273.3	116.8	134.8	58.9
1944	285.0	116.8	134.8	55.8
1945	264.7	119.4	148.0	55.8
1946	244.8	131.0	198.4	62.8
1947	298.7	146.9	248.0	62.8
1948	331.4	167.4	237.9	67.4
1949	283.9	181.0	222.0	65.9
1950	352.0	188.3	261.7	76.7
1951	383.8	201.4	277.7	76.7
1952	419.6	206.6	301.4	76.7
1953	404.8	220.3	331.1	76.7
1954	388.6	229.9	380.7	78.4
1955	439.5	242.7	444.1	78.4
1956	512.3	261.2	475.9	92.2
1957	464.5	282.8	411.4	92.2
1958	404.4	295.5	331.4	88.4
1959	478.4	302.1	377.1	83.7
1960	485.8	302.1	393.3	86.8
1961	489.0	302.1	371.4	82.9
1962	547.4	302.1	377.3	82.9
1963	594.4	303.9	377.3	82.9
1964	715.3	306.0	382.6	82.9

Source: James F. Lincoln, *A New Approach to Industrial Economics* (New York: The Devin-Adain Company, 1961).

Of course, one should also evaluate the program in terms of its impact on human variables in the organization. In distribution of the number of years employees have spent with the company, Lincoln compares favorably with similar firms in the electrical industry. The number of "old timers" seen during a tour of the plant shows that the program is well accepted by many employees. Employee turnover figures would not give as strong an indication; but upon closer examination, one sees that a high rate of turnover occurs during the early stages of an employee's association with the company. Apparently, there are a certain number of employees who are not able to adjust to Lincoln and the "Lincoln system." The turnover rate, though, is very low among employees who started with Lincoln below the age of 25. Apparently, workers with experience in other industries or in comparable firms, who formed expectations under entirely different compensation systems and organizational climates, experience dissonance and find it difficult to accept the Lincoln system. The employee's expectations of the work atmosphere, his relationship with his superiors, and other intrinsic rewards of employment are apparently important factors in determining whether he will be happy at Lincoln. It seems there is a strong incompatibility between James Lincoln's philosophy and the philosophy that prevails in most American industrial firms.

ORGANIZATIONAL CLIMATE AND INDUSTRIAL ATMOSPHERE

A unique climate or atmosphere is evident to the visitor immediately upon approaching the Lincoln plant. One first drives through a very large parking lot, distinguished from the usual factory lot by the absence of assigned parking places. No places are labeled with the names of high officials. All parking places are on first-come, first-served basis. The absence of such a status symbol is quite startling to a visitor who has been to many other industrial installations. There is no visitors' parking lot, so the visitor must make the long trek from the last available parking place to the front of the building. The factory building is a single, long rectangular structure. There is no separate office building. Squarely in the center of the building, as one approaches it, is the single entrance through which *all* employees pass: production workers, administrative personnel, and officers. This entrance effectively divides the building into two parts. To one side is the rotating equipment division, where power supplies for welders and electric motors are produced. In the other side of the building is the area for construction of the welding rod, which is essentially wire cut to length and coated by various materials. The building is thus efficiently divided along technological lines, as the production and technological processes and skills are quite different for these two product lines. A gigantic hallway in the center of the building reminds one of a hotel lobby.

Starkly evident in this hallway is a very dramatic sign against a brick wall:

THE ACTUAL IS LIMITED
THE POSSIBLE IS IMMENSE

Such an exhortation is reminiscent of THINK signs that one sees throughout IBM installations. All employees pass beneath this sign when entering the plant each day.

Part of the atmosphere is immediately evident to the visitor in the way the building is constructed. The walls of the lobby are brick. All the furnishings and facilities, such as ashtrays and handrails, are aluminum. The effect is one of starkness, spareness, and cleanliness. It is the most uncluttered installation that this observer has ever seen. There is no evidence of litter or disarrangement anywhere in the lobby. Cleanliness seems almost a fetish. Few hospitals appear as well supervised and maintained. There is no evidence of a single piece of equipment or furniture in a state of disrepair. The design of all the facilities is functional to a degree that make the artistic seem absent. There are no pictures on the wall. *Function* seems to be the primary criterion and is evident from the front door right on through the rest of the plant. To leave the lobby one ascends a wide ramp to the right or to the left, depending on which aspect of the business or which product line is to be observed.

At the top of the ramp the visitor chooses one of two doors leading to the production area or to the office area. Stepping into the corporate offices one has the feeling that they were designed and furnished in the 1930s or 1940s and have not been refurnished since; yet the degree of maintenance and cleanliness is startling. The desks are all one style, and so is the rest of the office furniture. The age of the equipment does not mean that it is nonfunctional, just unimpressive. There are very few personal touches such as flowers or plants or paintings or pictures throughout the office. The office equipment is roughly the same vintage and without any status distinctions. In other words, there is no difference between the office equipment of a clerical worker and that of a vice president. Very few private offices exist. Most of the employees work in large rooms at adjacent desks. The few private offices are at the vice-president and plant-management level and above; and these have glass partitions that act as sound barriers rather than visual dividers to separate the managers from the subordinates. Very few doors to the offices were closed. In most cases the doors were open, and employees moved freely in and out of their superiors' offices. There could be no better evidence of an "open" organizational climate.

In summary, there was very little evidence of amenities. At the same time there was no evidence of sloppiness or disarray. Wastebaskets were not full, there was no litter on the floor, simple asphalt tile was well polished. The impression is one of solid value and excellent maintenance.

It was startling to observe that when an employee tossed a piece of paper toward the wastebasket and missed, another employee reached down immediately, picked it up, and properly disposed of it. Apparently this fetish for neatness and orderliness is a group norm for cooperation and maintaining the cleanliness. Orderliness was starkly evident in contrast to many other installations this observer has visited.

In general, the atmosphere in the office was one of business without commotion, disorder, confusion, or noise. Each employee seemed to have a sense of purpose and an objective toward which he was working at the moment. Very little activity for its own sake was observed. Communication appeared to be smooth and direct, with little conversation for its own sake. The employees seemed to be busy rather than antisocial.

The climate in the factory portions of the building reflected many of these same characteristics. The factory floor was remarkably clean and there was no evidence of litter. All material was stacked neatly or enclosed in containers. Employees' workbenches were as neatly arrayed as the desks in the office. Necessary tools were arranged in an orderly manner at the work place, and litter and scraps were deposited in containers. There was no evidence of scraps on the floor or mixed into the raw material containers.

The atmosphere in the factory was placid by most industrial standards. There was a minimum of noise and confusion. The noisier manufacturing operations, such as punch presses and rolling mills, were set apart in one portion of the plant against the wall and effectively isolated by large stacks of raw materials in containers that essentially baffled the sound. Production employees worked in small production lines which ran the width of the plant. These production lines included from 4 to 12 people each, either because the products are relatively simple, requiring a few simple operations, or because the complexity of the assembly operation was reduced by the use of subassemblies. Each production worker was separated from the others by a distance of 12 to 20 feet. Between the production workers were large stacks of in-process materials. It seemed as though each worker was surrounded by a huge pile of in-process inventory. It was all "good work" ahead of the man. It effectively represented to the worker a certain amount of job security: there was work to be done. Upon completion of his assembly task, the worker placed the item upon a roller conveyer that moved it to the next work station where they were piled in front of that worker and became a portion of the "backlog of work in process" or "float." In one sense, the manufacturing floor at Lincoln represents a gigantic warehouse of in-process inventory with the minimum of aisles and almost no traffic down aisles or past work stations. Materials proceed directly from one work station to the next and do not wind between stations and around piles of material. The flow is direct from the beginning of each short production line to its end. Each production line ends next to a shipping area, with a railroad dock and a warehouse section of the plant. Upon completion of the production operation (usually a final test and then painting), the item is shipped to a customer or consigned to a warehouse.

There was no evidence of the usual amount of horseplay or of activity for the sake of activity that one finds in a factory. There was very little activity other than the direct production work.

Workers at first appeared to this observer to be quite isolated from one another. But the managers, from foreman to vice president, took frequent trips up and down the various production lines in the plant, observing, listening, and questioning so that the contact between the worker and various levels of management was quite noticeable. Analysis of the organization shows that the organizational distance at Lincoln Electric is on the order of three or four. This means that communications from, say, the lowest levels of management pass through only two sets of filters in addition to the engineer and the president; there are only two intervening levels of management. This short organizational distance should both speed the rate of communication and reduce sources of distortion. The organizational distance observed in other firms in this industry, of a size similar to Lincoln Electric, was found to be two or three levels greater.

The arrangement of the work load in the plant is consistent with several of Jim Lincoln's purposes. The work-in-process inventory is arranged so that it presents a visual image to each worker that says: "There is work available for you in this amount which will keep you busy and on the payroll." Such work-in-process float is symbolic of the delays between operations. In the way the plant is laid out, Lincoln Electric uses this necessary work-in-process to literally show the worker that he is needed; there is work for him to do. This is consistent with James Lincoln's philosophy which includes providing a feeling of security and freedom from periodic layoffs. Such layoffs are quite common in this industry when demand slows and the rate of production is cut back. At Lincoln Electric, however, under such conditions the plant is kept operating and production is stockpiled in inventory. There is a basic policy of the company to maintain continuity and uniformity of production rate and therefore of employment. One side effect of such continuity of production is a lower fluctuation of production, which is also consistent with the major policies of the company. In this way, the company avoids "coasting" by employees as they observe the production rate slowing down. Production employees usually sense an impending layoff because of a reduction in the in-process inventory. This leads to increasing costs or lower productivity per man-hour as the production rate is reduced; and layoffs necessarily follow. Then when production is increased, the company must start out at a lower point of the learning curve and gradually work its way back up. Both these events lead to lower output per man-hour, which is inconsistent with the basic philosophy at Lincoln Electric. Therefore, such stop-and-go production planning is avoided, and a steady work flow is a primary objective of the production planners.

EVOLUTION OF THE LINCOLN PHILOSOPHY

James Lincoln's father was an ordained minister of strong moral convictions. He was very active in the abolition of slavery and the encouragement of individual initiative. It was in this strong moralistic home life that James Lincoln was brought up. James spent his boyhood working on the family farm, for he was a brawny, strong young man. Work was no stranger to him; it was a vital part of his existence. Hard work was also consistent with the strong moralistic environment of his early childhood. In the evenings after the completion of his farm chores James would sit and listen to his father read aloud from the Bible. Consistent with the Protestant ethic, James saved his money from work on the farm and, at age 20, enrolled at Ohio State University where he took up the study of electrical engineering. An average student scholastically, the tall, strong young Lincoln performed exceptionally well on the Ohio State football team for four years. His senior year he was captain of the football team and played every minute of ten games, during which Ohio State's goal line was never crossed.

Jim's oldest brother, John, 17 years his senior, had worked for a number of electrical companies. In 1895 the Lincoln Electric Company was started in the basement of John's home. Financed on $150 of borrowed capital, its purpose was to repair and build electric motors. During

Jim's summer vacation from college he worked with John to get the infant company off the ground. This gave James exposure to the practical side of electrical engineering, and was a leavening of the theoretical training he was receiving at Ohio State University. John's interests were primarily in engineering and product development, so James became the company's salesman and focused the business side of the enterprise. The Lincoln Electric company went through its infancy at the same time that the electrical industry did. And the Lincoln company has grown along with the industry and the demand for electricity.

During World War I the company began to grow significantly. At this time James was appointed general manager of the firm. One of his first actions was to call together the people of the company and ask them to elect representatives from each of the departments to meet with him and advise him on the company's operations. The group was strictly advisory, but was to have no limits on the scope of its interests and concerns. The advisory board has continued until the present, meeting twice a month, every month. With the events surrounding World War I, a dramatic change in the technology and market demand shifted the focus of the company away from motors and arc lighting and brought to attention the potential of arc welding. James went to Washington, D.C., in an attempt to convince the navy that the use of welding could permit the building of lighter and stronger ships than could riveting. Because proposal was met with doubt, James started a welding school to train welders and provide demonstrations of the capabilities of electric welding. It was necessary to provide the skills and trained personnel and demonstrations simultaneously to build a market for electric welding.

Lincoln Electric was innovative not only in the technical area but also in the management area. In 1915 each employee was given a paid life insurance policy. In 1919 the employees organized an association for health benefits and social activities. In 1923 employees were given two-week vacations, and the shop was operating with a piecework plan. At the same time, all earnings were adjusted automatically up or down according to the fluctuations in the cost of living index produced by the Bureau of Labor. In 1925 an employee stock purchase plan was started, and in 1929 a suggestion program was begun. None of these programs, all of which are quite common fringe benefits today, were initiated under any form of pressure. All apparently have been successful, for they continue to operate today. Each of these programs appealed to James Lincoln as the "right thing to do."

In the 1930s Lincoln Electric experienced the same problems of reduced sales that affected all of American industry. In 1934, through the advisory board, the employees asked if hours could be increased. This was done at the same time a bonus plan was established. At the end of the year, as a result of greater operating efficiency, the company was able to distribute a cash bonus consisting of additional earnings after taxes and dividends were paid. That year each employee received a bonus which, on the average, amounted to 30 percent of his earnings during the year. This was the beginning of Lincoln's bonus plan.

The fringe benefits, and a concept of the bonus plan, were all consistent with James Lincoln's philosophy and moral values: A worker is worth his hire; and those who perform should share in the benefits and gain from his labor. A merit rating system and an evaluation of each employee by his supervisor were required to determine the individual appropriate shares of the bonus fund. Tying increased productivity to the ability to reduce prices resulted in Lincoln Electric becoming, by 1940, the world's largest manufacturer of arc welding equipment, exporting to a number of foreign countries and licensing manufacturers to produce products in others.

Despite the fact that James Lincoln based his workers' compensation on the Sermon on the Mount, he found himself in trouble with government agencies during the 1940s. The government sued the company on the basis that because it was overpaying its workers, it was not reporting profits in as large an amount as it should, and was thereby reducing its tax liability. It was necessary for the company to prove that it was getting a performance from the organization and its employees commensurate with its high rate of pay. The case dragged through the courts for ten years, at the end of which the former Ohio State fullback prevailed. During the war, Lincoln Electric was also called to question for the profits it made on welding equipment it produced for the government program. James Lincoln claimed in fact to have reduced the cost to the government. He offered to visit his competitors and to show them how to reduce costs appropriately. This case also was resolved in favor of Lincoln Electric. The government was unable to prove that it could have acquired equivalent equipment and supplies from any other source at a lower price. The rapid expansion of welding to produce shipping for the war effort resulted in rapid growth of the Lincoln Electric Company, which operated three shifts per day to meet more demands.

While other firms faced the problems of conversion from wartime to peacetime, in 1945 Lincoln Electric established a goal of reducing its labor and material cost 10 percent every year. As a result of such reduction, they could reduce the prices of welding equipment and hopefully expand the market for their products.

The history and philosophy of the Lincoln Electric Company have been characterized by the value system of James Lincoln. This includes the virtues of hard work, with emphasis on the Protestant ethic, and to offer an increasing value in products at lower prices, and increasing benefits to employees, whose greater effort and productivity are rewarded with greater salaries. All these elements are consistent with the upbringing and the strong physical drive of James Lincoln. Loyalty is basic. Loyalty to the company and effort expended for the benefit of the company lead to a reward for the employee. Each employee shares in the benefits of the company's productivity and its market growth. He shares in a very tangible way in terms of dollars. The philosophy of James Lincoln could very easily be construed as empty moralizing, but it avoids this by the way the program is carried out. Each supervisor regularly evaluates the performance of his subordinates, and based on this evaluation employees share, in a proportionate manner, in the total bonus package. And the total bonus package is a function of the total sales and profitability of the whole firm.

Basic to James Lincoln's philosophy was the concept that the welfare of the employees, the welfare of the firm, and the welfare of the company's customers are all interrelated. As the company has grown, so has its bonus fund and the employees' share in the earnings of the company. And at the same time the prices that the company charges for its welding equipment and electric motors are today at levels the same or lower than they were in the 1930s. This is an effective definition of productivity.

One might expect that a company that so strongly reflected the personality of the key man would, as it grew to more than 2,000 employees, have difficulty reflecting these values, especially when the key man who initiated and personified most of these programs died. With James Lincoln's death, William Irrgang assumed the leadership of the company. With the firm's growth in size and change in leadership, much more emphasis must be placed on the organization to carry out the policies and principles upon which the firm operates.

The policies have not been changed at Lincoln Electric. Instead, the organization has been developed to reflect the policies and to continue to carry them out. Product design begins at the conception stage where, to avoid inhibiting ideas or creativity, no thought is given to manufacturing costs. Then, at a critical point, the design department is interfaced with production, when the cost-reducing efforts are given emphasis. Conscious effort is made to separate the functions of creativity and cost reduction. This is reflected in the organization structure of the firm and the communication patterns within the organization. This interfacing is built into the organization in the form of something of a "specials department." All this department does is to make pilot runs in small quantities. These pilot runs permit the manufacturing problems to surface, provide an idea of cost and opportunities for cost reduction, and permit the organization to work up the learning curve.

Continuity of employment has been certified into policy. A continuous employment program guarantees everyone who has been continuously employed by the company longer than two years a job or income for 49 weeks a year with the minimum of 30 hours of work per week. In addition, it is company policy to promote from within the organization whenever possible. Bringing in persons from outside to fill new openings is rare. This reflects to all employees the importance that management attaches to each person on the payroll. The policy statement is "we put the best man that we have in any kind of job." All job openings are posted publicly in the plant. Another company policy states "there are no unimportant jobs: consequently, there are no unimportant people in the company." In continuation of past practice, the advisory group of employees meets every two weeks with the president, during which new opportunities and problems are discussed and decisions are made.

Year-end bonuses for employees normally range from 60 to 150 percent of their regular salary. The size of an individual's bonus depends on three factors: his merit rating, his base salary, and the size of the total bonus pool. The actual bonus is computed by multiplying the employee's salary times his merit rating times the bonus factor. The bonus factor is the dollars of the total bonus pool divided by the total dollars of the company's payroll. Each department head must rate his employees, and these merit ratings for his department must normally average out to 100.

One method of keeping costs low is to keep the organization and its overhead small, to run a tight ship. At Lincoln one sees little supervision; there are few memos or lengthy reports. Lines of command are kept short so communication is both easy and direct. Both of these factors are aided by a lower turnover rate among employees.

Merit ratings are standardized by using a set of four cards—the same four cards for all employees whether they are engineers or production workers. Each individual is scored on the basis of four equally rated factors: workmanship, supervision, ideas, and output. Managers have a wide latitude in applying these factors to their employees. Control is maintained over the application of the system by comparing scores and ratings between departments. Thus, "hard markers" are picked out and identified and reasons for such hard marking may be examined.

One might expect that a rating system would tend to emphasize uniformity and inhibit creativity. This problem is avoided by other programs and other incentives that are as important as a cash bonus in motivating employees. An outstanding performance citation is given to ten people each year who are recommended by department heads to the president. Anyone is eligible for this award, including a floor sweeper. The winners of these citations get an additional bonus, which is determined by the president. Another incentive is selection of promising employees to the company's junior board of directors. This is an advisory group of ten people selected from among employees who are identified as exhibiting executive potential. This group meets once a month and can make recommendations on any subject to the company's board of directors. This junior board of directors is given a high degree of visibility within the company.

PROFITS HIGH, PRICES LOW, AND EVERY EMPLOYEE BENEFITS

The elements of the Lincoln approach may be summarized as follows:

1. The company must have an objective that makes sense to every employee, such as making better products to sell at lower prices. Profit is a by-product. Making profit as such is not an adequate objective for people on the production floor, because they have little control over this management goal.
2. Each employee's contribution is evaluated by a merit rating of his performance. Each individual is given responsibility, and each gets recognition in terms of pay and promotion.
3. Each employee is brought to recognize that his earnings are determined by the extent of his contribution to the success of the company as a whole.

4.   Guaranteed continuous employment assures employees a minimum of 75 percent of the number of hours in a standard work week.
5.   The company aims at constant profit, raising or lowering prices as costs increase or decrease. Once the profit standard has been achieved on a product, everyone benefits; the customer through lower prices, the distributor through an improved competitive position, and the company employees through an increased volume of sales resulting in greater profit to the company and greater bonus pool.
6.   Every employee is made aware that his contribution to reduce costs in production as well as to improve quality will be of direct benefit to him in terms of profit sharing.
7.   The company stays on top of its market and keeps itself thoroughly informed of economic changes to assure that it operates in businesses where there is a continuous increase in demand.

EXHIBIT 2
Press Release
Seattle Times—December 1975

Firm's 2,369 Employees Split $27.5 Million Christmas Bonus

CLEVELAND—(AP)—A practice begun in 1934 when a welding firm's employees asked for higher wages has paid the company's present 2,369 workers a record $27.5 million bonus—just in time for Christmas.

The checks the Lincoln Electric Co. employees took home Saturday represented the fourth record year in a row and the 42d in which the bonus was paid. Last year 2,421 employees shared $26 million.

The total yields an average of $11,608 an employee.

"It's astounding when you consider the general state of the economy," said Richard Sabo, manager of publicity and educational services. "We're very dependent on construction, and you know how that's been doing."

The firm produces arc welders and electrodes. It is a corporation in which present or former employees and members of the Lincoln family hold a majority of the stock.

Every employee on the payroll before October 31 got a part of the bonus, the amount depending on a variety of factors, Sabo said, but he declined to indicate how much.

It's all a part of an effort "to produce better products faster," Sabo added. "They receive what they have earned during the year. All are merit-rated, and they know their rating. Once they get the percentage, they pretty well can figure out what they're going to get individually."

Sabo said the majority of employees are on piecework.

James F. Lincoln, a brother of the company's founder, John C. Lincoln, originated the bonus program, Sabo said. Workers had asked for higher pay, and Lincoln had told them the firm just didn't have the money for it.

"So they simply said, 'If we could make more money for you, would you pay it to us?' and Lincoln said yes," Sabo said. "It's a one-time payment. They are sharing in the profits, but it's not a profit-sharing program in the usual sense of the word. And there's nothing guaranteed—it depends each year on how well the year goes."

Sabo credited the company's strong financial showing to such factors as work on the trans-Alaska oil pipeline, offshore-plant construction, shipbuilding activity, and other energy-related operations.

Case 1–8 ————————————————————————————————————

The Individual-Organizational Fit: Ethics and Style

Robert Knapp

Alternating between tapping his fingertips on his desk and propping his head with them, Dr. Mike Maynard stared at the memo in his office at Energy Research Labs. He had studied it most of the previous night, after it had been pushed under his door just before leaving his office the day before. Shortly he would have to decide what position to take on it. The memo was signed by the "Committee of Concerned Researchers," who wished to meet with Maynard in his office at 9:00 A.M., which was approaching.

He studied again the list of "grievances" against his boss, Wayne Newsome, president of Energy Labs. Trying to be objective, he felt some charges were exaggerated and a few untrue. Nevertheless, he had to concede that on the whole they were well founded.

More troubling was the section titled "alternative recourses." The memo asked its readers to consider which actions they would support regarding president Newsome and the problems at Energy Labs. Three possible actions were proposed.

The first advocated an all-out effort to replace Newsome by perhaps "going public" with a campaign to embarrass him in the media and among other important outsiders, by going over his head and taking their grievances to the board of directors, or by taking a vote among the organization's professional employees to express "no confidence" in the president.

The second approach advocated that a committee of department heads see Newsome in private about their concerns, hoping to turn him around and salvage both the deteriorating situation at Energy Labs and Newsome's job.

The third action advocated doing nothing, partly out of fear of making a bad situation worse and of avoiding wrathful revenge from the president, and partly in the hope that things would improve naturally.

Maynard had heard all these before in many different conversations, and had, in fact, contemplated doing some of them on his own. He knew he was in a unique position at Energy Labs because of his long tenure, his personal relationship with Newsome, and his close contacts with some members of the board of directors and other outsiders. Moreover, Maynard felt he, and perhaps only he, knew the root cause of the whole bad situation.

REFLECTIONS

Maynard lay back in his chair and reflected on the course of events that had led to this unfortunate but not totally surprising crisis. The drama of events tightly linked Energy Labs, president Newsome, and himself in such a way that Maynard felt himself moving to center stage.

The company was started nine years ago as a small energy research "think tank" by three university faculty members and two corporate energy specialists. Maynard was one of the original founders still at Energy Labs, and now was head of one of its major research departments. From the beginning, there was some conflict among the organization's principals about whether it should be run more like a university research lab or a profit-seeking private corporation. In the early years, those favoring a collegial or horizontal organization prevailed over those wanting a hierarchical or vertical organization, reflecting the largely academic background of its founders.

Shared decision-making seemed to work well enough until Energy Labs began to grow. Funding of research grew faster than even the most optimistic of its founders expected. A critical point was reached five years ago when both government and private funding agencies required that Energy Labs reorganize itself more like a business, implement better management and financial control systems, and hire a professional administrator with proven managerial experience.

Everyone was delighted when Wayne Newsome was successfully recruited to become president of Energy Labs. His background seemed perfectly suited to the firm's needs. He was recruited from a billion-dollar corporation, where for three years, he had been vice president of a reputable research division many times larger than Energy Labs. Before that, Newsome had retired as a two-star Air Force general. He had worked primarily in staff and management functions in the Air Force, and after receiving his MBA, spent almost five years managing high-level military research offices. He knew personally just about every important energy expert in Washington. He had the reputation of a high-energy, take-charge person, who was also a supersalesman.

Maynard remembered how hard he worked, first to get Newsome to take the job at Energy Labs, and later to assist him in adjusting to the new job and community. Perhaps it was because of this that the two became such close friends. But Maynard always believed their friendship was based more on personal qualities and mutual respect beyond their professional association. Even their wives and children had become very good friends, sharing much more than is typical among families of professional colleagues.

Maynard was touched and flattered when Newsome embraced him as his best friend at Energy Labs and took him under his wing. A rather cloistered academic craftsman-scientist, Maynard learned a great deal from Newsome about people, the business of life, and the life of business. From his relationship with Newsome, he learned how important a mentor could be, even though only 14 years separated them.

Maynard was especially proud of his involvement with Newsome during the latter's first years of leadership. The organization prospered, growing from 40 persons before Newsome took over to almost 120 persons, mostly high-talented professionals, five years later. The number of major divisions and departments had almost tripled.

Newsome proved especially talented in developing and, as he liked to say, "seducing" major funding agency heads. In those early years, everyone at Energy Labs admired Newsome, rallied behind him, and gave their extra for him and for the organization. No one could fault Newsome, not even now, for lacking aggressiveness or for failing to increase Energy Labs' national visibility. Newsome's extremely effective efforts on the outside earned him considerable respect and support from major funding agencies, as well as a respect that bordered on fear from competitors.

Anticipating who would make which arguments at the approaching meeting, Maynard recalled the many hours he had spent discussing Energy Labs' internal problems. Such a waste of time, he thought. Yet the endless discussions seemed necessary—to comfort a subordinate who had suffered an unnecessary lash from Newsome for a minor or nonexistent misstep; to sort out with other department heads the causes and possible solutions to the growing employee disaffection; to counsel people, including some of the organization's best, who were planning to leave Energy Labs out of frustration or anger at Newsome's personal antics or at his refusal to support their recommendations without any explanation.

STAFF MEETING

Last week's meeting of the five research department heads and their senior staffs highlighted the key issues, he thought. The meeting was called to work on the budget with president Newsome, but, as was happening increasingly in recent months, Newsome's secretary informed the group that the president had to leave the office suddenly on urgent outside business and could not attend. Then, as was also happening all too often, the majority of the two-hour meeting was given to discussion and debate about Newsome's performance and Energy Labs' problems.

"Here we go again," one department head said. "We all prepare for hours for another important meeting and Newsome cancels out on us again. I needed his decision yesterday on a new equipment contract, but the supplier agreed to extend the discount period until this afternoon. I really need that equipment and I'll never get that low price again. I am just going to go ahead and order it without Newsome's approval."

"He will have you on the carpet as soon as he finds out," someone commented. "I was in the same bind two weeks ago and ordered some lab remodeling when he wasn't around to approve it. I never saw him pound his desk so hard nor curse so loudly."

All of them had experienced Newsome's fulminations in recent weeks, whenever they posed a problem or even with an innocuous comment roughed some raw nerve no one really understood. Mostly the outbursts came in response to any hint, however slight, that something was not quite right with Energy Labs or with Newsome's performance.

"This guy is so edgy and explosive, I am afraid to say 'good morning' to him," one person said.

"I think he is becoming a little unbalanced, really paranoid—he even looks ill," another added.

"Thank God he is away from the building so much; at least when he is gone, I am not worried about his temper tantrums ruining my day or that of one of my people," was another comment.

"Yeh, but the guy is gone so often things are piling up and important decisions postponed; we are like a fast-moving ship with a half-time captain," another said.

Dr. Mary Richards, one of Energy Labs' brightest, most promising young prospects, had said little on previous occasions. Now, she said: "I am new here and I have been too busy trying to figure out just what the heck is going on to say much, until now. Newsome's paranoia, outbursts, and absenteeism are bad enough. But what really gets me is his macho street-fighter behavior. He even tries to cultivate that image. Every time I see those stupid quotations around his office, I cringe."

"You mean like the Vince Lombardi line about winning is the only thing?" someone asked.

"The worst is that inane rhyme by General Patton," she responded.

They all knew she was referring to the inscription on a plaque behind Newsome's desk. He loved to quote it: "In war as in loving, you've got to keep shoving."

Newsome's locker-room talk and mannerisms had been received cheerfully and without objection in his early years. They seemed a harmless part of his affectionate way of figuratively and at times literally wrapping himself around each employee and making him or her feel loved and appreciated. Now the talk seemed crude, and the backslapping and stroking, phony.

In recent months, almost all of them had experienced being stroked verbally and sometimes physically one day only to learn that Newsome had maligned them to someone else the next day.

"The guy's personality and style fit him to run a used-car lot or a mental institution, but not a research organization," Mary Richards said.

Maynard listened to the long list of complaints, as he had many times before, without saying much. As Newsome's closest associate, but also as one who had gained the respect of Energy Labs' senior employees over many years, Maynard knew they expected him to challenge or at least temper their rising chorus of complaints.

He didn't disappoint them. Partly out of conviction and partly to play the devil's advocate—for his own thinking as well as theirs—he spoke out.

"Isn't it possible," he suggested, "that our problems may not be all or even mostly the president's doing. Our growth rate has soared since he took over. Maybe we are suffering organizational growth pains that neither he nor we can handle through no fault of anybody. We have all become overworked and strung out, and the president most of all."

Someone commented that after Newsome returned from his last one-week vacation, he seemed more relaxed and in control, at least for a while.

"Let's not forget," Maynard continued, "how most of the same people in this room publicly applauded the president just two years ago for the great job he was doing. Before he came, we were floundering without any leadership at all. He was our white knight savior, one of you said. He put the pieces together around here. More importantly, his personal commitment to Energy Labs, his drive, and the way he made us feel appreciated—these energized all of us to really put out. This place suddenly came alive with excitement and promise. You've got to admit he provided us great leadership, at least until recently."

Another department head added a supporting comment: "Despite my alarm about our internal problems with Newsome, I've got to admit he does a hell of a job for us on the outside. He hasn't lost *that* touch."

He continued: "Just last week I watched him put on a stellar performance when he made our proposal before the Energy Development Department in Washington. He had them eating out of his hand, and I know he arm-twisted the agency's chairman at a private party afterward. The guy is an old crony of his. I'm sure we will get the contract."

Matt Blackburn, who was at the same presentation, said: "I agree it was another virtuoso performance, but it bothered me that he wasn't quite truthful in the performance specifications he promised we could meet. And his digs at our competitors were not really fair or true. I am afraid that in time outsiders will see through the bravado and b.s., just as we have. There is no doubt he is politically slick and, so far, very effective with outsiders. He'd probably make a great politician. But we need a manager who can keep things humming internally, not just a slick outside p.r. type."

"And we sure will suffer badly if, as Matt says, our credibility becomes suspect on the outside," someone commented.

"Maybe it's not so much that Newsome has changed as that we have," another speculated, going on; "maybe Newsome was the right guy for putting this organization together and sparking its early takeoff. Maybe now we need a president with different skills, one who doesn't lead so much by his own personality and by more selling, but one who can manage what we have already got going. I admit Newsome did a great job getting us launched; maybe now we need someone different to sail the ship."

Many heads nodded in agreement. There ensued a long discussion about Energy Labs' problems and needs, followed by a discussion of whether Newsome could change his style and adapt to the new needs.

Lunch hour was approaching. Danny Martinez, one of the younger but more outspoken people, said: "We've been over these same points time and time again. After lunch we will all go back to our offices to the same pile of problems, and they are never going to be solved as long as Newsome is around."

"What do you propose doing?"

Martinez had his usual ready answer, but this time it came from his close colleague, Mary Richards. Both of them had recently left major universities to join Energy Labs. At their universities, both had also experienced faculties taking "no confidence" votes on their administrators. In one case, a dean was subsequently replaced, and in another, a university president.

Richards asked the group to consider taking a "no confidence" vote on Newsome. She and Martinez seemed to persuade the more skeptical people who had never experienced such an action, that it might make sense at Energy Labs, which they pointed out was closer in nature to a university than a factory, where such votes are unheard of.

Among the various courses of actions frequently discussed, this was becoming the most popular one, at least in recent weeks.

"I am not sure," cautioned Maynard, and he asked: "How do we know how it will turn out? How do we assure it is done honestly and completely? Who will be asked to vote? What do we do with the vote after we have it?"

Martinez began to answer: "We can . . ."

But Maynard continued: "Look, we can't decide anything definite now, and I have to run to a luncheon meeting in a few minutes. I really am not sure in my own mind what or who is really the cause of our problems. There are so many different possible explanations." He paused and chose his words carefully: "There has just got to be something else going on that can explain what's happened over the last year or so. Until we are sure of the cause, we can't choose which action is best. Doesn't anybody have any new insights or information to consider before our next discussion?"

He carefully surveyed all the faces for some hint. The looks were all tired, blank, unrevealing.

"Let's get out of here," Martinez said.

The meeting ended.

TROUBLING TRUTH

Maynard knew he had lied about his ignorance. He knew the answer to his own question and now he was confident no one else did. But this knowledge only increased his burden and sense of responsibility.

His first suspicions of Newsome's drinking problem came from comments from Newsome's wife over many months. Now, in retrospect, he realized she had been growing alarmed at her husband's declining condition and sending out appeals for understanding and help.

Then there was the night when the Newsomes dined at the Maynards' house. That day Newsome had been pounded pretty hard at the board of directors meeting. Newsome drank too much and Maynard had to drive the Newsomes home. He felt at the time it was odd for Mrs. Newsome to break down so much over one too many martinis on one night.

A more definite indication had come two months ago and strictly by accident. Maynard found out from a friend at another firm that Newsome's last vacation was probably spent at a drying-out institution in another state. The friend's wife had been at the same institution at about the same time and thought she had seen Newsome there.

After much soul-searching together, the Maynards decided to reveal their suspicion of Newsome's incipient alcoholism to Mrs. Newsome. Maynard felt he had to do this both out of concern for his friends and for what was happening at Energy Labs.

After initially denying it, Mrs. Newsome confided that their suspicions were true. But she insisted that the problem was temporary and the result of special personal and business pressures that would pass.

She said that her husband developed a similar problem midway in his military career under similar pressures, but that he licked it. After a temporary setback, he resumed and, in fact, improved his successful performance on the job and progressed rapidly. She was confident that he would do the same thing again. She asked Maynard not to reveal anything about this at Energy Labs. In response to Maynard's question about whether he should reveal his knowledge to her husband and offer his help, Mrs. Newsome said she really didn't know.

Since the confirmation by Mrs. Newsome, Maynard felt better for knowing the truth, but also more troubled by what to do. He could not decide whether Mrs. Newsome's confidence that the drinking problem would pass was based on reason or simply hope.

Moreover, Maynard wasn't sure that even if Newsome beat his drinking problem, he would still be able to perform what was needed at Energy Labs. Maybe the organization *had* outgrown Newsome's skills and talents. Maybe a leader who excels at selling and dealing, at stimulating people by his individual drive and personality, isn't suited to manage an organization grown large, complex, and more impersonal.

At one point weeks earlier, Maynard made up his mind to openly discuss the matter with his boss and friend, and to offer his understanding and support. He asked to have lunch with Newsome. He tried to open the matter by mentioning how concerned he was about the growing talk of unionization and other problems at Energy Labs, and also how worried he was about Newsome's well-being under such pressures.

Newsome came unglued, wildly waving his arms, cursing the union advocates as "ungrateful Judases." Nobody appreciated all he had done for Energy Labs, Newsome yelled. Nobody knew all the goddamn constituencies he had to serve. Nobody worked harder at Energy Labs than he did. The outburst lasted throughout lunch, with Maynard hardly saying another word for an hour and a half.

Afterward, Maynard wondered if his timing had been bad, and whether he should try to broach the subject another time in another way. He also wondered what was on the mind of his close friend on the board of directors. When the friend asked to meet with Maynard, ostensibly about a funding proposal, he kept probing about Newsome and internal problems at Energy Labs. Did his friend know? Did he suspect? Should Maynard tell him and seek his advice?

There was a knock on Maynard's door. He looked at his watch, saw it was 9:00, and braced himself for another tense meeting.

Case 1–9
Stewart Steel
Geraldine Byrne Ellerbrock

Stewart Steel's plant has been in operation since 1950. When it became automated in 1970, there was an increase of 20 percent in its production of steel castings and bearings. The automation of the assembly line resulted in increased production and quality, but caused a large debt. The company is seeking to maintain the benefits of the automation while decreasing its debt.

The factory is noisy but clean. The women wear attractive pant suits and the men colorful sport shirts and slacks. When possible, the work is arranged so the employees can converse and socialize on the jobs that require only surface attention. The employees earn as much as $9 an hour, including benefits. They're given two break allowances of 15 minutes each, and by arrangement, are given 30 minutes for lunch. There is no incentive plan. The employees are on a "fair-day's work for a fair-day's pay" basis. It is not easy to fire an employee for low productivity. A dismissal must go through these stages: a normal warning, a written warning, one-day suspension, one-week suspension, one-month suspension, three-month suspension. If the employee still does not perform well, he is given terminal suspension with a six-month's probationary period for reevaluation.

Stewart Steel has been operating smoothly with little down time. The supervisors agree, ". . . by far, the main cog in the operation is people." Absenteeism, however, is a big problem. One of the foremen reported, "Today is the first time in over two weeks that all my people have been here." Absenteeism necessitates employing 12 percent more employees than needed, so a section of the line will not have to be closed down, necessitating work stoppage throughout the plant. Another foreman commented, "It seems we are hiring more young people and women. I don't know whether that is our problem or not."

A third foreman said, "The young people are a lot smarter than they used to be, and the women must feel good about this place or they wouldn't go to the bother of fixing their hair and selecting their clothes. It is a puzzle to me."

The automated plant has made it possible for Stewart Steel to improve the quality of their products. This has resulted in increased sales orders. They find that it is necessary to promote one of the foremen to the position of assistant plant manager. The three leading candidates are Dave Ashland, Frank Bates, and Mike Citz. Dave, a college graduate, believed that being a foreman was a necessary step to advance his career in management. Although some people of a minority group would not have accepted the low-status job as foreman, he felt it was a position which would give him valuable experience. Although he is a minority member, he feels very comfortable in his position and in his relationships with the workers. He is proud of the fact that he is to be sent to an out-of-town supervisory training seminar. Dave said, in conversation with Frank, "I have plans to redesign some of these jobs, so the people will get an opportunity to do more than one operation. It will make them feel good if they can see the whole part completed." Frank replied, "Well, I try to get the guys working together, even if they do the same thing all day. If they can help each other out, it gives them a good feeling." Dave said, "I know they like to do things together since they have worked in this place so long and know each other well. The problem is that some jobs don't lend themselves to teamwork."

Dave can be seen in the plant talking to employees: "Cal, why do you suppose that part gets jammed in the machinery?" or "Bob, I can always count on you to keep a smooth operation here. There hasn't been a breakdown in your section for over a year. I believe it is because you are always so alert to possible problems and do preventive maintenance. There is an opening coming up for foreman. I am going to recommend you. Would you like the job?" Bob said, "No thanks, I have worked on this job for 15 years. I know more about it than anyone in the plant. The guys get along together. I don't want a foreman's grief. Thanks, anyway."

He was disturbed when one of the men, after having been moved from his line because of an extended sick leave, filed 13 grievances in three weeks. He would have promised the man the first opening that came up on his old line, but was afraid that five or six commitments of this sort would "box him in." He values his reputation for trustworthiness and does not want to make commitments to the workers that he might not be able to fulfill.

Frank Bates knows the job well, having been employed on the line for 12 years before his promotion to foreman. He still lives in the same section of town as formerly and is in the same car pool. He bowls on the plant team. He prides himself on being foreman of the section with the highest productivity in the plant. He has not mentioned that his department also has the highest absenteeism and turnover. Frank can be counted upon to work late hours or come in early to set up a job. He is able to make minor repairs and keep his line in operation. The other foremen respect him.

Mike Citz has been with Stewart Steel since his college graduation 20 years ago. He knows the operation well and is considered a real "company man." The company's goals are his goals, and the company's goals are increased production and cost reduction. He expects reasonableness and cooperation of the workers but believes he must maintain control. One of the other foreman has said about him, "Mike is a combination of scout leader, army sergeant, and everyday problem solver." Although always actively engaged in problem solving, he does not lose his patience. Both self-disciplined and self-motivated, he does not seek more autonomy nor does he give those he supervises more autonomy. He receives his orders from his supervisor and can be trusted to carry out the assignment at the least cost. He is deeply involved in each facet of his own department but pays little attention to how the other departments operate. He is respected, however, by the foremen in these departments.

The plant manager, Paul Rolf, has the responsibility for selecting the new assistant manager. Paul called the personnel director, Fred Eddy: "Fred, I know the three guys who are up for promotion to assistant plant manager. That is a key job and it is a chance to bring some new blood into management. I like each one of those guys. In fact, I hired them. I want you to evaluate them and then send the reports to me so I can make the final selection." He had just hung up the phone when John Stewart, the president, came in the office and showed him some handbills that some of the employees were passing around.

"Would you believe it, now they want a union! As if we don't have enough problems. Some of the men are trying to get enough support for a unionization election. A union could make it tough for us. I know we are going to be getting a new assistant plant manager. Before we choose one, I want each of those being considered to make a full report on this union- ism deal. This will help us choose the best man for the job."

Paul said, "I just called personnel and asked for their evaluation of each man. We can ask Dave, Frank, and Mike to make a complete assess- ment of the proposed unionization and how they react to the situation. We can find out what effect a union would have on us, and why. We can determine what action we should or should not take."

Case 1–10 ————————————————————————————————————

Which Style Is Best?

W. D. Heier

The ABC Company is a medium-sized corporation which manufactures automotive parts. Recently, the company president attended a leadership seminar and came away deeply impressed with the effect various leader- ship styles could have on the output and morale of the organization.

In mulling over how he might proceed, the president decided to utilize the services of Paul Patterson, a management consultant, who was cur- rently reviewing the goals and objectives of the company. The president told Paul about the leadership seminar and how impressed he had been and that a leadership survey of the company was desired.

It was determined that the division headed by Donald Drake should be the test case and that Paul would report to the president upon completion of that survey. Some of the notes made by Paul in his interviews with the key managers in Drake's division follow.

Ancil Able

Ancil is very proud of the output of his section. He has always stressed the necessity for good control procedures and efficiency, and is very insist- ent that project instructions be fully understood by his subordinates and that follow-up communications be rapid, complete, and accurate. Ancil serves as the clearinghouse for all incoming and outgoing work. He gives small problems to one individual to complete, but if the problem is large he calls in several key people. Usually, his employees are briefed on what the policy is to be, what part of the report each subordinate is to complete, and the completion date. Ancil considers this as the only way to get full coordination without lost motion or an overlap of work.

Ancil considers it best for a boss to remain aloof from his subordinates, and believes that being "buddy-buddy" tends to hamper discipline. He does his "chewing out" in private and his praising, too. He believes that people in his section really know where they stand.

According to Ancil, the biggest problem in business today is that subordinates just will not accept responsibility. He states that his people have lots of opportunities to show what they can do but not many really try too hard.

One comment Ancil made was that he does not understand how his subordinates got along with the previous section head who ran a very "loose shop." Ancil stated his boss is quite happy with the way things go in his section.

Bob Black

Bob believes that every employee has a right to be treated as an individual, and espouses the theory that it is a boss's responsibility and duty to cater to the employee's needs. He noted that he is constantly doing little things for his subordinates and gave as an example his presentation of two tickets to an art show to be held at the City Gallery next month. He stated that the tickets cost $5 each but that it will be both educational and enjoyable for the employee and his wife. This was done to express his appreciation for a good job the man had done a few months back.

Bob says he always makes a point of walking through his section area at least once each day, stopping to speak to at least 25 percent of the employees on each trip.

Bob does not like to "knock" anyone, but he noted that Ancil Able ran one of those "taut ships" you hear about. He stated that Ancil's employees are probably not too happy but there isn't much they can do but wait for Ancil to move.

Bob said he had noticed a little bit of bypassing going on in the company but that most of it is just due to the press of business. His idea is to run a friendly, low-keyed operation with a happy group of subordinates. Although he confesses that they might not be as efficient in terms of speedy outputs as other units, he considers he has far greater subordinate loyalty and higher morale and that his subordinates work well as an expression of their appreciation of his (Bob's) enlightened leadership.

Charles Carr

Charlie says his principal problem is the shifting of responsibilities between his section and others in the division. He considers his section the "fire drill" area that gets all of the rush, hot items, whether or not they belong in his section. He seems to think this is caused by his immediate superior not being too sure who should handle what jobs in the division.

Charlie admits he hasn't tried to stop this practice. He stated (with a grin) that it makes the other section heads jealous but they are afraid to complain. They seem to think Charlie is a personal friend of the division manager, but Charlie says this is not true.

Charlie said he used to be embarrassed in meetings when it was obvious he was doing jobs out of his area but he has gotten used to it by now, and apparently the other section heads have also.

Charlie's approach to discipline is just to keep everybody busy and "you won't have those kinds of problems." He stated that a good boss doesn't have time to hold anybody's hand, like Bob Black does, and tell the guy what a great job he's doing. Charlie believes that if you promise people you will keep an eye on their work for raises and promotion purposes, most of the problems take care of themselves.

Charlie stated that he believes in giving a guy a job to do and then letting him do it without too much checking on his work. He believes most of his subordinates know the score and do their jobs reasonably well without too much griping.

If he has a problem, it is probably the fact that the role and scope of his section has become a little blurred by current practices. Charlie did state that he thinks he should resist a recent tendency for "company people above my division manager's level" to call him up to their offices to hear his ideas on certain programs. However, Charlie is not too sure that this can be stopped without creating a ruckus of some kind. He says he is studying the problem.

Donald Drake

As division manager, Don thinks things are going pretty well since he has not had any real complaints from his superiors in the company, beyond the "small problem" type of thing. He thinks his division is at about the same level of efficiency as the other divisions in the organization.

His management philosophy is to let the section managers find their own level, organizational niche, and form of operation and then check to see if the total output of the division is satisfactory. He stated that he has done this with his present section heads. This was the policy being used when he (Don) was a section head and it has worked fine for him.

Don considers his function as that of a clearinghouse for division inputs and outputs, and sees his job basically as a coordinating one, coupled with the requirement for him to "front" for the division. He believes that you should let a man expand his job activities as much as he is able to do so. Don noted that Charlie Carr had expanded greatly as a manager since he (Don) had arrived. Says he frequently takes Charlie with him to high-level meetings in the company, since Charlie knows more about the division's operations than anyone else in it.

Don noted that both Ancil and Bob seem to do a creditable job in their sections. He has very little contact with Ancil's employees but occasionally has to see one of Bob Black's boys about something the employee has fouled up. This results from the fact that Bob considers such a face-to-face confrontation between the division manager and a lower-level section employee a good lesson to impress upon the subordinate that he has let down his boss. Don Drake said he is not too keen on this procedure but that Bob considers it a most valuable training device to teach the employee to do a good job every time, so Don goes along with it.

Case 1–11
Gladstone Company
Ronald M. Zigli and W. Daniel Rountree

BACKGROUND INFORMATION

The Company

Gladstone, a family-owned company, has been in the textile business for the last 50 years. It has grown from a small firm struggling for existence in 1926 to a national company in 1976 with gross sales in excess of $100 million. Gladstone has always been a paternal organization, concerned with the personal welfare of its employees while demanding a high level of productivity. For years Gladstone has enjoyed an excellent reputation for its efforts toward social betterment in the community. Many members of management are actively involved in community programs and projects with the full support of Gladstone's top management.

The company manufactures a complete line of textile products and has its own national sales force selling to both wholesalers and retailers. Gladstone's products are sold for commercial use and to ultimate consumers. Both branded and nonbranded items are sold. In general, Gladstone's product line is considered to be of moderate to high quality. Nine major plants produce most of Gladstone's line. Most plants are located in Burnsville, a small textile-industry-dominated town of approximately 60,000 people in the southeastern part of the United States. A few plants are scattered in parts of the eastern United States.

Each of Gladstone's manufacturing plants carries on most of its operations autonomously. Only questions involving marketing and sales, major financial investments, or other issues of companywide impact are decided at the company office. All other decisions remain the prerogative of the plant manager, whose effectiveness is usually measured against profit for his plant. Some plants manufacture intermediate items that are subsequently converted into finished products by other plants. Even in these instances, where profit cannot be measured directly, decisions are still largely the prerogative of the plant manager.

Gladstone employs 3,000 people, including management. The non-supervisory labor force is not unionized and consists largely of semiskilled or unskilled workers. These workers typically have relatively low job aspirations, are not likely to leave the immediate geographic area, but may move from one textile firm to another within the local community. Unskilled workers are more likely to change jobs because of unpleasant working conditions, uninteresting work, or a combination of both.

The Industry

The textile industry is rather unusual in several respects. Perhaps most apparent is the fact that it is one of the few industries that approaches pure competition in the economic sense. Even the largest firm captures no more than 10 percent of total industry sales (in dollars). Another characteristic of textiles is the concentration of firms in the southeast. From a marketing standpoint, competition in the marketplace is fierce. "Cutthroat" practices are not uncommon. Finally, the textile industry is quite sensitive to buyer preferences and endeavors to produce what the customer wants. As a result, textile products are constantly changing in style and composition.

In the last several years, the industry has undergone a number of changes. More and more companies have expanded their operations. Many have merged with other companies (in and out of textiles), diversified and "gone public." Many of the largest manufacturers are actively investigating vertical integration. In addition, billions of dollars have been spent on plant modernization in an effort to become less labor-intensive and more capital-intensive. Nevertheless, most experts agree that some art or craftsmanship will always be an integral part of the industry.

Changes in raw materials and raw material sources have also occurred in the last several years. Synthetics are being substituted for more basic materials. Although many buyers still prefer the use of "natural" materials, more and more consumers are convinced of the superiority of synthetics from the standpoint of durability and strength, with no discernible difference in appearance.

In spite of all these positive changes, the textile industry still has several major problems to resolve. One of the more important and difficult issues facing many textile manufacturers is that of high turnover. This problem is particularly acute in areas where unemployment is low and a shortage of needed labor exists. In fact, availability of labor in some areas is so low that many companies have turned to less conventional sources for labor. Other companies have changed fringe benefit programs hoping to induce a greater sense of loyalty and tenure on the part of employees; still other companies have tried a wide variety of financial and benefit-oriented, nonfinancial incentive programs. For almost all of these firms, success has been minimal. A comparative statewide study of benefit programs was conducted in 1974 in Gladstone's home state. The results, for selected industries are shown in Exhibit 1.

THE SITUATION

Casual-Wear Plant 5

Gladstone is one of several large textile manufacturers in Burnsville. As a group, these firms represent the dominant industry and major employer in the area. Because of this, competition for the existing labor force has been fierce, and, at any one time, a sizable proportion of textile employees are in transit from one textile manufacturer to another.

One of the largest manufacturing plants in the area for Gladstone is Casual-Wear Plant 5. (See Exhibit 2 for the organization chart.) Employment at this plant fluctuates over the year from, roughly, 300 to as high as 700 employees. This fluctuation is the result, in part, of a high turnover rate, one of the most frustrating problems at Casual-Wear Plant 5. Although the rates are not atypical for other similar plants in the area, the plant manager has been pressing hard for answers to the problem. Clearly, the costs of turnover are high. The personnel processing costs of recruitment, selection, and training, not to mention interruptions in production, have a serious impact on profitability. A number of things have been tried to reduce turnover, but none has been successful thus far.

One such experiment has been the employment of prison labor. Essentially, the program consists of releasing prisoners during the day to work at Casual-Wear Plant 5. Each evening these employees return to prison. These workers are paid comparable wages and are excused from other prison work. The only additional expenses incurred by prison workers are travel expenses, which are paid to the state by the prisoner from wages earned.

For the past eight years, under the direction of Dave Packet, Plant 5 has employed between 5 and 30 prison workers. In addition, several other efforts have been made to reduce the turnover rate, including a merit review system whereby merit pay raises are given throughout the year. Also, Casual-Wear Plant 5 has had, for years, an "open door" grievance system which allowed any employee to walk right into the plant manager's office with any complaint. In spite of all these efforts, turnover remained high, as evidenced by Exhibit 3. Until recently, the prison release program has been moderately successful. However, Dave Packet was just informed that the state plans to move the facility housing prisoners that participate in the release program at Casual-Wear Plant 5 to another geographic location which would be too remote for continuance of the program. As a result, the entire issue of turnover has been raised again.

The Plant Meeting

The plant manager, Frank Brumbley, has called a meeting in his office. Attending are Dave Packet, Jean Britton, and all shop foremen. The pros and cons of the prison release program becomes the first order of business. It is pointed out by one foreman that prison workers are not accepted by other employees socially. As a result, problems have occurred on the job

EXHIBIT 1

Fringe Benefits for Selected Industries on a Statewide Basis
(all items expressed in percentages)

	All Industries	Textile	Primary Metal Industries	Furniture and Fixtures	Paper and Allied Products	Chemical and Allied Products	Rubber and Miscellaneous Plastics Products	Stone Clay, Glass, and Concrete Products
Percentage Coverage of Establishments in Survey	12	17	20	9	31	10	20	6
1. Paid vacation of 1 week (less than 1 year service)	21	25	0	28	17	42	24	4
2. Paid vacation of 2 weeks or more (1–5 years service)	26	18	31	30	36	83	40	25
3. Paid holidays of 5 days or more	72	51	100	53	93	100	96	83
4. Paid rest periods of 20 minutes or more	79	80	85	79	78	50	88	54
5. Annual or semi-annual bonus plan	45	58	31	52	22	29	40	46
6. Annual savings or stock purchase plan ...	15	13	15	14	7	46	16	4

7. Cost-of-living pay increases	13	10	23	9	7	13	24	8
8. Paid sick leave (less than 1 year service)	9	2	15	2	15	25	28	8
9. Paid sick leave (1–5 years service)	13	3	23	2	15	33	38	21
10. Life insurance (employer paying more than 50 percent)	77	74	84	75	85	88	92	88
11. Hospital insurance (employer paying more than 50 percent)	76	75	92	69	85	95	92	96
12. Income protection plan (employer paying more than 50 percent)	31	23	38	38	46	71	40	33
13. Retirement pension plan (employer paying more than 50 percent)	55	53	69	55	74	95	56	67

NOTE: Statistical data compiled by state agency. Identification withheld for reasons of confidentiality.

EXHIBIT 2
Casual-Wear Plant 5 Organizational Chart

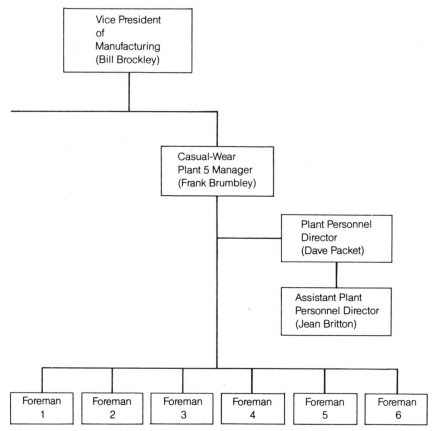

from time to time. George, another foreman, counters this argument say-ing that these problems are minor and are more than offset by the fact that prison workers learn fast, are the most reliable, and are among the top 10 percent in productivity. Most of the other foremen agree with this observa-tion. Jean asks Dave how long the average prison worker stays at Glad-stone. Dave replies, "Approximately 15 months." The basic purpose of the use of prison labor also comes up. "Are we interested in rehabilitation, profit, cost savings, or an assured labor source?" asks one foreman. After some discussion Dave, Jean, and Frank agree that business interests must come first; however, the four issues are not necessarily mutually exclusive. Dave asks the question, "Do any employees show any resentment toward prison workers, perhaps feeling that a job has been taken away from

EXHIBIT 3
Gladstone Annual Average Turnover

Year	Turnover Rate (percent)
1965	100.00
1966	110.00
1967	115.00
1968	110.00
1969	126.00
1970	140.00
1971	140.00
1972	110.00
1973	125.00
1974	144.00
1975	75.00
1976	n.a.

Source: Company records.

someone else by the prison workers?" Again, most foremen indicated that they found no evidence of that on the job. Frank suggests that the discussion of prison labor may be a moot argument since this source was not going to be available in the future. He then asked Dave and Jean whether there were any alternative sources of prison labor. Dave indicated that a younger group of prisoners, most of which were serving terms for drug abuse, would be close enough to the plant for employment. At this point, several foremen raised objections citing a number of problems experienced by other companies that attempted to use such labor. On several occasions, other firms found these younger prisoners "pushing" narcotics and generally creating disharmony on the job for other workers.

The Challenge

Frank asks the question: "Is it necessary to seek employees from less conventional sources? Could we offer additional direct and indirect financial and nonfinancial inducements to draw and develop a stable labor force?" "Possibly," says Jean, "however, we will have our work cut out for us." She shows the group the annual average rates of employment for the United States and county for the last 14 years. (See Exhibit 4.) Jean goes on to point out that, job for job, pay scales are comparable to any in the county or state. She also cites a personal observation that the highest turnover seems to be in departments that have the most unpleasant jobs and highest unskilled labor ratios. Frank finally charges Dave, Jean, and two of the senior foremen to develop a plan to reduce turnover and stabilize the work force.

EXHIBIT 4
Average Annual Unemployment (in percent)

Year	Capitol County	U.S.
1963	4.5	5.7
1964	4.2	5.2
1965	2.8	4.5
1966	2.2	3.8
1967	3.1	3.8
1968	2.1	3.6
1969	2.0	3.5
1970	5.0	4.9
1971	5.2	5.9
1972	3.4	5.6
1973	2.9	4.9
1974	4.9	5.6
1975	n.a.	8.5
1976	n.a.	n.a.

Source: State Employment Agency and Manpower reports to the President in 1971 and 1975.

Case 1–12

Credit Comes South

Virginia Geurin and Edward F. Mills, Student

Birmingham Industries is one of the nation's leading producers of textiles for apparel, home furnishings, and industrial markets. Their expected sales for the coming year should be in the vicinity of $500 million, with a net income of over $20 million. The main headquarters are located in New York City, due mainly to the proximity of the apparel and money markets. These offices house the chairman of the board, several vice presidents, the treasurer, controller, sales functions, and credit department.

The southern headquarters for the corporation is located in Raleigh and is the hub for the over 25 plants located in the southeastern United States. These offices are manned by 250 employees, headed by the corporation's president. It functions as a service center and supplies the plants with centralized staff departments, such as purchasing, engineering, accounting, information services, industrial engineering, transportation, and research development.

Birmingham Industries deviates somewhat from traditional textile administrative customs, probably due to its diversity of products. Such a deviation is the credit operation, which is normally a function factored by most companies in the textile industry.

Until June of this year the entire credit function was handled from the New York office. The various company divisions were spread among three credit managers who reported directly to the treasurer. Each manager had several credit analysts (ten altogether) directly reporting to him, and some of the analysts had assistants with the title of collection men.

At the beginning of the year the decision was made to consider moving a portion of the credit function to the Raleigh office. The final decision was to be based on the following:

1. The availability of qualified personnel, in the immediate area, to staff the department.
2. The number of experienced workers in the New York department that would move South.
3. The effect, on the remaining staff, of terminating those personnel who would not relocate.
4. The divisions or areas of credit that could be handled as well in the South as in New York.
5. The expenses and savings of such a move.
6. The availability of resources (space, equipment, communication) in the Raleigh office.

Many other criteria were also used in making the final decision; however, it all ultimately culminated into the newly formed "Southern Credit Office."

One of the present credit managers in the New York office was offered the top post in the new department. However, he turned it down when the company would not meet his demands for a substantial salary increase (he was subsequently terminated). Jack O'Brian, an aggressive young credit analyst, was then given the opportunity to make this new department work . . . and he accepted.

The staff was to consist of one manager, four credit analysts, two collection men, and three secretaries. Only one other man from the New York credit department accepted the offer to move to North Carolina. The remainder of the staff was recruited and hired by the personnel department in the Raleigh office. The men were interviewed personally by both Jack and Mr. Donivan, the treasurer of the corporation. The secretaries were first screened by personnel and then interviewed by Jack alone.

By June 14, the construction required to expand the new office area was complete and most of the file cabinets and equipment were in place. In a few days the office was buzzing with the sounds of a busy staff trying to get oriented to the new environment. A sketch of the office shows the final layout as designed by the treasurer (see Exhibit 1).

On July 21, Bobbie Leigh, the manager's secretary, quit after working for just over one month. This came as quite a surprise to Jack O'Brian, as well as to the personnel department. There didn't seem to be any problems, then all of a sudden she was handing in her two weeks' notice. The following is an excerpt from her exit interview:

Q. Why did you quit?

A. So many reasons, it's hard to put in a nutshell . . . It's more or less working "for" instead of "with" . . . I want to feel I'm part of the team . . . I want to feel equal . . .

EXHIBIT 1

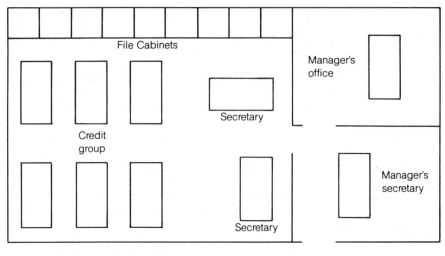

Q. Equal to the other girls or the men in the office?

A. The men . . . I want to feel equal to the men . . . that's terrible isn't it!

Q. What made you feel unequal?

A. I don't know . . . I felt he *[the manager]* didn't trust my judgment . . .
I feel that this whole corporation is very male-oriented . . . I can see
men getting special privileges within our department and that doesn't
seem right . . . they don't work as hard as we do . . . yet I'm sure
they're paid on a far larger scale . . . even their paychecks aren't distributed like ours . . . special handled *[monthly versus weekly payroll]*
. . . And I guess those things make them appear special . . . I'm not
really for women's lib in the violent, dramatic sort of way, I just feel
that a woman can handle a job as equal as any man . . . In fact I can
see in our office that the women are, more or less, doing the work for
the men as far as the actual paperwork involved and they are chatting
on the phone . . . I'd rather be chatting on the phone than doing paperwork . . . I feel I could handle any credit analyst's job, with more
finesse than I've seen there . . . and I don't see any future for me . . .
you know, in credit . . . I'm always looking for a chance for advancement and I can see that there would be none available . . . I also don't
feel appreciated, I don't mean that I want to be pampered or babied
. . . but just to be appreciated would be so great . . . I think in any
office that, sure you should get your work done, but also I think it
would be the ideal situation to be able to have a rapport where one can
have a friendly conversation with their superior, I think this is good.

Q. Could you talk with your manager?

A. No . . . I tried to . . . maybe I'm too pushy.

Q. Do you think you're too pushy?

A. Yes . . . you should have seen me at my last job at Biscayne *[two-year
business college]* . . . I was . . . well, admissions secretary, but just before I left we had new accounts to sell and I took over and that was a

man's job . . . Money started coming in because I was on commission
. . . it was easy . . . of course, if someone needed me I would have to
be there, even at 8:30 in the evening . . . my hours were very flexible
because it depended on when I had an appointment . . . I could even
play tennis for a couple of hours in the day if there were no appointments . . .

Q. Why did you leave, was there more money here?

A. Oh, no! I was paid better there; however, they were in the process of
cutting salaries and tightening their belts to improve profits . . . The
competition from a local technical school was beginning to hurt
them.

Q. That sounds like a selling type of job. Have you done pure secretarial
work before?

A. Yes . . . but what I'm doing now has no challenge—it's a very dull
type of atmosphere . . . I'm sure it's exciting for the men because they
have a little bit of power there.

Q. What kind of power?

A. You know, they can refuse a customer . . . decide on how much credit
to give him.

Q. Were you given a complete job description before you were hired?

A. No one is going to believe me, no one has believed me, but I swear he
just kept saying "my secretary, my secretary" . . . Peggy [personnel]
kept saying Mr. O'Brian's secretary . . . if he had said "secretary to
me, also to two other people," I'd have said, "Hey, this is not enough
money" . . . 'cause it isn't . . . Don't get me wrong, I like to stay busy,
I like working hard, in a way, because it keeps the day from dragging
. . . What bothered me was that on the second week when the men
came in it was then that I realized I was working for three instead of
one.

Q. How were you told about the other two men?

A. I was so stupid . . . Jack told me there was to be some phone switches
installed, one to his desk and two more at the rear desks so that if
those men were out or busy I could pick up . . . but he felt that there
would not be much need for that . . . I still didn't catch on that I'd
be working for them . . . I didn't stop to think . . . I knew that during
the interview he said I would be preparing tickers for some of the
other men . . . but I still didn't tie it together . . . But I think it was a
matter of self-importance [the manager's self-importance] . . . He
kept describing himself, his duties, his power, his contacts, and things
like that . . . and how it would relate to me . . . being his secretary and
all, that I didn't realize that anyone else was involved and he did the
same thing to my replacement, Mary. He kept saying as my secretary
this, and as my secretary that . . . But of course she already knew
[about the additional duties] . . .

Q. How did you get along with the two other men, once you realized
you'd also be working for them?

A. Well, I don't think it would have mattered that much but . . . well, let
me give you an example . . . I had been working through breaks and
after five trying to get my head above water and Fred said, "Tiger,

when are you ever going to get my filing done, it's stacking up over my head!" . . . and he was right, it was piling up . . . But then Jack said, "Well, what have you been doing" . . . I didn't feel I had to stop and tell him what I'd been doing when I had been going as fast as I possibly could . . . Nothing was said like "You've been doing a good job" . . . just "What have you been doing?" . . . There was no appreciation for what you did, just accountability for what you didn't do! . . .

Q. Did the other two men give a lot of orders?

A. Well, I heard one of the men say *[when they were first organizing the department],* "When my secretary gets in she'll be doing everything for me" . . . and I think this is about the attitude that they have . . . When your desk is next to the file cabinets and you need two files pulled, and your secretary is in an entirely different room and it will require you to walk 40 feet to get her, wouldn't it be easier to go to the file cabinet yourself, pull the two folders and return to your desk? . . . Well, they would come all the way into my office, give me the ticket and I would follow them back to almost their desk to pull the folders.

Q. Do you work in teams, either with the men or the other secretaries?

A. Mary has a credit analyst and a collection man, so does Lynn, where I have two credit analysts and the manager . . . You see this department started from scratch, down to the pencils . . . I've bugged purchasing to death . . . they hate to see me coming . . . My name's mud everywhere—the storeroom, maintenance, engineering . . . you know! . . . Jack had to look at a dozen catalogs to buy one ashtray for his office.

Q. Who did you like best in your office and why?

A. Scott *[no reporting relationship]* because he's cheerful, friendly, very easy to work with, and easy to please . . . He's businesslike but comfortable to be with . . . I think working for him would be fun!

Q. Who did you least like working with, and why?

A. Lester *[direct reporting relationship]* . . . Hey, this is hard to say . . . well, for example these files that came down from New York go back years and Lester feels we should go through and update all the files . . . I know they're in bad shape, but we're just trying to get started and every night Lester would have 25 or 30 folders to update that would need eight letters for references . . . He makes me feel subservient.

Q. Are you training your replacement?

A. Jack called me in to tell me that Mary was going to get my job and the training period will start next Monday and that since both our jobs were so similar that all I would really have to do is show her where I kept the pencils . . . It really hurt my feelings because I had worked so hard to accomplish this, that . . . gee, I really thought I had something . . . I have a two-year degree in secretarial science, keep house, raise a family, and work all at the same time . . . I thought I had really accomplished something. I guess I felt almost as arrogant as he did! . . . So I figured here is this person who was a beautician *[Mary]* for ten years and worked for Sears on the floor . . . and she was taking over my job ... Jack had a way of making me feel inadequate.

Q. Is that the main reason you're leaving?

A. No, the main reason I'm leaving is because I'm not happy, I don't feel comfortable ... Think about it, most of your waking hours are spent on the job ... then why can't your job be something delightful? People don't realize how much I'm by myself ... my office is separated from the others and the only contact I have is when they bring me some work to put on my desk ... They'll be in the outer credit office talking and laughing and they can enjoy each other, but I can't! Oh, that reminds me of something that happened ... I think Mr. Donivan is a really nice man *[the treasurer of the corporation, whom she has never met]* ... I really like him ... I liked him immediately as soon as I heard his voice on the phone ... his voice had character ... He would call several times a day ... and he would call me Bobbie and I would say, "Well, how are you?" and he'd say, "I'm fine, Bobbie, how are you?" and I'd say, "Well, how's the weather in New York?" and he said "Oh, not too good!" and I'd say something like "Oh, it's beautiful here today and what a beautiful view we have out the back window, you should be here!" and he'd say, "Well, I'll be coming down soon" and I'd say, "I'm looking forward to meeting you, hurry down!" ... Well, Jack overheard this one day and nearly had a stroke! He said, "Oh, Mr. Donivan is such a professional, I just don't think it would be advisable to chit-chat with him over the phone, he's just too busy!" ... I couldn't believe it ... I thought, "Well, is he ashamed of me? ... does he feel I'm not capable of carrying on a normal conversation with his superior?" ... He may be scared to death of him, but I'm not a bit afraid of him ... I'm just as good as Mr. Donivan! ... You know, people with positions like Mr. Donivan ... they don't feel as important as Jack does!

Q. Did you ever try to make suggestions to Jack which might improve conditions in the Credit department?

A. I tried ... I went in three weeks ago and told him that I just can't seem to get everything done ... keep up my filing, sort mail, get the reports and everything else ... He said, "Why is it you can't? You don't seem to realize that everybody has a lot of work to do!" ... and I thought, well, if you can't talk to him ... if you work your butt off and that's not enough and you go to him for some help ... and it does no good, why bother?

Q. When you told Jack that you planned to quit, did you leave him any options?

A. I went into his office Friday afternoon ... I realize it was a bad time 'cause he was getting ready to go out of town around six ... this was around four ... Fred had just asked me why I hadn't gotten his filing done and Lester wanted to know why I didn't get his letters sent out ... and I went in to tell Jack that I hadn't had time to get those things done ... and Jack said, "What have you been doing?" ... I told him that I didn't think that anyone should be on my back wanting to know why I hadn't done something! ... I don't think this is asking too much ... I had been working hard all day! ... I told him that I didn't think the workload was fair . . . working for these three men was like working for six . . . and the other girls had only two each . . . I just don't think it's fair . . . And he said, "Actually Lynn and Mary have more paperwork than you do! . . . So what's your problem?" . . . So I said my problem is that I want to leave . . . that I'm not happy here . . . he said to hold off until we could discuss this on Wednesday when he got back.

Q.   Did he discuss it when he got back?

A.   He said, "Well, did you decide that you want to leave?" . . . and I said, "Yes" . . . so that was it! . . . He doesn't care, don't ya see, he just doesn't care . . . He thinks that I'm stupid!

*   *   *   *   *

After the interview someone from the personnel department went to the credit department to find out more about Bobbie. His first stop was at Jack's office, where the following conversation took place.

Personnel: Jack, did Bobbie get a complete job description on her interview?

O'Brian: Absolutely . . . she knew exactly what her job was going to be like . . . as best as I knew it at the time! You know this was a completely new department and in the beginning a lot of changes had to be made . . . But I definitely told her she'd be working for some other credit men as well as myself.

Personnel: What were your feelings about Bobbie after the initial interview?

O'Brian: She was "gangbusters" . . . really came on strong . . . seemed bright, and with her skills and education she was more than qualified. In fact, I was joking with some of the guys in New York . . . that she'd probably have my job in a couple of weeks.

Personnel: Did your feelings about Bobbie change?

O'Brian: Well, . . . her work was acceptable, but she wasn't grasping some of the department concepts as rapidly as I first thought she would . . . She also started directing the other girls . . . so I had to call her in to put a stop to that . . . I told her that Mary and Lynn report to their respective credit men and not to her!

Personnel: Was there anything else?

O'Brian: Yes, . . . she treated Fred and Lester as though they were a secondary portion of her job . . . a nuisance . . . it bothered her to do anything for them . . . I was afraid this would lead to additional conflicts in the department morale.

Personnel: I guess that's it then!

O'Brian: Another thing bothered me . . . she was a "people person" . . . she would strike up an immediate conversation with a complete stranger . . . If a customer came in she'd start right off by telling them about her family life, her vacation . . . about anything . . . She did this with the treasurer! . . . And she was always too nice!

Personnel: Too nice?

O'Brian: Sounds crazy, doesn't it! . . . but she would "please" and "excuse me" and "thank you" and "pardon me" and "I appreciate it" and "you are welcome" me to death! . . . With all these adjectives it took her ten minutes to tell me who was holding on my line! *[phone]*

Personnel: When she quit were you surprised?

O'Brian: Surprised? . . . yes, but also somewhat relieved . . . I could see some more serious problems developing and this would solve several of them.

Personnel: Do you mind if I talk to some of your men?

O'Brian: No, go right ahead.

* * * * *

The next day in the office cafeteria the man from personnel saw some of the credit men gathered around a table sipping coffee.

Personnel: Mind if I join you all?

Credit Men: No, sit down.

Personnel: I hear Bobbie is leaving!

Lester: Ya, thank God!

Personnel: You didn't like her?

Lester: She was dumb.

Personnel: Oh, really, . . . she seemed pretty bright to me!

Fred: Oh, he doesn't mean that kind of dumb . . . She just had no common sense . . . she was naive to normal business rapport.

Lester: Last week she addressed a letter to a customer using just the city, in this case it was New York . . . so the letter came back today! . . . Also, the other day I gave her five "short payment" notices for the same customer . . . She wrote five separate letters instead of attaching all five to one letter . . . that's dumb!

Fred: I don't think she ever worked in an office before . . . She would interrupt a meeting between Jack and I just to see if it was alright to buy a pair of scissors and if you needed something . . . like a tape dispenser . . . it would take her three days just to get the order up to the purchasing department.

Personnel: I take it you're glad to see her go?

Lester: You bet!

Fred: To be honest, Lester, you'll have to admit she had a good personality . . . and her attitude wasn't that bad.

Lester: She talked too much!

Fred: She did give us more information than we really needed . . . like when she took a call she'd tell us who it was, the company, what they wanted, etc. . . . All I wanted was his name!

Lester: . . . and she was too damn nice!

Fred: Ha-ha! . . . he's right you know . . . she was so sugary it was sickening . . . When she came in the room everything got syrupy.

Lester: I guess that wouldn't be bad under normal conditions but we talk with irate customers and obstinate salesmen all day . . . I guess the contrast was too great.

Fred: Ya, . . . I think she'd make a good receptionist!

They all got up and went back to the credit department.

Case 1–13 ————————————————————————————————————

*People Problems at Healer's Hospital**

Barbara Karmel and Patrick E. Connor

Michael Flaherty is director of nursing at Healer's Hospital. He is talking about problems of staffing and training in the hospital, especially as related to the care of aged patients:

"The primary goal of this hospital is to provide care for the acutely ill and the injured—not of providing care for ill or injured young people or old people. There is no differentiation as to the types of people we care for other than between the ill and the injured; the idea is that our purpose is to care for acute problems as opposed to chronic illnesses. In this context, the fact that some of our patients are aged, some are chronically ill, and some are both aged and chronically ill, in addition to the acute problem that brought them here, is not reflected in our organization structure. We have a medical department, an obstetrical department, a surgical department, a pediatric department, and an outpatient department as major divisions. We do not have a geriatric department. The patients are segregated by the general type of problem they have rather than by age group (except that children are placed in pediatrics).

"Where staff training is concerned, the fact that some of our patients are aged, or more specifically, have one or more of the chronic conditions generally associated with aging, in addition to the ailment or injury that brought them here, does constitute a problem. The problem is actually twofold. One is the technique problem where we are concerned with the physical differences related to aging as they affect the acute problem.

"The second training problem is one of attitudes. Our nursing personnel are not exposed to, for instance, a great number of cases of senility. It is difficult for them to accept the fact that although these patients are adults, their behavior is sometimes more analogous to that of small children, and they can't be expected to carry out instructions or remember to use the call button when they need assistance. So when one of them wets or dirties the bed, the tendency is to think of the patient as a 'dirty old man' or 'dirty old lady' or as one who has done it deliberately—either to aggravate the staff or to make more work for them. Many of our people get very impatient with some of the older patients because they are slow and require more time to heal and, consequently, stay longer, or because they require more physical care and assistance, such as care of their dentures and support in walking and having to be lifted in and out of bed, or because they are irritable or have unpleasant dispositions or complain a lot, or because they just 'don't smell good.' Some of the complaints regarding aged patients are real, but may be the result of medications they are already taking interacting with medications for the current illness or because of removal

---

* From *Organizations: Theory and Design* by Patrick E. Connor. © 1980 Science Research Associates, Inc. Reprinted by permission.

of some medication they usually need and have due to possible unwanted interactions with current medications. Also, some of the people just don't like to touch old people.

"This attitude problem is not insoluble so far as the professional staff is concerned because they are with us for an extended period and we have time to work with them and derive some benefit from the training. Our nurses' aides and orderlies, however, are a much more difficult problem. The turnover rate is quite high. Most of them don't stay with us more than a year and may stay just a few months. It is a continual job, just trying to maintain the minimum level of competence and an almost impossible job to get above that level. We have to rely mostly on the nurses supervising these people to take care of these attitude and behavioral problems as they become manifest."

Case 1–14
The Electronics Corporation
Margaret Fenn

PART A

Dan and Tom were sipping coffee in the back of the laboratory. Dan was a design engineer, and one of three people working on the project. Tom was visiting from the government agency sponsoring the project and was performing one of the required periodic progress reviews. Since the two were the same age and had remarkably similar backgrounds, Dan's supervisor, the project manager, had found it quite convenient to let Dan handle all the necessary social obligations during these visits.

Tom was saying, "I've been thinking about a career in marketing."

"That's a coincidence," remarked Dan. "I've been thinking the same thing and have been passively looking for a job myself."

"What have you done, so far?" asked Tom.

"Nothing really. I've never satisfied myself that I could get a job in technical marketing that would be interesting. I'd hate to push some catalog line of components; but most marketing done in the advanced technical areas is done by the older, more experienced guys. The two jobs I've had here—this laser project and that moon shot—have been fun, and I'd hate to leave the R&D side of engineering."

"Then why are you even thinking about marketing?" countered Tom.

"I'm restless," said Dan. "With the exception of those two trips I made last year, I haven't left this building in two years! I'm not an analytical researcher who wants to be locked in an office with a slide rule all his life. I need to get in contact with more people—either customers or vendors or something."

"You know," he continued, "I always had my advisors confused when I was in college, because I was the only engineer in graduate school who took his electives in business-oriented courses."

"I know a guy who's looking for you," said Tom. "He works for Electronics Corporation, in the Midwest, and is looking for six guys with exactly your background and interest."

"How do you know about him?"

"He offered me one of the jobs."

Tom continued on and described, in generalities, what he knew about the job. When he finished, he asked Dan if he wanted him to pass the word along to the Electronics Corporation that Dan was interested also.

"Yes, I'd like to at least follow up on it," said Dan.

"If they're interested," said Tom, summing up, "a guy named Jim Brant will be calling you, probably within the next few weeks."

Jim Brant called Dan four days later. They spoke about the job and Dan's interests, and finally Brant said, "Well, listen, Dan, we'd like to have you come back here and see our operation firsthand. Can you come this Friday?"

"Well, I kind of want to make one thing clear before we go to too much trouble," replied Dan. "You're the world's largest component manufacturer, and I'm not particularly interested in marketing components. I want to stay involved in the advanced R&D areas."

"Don't worry about that," countered Brant. "I know all about that. Believe me, we need guys with your kind of background to sell our R&D programs. Get back here this Friday and I'll show you where you'll fit into the organization. Then you'll see how far away from the components area you'll be, and what a good position you'll be in."

Dan's interest was aroused, and he arranged his schedule that week to make the trip.

During the first part of the interview that Friday, Brant explained the company's history and organization (see Exhibit 1). The company consisted of two major divisions, the Components and the Systems divisions. Components Division consisted of three product departments, A, B, and C, an R&D Department, a Marketing Department, and various administrative departments. Each product department was relatively self-contained, and each one produced components at the rate of several million per month. Each department manager was responsible for manufacturing, product engineering, some product development, quality control, product marketing, and the profitable operation of the department. Division C did $200 million in sales each year, which was about double that of either Division A or B.

The R&D Department was relatively small, and was responsible for the development of products and technologies benefiting the division in the medium-term—i.e., two to five years. Marketable developments generally were either merged into one of the existing operating departments or became the core of a new operating department. Department C, for example, had evolved eight years previously out of a development project.

There was a central marketing department managed by Mr. Hanson. All sales activities, long-range market research, merchandising, customer

EXHIBIT 1
The Electronics Corporation

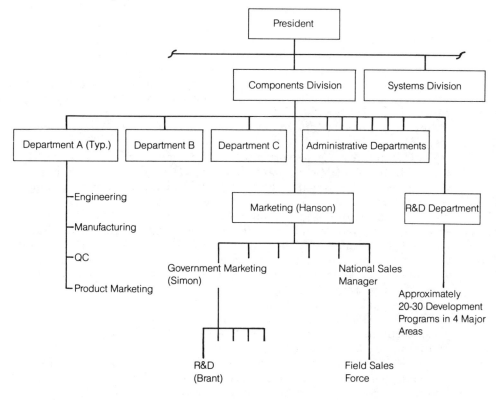

service, order entry operations, etc., were responsible to him. The field sales branch, about 150 people in 30 major cities, was responsible for all customer contact. They would take the orders, negotiate the contracts, and handle the customer relations for the division. Since the division marketed a catalog line of over 3,000 components, the salesmen were not expected to be experts in any one product. Therefore, when technical negotiations were involved, the salesmen would rely on product marketing engineers within the marketing branches of each product department. These marketing engineers were technical specialists, or "experts," in particular product lines, and were not involved directly with the customer unless specifically needed. Their approval was necessary, however, before the salesman could accept and schedule orders for (1) unusually large quantities, (2) ambitious delivery, (3) technical exceptions to catalog specifications, or (4) quantity discount or competitive pricing.

The products made by Departments A and B were equally complex. The devices built by Department C were inherently more complex, but most salesmen could handle all three product areas equally well. The salesmen were paid strictly by salary; although there were monthly sales quotas established by the office managers, neither a commission nor a bonus was received for exceeding this quota.

Mr. Simon's branch within the Marketing Department was responsible for all military marketing—i.e., all device sales and contracts with government agencies. In general, these sales were small. But public relations was a very important consideration. The customers whom the people in Simon's branch called on often were directly responsible for very large programs within the aerospace industry. Thus, Simon's branch was in a strong position to influence sales that would be entered through a field office.

Brant continued to explain to Dan some of the specifics that concerned his particular area.

"I hired in a year ago to work directly for Simon. At that time, our R&D support from outside the company was only $2.5 million. Most of that was given to us by government agencies who had to spend the money somewhere before the fiscal year was up. When I took over the R&D sales, I increased that figure to $5 million in the first year. Now that Hanson has seen what we can do with a little effort in this area, he wants to do what I have suggested and establish a group responsible for R&D sales. There will be six people added under me. Three will stay here in the home office, and three will take positions in the field near major government installations. You and Tom will be based here."

"Has Tom accepted the job yet?" asked Dan.

"Not yet," said Brant. "But I'm working on him. He thinks he's going to get a 'Distinguished Service Award' toward the end of the year, though, and wants to stay where he is until then. We'll get him, though.

"We want you to be the 'expert' and take over the marketing for those three programs in the R&D area that we discussed earlier. We need about four new contracts for each one within the next 12 months. These are all key programs and each will play a major part in our product mix in about five years. If you do a good job, you'll be able to follow along with whichever one you want and become the marketing manager for it. Or, if you want, you can stay here and keep on working with the new developments.

"You know, you'll be in a prestige group, here. Everyone in the company looks up to us. We've got no quotas to meet, deal with the big men in the industry, not just the purchasing agents, and work on the interesting programs.

"And, not only that," continued Brant, "if you do a good job for Hanson, you've got it made. He started here seven years ago as a field salesman, and now he's a v.p. He's got 'his men' placed all over the company, and no one gets a promotion or a big raise unless he's one of 'Hanson's boys'. The division manager doesn't do anything without Hanson's OK. He's really hot for guys with your background, and when I told him about you, he was really interested. He wants to meet you."

At that point, Hanson came into the office and sat down. The conversation was general and low-pressure. After about ten minutes he left, signaling Brant to follow. A few moments later, Brant returned.

"I knew he'd like you," he said.

He then made Dan a firm offer, at a substantial increase over his present salary. Dan accepted it on the spot.

Dan reported to his new job on September 15. The local university was just beginning its fall semester, and apartments were hard to find. Although he was paid full-time, Brant gave him at least half a day off every day for three weeks until he could locate a suitable place to live. The remainder of Dan's time was spent reading reports and working alongside the engineers, learning as much about the technologies as he could.

One day Brant signaled Dan to come into his office and have coffee with him. "How're things going?" he asked.

"Fine. Some of the engineers seemed a little distrustful of a marketing guy at first, but we speak the same language and things are coming along pretty well."

Brant nodded. "I've been hearing good reports from the managers down there. Keep up the good work."

He paused a minute and then changed the subject. "Those bastards in C Department are really screwing me up. We're trying to land a $200,000 contract for B Department, and need about one man-month's worth of support from C, but they won't cooperate. Those prima donnas think they own the world."

"So why won't they support it?" asked Dan.

"They say that there isn't enough in it for them. Hell, it's a big chunk for B Department—just what they need. But C is fighting all the way. We can't ever get any cooperation out of them."

"It's all part of the same division, isn't it?" commented Dan. "Why should they even have a choice in a situation like this?"

"They won't cooperate with anyone unless they make a lot of money, handle the negotiations themselves, and think up the idea first. They're the only people around who don't cooperate with anyone else."

By mid-November, Dan had begun to contact potential customers. He received his leads through the people in the government marketing branch, the field sales organization, or his own knowledge of developments within the industry. Whenever he called on a person in the industry, he always made it a point to notify the salesman handling the account ahead of time and invite him to go along. The salesmen were anxious, themselves, to learn about the new technologies, and invariably accepted Dan's invitation.

On one of his trips, Dan and the salesman were relaxing at the bar in an airport waiting for Dan's return flight home.

"I'm glad we've got someone like you handling this job," commented the salesman. "Before, we never had anyone we could call on back there to find out what was going on. A guy from C Department came out once, but they're so inconsistent and independent, that we weren't able to follow up on anything. I hope you won't be like those guys."

"Don't worry about that," said Dan. "I'm going to run you guys to death!"

"Good," replied the salesman. "We try not to even take any orders for those guys in C because we can't even get delivery. You'll be a hero out here if you don't let us down."

Because he had been with the company only three and a half months, Dan wasn't eligible for a merit review at the end of the year. Brant asked him, however, to come into the office.

"Hanson's read over your last two monthly reports and is pretty impressed."

"Good," said Dan.

"What odds do you give for these potential contracts coming in?"

"Two almost for sure," said Dan. "The big one will happen if Congress decides to go ahead with the missile program. The rest depend on the internal R&D budgets of the various companies. They won't know till January or February whether they'll have the money."

"Like I said," repeated Brant, "Hanson's hot for what you've done. Keep up the good work and you've got it made.

"Say," he said, changing the subject, "you want to go South with me next month? I'm going down to see Tom and try to get him signed up. He won that award, you know."

"Great! Sure," said Dan. "Got anybody else lined up for the other four jobs?"

"Nope . . . Good men are hard to find."

PART B

On January 2, Dan was at his desk when a messenger came by distributing a company news bulletin:

> Mr. ——, Manager of the Components Division, has been reassigned to a newly created post, Director of Personnel Policies.
>
> Mr. —— will assume the responsibilities of Components Division Manager, effective immediately. He has effectively contributed to company growth in his previous position as Manager of the Systems Division, and we all wish him success in his new assignment.
>
> An announcement will be made shortly concerning Mr. ——'s successor as Manager of the Systems Division.

> (signed)
> (Company President)

For the next few days, rumors flew concerning the change. In Dan's conversations with others, however, the only general agreement seemed to be that the announcement seemed rather abrupt, and that "Director of Personnel Policies" did not seem to be a particularly significant title for a man who had formerly managed $400 million worth of business.

Then, on January 15, as Dan was coming into the office, Brant stopped him and said, "You'll have to clean up your business by the end of the month—you've been transferred to the product marketing branch in C Department."

"What do you mean?" said Dan.

"There's nothing I can do about it," said Brant. "Hanson called me last night and told me to start the paperwork moving on the transfer. I asked him why, but didn't get much of an answer. All I know about it is that you've gotta go. Hanson did say that it would be a temporary deal and you'll be back in six months. That's all I know. I gotta go down to the legal department and see about something."

Dan didn't get much done that morning. In the afternoon, he waited for a chance to see Brant again. As he entered the office, he began, "How the hell can I finish up a bunch of contracts I've got no control over? I can't get them in here until the customers know if they've got the money."

"I know, I know, I know, I know," repeated Brant. "Look, I can't do anything about it. You'll just have to go over and do a job and wait. It's just for six months."

"You also know I made it pretty clear when I hired in that I didn't want to work over there peddling components. What's going on?"

"I don't know. But I've got no choice. Besides, the experience will do you good. And remember, it will only be for six months, like I said."

"It wasn't *ever* going to happen when I hired in," said Dan. "Who's going to take over the marketing I've been doing?"

"I'll have to do it myself," said Brant.

Later that week Dan went to see Simon.

"I'll tell you what the story is," Simon began. "C Department, we just learned, has been operating at a loss this past year. Profits for the division took a deep plunge. That's why we have a new manager. He's decided the reason is that we haven't sold enough C Department devices. So he's moved 18 product marketing engineers from there out to the field to boost the sales force, and we have to move 18 guys from around the division in there to take their places. You're one of them."

"You know, I feel like you guys have let me down," said Dan. "This was the one thing I wanted least to happen, and you all assured me it wouldn't. . . . unless I was really screwing up," he added.

"You've been doing a good job," said Simon. "But we haven't any choice. Just be glad you weren't transferred out into the field. Besides, it's only for six months, like we've been telling you."

"I hear you talking," replied Dan, "But I think I'd like to hear that from Hanson himself. You always said that I was one of 'his boys'; I think I'll go see him."

"I wouldn't do that," said Simon. "He's got his own problems."

PART C

Dan took his vacation the following June. One night, after dinner, he was sitting in the living room with his father-in-law describing what happened following his transfer.

"I didn't do a single thing for C Department the whole time I was there. I stayed away from my desk as much as I could, but continued following up a little on my other contract potentials. I'd already talked to my old boss in the aerospace company, and he said he'd welcome me back if I wanted to come. So I really didn't care what anyone in C Department thought.

"But at the same time I did a little of my own politicking and arranged a transfer back into the R&D Department. Now, I'm nestled out of the way there waiting for things to calm down. The R&D Manager liked the contracts I brought in, and, in a sense, he's protecting me. The supervisor in C Department was glad to see me go; I was such a drain on his budget.

"Hanson is almost stripped of his power. All he has left is the field sales force. Everyone else reports to the new men that the Division Manager brought with him from the Systems Division. The Government Marketing Branch doesn't exist any more—most of the guys, including Simon and Brant, are working in the product departments, but a few of the guys were fired. Every single manager in the division has been affected. A couple got promoted, but a lot of them have been "shelved."

"Morale everywhere is low. No one knows what will happen next or what to expect. The reorganizations are coming so fast it's almost a joke. Some people say that they've seen organization charts that were not only dated, but *timed!*

"Morale in the sales force *really* went down. They always felt that they could have sold twice as much for C Department if they'd just had a little cooperation and if the delivery promises had been kept. When those 18 guys were sent out, it was like a slap in the face to them—like they couldn't do the job. Most of the salesmen feel that they ought to take those 18 and put them in the Manufacturing Department. One entire office—7 salesmen, the manager, and 3 secretaries—left the company and set up a distributership in direct competition with us in that area. You better believe they've been doing OK already! Overall, we've lost about half the sales force in the last six months.

"Incidentally, only 1 or 2 of the 18 have been able to transfer back into the plant. The rest will probably be stuck out there forever.

"As for myself, I'm afraid if I leave the company I'll begin to look like a job-hopper. But on the other hand, it sure wouldn't take much to get me away. We haven't met *any* of the commitments we made to my customers, and I'm afraid things are going to get a lot worse before they get better. I don't know what I'm going to do."

Case 1–15 —————————————————————————————

Ripping Off Mr. Gold's (A)

Jerry Saegert and George Eddy

As the president and sole stockholder of Goldsmith's Lumber Company, Jake Goldsmith decided to seek the advice of his general manager, Daniel Rosenberg, about administering a polygraph test to all his employees. As he waited for Rosenberg to come to his office, Goldsmith wondered how things could get into such a bind when his business was doing so well. When Rosenberg appeared, Goldsmith said,

Well, Dan, what do you think we ought to do? I can't bring myself to believe that some of my long time employees are robbing me! After all these years? How can it happen? And the kids—! You know the security company is pushing me to give all our employees a polygraph test right away. But . . .

Jake, Jake, I agree with them wholeheartedly! I felt we should have done this a long time ago and gotten rid of these bums who are taking advantage of you. These three students I caught stealing materials should be fired immediately and we should contact their parents to let them know what kind of kids they've got. We might also want to contact the police to see whether or not we should file any charges. Also, if the polygraph tests should show that any other employees are stealing, I think we should fire them immediately, too. What are we waiting for?

*   *   *   *   *

Goldsmith had become alarmed when he first was approached by several customers who told him that they had been offered merchandise by employees working in the yard section of the store where lumber, sheetrock, cement, steel products, roofing materials, and related items were kept and sold. The customers related that the salesmen told them they didn't have to go inside and pay for the materials but that they could just give a few dollars to the salesman outside and no one else would be the wiser for such a transaction. Most of the employees in the yard section had been with Goldsmith's Lumber Company for many years prior to coming to Mr. Gold's Home Center, and he considered all of them to be quite loyal. Their jobs could be described as semiskilled; however, with pay above average for the Laredo area, with many benefits provided by the company, and a close association between employees and management. Goldsmith had delegated authority to these men so that they would consider themselves an important part of the company. Most of the employees of Mexican background regarded Goldsmith as *the* boss, with total authority. Seldom were his decisions questioned.

After several years in the construction business in Laredo, Texas, Jake Goldsmith decided in 1953 to open his own lumber yard under the name of Goldsmith's Lumber Company. The purpose was to supply his own construction work and to have a place to store his equipment. For over 20 years, the lumber yard prospered and grew, with its success coming not only as a supplier for Goldsmith's construction business but also in sales to other customers. By 1970, as a result of the increasing demand for building supplies and home furnishings, he believed he should expand. Initially, he hesitated whether he should enlarge the present location or move to another one. He thought the problem in trying to decide whether to expand the present facilities of Goldsmith's Lumber Company was one of a cultural nature. He wondered, too, what to call the new facility. Laredo, Texas, a border city with its sister city lying in Mexico, has a population predominant in Mexican backgrounds. In addition, Laredo's economy has been dependent significantly on its neighbors to the south for much of its business. The size of the store that Goldsmith wanted to open was an unheard-of type in this part of the state. Laredo still was considered a small town where people are suspicious of "big-time" operations. The possibility of alienating long-time customers who might be ill at ease in a store of the size Goldsmith had in mind needed to be considered.

After extensive planning and replanning, checking with people in the field, as well as traveling in various parts of the state to see if a trend could be detected, Goldsmith made the decision to go ahead. Accordingly, Mr. Gold's Home Center—his choice for a name—was started in March of 1974 with a 30,000-square-foot building, housing a full line of building materials, home furnishings and do-it-yourself tools and materials. In addition, there was an open-shed lumber yard connected to the property, from which standard lumber and building materials could be purchased.

Many of the employees from Goldsmith's Lumber Company were moved to Mr. Gold's Home Center to handle the business of the new store. The older employees had been with the firm for many years and Goldsmith considered them as traditionally hard-working and loyal. In addition, Goldsmith brought in his younger brother-in-law, Daniel Rosenberg, to be general manager of the store. Rosenberg had been a store manager with a large jewelry store chain in Houston, Texas, for a number of years and had developed a style of leadership which was somewhat different from Goldsmith's. This style of leadership had been developed as a result of his experience in supervising a large operation in a highly competitive urban market.

As business increased at Mr. Gold's, it was obvious to Goldsmith that the skeleton work force would no longer be enough to handle the growing business. More qualified office personnel were hired, receiving became centralized under a separate department, and older employees were delegated more authority. Additionally, many high school students were hired for part-time help, as the store was open seven days a week.

The store began to prosper as sales doubled through the first year and a half. With this tremendous growth, Goldsmith's problems began, foremost of which was internal shrinkage (commonly known as stealing). Goldsmith was well aware that in this type of retail business it is inevitable that some kind of internal shrinkage would occur. Accordingly, he made an even higher than usual allowance of 4 percent, which he built into his accounting criteria. Goldsmith realized that many small items would be shoplifted by professional shoplifters and others as a "hobby," but he was unaware of the extent of internal shrinkage practiced by his employees. He did not expect this development due to the long-time employment of the majority of his employees. Mr. Gold's employed between 45 to 60 employees for sales, depending on the peak period.

After contacting a security company in San Antonio, Goldsmith decided to use store walkers as a security team to try and stop the internal shrinkage. He considered some theft to be a normal consequence of doing business, and in the past had made no reference to it, believing that it was not important. In fact, he thought that some of the items that were taken were those which were left over and not salable, or scraps which could not really be sold for a profit. The security survey, however, suggested otherwise. After making its investigation, which included playing the part of customers in approaching salesmen in different areas of the store, the security team reported to Goldsmith in November of 1975 that two people had been willing to sell goods in the yard without requiring the customer pay the store, but paying the salesman directly. In one case, the security investigator was not absolutely sure he could identify the salesman. In the other case, Goldsmith's legal counsel concluded that it was entrapment, and that he should not proceed against the employee. Moreover, this employee had eight years of service with the company, which Goldsmith considered had been outstanding.

Another factor which complicated the investigation was that business was progressing so rapidly and so well that all available personnel, including members of Goldsmith's family, were being used to keep the store going. Goldsmith doubted that it was sensible to terminate any employees who had experience due to the lack of time available to rehire and retrain people in the midst of the tremendous sales volume he was experiencing. Besides, Goldsmith still did not consider the theft problem to be of a sizable nature.

Nevertheless, he took several steps: (1) the one employee of eight years service who had been identified by the security investigator was transferred to another department; (2) Goldsmith moved an additional cash register closer to the lumber yard section of the store so that there would be little excuse for customers to have to go back into the store to pay for goods; (3) a voucher system was established whereby the customer was required to produce a paid receipt for any materials before they were taken from the yard; (4) the security people instructed several of the trusted employees to check on exits in departments other than those they were in charge of; (5) a system of two people was established in checking merchandise so that both would be responsible and no one person would have authority without the consent of the other; and (6) a standardized security program was established which provided closer scrutiny and more control.

With these changes, Goldsmith considered operations to be moving along well. Business was still good and new people were hired for the lumber yard to keep up with the expanding customer demand. Most of these were high school students who worked afternoons and weekends. Due to the previous security problems, the entire hiring procedures were being revised. However, these were not totally implemented due to the lack of time, since all available people were fully utilized to make ends meet in just keeping the store going. After several months without further incidents, Goldsmith began to think that the problem of internal shrinkage was back under control. Unfortunately, his satisfaction was premature.

It was Rosenberg who told him, enraged by the incident. Three high school students who worked in the lumber yard department were discovered to have taken several 50-pound boxes of wire fence staples, and some PA system speakers which had been attached to the walls for calling employees, but which were not used very often. These items apparently had been thrown behind the building in tall weeds at the end of the late shift. For some reason, these part-time employees had failed to retrieve the items that evening and Daniel Rosenberg saw them the next morning picking up this material when they were not supposed to be on the premises.

When accosted, two of the students denied any part in an illegal activity, while the other secretly approached Goldsmith and confessed that they were stealing. He also declared that other employees in the store were doing the same thing and had been for some time. Goldsmith was stunned. After his initial dismay, and before making any decision, he contacted the security company in San Antonio that was still on retainer. Previously, the security company suggested that Goldsmith give a polygraph test to all his employees, but Goldsmith had rejected the idea because he concluded that internal shrinkage was not such a large problem. With this latest development, the company urged immediate polygraph testing of all employees.

Still Goldsmith hesitated. Countering Rosenberg's agreement with the security company as potentially troublesome, he demurred:

> I'm not so sure. As you know, we have been working up to 12 hours a day, almost seven days a week. We really can't afford to fire anybody! To make matters worse, I've talked with some of the department heads, who say that its already known around the company that we've discussed the possibility of giving everyone a polygraph test. They tell me that many of the employees have said they would quit if they were forced to take it. Dan, I don't feel we can handle the store if all these people leave at once.

Rosenberg's response was emphatic:

> Well, Jake, I just don't agree with you! There's no question that you've got to take action against these high school students we've caught . . . and for the rest of them, well, if they're stealing from us, then I don't want them working here either. I'd rather work all day every day to keep those thieves out of this company. As fair as you've been with your employees and all the benefits you give them and the fact that they get wages as good as or better than any other place in this town, I feel we're just making too many concessions. Jake, you just can't stall this off any longer!

Case 1–16 ───

Things Are Different around Here

Ann Marie Calacci, with the assistance of Frank Yeandel

"Things are different around here" were the first words that Jill was told by the new manager. Mr. Tyler was welcoming Jill back to another summer of working at Trams, a nationwide discount store. Jill was not at all thrilled with the prospect of another summer at Trams.

Reluctantly, Jill had returned to Trams where she worked in the ladies' and children's apparel department. Her job consisted of folding clothes, fixing the racks, and going to the registers for "price checks." In the summer after her sophomore year in college, Jill had hoped to find something a bit more stimulating or better paying. But jobs were hard to find, so Jill had returned to Trams to work the 6:00 P.M. to 8:00 P.M. shift.

Her past memories of Trams were filled with strong disdain. She was originally hired since the management found that college students work hard, and work hard she did. Under the regime of Ms. Williams, Jill began her employment at Trams. Ms. Williams had strict rules that were to be adhered to or else you were fired.

Jill's stomach tied in knots as she remembered Ms. Williams and her rules. There was to be no talking between employees, or to friends or family who entered the store. Since the department was located by the main doors and the store was only a block from Jill's house, it was a difficult rule to comply with. Each of the four girls who worked the night shift was assigned a section of the department and would be held responsible for it. With the clientele and the amount of price checks, it was nearly impossible to finish. Yet each night, Jill would do the impossible as she would race against the clock to finish her section. Exhausted at the end of the night, Jill would gaze at her completed job and think of the fruitlessness of it all. For the next day, the customers would ruin it all and she would again do it over.

It seemed from the minute she got there until the minute she left, there was not even time to breathe. She did have a 15-minute break, but it could not be a second more than that. Ms. Williams would look through a one-way mirror, so everyone was alert at all times. The pressures of being silent in front of friends and relatives who did not know there was a silence rule, trying to beat the clock and trying to keep her mind occupied as the taped music droned on repetitiously, made Trams an unpleasant place for Jill to work.

As she talked to Mr. Tyler, she sensed that things really were different. He seemed like such a nice man. One by one, the new girls she would be working with were introduced to her. Surprisingly, they all seemed to know each other well. Jill was shocked to see them actually smiling as they came in to work. Jill was anxious to see how things were now run. Mr. Tyler then left at 6 P.M., leaving the night crew under no supervision. Jill asked Tara, one of the only remaining old employees, who was in charge. Tara explained that no one was in charge of assigning sections any more, they all worked together as a team.

Jill noticed how the talking ban was lifted. There was a constant chatter among the girls and they eagerly asked Jill about college and how Trams was under Ms. Williams. Jill was hesitant in talking at first, but after a while she became comfortable talking and working, a thing she had never attempted in the past. The girls teased her for working so quickly as they reminded her they were a team and they would all pitch in to complete the section. At break time, Jill became very uncomfortable as the time was going on 20 minutes and no one attempted to move. Her past training was making her very uncomfortable in the new way of working. That night, amazingly to Jill, all the work was finished with time to spare.

All the girls sat around or ate popcorn, while Jill nervously double checked to make sure everything was done.

At first Jill was appalled at the amount of goofing around the girls did, but as time passed Jill found herself enjoying it and participating, too. She actually enjoyed coming in to work. It was so different for her to get to know the people she worked with, especially because they were so different than those she went to school with. The night crew was a team. They had so much fun, Jill felt guilty, as if she was getting paid to do nothing. She still was teased good naturedly about being a worrier, a clock-watcher and a workhorse. They reminded her that the kind Mr. Tyler was in charge and Ms. Williams was long gone. Jill, a lazy person by nature, began to act more and more like the others.

Then one day the district manager came to the store and said that things were to be done much neater since sales took a turn for the worse. Suddenly Jill was thrown back into the time-watching method. As the new girls complained, Tara and Jill saw how little they had been doing before. Mr. Tyler enforced this new method for a week and then, slowly but surely, the old ways started to surface, and then came out with a bang.

Breaks turned into 45-minute affairs. Eating was done after and during work. The girls became sloppier than ever in their work. They started calling in sick often. Jill liked the relaxed atmosphere, but thought that this was ridiculous.

Jill felt responsible for the decline in sales, since the department was so untidy. She hated to see inefficiency and for the sake of the store wanted to do something about it. She began to suggest things to the girls, but they rejected her ideas. She knew she was in a bad position to suggest things since they were wary of her education. They resented her level of education, referring to her language as college talk and too difficult for them to understand. So that they would not call her a college snob, Jill made her suggestions to Mr. Tyler. He agreed that they were excellent suggestions, but he never mentioned them to the others. Jill was frustrated.

The behavior became even more lax, with no comments from Mr. Tyler. Jill enjoyed this freedom less and less. One day, Sue did not come in to work or call in sick. This meant that three had to do all the work that four were to do. After this kept up for a week, the girls were sure that Sue would be fired. But Mr. Tyler could not bring himself to fire Sue, so he gave her a warning. The girls were outraged.

In rebellion, the breaks became an hour long. They reasoned that if Sue could miss days and not be fired, certainly ten minutes here or there would not make a difference. They did not do their job completely, and what they did was done sloppily. Jill participated in the breaks and the quality of her work went down, but she still tried to do her job and the job of the others. Again Trams became a nightmare to her.

Then one day, Tara approached Jill and asked her to ring up a dress for $2. Jill replied that the tag said $25 and not $2. Tara said that Jill was right, that was what the tag said, but it made no difference. Tara explained how she had worked hard for years, did her job and never received any reward. She reasoned the store owed her this "discount." Jill adamantly refused to ring it up. Tara went to the register and rang up $2. Jill knew now it was time for her to act.

On the Firing Line

Herbert S. Kindler and Steven A. Lippman

THE SITUATION

Henry King learned the "business" of executive management, in general, by trial and error—relying heavily on his strong analytical skills. His systematic logic, honed by an engineering education, helped him move from a research and development (R&D) job in industry to educational director of a major international engineering association, the American Automation Society (AAS), headquartered in Washington, D.C. After seven years with AAS, he was appointed its executive director in 1963 at age 35. The AAS board of directors promoted Henry largely because of his problem-solving skills, diligent implementation, verbal ability, and charismatic charm. Some board members opposed Henry's promotion, expressing the view that he was too young, too inexperienced, and emotionally immature.

Although married, Henry was basically a "loner" with virtually no intimate friends either at work or in his personal life. He kept his feelings pretty much to himself, and went about his activities both at work and at home in an orderly, organized way. He had a strong drive to achieve success and recognition. Henry's interests included doing things with his three children, home improvements, tennis, and woodcarving. He frequently wrote articles for the AAS journal; occasionally, he wrote poetry that he shared with no one, not even his wife.

Shortly after assuming the executive directorship, he realized that his knowledge of personnel administration was minimal. Henry found himself particularly inept at the process of selecting (from among candidates) for managerial level positions. Despite these deficiencies, under Henry's leadership, AAS prospered as reflected in Appendix B. The Society's financial success helped Henry to feel more self-confident. Initially, he had felt quite insecure about holding his job—partly because he knew that several elected society officers had applied for the executive directorship, which paid considerably more than typical salaries for engineering management in industry. Henry suspected that these unsuccessful candidates, some of whom later served on the executive board, secretly wanted him to fail. He also vividly remembered that his mentor, the previous executive director, had been fired by the board the first time AAS experienced a deficit under his regime. (AAS background information is presented in Appendixes A and B.)

Henry's management style, like that of his predecessor, was basically autocratic—he made all final decisions for new policies and major programs unilaterally, subject to approval by the executive board. Unlike his predecessor, Henry more actively solicited inputs from subordinates, conducted frequent staff meetings, and, gradually, delegated to his department heads full authority for implementing approved policies and programs. (See Appendix C for headquarters organization, Appendix D for salary schedule.)

As Henry mastered the details of each of his subordinate's jobs and let them "run" their operations, a metamorphosis of his role took place. He functioned principally as a "boundary manager." He was a buffer between the five headquarters departments as well as between headquarters personnel and the executive board. He also served as a bridge between his staff and the executive board, linking their interactive needs. In addition, he helped resolve internal conflicts, and he scanned the external environment for trouble signals as well as for new opportunities.

The five headquarters' department heads who reported directly to Henry differed considerably in personality, education, skills, and experience. Brief biographical sketches follow:

Ed Green: Director of Finance, Personnel, and Administration

Ed had a reserved personality that, combined with an ingenuous quality, made people feel he was trustworthy beyond question. Ed, a CPA, was Henry's age, a bachelor, and a hard-working, dedicated person who got to work early and stayed late. His subordinates were loyal, admiring his sense of integrity and industry. Perhaps the only qualities he lacked to be the top executive were a more dynamic personality and an engineer's understanding of the automation technology.

Reporting to Ed were Angie Cee, a highly capable accountant supervisor; and two efficient technician supervisors, Dave Deed, who handled data processing, and Andy Mather, who ran the printing-reproduction operation.

Ed was hired in 1959 and had been a tremendous help to Henry King during the early period of Henry's executive directorship, when he didn't even know the difference between exempt and nonexempt employee status under the provisions of the Fair Labor Standards Act.

Vern Gibson: Director of Technical and Educational Services

Vern had been hired in 1969 to integrate and improve activities involving automation engineering information: symposia, standards, book publications, short courses, and learning materials. Vern was five years older than Henry. He had been employed by an automation manufacturer developing technical support materials. He wanted to change jobs because his employer was starting a corporatewide, employee reduction program. In deciding to hire him, Henry experienced a flicker of doubt about Vern's supervisory abilities, but the fact that Vern had risen to the rank of major during World War II seemed to negate this vague concern. Accordingly, the Society had moved Vern and his family, which included seven children, from Philadelphia to Washington where Vern purchased a home. Vern turned out not to be a very effective supervisor; he was more a buddy to his subordinates than a leader. He avoided risk and tended to consume a disproportionate amount of time, including Henry's, checking and counter-checking minor details. However, Vern was skillful in personnel selection and hired Greg Happe, a former high school science teacher, to manage educational services and book publications. Greg quickly became an effective, reliable, and imaginative young executive—who, on occasion, tripped up because of his lack of experience in the business world.

Vern also hired Bob Berg, a capable technical writer, who coordinated the engineering standards activity, and Alice Karp, an effective meetings coordinator.

Phil Marlow: Director of Communications Services

Phil's title was a euphemism, common to nonprofit corporations, for what his department actually did. It promoted the sale of advertising and exhibit space, books and subscriptions, and Society membership. Phil, slightly older than Henry King, had dropped out of college to become a salesman. He was hired by the Society, about the same time as Henry, to sell advertising in the northeast region. Phil had been a hard-driving, hard-drinking salesman and a tough, autocratic executive. He had an "old line" work ethic and demanded that all his subordinates rigorously observe work hours and a conservative dress code. Phil was an effective sales producer, but he lacked creativity and tended to promote, rather than curb, interdepartmental rivalry.

Phil had one long-term subordinate, Dan Stum, the public relations manager—who wrote better-than-average copy, but with little innovation or flair. Diane Shaff and Dave Mitch were newer people that Phil hired. Though relatively inexperienced, they appeared to be highly capable.

Sue Pace: Manager, Member and Section Services

Sue was a high school graduate who started as Henry's secretary. In her late thirties, Sue was married and dedicated to her career. Henry promoted her in recognition of her strong administrative capability. As the organization's first woman manager, she experienced some problems (being labelled as bitchy by subordinates and aloof by Society members with romantic intentions), but she resolved these issues reasonably well. Sue was methodical, personable, and set a high performance standard.

Fred Murphy: AAS Journal Editor

Fred was divorced, with no children. When hired, he was 35 years old. Fred had an engineering degree and solid editorial experience, including seven years with a competitive automation journal. The two previous editors that Henry hired had not worked out, and Henry was delighted with the new standards of writing and the design quality of the AAS monthly journal under Fred's direction. Fred's staff worked well as a team. However, they operated with Fred in a much more relaxed mode than other headquarters departments—they dressed more casually, rarely started on time, or returned from lunch on time; but they worked late when necessary to meet deadlines. His art and production manager, Ben Blue; associate editor, Dick Kain; and most recent staff addition, assistant editor, Marion Jafe, were all capable professionals. Fred denied that he drank excessively, but in Henry's view, Fred's drinking habits occasionally interfered with his work.

THE PROBLEM

During 1970, anticipating the severe national economic downturn, Henry considered measures that would help the Society cope with the impact of probable reductions in Society income. On his initiative, a membership dues increase of 33 percent (from $15 to $20) was approved and went into effect in 1970, increasing total dues income, despite a slight decline in active members (from 20,400 to 20,000). Also, there was a reduction in spending "frills," such as Society funds paying for committee lunches and headquarters social events.

As 1971 progressed, the extent of the recession became clearer, and income dropped precipitously. Companies reduced their budgets for promoting automation equipment with the result that by the end of 1971, AAS income from exhibit booth rental (where manufacturers display new products) dropped 35 percent, a $175,700 loss of revenue from the previous year, and advertising in the AAS monthly *Automation Technology* journal dropped 10 percent, a loss of $44,800. Additionally, membership dues income declined about $12,000 while the only income increase, which was in publications sales, just offset the dues decline. (Of course, these precise year-end declines were unknown as 1971 began.)

The problem that faced the Society at the start of 1971 was this: Knowing that there would be a sizable drop in 1971 income, relative to the 1970 level (the drop ultimately amounted to $228,000), what course of action would be most appropriate? The executive board didn't wait for a headquarters proposal. At its regular meeting in January, the board approved the following directive:

> The executive director shall: (1) Cut staff salaries in 1971 by $80,000.
> (2) In view of the current economic recession, and in consideration of the Society's accumulated surplus position, a total combined deficit of no more than $100,000 shall be tolerated during 1971 and 1972 in order to maintain continuity of Society Services. (3) During 1973 a surplus of 4 percent of gross annual income shall again be the Society's fiscal goal.

One constraint upon which both the headquarters staff and the executive board agreed was that reductions in promotional budgets by industrial firms (affecting AAS income from exhibits and advertising) were essentially beyond the Society's power to influence, at least during 1971.

APPENDIX A

About The American Automation Society (AAS)

The Society was founded in 1945 "to advance the arts and sciences of engineering related to automation equipment theory, design, manufacture, and use in science and industry." AAS is international in scope with about 85 percent of its members residing in the United States. Most members are employed in technical positions in industry and government. Local sections are organized in 140 cities with considerable autonomy to elect their own officers and conduct their own business. Sections are grouped into 12 geographic districts to elect representatives to the executive board. As the Society matured, five membership service areas evolved as follows: Publications; Education and Research; Standards and Practices; Technology (comprised of several divisions with which members affiliated); and Industries and Sciences (also comprised of several membership divisions).

The executive director has the responsibility for maintaining and directing a headquarters staff to conduct the Society's business operations and to administer, coordinate, and promote membership services. Organization of the headquarters staff in 1970 is shown in Appendix C.

Data regarding economic performance, membership growth, and the number of full-time equivalent employees is shown in Appendix B.

APPENDIX B

TABLE 1
American Automation Society Economic Performance Data

Year Ended December 31	Highest Number Headquarters Employees‡	Gross Income ($\times$ $1,000)	Annual Surplus or Deficit ($\times$ $1,000)	Accumulated Surplus ($\times$ $1,000)	Ratio of Surplus to Gross Income (percent)	Total Number of Members ($\times$ 1,000)
1960	47	818	(104.6)	297	−12.8	12.5
1961	37	865	4.6	192	.5	13.3
1962	38	814	44.1	197	5.4	14.0
1963*	38	831	34.6	231	4.1	15.0
1964	40	977	31.1	262	3.2	15.1†
1965	39	1,049	44.0	306	4.2	16.5
1966	39	1,123	57.4	363	5.1	17.4
1967	43	1,276	72.6	436	5.7	18.5
1968	46	1,402	52.1	488	3.7	19.8
1969	47	1,522	73.5	562	4.8	20.4
1970	47	1,637	63.4	625	3.9	20.0†

* Initial year of new chief executive officer.
† Year in which membership dues were increased.
‡ Does not include eight persons who sell journal advertising and exhibit space part time on a commission basis.

APPENDIX B

TABLE 2
American Automation Society
Income and Expense Data, 1961 and 1970 ($000)

	1961	Percent of Total Income	1970	Percent of Total Income
INCOME (× $1,000)				
Member dues	102	12.6	288	17.6
International exhibit booth rental ...	440	51.3	502	30.6
Journal advertising	248	27.5	448	27.4
Publications sales	54	6.2	203	12.4
Interest, registration, misc.	21	2.4	196	12.0
Total	865		1,637	

	1961	Percent of Total Expenses	1970	Percent of Total Expenses
EXPENSE (× $1,000)				
Salaries, other employment costs ...	301	34.9	480	30.5
Contracted services	61	7.0	123	7.8
Printing, cost of publications sold ...	181	21.1	395	25.1
Promotion	73	8.5	121	7.7
Administrative	89	10.4	161	10.2
Commissions (ad and exhibit sales) .	64	7.5	94	6.0
Rent (exhibit and office)	81	9.4	122	7.8
Miscellaneous including depreciation	10	1.2	78	5.0
Total	860		1,574	

APPENDIX C

Headquarters Organization

EXECUTIVE BOARD
Society President

Executive Director — Henry King

Finance Personnel and Administration

- Accounting and Billing
- Data Processing
- Printing and Reproduction
- Personnel Administration

Director:
Ed Green

Accountant:
Angie Cee

Supervisors:
Dave Deed
Andy Mather

Technical and Educational Services

- Division Meetings
- Publications
- Standards and Practices
- Educational Services

Director:
Vern Gibson

Supervisory Personnel:
Greg Happe
Bob Berg
Alice Karp

Marketing and Public Relations

- Exhibits and Advertising
- Membership and Publications Promotion
- Public Relations

Director:
Phil Marlow

Supervisory Personnel:
Dan Stum
Diane Shaff
Dave Mitch

Member and Local Section Services

- Application Processing
- Local Section Meetings
- Membership Recognition Services

Manager:
Sue Pace

Monthly Journal Editorial and Production

- Manuscript Review and Editing
- Artwork and Design
- Printing and Production

Editor:
Fred Murphy

Production Manager:
Ben Blue

Associate Editor:
Dick Kain

Assistant Editor:
Marion Jafe

APPENDIX D

AAS Headquarters Personnel (1971 annual salaries)

Incumbent	Position	Salary
Henry King*	Executive director	$38,000
Ed Green*	Director, finance and personnel	23,000
Angie Cee	Accountant	13,000
David Deed	Data processing supervisor	11,000
Lois Love	Keypunch operator	7,000
Andy Mather ...	Printing-reproduction supervisor	18,000
John Grey	Press operator	8,000
Vern Gibson* ...	Director, technical and educational services	22,000
Greg Happe	Manager, publications and educational services	15,000
Bob Berg	Coordinator, Engineering standards	13,000
Alice Karp	Coordinator, meetings and division member services	12,000
Phil Marlow* ...	Director, communications services	25,000
Dan Stum*	Manager, public relations	16,000
Diane Shaff	Coordinator, membership and publications promotion	13,000
Dave Mitch	Coordinator, exhibits and advertising promotion	13,000
Sue Pace	Manager, member and local section services	14,000
Fred Murphy* ...	Editor, *Automation Technology*	23,000
Dick Kain	Associate editor	18,000
Ben Blue	'Art and production manager	13,000
Marion Jafe	Assistant editor	12,000
	Senior secretaries	8,000
	Secretarial typists	7,000
	Clerks	6,000

* Has senior secretary.

Section 2

THE GROUP

Factors, Situations, and Processes Which Affect Group Behavior in Complex Organizations

The cases and incidents in this section have been collected to address four groups of topics generally discussed at the level of the group or team. Many cases, however, have a secondary issue at the individual level. Students will quickly observe that the cases in this section address issues and problems under the general headings of group dynamics, communication, conflict, leadership, and control.

As technologies and social issues continue to become more complex in organizations, there will be more and more management emphasis upon group decision-making. No one person will have the total expertise to solve these complicated engineering, scientific, or human problems. Already we have seen examples of project management and matrix organizations used successfully in designing aircraft, NASA flights, and computer systems.

When groups are formed in organizations, two major problems should be considered by management. First, groups must be structured so that organizational goals are accomplished while the group members meet their own individual goals. Second, management must define and structure working relationships between groups that enhance the productivity of each working group while decreasing the incidence of conflict and destructive competition.

As groups are formed, two different levels of analysis and skill are helpful to the organizational participants. The first concerns the processes and events occurring within each competing group. The second level of analysis is the events, actions, and processes occurring between each competing group.[1] Readers should also be aware of the consequences of competition. For example, what are the effects on group dynamics within a losing team? What are the effects of winning on the group dynamics of

[1] For a detailed discussion of these dynamics see Edgar H. Schein, *Organizational Psychology* (Englewood Cliffs, N.J.: Prentice-Hall, 1970), pp. 96–102.

the team? Further, how does a manager prevent intergroup conflict?[2]

Several cases in this section provide the reader with the opportunity to apply the theories and concepts of group dynamics. Cases vary from the rather simple, straightforward situation described in "IR 444" to the complex case of "Acme Wholesale Distributing Company."

Understanding communication, another topic in this section, is important for success at work as well as in personal life. Communication is an idea transplant. Managers may think they are communicating but the real test of the effectiveness of the communication is whether it accomplishes the sender's purpose. Communication consists of the sender, encoding, noise, decoding, and the receiver (see Figure 2–1). The sender is the person attempting to communicate. The sender encodes the message by some form of writing, speaking, or other language which is possible to transmit. Noise enters the process because of the differences in perceptions, attitudes, feelings, and sentiments of the sender and receiver. Each has experienced life differently and gives meaning to the message based upon their learned frame of reference and a unique set of biases and values. Decoding consists of receiving the message in the brain and attaching meaning to the message. Hopefully, the receiver decodes a message that is similar to the original idea.

FIGURE 2–1
The Communication Process

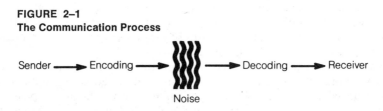

Communication can consist of many types and forms. Three common forms are downward, upward, and horizontal communication. Harold Leavitt[3] experimentally tested communication networks which he labeled the wheel, the chain, the circle, and the all-purpose channel (see Figure 2–2).

FIGURE 2–2
Types of Communication Networks

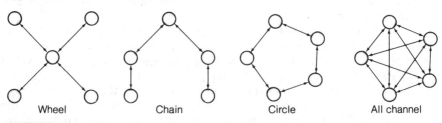

Wheel   Chain   Circle   All channel

---

[2] For the answers to some of these questions see Schein, ibid.

[3] Harold Leavitt, *Managerial Psychology* (Chicago: University of Chicago Press, 1972), pp. 115–21 and 189–98.

The position of the central figure or leader produced the most personal satisfaction. The most satisfied person was the person at the center of the wheel, while the least satisfied was at the end of the chain. Satisfaction for all organization members was the highest in the circle and all-channel forms. Simple tasks were accomplished faster by the wheel and chain communication channels. However, as the task became more complex, the circle, chain, and all-channel structure became more advantageous. Two rather detailed cases dealing with communication problems permit the readers to analyze communication patterns, interpersonal communications, and organization communication channels (both formal and informal). Some issues and questions the reader should consider are:

1. What are the means by which a message can be conveyed?
2. How accurate is the grapevine in an organization?
3. What processes or people distort the message?
4. Can a communication system be overloaded? How?
5. How do the personal attributes of the sender affect the nature of the message?

A common view of leadership, a third major topic in this section, is to define leadership from the point of view of the attributes or behavior of the person in a position of authority. A somewhat broader view of leadership is ". . . the aggregate patterns of reciprocal influence by all members of a group or organization."[4] The cases on leadership in this section also raise issues on the topics of control. These cases were selected to highlight the attributes of leaders, the behavior of leaders, and the situational (contingency) nature of leadership.

FIGURE 2–3
Key Variables and Leadership Styles

	Variable	*Style*	
	—		—
	Time	Autocratic	
Ownership	Quality	Consultative	*Participation*
	Commitment	Consensus	
	+		+

Vroom and Yetton[5] have described a situational leadership system by using a series of variables to diagnose the situation. The leader must then apply the appropriate style to fit the situation (see Figure 2–3). This theory assumes that leaders are adaptable and can change their style.

---

[4] W. Clay Hamner and Dennis W. Organ, *Organizational Behavior: An Applied Psychological Approach* (Dallas: Business Publications, 1978), p. 381.

[5] V. H. Vroom and P. W. Yetton, *Leadership and Decision-Making* (Pittsburgh: University of Pittsburgh Press, 1973).

The time available for the decision is the first key variable. The quality of the decision refers to the "feeling of importance" the organizational participants place on the decision. Where to place a bulletin board is a low-quality decision while defining the organizational criteria for annual merit increases is a high-quality decision. Commitment is defined as the needed attachment or support the employees must give to the decision.

In an autocratic style, the leader makes a unilateral decision. The consultative leader consults with two or three key subordinates, receives their recommendations and then makes a decision. The leader may or may not use subordinates' recommendations. The true consensus style consists of the leader telling the management team about a problem and asking them to come up with a recommendation. The leader is then responsible for implementation. The theory is that if the leader has selected and hired outstanding people then the leader should use their expertise to increase the probability of arriving at a correct decision.

The model suggests that if time is short the leader should be autocratic and make the decision. Consultative and consensus styles require more time. Employees may actually resent a leader who uses a consensus style when time is critical. They want quick decisions in a crisis! Further, as the needed quality of the decision changes from low to high (as perceived by the employees) the leadership style should change from autocratic to consultative or consensus. Finally, if commitment by the participants is important in implementing the decision, then the leader should shift his or her style toward the consensus end of the scale.

The consultative style of leadership, although often used, is very susceptible to "turnoff" by the subordinates. If subordinates are asked for their input, but find after two or three attempts that the leader never uses it, they become "turned off" and do a superficial analysis of the problem. After a time, they may do only the minimum level of effort required to keep from receiving negative attention from their supervisor. Proper feedback is the key. Successful consultative leaders create a good psychological contract when they ask for input from their subordinates. The contract should consist of: (1) I *really* want your input; and (2) I may or may not use your input; however, I will give you feedback on those recommendations I implemented and why. The more effective consultative leaders will choose *one* recommendation, implement it and be sure to give feedback!

ADDITIONAL SELECTED READINGS

Davis, James H.   *Group Performance.* Reading, Mass.: Addison-Wesley, 1969.

Filley, Alan C.   *Interpersonal Conflict Resolution.* Glenview, Ill.: Scott-Foresman, 1975.

French, Wendell L.; Bell, Cecil H., Jr.; and Zawacki, Robert A.   *Organization Development: Theory, Practice, and Research.* Dallas: Business Publications, 1978, pp. 69–112.

Gibson, James L.; Ivancevich, John M.; and Donnelly, James H., Jr. *Organizations: Behavior, Structure, Processes*. Dallas: Business Publications, pp. 161–79 and 407–25.

Hamner, W. Clay, and Organ, Dennis W. *Organizational Behavior: An Applied Psychological Approach*. Dallas: Business Publications, 1978, pp. 340–60 and 381–407.

House, Robert J., and Baetz, Mary L. "Leadership: Some Empirical Generalizations and New Research Directions." In Barry M. Staw, ed., *Research in Organizational Behavior*, vol. 2. Greenwich, Conn.: JAI Press, 1979, pp. 341–423.

Manners, G. E. "Another Look at Group Size, Group Problem Solving and Member Consensus." *Academy of Management Journal* 18 (1975), pp. 715–24.

Rogers, Everett M., and Agarwala-Rogers, Rekha. *Communication in Organizations*. New York: The Free Press, 1976.

Schemershorn, J. R. "Information Sharing as an Interorganizational Activity." *Academy of Management Journal* 20 (1977), pp. 148–53.

Shaw, M. E. *Group Dynamics*. New York: McGraw-Hill, 1976.

Stagner, R., and Rosen, H. *Psychology of Union-Management Relations*. Belmont, Calif.: Brooks-Cole, 1965.

Stumpf, Stephen A., Zand, Dale E., and Freedman, Richard D. "Designing Groups for Judgmental Decisions." *Academy of Management Review* (October 1979), pp. 589–600.

Stogdill, R. M. "Historical Trends in Leadership Theory and Research." *Journal of Contemporary Business* 3 (1974), pp. 1–17.

Yukl, G. "Toward a Behavioral Theory of Leadership." *Organizational Behavior and Human Performance* 6 (1971), pp. 414–40.

IR 444

Geraldine Byrne Ellerbrock

IR 444 was the last course in the "Behavior in Organization" series. It reviewed concepts and theories learned in other courses and integrated and applied them to the solution of cases. On the first day, Prof. Brock gave the students a syllabus, and after explaining the objectives of the course, she called to their attention the section of the syllabus which said, "The examinations in this course will be take-home exams. They are a learning experience. You may consult your text or any books or library materials. You may not consult your fellow students or other individuals."

As a scheduled midterm examination, a case was given to the students. Prof. Brock reminded them that this was an individual project. "Students have told me that if I give them a week to do a case, they wait until the day before. You will have the weekend to work on it. I suggest that you read it over several times today, and make notes on the margin provided. You will have better recall of information if you give yourself an extended time before you begin your actual solution. They are due Monday in the suggested typewritten form. Are there any questions?"

When grading the test, Prof. Brock discovered that two students had almost identical papers. She handed back all the papers except these two and said, "If you did not receive your paper, please come to see me." Harry Homes came first. Prof. Brock said, "Harry, your paper and that of Andy were almost identical." Harry retorted, "Sure, they might be similar because Andy is my roommate and we share the same book, but we didn't copy from each other. Both of us work, so we were working on the case at the same time. We discussed the case at the same time. We discussed the case and the questions. It made the case clearer. It helped our thinking." Prof. Brock said, "Do you think it is fair to give you a higher grade than someone else in the class who read and stuck to the directions?" Harry answered, "Well, you said it was a learning experience. Andy and I discuss any class we are taking at the same time. It makes sense. I remember things a lot better if I talk about them than if I just read things in a book. What are you going to do about this? I've got to have a good grade in the course. It's my major." Prof. Brock said, "I will have to think about it further. I will talk to Andy first and see what he has to say." "I'll send him around," Harry replied.

Then the second student, Andy Biene, came to see Prof. Brock. He said, "It is illogical to expect students not to share the information. I'll bet half the class did the same thing we did." Prof. Brock maintained that it would be logical and fair for her to give each of the students half the grade earned for the exam. Not to do so would penalize students who needed information, but followed the instructions. Andy argued, "I'll bet most of the other students worked together. They just disguised it." Prof. Brock said, "I don't believe they did. But I want to be fair to you. Let's see if they did share information. At the next class meeting you may pass out slips of paper. I will ask each student to answer the question, 'Did you discuss the case and/or questions with anyone? Indicate your answer by writing either, 'Yes' or 'No'.' I will tell the class that you will collect, tabulate, and then destroy the slips of paper." Andy said, "You'll see I'm right. Students work together all the time. They are used to doing it."

At the next class session, Prof. Brock announced, "Two students submitted almost identical papers, and when questioned had contended that many of the other students had probably worked together also. This is a senior-level course. You are majors. Hopefully we prepare you for careers. That does not mean that we give you only facts, techniques, and an encouragement to think. It means that we help you to develop work habits and a modus operandi you can use in your careers. When your boss asks you to do something, he expects you to do it, unless you give him a good reason not to do so at the time he requests it. This is the way I see it. Andy says students don't see it this way. He says many of the students discussed the case and questions. I suggested that he poll you to see whether or not you worked alone on the test. Only Andy will see the answers, but he will announce them to the class and then destroy them. We will discuss the results."

Andy tabulated the results of the question, "Did you and another student in the class help each other on the test or do the test together?" In a class of 24 students, 9 students answered "Yes" and 14 students answered "No."

Case 2–2

Five Young Men

Jerry L. Geisler

The Feathers Company[1] was established in 1960 in a small midwestern town. Retail poultry sales had been growing rapidly and area feed suppliers, growers, and processors were expanding to keep pace. Economic activity was a community concern and the Feathers Company's incorporation had been supported by a local development corporation that assessed each worker 0.5 percent of his earnings. For each $20 collected, the development corporation issued the employee one share of stock. Participation was voluntary and the receipts were used to attract more industry to the area.

From the outset, the Feathers Company utilized the most modern plant

---

[1] All names have been changed.

and equipment. The majority stockholder, Bill Thomas, assumed the presidency and spent much of his time communicating with suppliers and customers. Both he and the general superintendent, Mr. Johnstone, had considerable experience in the broiler processing industry, because of their external work and relations with area growers and feeders.

PROCESSING

Upon arrival at the plant, chickens were removed from coops, hung upside down on a line which moved at a speed of 45 to 60 chickens per minute, killed, scalded, picked by machines, singed, rinsed, transferred to another line, entrails removed, inspected, chilled, weighed, packed in boxes, iced, and stored in a cooler awaiting shipping. Processing averaged about 60 minutes with one half of the time involved in chilling. Nearly 100 workers performed very specialized tasks during the process. The line speed was set to handle about 25,000 chickens per day. If four workers performed the same operation, each person's quota would amount to 6,250 per day or 782 per hour. During peak periods the day's run might hit 30,000 chickens. Fatigue became a major factor when the work day extended past eight hours.

Occasionally, trucks would arrive late and the line would stop. Employees clocked out and waited without pay for production to resume. Because all were paid the minimum wage, overtime (at time and a half for more than 40 hours per week) was important.

PACKING

Eight workers, including a foreman named Baylor who helped where needed, handled the packing department. As chilled chickens passed over a scale, they were tipped from the line into bins ranging from two pounds to three pounds and over. Workers then filled, weighed, iced, and closed the boxes before stacking them in the cooler. The packing crew later loaded them for shipping to retail stores after the normal day's work was finished. This led to about five hours per day (per person) of overtime, plus a half day on Saturday. Because of the potential for high earnings, the packing crew was considered a choice assignment. Turnover was low, however.

CLEANING UP

Nothing is wasted in a broiler processing operation. Feathers, entrails, and even blood are sold to rendering plants for use in making fertilizer. Thus, the plant is carefully washed down with high-pressure hoses and the debris placed in barrels for transportation to market. After the hosing, all equipment is scrubbed with detergents and brushes and steam cleaned. The last job of every cleanup shift is to scrub all floors with a strong detergent. The entire plant is inspected by the foreman. The next morning the plant is again examined by a federal inspector, who has the authority to delay the start of production if plant or equipment is not satisfactorily cleaned.

The crew was comprised of 15 men ranging in age from 17 to 62 years. Turnover was high for a number of reasons: no shift differential, erratic hours (normally from about 5:00 P.M. to 1:00 or 2:00 A.M.), and friction within the crew. About half the crew members were under 25 years of age, single, and uninterested in earning overtime. In addition, one group of five young men graduated from the same high school class and were good friends. The overtime issue and age were factors in creating a less than harmonious work situation.

Job standards had developed from experience. They were loose, as each person's abilities varied widely. Each crew member was assigned a number of tasks. After completing his job he was assigned to aid other workers as needed. Early in the work week, eight to nine hours were generally required to finish all jobs. However, on Friday evenings, or prior to holidays, the young men would very often complete their jobs in four to five hours and then pitch in and finish the entire plant within six hours. The older workers grumbled constantly about their inability to earn overtime. The youngsters retaliated by pulling pranks.

The favorite prank involved placing a water hose with 90 pounds of pressure into a knee-high boot—usually an older person's boot. Another prank was the spraying of water into a large wall fan that divided two rooms in the plant. The instant rain shower nearly always produced shouted curses and threats. Minor pranks involved an occasional soaping of the already slippery lounge floor where nightly breaks were held, as well as general horseplay. The situation smoldered for about a year.

REORGANIZATION

Without explanation, one day the five young men were reassigned to a loading crew. The loading crew's duty was to load outgoing dressed poultry on trucks for shipping to grocery chains. They were not replaced on the cleanup crew, which resulted in considerable overtime for each of the remaining ten members.

At first, the crew's only task was to load trucks. However, the five young men now loaded each truck in 2 hours, where it had previously taken the packing crew 3 to $3\frac{1}{2}$ hours. The packing crew no longer earned overtime unless the week's production run exceeded 40 hours. The resultant drop in their earnings led to an outcry exceeding that of the cleanup crew.

In the meantime it became exceedingly difficult to keep the loading crew busy. Workers cleaned trucks, trimmed shrubs, unloaded boxes, washed the president's cars and airplane, and performed any tasks required of them. The crew was commended several times by Mr. Thomas. The next year passed quickly.

One day the crew reported to work as usual. Upon arrival they discovered that their time cards had been pulled. A supervisor told them that they were laid off—forever. No other explanation was offered. The company never called them back even though no replacements were hired. In addition, the company held up their unemployment benefits for six weeks.

Case 2–3 ——————————————————————————————————
Why Was Production Sticky on the Glue Line?

Donald J. Petersen

BACKGROUND INFORMATION

Kenilworth Electric is a very large, international corporation, producing a wide array of electrical products and services, from household appliances to industrial transformers. Five years ago, Kenilworth erected a large manufacturing plant in a midsized city in central Indiana, for the production of million-volt transformers. The plant created 3,200 new jobs for the community, which already had a large industrial and manufacturing base and a ready supply of workers, many of whom had recently moved north from Kentucky and Tennessee. In the five years since its erection, the plant has yet to have a profitable year. Almost as soon as it opened its doors, Kenilworth became unionized. Two years later the plant suffered its first strike, which lasted 95 days. One year after this strike, the workforce was still generally hostile, espousing the motto, "Screw the company before the company screws you." Union stewards were kept busy filing grievances on a common gripe among workers—the allocation of overtime. Many of Kenilworth's production workers were even heard to express concern about overtime running out.

Despite all of this, the Kenilworth plant was still enjoying a backlog of orders. Adding to the production pressures were several transformers which did not test out in the field and had to be torn down and rebuilt. Consequently, 12-hour days were common in most departments, with occasional 16-hour days offered on all three shifts. Hourly pay was lower than the prevailing area rates in the lower level jobs, but above community average in the higher level jobs. Workers could bid on higher level jobs which were awarded by seniority. There was a rather large turnover of workers, so advancement to higher jobs was quite common.

THE SITUATION

For some time Jack McKay, third-shift foreman of the paperboard washer department (paper washers which surround the coils in huge transformers) had been unhappy with the low production in his department. Production had been only about 62 percent of standard. At a meeting with the plant superintendent and the foremen from the other two shifts, he learned that the production rate was similar on the other two shifts as well.

The heart of McKay's department is an assembly line, which glues small blocks of paperboard to the large washers at precisely located spots. Each washer requires a team of eight men, four on a side, working together to cover the spots with blocks as the washer moves slowly past them on a belt.

Any exposed glue must be removed completely, as it will cause a short in the transformer.

One Tuesday evening, Jack had just completed a tour of the department, noticing that most of the shear presses were operating at acceptable paces. However, the line, which should never have to be stopped if production is maintained at a reasonable pace, had already been stopped four times to allow the gluers to catch up. He noticed also that two of his newest linemen were finished with their sections, while the rest of the men were only half through. Several of the slower men were looking angry, so Jack thought he would observe from a distance what was happening. From a back corner of the department, on top of a pile of paperboard, Jack could sit and watch the entire department, without being seen.

Jack observed the belt moving again, slowly. As a new washer approached, the men began gluing blocks, very lethargically, except for the two new men, who seemed to be racing each other and having a good time at it. Suddenly, one of Jack's men located on the far side of the line tossed a block, which had been glued on all sides, right into the middle of the area being completed by one of the new men, George Crawford. Because of the problem as mentioned before, of exposed glue causing shorts, the block had to be removed, as well as all excess glue. While George went about this task, two more blocks hit in his area, and three were tossed into the area of his companion, Dave Sickles. Neither man seemed overly perturbed and they cleaned up the mess. Despite these interruptions, they still finished well ahead of the others on the line. In the meantime, the other men were moving so slowly that the belt had to be stopped again, this time for five minutes.

Jack had seen enough. He climbed down from his vantage point and went into his office to draft a letter to the third shift supervisor, Wendell Caudill, detailing his observations.

Case 2-4 ———————————————————————

Acme Wholesale Distributing Company*

Gary Whitney

In February of 1973, I was hired by the Acme Wholesale Distributing Company, a local firm in Portland. The work group consisted of ten students from the local university We found the job through the university's placement center.

The group members were approximately the same age, ranging from 18 to 23. The reason for the majority of the workers to seek employment was to earn money for school. The social backgrounds of the group were hard to estimate; however, I believe a middle-class background prevailed. Of the ten, I only knew two, my roommate and a friend of my brother.

The job consisted of about a week's work in the evening from 8:00 P.M. to 2:00 A.M. It involved opening old boxes of a nationally distributed brand of imported, and now moldy, salami; separating the salvageable from the unsalvageable salami; cleaning the salvageable salamis with vinegar and a scrub brush; drying, rewrapping, and reboxing them.

The building was an old, cold, gloomy structure, which was primarily used as a warehouse, with a small office in the front. We worked on the second floor, which was accessible by means of an old open-style elevator used to haul the products. Stairs near the front office also gave access to this floor. The floor was filled with boxes of various products, with all but one dirty brick wall covered. The few windows were too high to be of any use.

We had one supervisor who was a day employee at the firm. He also had attended the university. His age was around 30. It was his duty to instruct us and see that we did our work. He also made periodic inspections of the finished product to see if it met quality standards. It became apparent at once that he did not like working nights, but enjoyed the overtime pay.

On the first night we were divided into two groups, based on where we were standing at the moment. Instructions were given to each person for his specific job and we started. The following is a diagram of the work area.

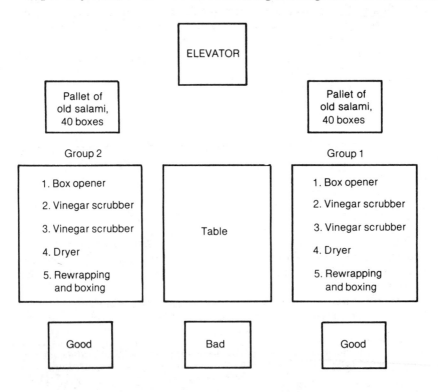

Bill, the supervisor, stayed with us the whole first night helping at each position. It was also his responsibility to see that a new pallet of 40 boxes was supplied at the same time the old one was finished. This kept an even flow through the line. We had one major break in the evening, which was at 10:30 for half an hour. This time we spent in a nearby tavern, eating and drinking. Bill and one other member who brought a sack lunch did not attend this gathering. Very little conversation took place that night. What did occur was primarily questions directed at Bill. By 2:00 A.M., we had achieved 170 boxes and ten sore backs. A thorough cleaning of the area at night's end was mandatory. So ended the first night.

On the second night Bill had been instructed to achieve a production quota of 240 boxes a night, and that we were to produce a higher percentage of good salamis. This meant that we would have to scrub more salamis and scrub them harder to get more mold off.

This, however, produced a conflict of goals between the group and management. We were to work at a rate that seemed impossible and to produce more for the same pay. The incentive was that if we reached this goal early, we were finished for the night, and would be paid for the full night. So the work began again, this time with Bill not present but staying in the office, returning only to supply us with more pallets, check our work, and leave again.

Things began slowly, with members changing positions periodically to relieve boredom. Specialization in each job developed and new methods evolved to increase speed. Rotation slowed when each member found a job he liked best and could do the fastest. If anyone was slow at one position, thus slowing the line and the production, he would give it up for another position. Thus, we all found our optimum spot in the line. On the second night I left group two for group one, in which my roommate and my brother's friend were working. This was the only transfer between the two groups to take place.

We developed a sense of unity which helped our group. Our group talked more, produced faster, and, in general, joked around more. The overall atmosphere changed, with laughter often heard. Someone brought a radio. Individuals were given nicknames such as "fat man," etc. Conversations were more within each group, with occasional satirical remarks exchanged between the two groups. It seemed to be our way of communicating to those we didn't know without feeling awkward or leaving anyone open for personal attack. No one spoke of their past. The talk was focused on the strange situation in which we were working. We all decided it was against the law, health codes, etc. No one seemed to care beyond that point. After all, it was money, which we all needed. Group two spoke little; our group dominated most of what was said. I felt they had less in common with each other. This hampered their overall production, as was demonstrated when short contests between tables took place. One of their members was the individual who didn't go to the tavern with the rest of us. On the fourth day, one of their members left for Washington, D.C., to protest against Nixon.

Members helped out at other positions on their table and at times crossed over to help the other table; this was done to finish faster before our break and at the end of the evening. Sloughing off was not permitted and when discovered, immediate verbal attack occurred. Production by the third night reached a surprising 240 boxes in four and a half hours.

The next night, Bill tightened up his inspections of the finished product, demanding better quality. This, of course, increased the time required to complete 240 boxes per night. Also, he stressed that his boss still wanted more of the 240 boxes done each night to yield good salamis. A good box received up to $25 and the rejects about $5 in resale value.

To make everyone happy, we cheated. Of course the consumer was the ultimate loser but that was not our concern. We hid the not-so-good salami at the bottom of each box and placed the boxes of ill repute in the center of the pallet, a hard place for Bill to reach to inspect. So more salamis passed as good ones, thus pleasing Bill; more boxes of good were packed, thus pleasing Bill's boss; all done in less time, pleasing us.

Case 2–5 ——

New Commissioner Is a Manager*

Virgil B. Zimmerman

Robert Jackson began his job as Commissioner of Social Welfare in Tripp County on a hot July day. The oppressiveness of the humidity only heightened the anxiety felt by the staff, for the new commissioner was a person about whom little was known. He was not a social welfare professional, but rather a retired ("fired," some said) district manager for one of the state's larger chains of supermarkets. He had worked at the firm's headquarters in the far corner of the state. One caseworker had heard from a friend on the county legislature's Selection Committee that Jackson was a "pretty good fellow" with the reputation of being a tough manager and a strict disciplinarian. As this rumor spread through the cavernous, century-old factory building in which the Department of Social Welfare was housed, the staff's apprehension grew.

Jackson's first day started off well, although his introductory meetings with Kevin McBride and Meyer Levine, the two division directors (who had, themselves, aspired to the commissionership) were somewhat strained. After meeting the heads of units and the members of his immediate staff, commissioner Jackson paused only briefly to examine the various papers that had been assembled on his desk: the organization chart; the budget; copies of pertinent state and federal statutes and regulatory guidelines; the comprehensive plan required for those social services

* This case was prepared for the Continuing Education Project of the School of Social Welfare of the State University of New York at Albany pursuant to a contract with the New York State Department of Social Services and partially funded by a grant from the U.S. Department of Health, Education, and Welfare.

reimbursed, in part, by the federal government under Title XX of the Social Security Act; and letters from the county Popular Party chairman and the state Department of Health and Social Welfare (DHSW) which seemed to merit his personal attention.

Jackson, a somewhat portly gentleman in his late 50s with ruddy complexion and a grizzled crewcut, then surprised his subordinates by spending a couple of hours wandering from office to office, introducing himself and chatting with whichever members of the staff happened to be available. In these visits he did not seem particularly interested in departmental operations but was cordially social, asking about the employees' education, families, and other such mundane matters. He even spent half an hour sitting in the intake waiting room pretending to be a "client"—to see whether the chairs were sufficiently uncomfortable," he said later.

Those with whom the new commissioner socialized that first day felt reassured. His easy, friendly manner, soft voice, and ready wit didn't seem to fit the image they had formed of a demanding boss. Just the fact that he had stopped to exchange pleasantries with several of the very lowest-ranking employees made him seem more human, more concerned, more approachable than the former commissioner had been.

In a lengthy conversation with Louis Macri, his administrative assistant, Jackson commented that he had found the staff to be surprisingly bright, seemingly competent, and cheery. He admired the care with which the building had been restored, the good lighting, and the colorful walls. Furniture in a majority of the offices seemed to be relatively new, efficient, and inexpensive, as befitted a public office serving the poor and troubled. Even the commissioner's office, he noted with an approving smile, was approachable than the former commissioner had been.

Toward the close of the day he asked his secretary, Alice Fanning, to bring together in his conference room all of his immediate subordinates. When they had gathered, he thanked them for the materials they had prepared for him and complimented them on the good order and harmonious working relationships he had observed. "There are some pretty sharp conflicts here that you didn't see," Tom White, the head of the Investigations Unit, thought to himself, "but you'll find out soon enough that this agency isn't all milk and honey." After the generalities he asked that each of them meet with him the following morning beginning at 10:00 to give him a detailed report on his or her area of responsibility and its objectives, legal basis, funding, staffing, problems, and the like.

Before he dismissed them, he began to ask some rather penetrating but quite unexpected questions about Tripp County, such as its population, ethnic composition, age distribution, labor force, types of economic activity, and number of unemployed. He seemed surprised, disappointed, and a bit put out by the inability of the staff to provide precise answers. Once when Jim Robinson ventured an answer beginning "All I can give is a rough guess . . . ," Jackson broke in, "Why don't you know? I'm not interested in guesses!" The hint of temper in his voice was noticed by all. "This old cat has claws under those velvet paws," the head of the food stamp unit thought to himself.

When it became apparent that the staff could not provide him with the data he sought out of their collective memories, he turned to Alan Rapp, the youthful head of the operations analysis and planning unit, and asked him if he could pull together basic information on the county and provide a brief note on it by the following afternoon (see Appendix A). Then with a broad smile, he asked if it would be possible to have the entire staff of the department assemble at the closing hour the following day so that he might speak with them. Macri spoke up to say that a meeting could be held, although the first floor hall, the only space in the building not divided into offices, was barely large enough to hold all the staff. However it would not be possible to reach everyone in so brief a time, as caseworkers who visited clients in the northern part of the county did not come in to the office every day. The meeting was then scheduled for the following Thursday afternoon. James Lincoln, the director of administrative services, was instructed to see that notices got out and the other necessary arrangements were made. With that the commissioner's first staff meeting ended.

COMMISSIONER JACKSON "DISCOVERS" SOCIAL SERVICES

The meetings which the new commissioner had with his unit heads on his second day in office were highly enlightening. He learned that he now directed a staff of some 340 employees who collectively were responsible for an extensive collection of programs and subprograms. All together, they would disburse roughly $75 million, of which approximately 33 percent was reimbursed by the federal government and 38 percent by the state. Most of these programs were subject to complex regulations and guidelines issued either by the Department of Health, Education, and Welfare (HEW) in Washington or by the state DHSW, or both. Reimbursement formulae varied with the program: some expenditures were fully paid for by Washington; some were partially federally funded; some were the sole responsibility of the county; and some were shared between the county and the state. The flood of regulations, directives, and guidelines coming to the department from HEW and the DHSW was of such a volume that Macri reported that he spent almost a third of his time reading the new circulars and seeing that the proper unit heads understood them and would follow their dictates.

As Jackson reviewed the organization chart (see Appendix B) with Macri, he saw that the department was split into three main divisions. One division was responsible for public financial assistance (often called "income maintenance" in the documents). Another division provided a long list of "social services." The third, called "administrative services," handled personnel matters, accounting, the data processing center, and miscellaneous necessary housekeeping activities like security and procurement.

The separation of financial assistance from social services originally had been mandated by the federal government. That mandate had been lifted in the summer of 1977, but the corresponding state statute had not yet been modified (see Appendix G). Kevin McBride, the director of social services, told Jackson that he and many of the lower-level unit heads thought that the separation had been dysfunctional because many of those who were eligible for and receiving financial assistance also had family and personal problems calling for intervention by experienced caseworkers, all of whom were assigned to the social services division. In fact, Meyer Levine, the director of financial assistance, began his session with Jackson by asking for the immediate assignment of ten caseworkers to his division so that they could give prompt attention to the nonfinancial problems and needs of those applying for or seeking recertification for financial assistance. To this request Jackson replied only that he would ask Macri and Rapp to look into the pros and cons and that he would be prepared to discuss the matter further with the two directors the following week. To himself he thought, "Perhaps some more basic reorganization of the department would be desirable. At least we should be prepared to give the state department our recommendation on the legislative changes we think necessary well before the next session of the legislature."

The county budget, he discovered, listed each and every individual authorized position in the department with its corresponding salary and listed lump sums for the several categories of programs. Expected federal and state reimbursements were listed by category in the revenue section of the budget (see Appendix C). It wasn't easy to reconcile these figures with the various categories of expenses listed in the last year's annual report, although his chief accountant told him that it could be done. On the one hand, there was an elaborate, computer-based accounting system which enabled assistance outlays and services purchased from adoption agencies, day care centers, medical facilities, schools, and other suppliers of services to be documented in support of claims for reimbursement. On the other hand, all of the department's expenditures for its staff and their travel, supplies, and miscellaneous expenses were classified for accounting purposes as "administrative." The fraction of those costs charged to each of the several programs or services for reimbursement purposes was determined by statistical estimation rather than by accounting means.

Both Rapp and Macri supported Levine's claim that operations in the public assistance division were in good shape. Procedures, eligibility rules, and grant amounts were all so stringently prescribed by state and federal regulations that the division's role was essentially that of being a processor and recorder of individual transactions, a task at which it had become highly efficient. Carefulness of review was evidenced by the large percentage of applicants who were denied medical or financial assistance of food stamps. At the time of the last audit, error rates on determinations of eligibility and on the amount of grants were well within prescribed limits. Such major problem areas as the cost of hospital and nursing home care were largely out of county control, since rates for reimbursement were set by the state DHSW. Minor problems, such as claims for duplicates of "lost" checks and of moves of clients among the various counties, seemed to be well under control. The chief of the investigations unit assured Jackson that in a year and a half after a couple of well-publicized "fraud" prosecutions, his men had uncovered only a few instances of significant misrepresentation.

With respect to social services, however, the picture was not quite so bright. Jackson had been quite impressed with the comprehensive plan for Title XX services (see Summary listing in Appendix D) which he had found among the papers on his desk, but McBride could not answer many of the questions which its data had raised in his mind. He could not, for instance, reconcile the cost figures for the various services as given in the plan with any of the headings listed in the department's budget. The federal government, McBride explained, reimbursed 75 percent of the cost of services authorized by Title XX, but each county was given an absolute ceiling based on a rather complicated formula. That ceiling, in turn, had been distributed among the various headings in the plan. Estimates as to the numbers of clients to be provided with various kinds of services were largely "guesstimates." Although purchased costs could be distributed in the accounts to the specific kind of service, that part of the department's "administrative" costs allocated to each service was not based on an accounting of the time spent on them by the caseworkers but rather was extrapolated from areawide statistical studies conducted by the DHSW.

McBride explained to the commissioner how the "random moment" system provided a basis for cost allocation. The state DHSW required that each caseworker be identified by number. Each month the state office sent out a computer-generated (randomly selected) list of employee numbers and the precise moment over a five-day period (day-hour-minute) at which the work on which each such employee was engaged at that precise moment was to be noted and reported on a prescribed form. These forms were assembled and forwarded to the state DHSW, which processed them by computer to determine the percentages of costs to be allocated to each kind of service under the various reimbursement formulae. Until recently, these had been aggregated by multicounty districts, a procedure which apparently satisfied HEW but gave little guidance to individual counties. "Now, however," he added, "we are going to get quarterly reports based on our own county forms. We have sent in the forms for the quarter ending last June 30, and we should have the analysis back shortly. I'll see that you see it as soon as it arrives." (See Appendix E.)

Because of his prior experience, Jackson was much given to ratio analysis as a means of making complex data meaningful. Whenever he saw a couple of columns of figures—as he did in the Comprehensive Title XX Plan—he almost instinctively reached for his pocket calculator and began dividing. To McBride's surprise he had done so and was loaded with questions. "Why does it cost $425 on the average per recipient to supply protective services to adults but only $315 to render such services to children?" "Are these average costs per recipient higher or lower than last year and by how much and why?" "What is the ratio between the number of recipients in each of these service categories and the number of staff available to handle them?"

Jackson had noted that the statewide comprehensive plan had included expected costs and numbers of recipients for all counties, and he had been interested particularly in the figures for Lake County—here he had formerly lived and worked—and for Adams County, which he considered similar to Tripp County in many respects (see Appendix F). McBride did not know of any attempt to compare the figures in the Tripp County Plan with those for any other county. His eventual response to Jackson's questions was to say that since both costs and numbers of recipients as stated in the plan were considered to be such rough approximations, it didn't seem worth the time to make such calculations. "I understand," the Commissioner put in sympathetically, "I sometimes let my curiosity run away with me; but I do wish you could tell me how the social services plan was put together and how we can use it to make sure that we are using our limited resources to the best advantage."

In a subsequent meeting with the new commissioner, Macri and Rapp expressed the judgment that although social services consumed only a minor proportion of the department's total budget, that was where the "fat" was. In their opinion, based on random observations, some caseworkers had too heavy a workload, others had too little. Because of the way in which clients were assigned, some caseworkers spent too much of their time in travel. Unit supervisors, they claimed, did not seem to know specifically what caseworkers were accomplishing. Once clients had been found to be eligible for services, they tended to be held on the roster of "open cases" more or less indefinitely. No one seemed to know what average unit costs per type of service were or whether such costs were going up or down.

Many of the others with whom Jackson spoke that day thought that individual caseworkers were probably doing a thoroughly professional, competent job, but that there was no way of telling whether some were more effective than others or whether, for that matter, the department was accomplishing results commensurate with the funds expended to provide services.

In the course of his discussions, commissioner Jackson picked up two additional pieces of information which he considered significant. Certain local judges, he learned, were much inclined to assign youths appearing before them to periods of "detention" or "supervision" in state or privately run training schools or "institutes" for delinquents or persons in need of supervision. Such assignments were frequently made without the advice of, or contrary to recommendations of, a DHSW caseworker. Such institutional care of delinquents, which had to be paid for by the department, was extremely expensive, and the uncontrollable and growing costs of such care were consuming funds which McBride thought might better be spent for more productive purposes. The other item was knowledge that the state department had circulated portions of a consultant's report which had recommended a pattern of social service casework management which seemed designed to give better control of cases by involving supervisors in periodic reviews of individual cases (see Appendix H).

The new commissioner's meeting with the assembled staff on Thursday afternoon was not an unqualified success, although many of the clerks and other subordinate staff were pleased that they had been included. "It's about time somebody pays some attention to us," one said. Some of the senior staff, however, grumbled that "meetings like this are a waste of time." Others resented the possibility that they might irritate members of their car pools, who would have to wait for their delayed exodus from the agency. The hall in which the staff—except for the inevitable absentees—assembled was clearly inadequate for their numbers and quickly became a steaming cauldron.

The commissioner was mercifully and intentionally brief. He greeted them cordially and thanked them for coming and for the cooperation and dedication which he knew they had given and would continue to give to the objectives and policies of the department. He explained that he wanted to tell them, as quickly and directly as possible, about the philosophy of management which he would practice.

> My cardinal principle is one of concern for all the employees of the department. I will insist that all employees be treated fairly and that due consideration be given to individual needs and desires in such matters as assignments and the scheduling of vacations. Above all, I want this staff to feel challenged, to feel that their judgments will be respected, to feel that they have an opportunity for personal growth. As a store manager, it was my aim to have every person acquire the skills and knowledge necessary to do the work of every other employee. This made work more interesting by providing a variety of assignments, permitted a more equitable sharing of the workload, prepared people for advancement, and made it easier for anyone to get another job if he had to relocate. I realize the limitations, but I hope we can do something similar here.
>
> My second principle is that I don't try to second-guess experts who work for me on matters which they have been trained to handle. Most of you already know much more about public assistance and social services than I will ever learn. Feel free to come to me with your problems, especially if they have political or community relations aspects, and you will receive encouragement and support. But I won't try to interpret regulations for you or tell you what should be done with or for a particular case.
>
> Finally, I believe that any large and complex organization—and this department certainly fits that definition—must be *managed*, and that is my responsibility, a responsibility shared with division directors and unit chiefs. Our task is to strive to make the best possible use of our limited resources, both human and financial. We have a duty to assign and reassign such resources from time to time to meet changing priority needs. To do this we must have detailed, ongoing monitoring of all our operations and the results we get from them. As a store manager I had to know the volume of sales and profits each week of each department per square foot of space occupied and per employee. On the basis of this information, successful departments were expanded and those which lagged behind the goals set for them were analyzed to determine what the reasons might be and corrective action was taken. I don't believe I am wrong in thinking that a similar approach might be effective here. But, I will need your advice and your help. We all know that our resources are limited and that the needs of those we serve are vast. We all can share in the pride of accomplishment if we can do more with what we have.

He then opened the meeting to questions, but the only ones he received concerned the possibility of salary increases. He responded noncommittally, repeated his thanks, and dismissed the meeting.

In the weeks that followed, things settled down into a customary routine. Crises arose and were handled in the usual manner. The commissioner spent a fair amount of time with each of his branch and unit chiefs "learning the ropes" as he put it. He seemed to have an inexhaustible capacity for listening, rarely made suggestions, and almost never gave what could be construed as an order. McBride became one of his favorites.

Jackson rapidly became convinced that social services provided a fertile ground for experimentation with a monitoring and reporting system which would provide a check on individual caseworkers and their first-line supervisors as well. McBride, though an old-line social worker and nearing retirement, seemed intrigued by the notion of attempting to measure caseworkers' accomplishments individually and collectively and of relating such accomplishments to the costs of providing services.

By the end of August, Jackson's mind was made up. He called together McBride; the latter's administrative assistant; Jones, the senior "systems analyst" in the data processing unit; Macri; and Rapp and outlined his tentative strategy to them. "I want you to constitute a 'task force' under Macri's leadership to go over all of the ideas on casework management we have been discussing, consider the proposals and suggestions which anyone in the state DHSW might have, add any of your own or your colleagues' and come up with the design of a monitoring and control system for social services which you think we should adopt. I want a fairly detailed report by the end of September, which at the very least, would cover the following elements:

1. Case opening and assignment procedures.
2. Case documentations.
3. Reporting on case progress.
4. A method of evaluating the quality of caseworks of individual caseworkers."

APPENDIX A

Demographic and Economic Characteristics of Tripp County

MEMORANDUM

July 22, 1977

TO: Commissioner Robert Jackson
      Department of Social Welfare

FROM: Alan Rapp, Administrative Analyst

SUBJECT: Demographic and Economic Characteristics of Tripp County.

The kinds of information regarding Tripp County that you were asking for yesterday are not easy to obtain. The best source I could put my hands on in a hurry was the County Economic Development Plan, but the data cited there are not always identified by source. Data are given for different years and are not carefully defined. I have supplemented the data found there with some from our files on the clients of the department.

Total population (1975)	381,084	Nonwhite population
Avon City	136,000	24,000, nearly all
Centerville	32,164	Black; Orientals and
Suburban	105,781	Indians fewer than 500;
Rural and village	26,819	about 800 of recent
area	721 square miles	Latin-American origin.
Estimated population		
(1980)	386,450	

Labor force 220,980
   Males 132,640
   Females 88,380

Occupational categories

Manufacturing	37,500	Agriculture	14,120
Other blue-collar	21,400	Miscellaneous	74,600
White-collar	51,630	Unemployed	21,650*
Median income per capita . .	$6,850†		

* 9.8 percent of labor force, 5.6 percent of population.
† 1973 estimate.

The population of the county has held steady over the past decade. Manufacturing employment has been declining by about 2 percent per year. Construction has been in a slump for several years. Growth in median income has not kept up with increases in incomes in more prosperous sections of the state.

Number of families 72,548
   Families below federally defined "poverty level": 6.3 percent

Age distribution of population

0–19	122,582	60–79	57,865
20–39	106,805	Over 80	9,173
40–59	84,659		

	Amount disbursed	Number of persons
Medical assistance (1976)		
Nursing homes	$14,320	1,570
Medical care	16,360	14,950

Individuals on food stamps 18,900
New applications received (1976) . . . . . . 3,670; Granted: 1,740

Children in institutional care 586

Adoptions arranged 63

APPENDIX B

Organization Chart of Tripp County Department of Social Welfare

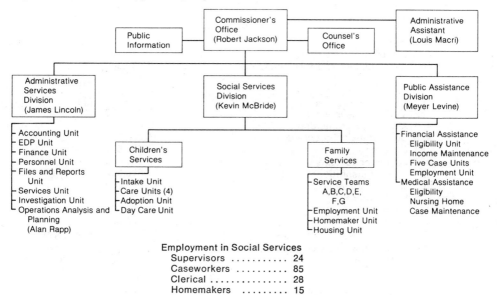

Employment in Social Services
Supervisors 24
Caseworkers 85
Clerical 28
Homemakers 15
CETA workers 12

APPENDIX C

Tripp County Department of Social Welfare Summary Budget
Fiscal Year 1977–78

Departmental expenses

401 Personal services	$ 7,720,360	
402 Equipment	75,000	
403 Rent, utilities and miscellaneous	1,980,000	
		$ 8,775,360

Program outlays

452 Medical Assistance	$ 27,830,000	
453 Aid to aged, blind and disabled	1,045,000	
454 Dependent children aid	15,230,000	
461 Children in institutions	3,800,000	
462 Foster child care	1,200,000	
463 Special institutional care	500,000	
464 Juvenile delinquents	3,055,000	
471 Home relief	4,200,000	
472 Emergency assistance	75,000	
473 Burials	100,000	
		$55,035,000

Revenues (other than county general fund)	$ 65,810,360	
X–423 Repayments and contributions	$ 2,385,000	$ 2,385,000

State aid

X–452 Medical assistance	$ 6,250,000	
X–454 Aid to dependent children	3,625,000	
X–405 Social services administration	1,957,000	
X–460 Child care	2,300,000	
X–464 Care of juvenile delinquents	1,050,000	
X–470 Care of adults	5,468,000	
X–471 Home relief	1,460,000	
X–472 Emergency aid	16,000	
X–473 Burials	45,000	
X–490 Other social services	574,000	
		$25,130,000

Federal aid

X–452 U Medical assistance	$ 11,300,000	
X–454 U Aid to dependent children	6,160,000	
X–405 U Social services administration	3,527,000	
X–490 U Other social services	1,479,000	$21,466,000
	$114,791,360	

APPENDIX D

**Summary of Number of Recipients and Costs of Title XX Services
Tripp County (1978 plans)**

Service	Number of Recipients	Estimated Total Cost
Adoption services	58	$ 53,415
Day care—children	2,099	1,307,335
Education	75	2,870
Employment (Non-WIN)	100	5,750
Family planning	590	10,410
Foster care—children	1,025	585,400
Foster care—adults	90	9,100
Health related	105	75,600
Home management	275	14,950
Homemaker	932	518,000
Housekeeper/chore	120	59,820
Housing improvement	1,225	50,325
Information and referral	7,900	79,525
Preventive	1,008	878,185
Protective—adults	256	108,746
Protective—children	1,782	562,360
Social group services—senior citizens	390	18,340
Social adjustment	255	29,150
Transportation	52	20,060
Unmarried parents	79	37,550
Total	19,326	$4,426,891

APPENDIX E

Random Moment Cost Assignments

October 5, 1977

Mr. Robert Jackson, Commissioner
Tripp County Department of Social Welfare
Avon City

Attention: Accounting Supervisor

Dear Commissioner:

Your random moment study percentages for the period July 1, 1977, through September 30, 1977, are as follows:

Family planning	1.21
ADC: ADC-U: ADC-FC	37.21
SSI	4.12
Eligible for MA-FP	7.78
Income eligible	25.72
Without regard to income	23.15
EAF	0.3
ADC–WIN	0.27
Personal care services	0.19
FNP	0.12
NR	0.02

These percentages are to be used in calculating your federal and state reimbursement amounts.

APPENDIX E *(continued)*

RANDOM MOMENT OBSERVATION FORM

	LOCAL AGENCY CODE NUMBER		SATELLITE (SITE) NUMBER

SERVICE WORKER'S NAME		WORKER'S I.D. NUMBER	DATE Mo. Day Yr.	TIME

INSTRUCTIONS: 1) Select from Section A the action which best describes the worker's activity at the time indicated above.

2) Complete Sections B, C, D, and E only for Section A, Items 01 and 02.

3) Do not check more than one box in any Section.

SECTION A - ACTIVITY

Direct Services

01 ☐ Service Related
02 ☐ Information and Referral
03 ☐ Group Services

Home Finding

09 ☐ Day Care
10 ☐ Adoption
11 ☐ Foster Care - Adults
12 ☐ Foster Care - Children

Indirect Services/Administration

04 ☐ Training
05 ☐ Meetings
06 ☐ Authorized Leave
07 ☐ Lunch Break
08 ☐ Other (includes coffee breaks)

COMPLETE THE FOLLOWING SECTIONS ONLY FOR ITEMS 01 OR 02 ABOVE

SECTION B - SERVICES

CASE NUMBER

01 ☐ Adoption Services
03 ☐ Day Care - Children
04 ☐ Education
05 ☐ Employment
06 ☐ Family Planning
07 ☐ Foster Care - Adults
08 ☐ Foster Care - Children
09 ☐ Health Related
10 ☐ Home Management
11 ☐ Homemaker - Other
12 ☐ Housekeeper Chore

13 ☐ Housing Improvement Services
15 ☐ Preventive (Counseling & Supportive Services)
16 ☐ Protective Services - Adults
17 ☐ Protective Services - Children
18 ☐ Social Group Services for Senior Citizens
19 ☐ Social Adjustment Services
20 ☐ Transportation
21 ☐ Unmarried Parents Services
22 ☐ Personal Care Service
23 ☐ Victims of Domestic Violence

SECTION C - CLIENT GOAL

01 ☐ Self Support
02 ☐ Self Sufficiency
03 ☐ Protection of Children & Adults
04 ☐ Community Home Based Care
05 ☐ Institutional Care

SECTION D - PRIMARY CLIENT

Who is the primary client?

01 ☐ Adult   02 ☐ Child

SECTION E - CLIENT STATUS

01 ☐ AFDC-WIN
02 ☐ AFDC-FC
03 ☐ AFDC
04 ☐ EAF
05 ☐ SSI-Aged

06 ☐ SSI-Blind
07 ☐ SSI-Disabled
08 ☐ MA-FP
09 ☐ Long Term Health Care
11 ☐ Group Eligibility

13 ☐ HR
14 ☐ Income Eligible
15 ☐ Without Regard to Income
17 ☐ FNP
18 ☐ Non-Reimbursable

☐ Posted on Daily Control Log   -17-   Initials _____   Date _____

APPENDIX F

**Summary of Recipients and Costs of Title XX Services (1978 Plans)
Lake and Adams Counties**

Service	Number of Recipients Lake	Number of Recipients Adams	Total Cost Lake	Total Cost Adams
Adoption service	450	85	$ 104,300	$ 23,400
Day care—children	4,000	130	865,000	50,000
Education		90		19,100
Employment (Non–WIN)	45	200	6,020	29,500
Family planning	260	100	56,000	10,000
Foster care—children	4,220	650	1,215,230	240,000
Foster care—adults	120	36	20,080	3,700
Health related	525	500	200,900	105,000
Home management	250	350	102,000	52,000
Homemaker	80	280	107,000	62,000
Housekeeper/chore	90	30	116,000	9,515
Housing improvement	290	235	262,000	41,500
Information and referral	2,500	1,440	30,400	41,200
Preventive	950	1,320	315,000	118,000
Protective—adults	140	155	150,000	34,000
Protective—children	6,920	600	2,600,000	241,000
Social group services—senior citizens ...				
Social adjustment	85	240	29,000	19,000
Transportation	55	400	17,000	39,900
Unmarried parents	125	70	46,500	13,000
Total	21,105	6,911	$6,242,430	$1,151,815

APPENDIX G

**Administrative Directive on Separation of Services Functions from Income
Maintenance Functions**

DEPARTMENT OF HEALTH AND SOCIAL WELFARE
15 Capitol Street, Capitol City

[An Administrative Directive is a written communication to local Social Services Districts providing directions to be followed in the administration of public assistance and care programs.]

ADMINISTRATIVE DIRECTIVE

TRANSMITTAL NO.:   77 ADM-83
[Administration]

TO: Commissioners of Social Welfare

Date: July 29, 1977

SUBJECT: Separation of Services from Income Maintenance

I.   Purpose

The purpose of this release is to inform local social service commissioners that the separation of Income Maintenance functions from Services functions

APPENDIX G *(continued)*

is no longer a federal requirement. However, Section 81 of the New York State Social Services Law still mandates separation. Nevertheless, within the mandate of Section 64, local social services districts will not be permitted certain latitude in modifying the current organizational system short of integration of income maintenance and social services functions. In addition, since local demonstration projects are permitted under Section 113 of the Social Services Law, proposals for demonstration projects involving integration of Income Maintenance, Medical Assistance, and Services will be considered for approval by the Department. Administrative Letter 71 PWD-23 is hereby repealed in its entirety.

II.   Background

In 1969, the Department of Health, Education and Welfare promulgated regulations recommending the separation of the administration of social services from other assistance programs. In 1971, the State Legislature enacted Chapter 109 of the Laws of 1971 (Section 64 of the Social Services Law) which mandated on all social services districts the separation of social services from the eligibility and assistance payment function. By Federal regulation, separation was mandated on January 1, 1973. Thus, since 1973 both the Federal and the State Governments mandated separation. Public Law 93–647, however, which became effective October 1, 1975, established a new Title XX of the Social Security Act which no longer required the separation of social services from income maintenance.

III.   Program Implications

In a survey of the methods used to administer the income maintenance programs in the upstate districts, we found a variety of methods used. Some districts have moved away from the functional approach which was installed in 1971 to some method of caseload management. Some districts have assigned cases alphabetically and integrated face to face recertification with other income maintenance activities as part of the caseload assignment. Other districts have assigned cases alphabetically to a team consisting of an application specialist, face to face recertification specialist, and income maintenance specialist.

Local agencies will undoubtedly wish to give some consideration to reorganization—either to a modification of the current system within the mandate of Section 64 or to an integration of Income Maintenance and Services as a demonstration project.

An example of a type of modification of the current system is the use of the team approach where the team consists of Income Maintenance, Medical Assistance and Services workers who perform eligibility functions and certain other activities. Administrative supervision of this team could be the responsibility of the Income Maintenance supervisor with technical supervision of the Services workers provided by a Services supervisor.

The functions of the team would include the establishment of eligibility and the furnishing of financial assistance to eligible public assistance recipients as well as an identification of the social needs of the applicant/recipient and his family in order to determine activities required to restore these families to a condition of self support of self care. This organizational structure would be consistent with the provisions of Section 401 of the Social Security Act which requires States to provide assistance in such a way as to maintain and strengthen family life and to help parents to attain or retain the capability for maximum self support and personal independence.

APPENDIX G *(continued)*

A.   The caseworker member of the team may perform the following income maintenance activities with an applicant for or a recipient of public assistance in order to meet the goals cited above:

1.   Determination of the needs of the applicant/recipient (A/R) so that referral may be made to appropriate resources of the community and/or agency. For example, the need for a mother to obtain counseling for her child who is having special problems is recognized. The caseworker talks with the family and motivates them to go to an appropriate family agency. If it is determined that the family needs specialized services such as foster care, protective services, homemaker, adoption, appropriate referral shall be made.

2.   Provide counseling and aid for an A/R unable to understand or cope with required contacts with outside community organizations (i.e., SSA, Family Court, Housing Authority, UIB, Workmen's Compensation, NYS Disability).

3.   Determine housing problems that are encountered by the A/R and take the necessary action as deemed appropriate (i.e., threatened eviction, need for relocation, building violations, etc.).

4.   Evaluate the need for the agency to provide an A/R with restricted payments pursuant to Department Regulation 381.3 and 381.4 and ongoing money management services as required by Department regulations. This would indicate counseling and/or referral to prevent an A/R from having recurring problems related to payment for fuel, rent, etc.

5.   Aid and counsel the A/R in locating and arranging protective payments to a protective payee.

6.   Contact with legally and socially responsible relative for the purpose of determining ability and willingness to assist financially or otherwise and to respond to requests from other units of the agency (i.e., foster care, protective services) as specified. This in no way impacts on the IV-D requirements.

7.   Assist clients who have been identified as physically or mentally unable to comply with income maintenance procedures. This might include assistance in securing needed verification necessary for completing the application, making home visits, etc.

8.   In a fuel (non-utility) crisis, search for a new vendor before recommending that payment be made to prevent termination of deliveries or to obtain a delivery from the debted vendor.

9.   Assist in the identification of those clients suffering from alcoholic and/or drug dependency and to refer such individuals for treatment while providing recommendations as to the payment of the grant.

10. Provide A/R's with apparent medical and psychiatric difficulties with aid in obtaining professional guidance and assist them in obtaining verification of their physical condition when an exemption of the work rules are claimed.

The activities listed above may either be charged to Title IV-A or if they are included in the Title XX plan may be charged to Title XX.

B.   *Under Section 64, caseworkers assigned to the team cannot perform initial and continuing eligibility determination for PA, MA, and FS. Nor can they provide social services such as foster care, day care, protective services,*

APPENDIX G *(concluded)*

adoptive services, and homemaker. If the need for these services comes to the attention of the team caseworker they shall be immediately referred to the appropriate Social Services Unit. In reorganization, a critical factor will be the allocation of costs for individual caseworkers. We realize that the caseworkers located in the Income Maintenance Units may be called upon to perform services that relate either to Titles IV-A, XIX, or XX. Allocation of the caseworker's time would have to be made dependent upon time spent by the worker on those services related to each of these titles.

APPENDIX H

Extracts from the Consultant's Report on Social Services in Richards County

Summary of Findings

*   *   *   *   *

3.   There is a lack of definition and structure within the services organization. It was not easy for persons receiving inquiries from the public to determine which service unit or which caseworker was handling any particular case.

*   *   *   *   *

6.   We found little or no supervisory control over either quantity or quality of casework. Supervisors were mostly concerned with crisis situations brought to their attention by persons outside of the County Department and with such internal housekeeping matters as personnel actions, reviewing travel vouchers, and approving formal documents requiring their signature. They typically did not know how many cases were being handled by each caseworker, whether cases were being handled in timely fashion, or whether the services provided were the right ones to fit client needs.

7.   We found the documentation in many case files seriously incomplete. Cases were carried as "open" cases despite the fact that no service had been provided over a period of many weeks.

*   *   *   *   *

9.   So far as we could tell, specific objectives were not being established either in terms of results to be achieved or as to the problem time required to accomplish such results of individual cases. Objectives or goals seemed to be carried mostly in caseworkers' heads or at best indicated in sketchy notes included in the file. Thus there was no way of ascertaining whether reasonable progress was being made on cases, whether they were behind or ahead of schedule. Moreover without the establishment of objectives it was hard for caseworkers to know when, and if, cases should be reported as closed.

*   *   *   *   *

11. We found that caseworkers tended to be arbitrary and haphazard in determining which cases would receive priority attention. Some tended to concentrate on certain kinds of cases—or certain categories of clients—

APPENDIX H *(continued)*

and neglect others; others tended to take easy and most recent cases first and neglect those which were most difficult or which had been open the longest. These all too human tendencies work an injustice upon clients and can only be corrected with regular supervision.

Recommendations

*   *   *   *   *

4. We recommend the development of a Case Management System which will leave a great deal to the professional judgment of the caseworker but will increase management control and accountability. Our aim is to propose a system which will indicate case results, not simply work activity. The three parts of the system are as follows:
   A. The Case Management Plan.   When any case is opened, a form "plan" should be prepared which will state specific case objectives, the services planned to achieve those objectives, and the time schedule by which each critical step should be accomplished. After the plan is formulated either in the intake or reception unit or by the caseworker initially assigned, the plan will be presented to the team leader or unit supervisor. The latter's professional judgment may lead to modifications in diagnosis, service prescriptions and/or time schedule—or, possibly, reassignment to another caseworker.
   B. The Case Status Chart.   This chart is a simple one on which each client is identified, the services to be rendered, and results expected arranged on a time line. These charts should be the basis for a monthly conference between each caseworker and his/her supervisor. This should enable the Team Leader to spot problem areas and work with the caseworker to assure that due progress is being made. It should enable supervisors to evaluate the performance of caseworkers to provide coaching or additional training as needed.
   C. Monthly Case Tally.   This monthly tally to be kept by each of the service units would be a month compilation of pertinent statistics. Basic data to be included would be:
   Applications received (by type of category).
   Applications accepted.
   Applications denied.
   Cases on or ahead of schedule.
   Cases behind schedule.
   Cases closed (by type or category).
   Cases remaining open (by type or category).
   D. Substantitive Case Reviews.   Each month each unit supervisor should select *at random* a limited number of cases being handled by persons in the unit and review these in depth by examining the case file, and by consultation with the caseworker. The purpose of this review would be to check the realism with which the case plan had been prepared, to identify problem areas on which assistance could be provided, and to determine whether changes in policy or procedure should be recommended to higher authority, and to give instruction or coaching as required to caseworkers.

   How many cases should be reviewed each month is problematic, but we are inclined to think that ten such reviews would be a good number.

APPENDIX H *(concluded)*

The fact that the cases would be selected at random could be expected to keep all caseworkers "on their toes" for no one could tell whose case or which one would be taken up for review.

We are inclined also to suggest that both the Director of the entire Social Services operation and the head of the County Department himself (or one of his immediate assistants) should periodically (monthly?) review a random sample of case files.

Case 2–6 ————————————————————————————

Why Did the Salesmen Quit?

Susan M. Szymanski, with the assistance of Frank Yeandel

Juan Campos, the general manager of Commun-Electro Company, leaned back in his swivel chair as he glanced through the morning paper and sipped a cup of coffee. The office was quiet in the early morning hour when there was a sudden knock at his office door.

"Come in," replied Campos, continuing to read his paper.

The door opened abruptly and in walked the five salesmen for the company. Campos glanced up as the men lined up in front of him and each simultaneously laid a piece of paper on his desk. The men ranged in age from 25 to 35 and had been working for the company five years or less. Before becoming salesmen, they worked as service technicians at Commun-Electro and other electronic equipment plants.

One salesman, Jose, started speaking for the group saying, "We have decided to turn in our letters of resignation. The five of us can no longer work in a company where we are deprived of fair treatment and freedom to think for ourselves."

Campos sat gazing at them as Jose continued, "It is difficult for salesmen like ourselves to make the proper kinds of sales if we do not have an expense account that will permit us to travel to our prospective customers and present clients. It is not that the organization has a small expense budget, but that you do not allocate sufficient funds for us to be reimbursed a rightful percentage of our gas mileage, which results in our paying gas expenses out of our own incomes. Although a number of our clients are within a fairly close vicinity to Mexico City, many of our new sales are in more distant places. If we are to be able to bring more sales into the company, we have to travel farther, and at present our expense budget is not nearly enough to cover these costs. In order to pursue a sale and be effective in acquiring it, we must have more freedom in regards to making suggestions and decisions on our own. For example, we think the amount of money allotted in our expense budgets should be greater. Since we are directly familiar with our areas, clients, and potential customers, we have a better understanding of what is needed for obtaining more sales. As you know, our present expense accounts do not cover these costs."

Enrique, one of the other salesmen, continued, "Ing. Campos, you are fully aware of these grievances because we have tried to discuss the situation with you on previous occasions but you do not seem to listen to us. Due to your inexplicable attitude toward us, we have concluded that our next step must be resignation."

"This is not what we really want to happen," added Pedro, "but our base salary and rate of commission that now hold do not provide us with much of an income. You do not realize how difficult it is to receive only $2,000 of your income in base salary and have to earn the remaining $6,000 in commissions to even equal the average yearly income for salesmen. It is not enough that you restrict our expense budget and income needlessly, but you claim credit for some sales that should rightfully be ours. You exclude possible additional commissions from us by treating some sales as 'house' accounts which you claim to have obtained."

"We got together and decided that the only solution would be to resign and work someplace else. Therefore, we are quitting, Ing. Campos. Good-bye!" stated Jose emphatically as he and the other salesmen left the general manager's office.

After the door closed behind them, Campos resumed reading the newspaper without appearing to have been fazed by the incident which just took place. Then he tossed his newspaper on the desk and began contemplating the audacity of the now ex-salesmen and his position in the situation.

Campos himself had been a service technician for Commun-Electro Company about six years ago, but he had already earned his graduate degree in engineering, unlike the five salesmen. In Mexico, this is quite a prestigious accomplishment and a person indicates his degree by using it as a title before his name, abbreviated Ing. Having worked as a service technician under the previous company owner, Mr. Brown, Campos had been promoted to manager when Brown sold the plant in Mexico to an American firm. Since Campos had more experience than the other employees and some of the capabilities needed to fill the managerial position, the new owner moved Campos into the position of running the plant. Committed to promoting from within the organization, the new owner was also concerned with filling the managerial position quickly, as well as having a person who understood the people and was familiar with this particular plant's operations. Campos was born and raised in Mexico City and was familiar with the area and the people. Now 35 years old, Campos had been general manager for the past three years.

Situated in downtown Mexico City, the small plant of Commun-Electro had been in existence for seven years when the entire sales division resigned in the spring of 1978. Conducting the servicing and selling of sophisticated electronic equipment and radio communications systems is a fast-action business because quotas have to be filled and shipping and delivery deadlines met. The sales division is a crucial part of this organization since it is responsible for obtaining new sales to fulfill the quotas. This division's importance needs to be fully understood by top management personnel.

Business in the electronic systems industry had been growing in the mid-1970s and was expected to continue an upward trend for 1978 and 1979. Therefore, sales and production should have been very good, but Commun-Electro's headquarters in New York discovered that their Mexican plant was not producing up to the statistical forecast and aimed at finding the reason why.

Early reports illustrated that the sales division had repeatedly failed to meet sales targets and goals, indicating that the plant's main problem was that it was not providing orders for the assembly and production divisions, and therefore not making a profit.

Mr. Johnson, company president, was planning to send an investigator to the Mexican plant to determine what solutions could be worked out about their profit losses when he received word that the entire sales organization had resigned. The high turnover rate in a sales organization is to be expected, but for an entire division to quit necessitates a logical explanation. He immediately assigned Mr. Whitman to the plant to determine what future actions should be taken to help the plant solve its problems, as well as fill the vacant sales positions.

Whitman was chosen because of his excellent technical background and knowledge of the product assembled in the Mexican plant. Johnson wanted to send a man who had this familiarity with the equipment the company sold so new models could be added to the plant's manufacturing division, but he did not want to send one of the top men of the U.S. division. The goal of the assignment was to help Campos improve the level of the plant and develop a good relationship with his workers, along with expanding the plant's manufacturing capacity to help raise profits and provide more jobs. Johnson realized that sending an American top management officer to suggest changes in the plant would humiliate Campos and cause him to lose his workers' respect. Sending Whitman as a technical consultant and the principal communication link to resources in the United States, Johnson believed Campos would be able to accept suggestions Whitman proposed and instigate them.

After spending several days at the plant, Whitman discovered some of the effects the sales organization had had on other divisions. He found a great deal of tension and frustration growing throughout the other departments caused by the sales division's inability to supply the assembly, shipping, and service departments with enough orders to keep them busy. Many of the orders submitted were given very short shipping dates, which required much overtime work from the production people. In trying to acquire sales accounts the salesmen had promised quick delivery of equipment ordered, and while this agreement resulted in orders, it needlessly pushed the production divisions beyond their work capacity load. This action caused the production divisions to be overwhelmed with work some days and have no work other days. It was evident to Whitman that there were other minor problems mounting that resulted in discontent among the employees and a subnormal communications level between the management and the work force.

Before looking into these minor problems, Whitman knew the immediate sales problem had to be solved by finding men to fill the vacancies in the division. Advertisements were placed in the local newspapers for people who had experience in selling industrial or technical products and who were willing to be trained to sell electronic equipment. Salesmen working for competitors were also contacted and were asked to work for Commun-Electro Company. Whitman realized that the plant needed more responsible salesmen with good judgement who would not promise more than the equipment was capable of producing. From the applicants who responded to the job offers, six new men were hired and trained as salesmen for Commun-Electro Company.

Whitman encouraged Campos to meet with the salesmen to work out the new sales areas each would be responsible for covering. He suggested that Campos instigate the new compensation package which had been modified to include a base salary of $15,000 a year and commissions equal to $9,000 a year. This new package was structured to give the men an opportunity to make more than $9,000 in commissions (which the old compensation package did not provide) if they applied themselves and worked hard to obtain additional sales. The salesmen would also receive larger expense budgets.

"In addition to the new compensation package, I think monthly reports would aid the sales organization in working more efficiently," Whitman told Campos. "Activity reports and sales reports would give a better indication of the salesmen's progress on a weekly basis. Don't you think this would result in improved control in the organization?"

"The reports would be good to adopt," agreed Campos sullenly.

"The reports serve as a good control over the salesmen's expenses and commissions. If the reports were to be posted monthly, the salesmen could see their progress in comparison to the other salesmen. There could be a reward for the salesman who achieves the highest quality sales for each quarter, in recognition of a job well done. This might become an added incentive for the men to compete with one another in acquiring worthwhile sales," said Whitman.

"It sounds as though they will be somewhat helpful." Campos continued sarcastically, "I suppose you would also suggest sales meetings?"

"Yes. Periodic sales meetings would develop a stronger relation between the salesmen and yourself."

"But why does the plant need six salesmen instead of five?"

"The New York branch thought that introducing additional models to be manufactured here would help the plant earn more profits and provide more jobs for Mexicans. It is the company's objective to have this plant operated solely by Mexicans. I am here to see what equipment will sell in this area. Additional models will provide more equipment to sell and will require more competent salesmen to obtain sales that will result in a profit for the company," explained Whitman.

"Oh," replied Campos.

Whitman continued, "Because this plant has such a low level of profits and sales goals in comparison to the current industrial trend and other plants, I have requested men from New York to come to instruct your workers in manufacturing and assembling the new models locally. These men will set up the manufacturing assembly line, establish manufacturing sequences, and test the equipment models. This action will eliminate some of the problems the plant has been suffering from."

"I do not think that there are any problems that have arisen that I am not able to handle myself," remarked Campos.

"Well, what did you have in mind?" asked Whitman.

"I was working on some possibilities when you came down from New York."

"Can you describe some of them to me so I can have a better understanding of what you plan to accomplish?"

"If you would have permitted me to work at solving the problems my own way, you would have seen results," Campos replied evasively.

"All right," said Whitman. "Why don't you see what kind of relations you can establish with the salesmen first? Maybe you could begin by acquainting yourself with efficiency methods and by opening lines of communication between all employee levels. If you delegate some responsibilities to other dependable employees, instead of trying to wield all of the authority yourself, the work load could be distributed. At the same time new ideas, opinions, and views could be voiced which might aid in resolving some problems in the plant."

"How will the problems be resolved by talking to the workers? I do not think it will be worthwhile to talk to them since they are not authorities on the subject."

Campos ignored the advice. He became irritated with what he considered to be lectures from Whitman on how to manage his plant. Even though Campos said he agreed with Whitman when they had met, he never took action.

Whitman offered to have Campos sent to several branch offices in the United States to become acquainted with various operation methods used successfully. Another option Whitman proposed was to have a management consultant firm visit the plant and submit recommendations, viewing the monetary investment as worthwhile if the firm's plans could be introduced into the Mexican plant's operations.

Whitman's objective was to give Campos a deeper understanding of some possibilities for reforming the plant's operations into an efficient and effective profit-making company branch. At this point, Campos displayed his resentment of what he considered the "gringo's" interference and disagreed with Whitman's suggestions of Americanized techniques and methods. Wanting to instigate his own ideas, which were still not in detailed form, Campos felt he could do a better job if Whitman left Mexico City.

Knowing that every possible means of achieving modification had to be exerted, Whitman felt he had to keep trying. He wanted to help Campos become a competent and successful general manager, but he realized

Campos's dislike of Americans and decided not to go to Campos anymore but to the workers themselves. The employees did not see Whitman as an authoritative figure working along with them, but as a technician who was instigating new techniques. He introduced the salesmen to the new equipment and tried to encourage them when they did a good job.

Campos sat back and watched Whitman develop a rapport with the plant employees as the new manufacturing and assembly systems were being constructed. Whitman strived to get the plant operating at a normal rate, knowing that the New York headquarters would support his actions. He had attempted to work with Campos, but it was an extremely difficult task.

When contemplating solutions to the management problem, several questions ran through Whitman's mind. Is Campos the right man for the job? Does Campos comprehend his managerial duties? Should the company look for a replacement? Should an American be brought in to assist Campos for an interim period? Is there enough U.S. control over the plant? Is Campos the problem or is it some other factor? Will it be good for the plant if a new manager is brought in or will it be better to keep Campos since he is acquainted with the plant?

Reflecting upon these questions, Whitman realized that he was supposed to call Mr. Johnson at the end of the week. Johnson was expecting the latest update on the situation in Mexico City. The new manufacturing and assembly techniques were progressing at a steady rate, which Whitman knew would please Johnson. Whitman was becoming more anxious about the answer he would give in reference to Campos and his managerial competence in the plant. Between that day and Friday Whitman would have to concentrate on finding answers to his list of questions.

Case 2–7 ——————————————————————————————

Is Anyone Irreplaceable?

Donald J. Petersen

BACKGROUND

Marilyn Owens has been employed by Enertrol Manufacturing Company for 32 years. Thirty of those years have been spent in the company's claims department as a secretary. Marilyn is one of two secretaries who work for the claims investigators. Because of her length of service, Marilyn is senior over the other secretary, but does not have any substantial formal authority. Marilyn is known as a perfectionist. Mr. Mills, the claims agent and department head, often relies on Marilyn to carry out the department's secretarial duties with expertise because Marilyn's quality of work output and her loyalty to the department are outstanding.

Janice Martin, a recent graduate of Adams Business College, was hired two months ago as the number two secretary for the claims department.

From her transcripts it could be seen that Janice excelled in shorthand, typing, business English, and had many other necessary secretarial traits. In her short time with the claims department Janice had shown her ability to communicate well with the public and had a friendly and cooperative attitude with the investigators in the office. Mills feels that she added to the professional and efficient atmosphere of the department.

In the past two years, there have been seven girls in the number two secretarial position. Most have had "personality conflicts" with Marilyn and departed within a short time.

INCIDENT

During the early stages of Janice's employment it seemed that she and Marilyn worked well together. Mills felt that the two women were a great asset to the department. One afternoon, however, Mills found Janice with tears streaming down her face. He asked her to step into his office. Through the conversation that followed, he learned that the secretaries were not as compatible as he had thought. It seems that Marilyn found some minute flaw with *all* of Janice's work and condescendingly pointed them out. Janice said she was losing her self-confidence and was finding it harder and harder to work under such pressure. Mills assured Janice that she had been doing a fine job and that he would speak with Marilyn.

Mills called Marilyn into his office. He related the incident that had just occurred with Janice and asked for Marilyn's views. She quickly became defensive and said, "I'm always the heavy around here." She went on to state that all the young girls hired as number two secretary "seem like they know it all when actually they know very little." She exclaimed, "It takes years of experience, not school courses, to become proficient in the secretarial field."

Mills told Marilyn he would have to think the matter over, but while doing so, she should display patience with Janice.

DECISION

Mills reflected over the past events. This was not the first time that Marilyn had unjustly turned against the girl in the number two secretarial spot. He felt that Marilyn was insecure about young competition; but he was torn in his decision—he needed Marilyn to run the clerical end of his department. She had always done an excellent job in the past and she continued to do so now. But he was also tired of the turnover that kept occurring in the number two spot. Is Marilyn irreplaceable?

Case 2–8

The Excellent Worker

James R. Bradshaw

Marie had returned to work after approximately 15 years of staying at home raising her four children to school age. She was very excited about doing a good job and believed she would enjoy the opportunity of working a few hours each day while the children were at school. She was known as very outgoing and very capable, and was well-liked and attractive. She is Oriental; and although English is Marie's second language, she speaks and understands it very well.

Helen had been working for another company and started working here shortly after Marie. She was approximately the same age as Marie. They had known each other casually the past several years and got along well whenever they met. Helen had indicated that she needed this job very much so that she and her husband could qualify for a home loan. Helen is quiet and reserved. Helen is Polynesian, but also speaks English as her second language. She preferred to let Marie do the talking whenever the need arose for information at work.

Mr. Williams was close to retirement. The impression most people have of him is that he is very good to work for. He was born and raised in the local area. One of his responsibilities is to oversee the company lunchroom where Marie and Helen were working. They were the only workers in the lunchroom, which feeds approximately 50 to 60 people each meal. The food is prepared elsewhere and brought directly to the lunchroom for heating and serving.

Mr. Phillips was in his late 50s or early 60s. He formerly worked as a construction foreman/supervisor. He is the vice president in his present company, a service organization. The president is a long-time close friend of Phillips, who had spent several years in the South Pacific area in construction work.

Marie had been asked to work for a couple of weeks as a temporary employee while one of the regular lunchroom workers was on sick leave. She found the work very interesting because of the people she saw each day—and they responded by saying that she brought a "ray of light" and enjoyment to the lunchroom. Comments came directly and indirectly to Marie about how the food seemed to taste better and how much more enjoyable it was to eat in the lunchroom when she was there.

Marie worked out a number of ways in which the lunchroom service and the food could be improved while reducing the total cost. Her suggestions were accepted and some were put into effect immediately. Her two weeks of substituting were very interesting for her. She showed great concern for her job by staying overtime nearly every day to put the area in shape by cleaning, debugging, and improving the general facilities. She brought vases of fresh flowers each day, and some of her own utensils from home to help improve the service. When her two weeks were up, the majority of the regular workers made it a point to express disappointment that she would not be working regularly.

After about one week away from her job, Phillips called Marie to see if she would work full time or at least part time on a permanent basis. She accepted the permanent part-time position eagerly. When Marie returned to work, she found that Helen had started a few days earlier, replacing one of the full-time workers who had quit. Marie began working, this time without formal orientation but merely with the comment, "We will fill you in later about your salary, and so on." She was not concerned because her main interest was working in an enjoyable atmosphere for a few hours every day.

Helen and Marie hit it off very well. Helen encouraged Marie to ask questions of Williams or Phillips whenever necessary, especially if it were to request materials or supplies that were needed. Helen was a good friend of the person she had replaced. She consistently wanted to do things in the same way as before, such as planning the menu, ordering supplies, and so on. Marie occasionally remarked that the former worker was no longer there and that she and Helen would be held responsible for whatever happened from now on. Also, since the comments had been very favorable about the changes Marie had instituted in the food and service, she felt that this was an indication that they should follow the new way of doing things. Helen seemed to agree, but periodically would revert to the old methods when Marie was not in the immediate area or had left for the day.

After about one week, Williams, in a joking sort of way, mentioned that "for the record" someone had to be listed as being in charge to fill out the time sheets, and so on. Helen and Marie looked at each other. Marie suggested that since Helen was full time she should be designated as "in charge." Helen did not object. Williams agreed by saying, "Okay, Helen is in charge, but Marie is chief cook." They all laughed and no one said any more.

Many times in the past, too much food had been ordered. The leftovers then had to be reheated to be served the next day, or even thrown away. Marie suggested that they work on this problem together, and Helen agreed. After one or two times, however, Helen somehow turned in the menu and the food was ordered before Marie arrived. This again resulted in the old problem of too much food and the serving of old or reheated food. Helen also served the old food first and put each day's fresh food in the refrigerator. Marie thought that she had finally convinced Helen that it didn't make sense to put fresh food in the freezer and serve old food— but Helen responded, "We always did it that way." Marie was concerned. She could sense immediately whether the workers who ate there each day felt the food was good or not. She finally decided to talk with Phillips about the ordering and serving. His initial reaction fit his reputation of being abrupt and somewhat brisk, as he stated, "I have worked for people younger than me and even though I didn't like it I had to do what they said." Marie asked if they weren't supposed to be working together on such things in a place with only two workers. Phillips said that he didn't see any reason why not. He also mentioned that he had heard many favorable comments and that it seemed the atmosphere and food had never been better.

Marie left his office feeling unsure of Phillips's feelings, but she believed that he was pleased with the work and that she and Helen should decide things together. Williams was also very complimentary about the work and the food, and said that Marie had brought a "ray of light" into the place.

Although there were minor differences of opinion, Marie and Helen always seemed to talk their problems through; and they nearly always drove to and from work together.

When Marie and Helen worked on the menu together, less food was ordered, less was wasted or thrown away, there was a greater variety of food, and a very pleasant atmosphere existed in the lunchroom. Marie was feeling more and more comfortable with her situation all the time.

About a week later, Helen once again ordered the food before Marie arrived. As before, this resulted in many leftovers; and there were the usual comments from the customers that the food was not as tasty as before. Marie decided to find out from Phillips exactly what the procedure for ordering the food was to be, but found him as brisk and unhelpful as the first time. Marie asked if they were satisfied with her performance. She explained how she liked seeing the people enjoy their lunch. Phillips and Williams both told her that had she wanted to work full time she would have been in full charge. They recognized her as the real organizer in the lunchroom and felt that much of the success experienced was due to her efforts. She was asked for her ideas about several things, including preparing some food items directly in the lunchroom. Marie agreed to prepare some of the items and was told that she had permission to buy and to store immediately in the freezer $200 worth of frozen food. When Marie arrived the next day, she found that Helen had already ordered the food at the request of Phillips. Marie expressed surprise and displeasure. Helen assured her that this order was an exception and that from then on they would always do it together. Marie forgot the incident and the remainder of the day (Friday) went very well.

Saturday, as Marie was leaving, Williams called her to his office. He was visibly shaken. He had great difficulty in telling her that because she had not been able to work harmoniously with Helen, Phillips had said he did not want "that woman" here any more. Williams said that Helen had gone to Phillips's office Friday evening in tears because Marie had been angry with her that morning over the ordering of the food.

Williams said that there was nothing he could do—once Phillips had made his mind up, no one could change it. Marie was shocked; and after thinking about it the rest of the day, went with her husband to Phillips's home. He was as brisk as before, insisting there was nothing more to say since she had been warned and had not changed her behavior in working with Helen. Phillips said that he needed harmony in the lunchroom and since Marie hadn't been willing to work with Helen, that was it.

Marie was completely dumbfounded. She had been told one day that she was an "excellent worker," and then fired the next.

Case 2–9 ——

How Time Gets Away!

W. D. Heier

Just after the planning conference broke up, George Cox summed up the general feelings of his peers by stating: "Hell, even a 'day-stretcher' wouldn't give us enough time to do our jobs around here!" When several of his colleagues fervently agreed, it made George reflect a little upon what he had said.

Later that evening at home, while talking to a friend from another company, George casually introduced the problem of time management in his job. When his friend, Pete, suggested George run through a typical day in his office, George started by saying that, as a section head, he was responsible for the activities of 25 people. As he described it: "That may be considered a lot of people to supervise but I have an assistant to help me. The lack of help isn't really the problem—it's finding the time to do anything even half-way.

"For example, I am expected in the office about 8:30 A.M., but I'm usually at the desk by 8:00 A.M. This used to be a half-hour's peace and quiet to get things arranged for the day, but not any more. It seems that the minute I walk in these days someone is waiting to hand me the first crisis-of-the-day. And, honestly, we have one 'brush fire' after another all day long! They've been coming so fast lately that I have had to resort to an odd kind of priorities system. First, we decide which ones are most urgent and place those in some order of precedence. Then, within that list, we decide which ones we have to do a thorough job on, those we can just give a reasonable amount of time, and those we can only give a 'lick-and-a-promise.' We know that we are probably going to see this latter bunch again, and at a much increased urgency level, but when we are really pressed for time and people to do the work, as a manager, I have to set priorities on resources like these. It is a shame, though, because many of the things that we suspect we'll be seeing again could be done right the first time around, if we could just give them the attention they deserve."

In answer to a question from Pete, George continued by saying: "No, the job of the section hasn't really changed that much. We're still doing about the same things we were before. It's just the fact that there seems to be a lot more urgent problems coming up now than ever before. We are getting increased demands for more sophisticated planning from up the line and that could create a big problem, if we had time to comply—which we don't! So far, this increased planning demand has taken the form of several conferences, which also used up valuable time we could have spent on solving our problems. Take the conference we had this afternoon. The division manager called a meeting to discuss the long-range planning goals of the division. Heck, we haven't even done any short-range planning in the last two years, let alone sit around dreaming about what our problems are going to be 10 or 20 years from now. Don't misunderstand me. I know the division needs to do some long-range planning, but they shouldn't expect the sections to drop everything and sit around thinking about what we should be doing, or will be doing, in 1990! I said almost exactly that in the meeting this afternoon but got no satisfaction from the division manager. He's one of those guys who thinks everyone should take time to plan whether a person has the time or not."

Pete interrupted the conversation to ask George whether he had some regular plan for operating during the day. George responded by saying that he used to have an informal staff meeting about 9:00 A.M. every morning and a regularly scheduled meeting each Thursday afternoon. The staff meetings were really coordination sessions used to check the progress being made on projects and current problem areas. The formal Thursday meetings were to review ongoing problems. George said he had been forced to discontinue the morning staff meetings "for lack of a quorum," and the Thursday meetings were abandoned after a series of unexpected, but necessary, cancellations. George stated that he, personally, did all of the coordinating now, since some one person needed to know everything that was going on during hectic times, such as the current ones.

George finished the review of his day, stating that: "By lunchtime, I feel like I've already been working 12 hours. The pressure never seems to stop! Lately, I've been eating a sandwich and a glass of milk at my desk. At least it's quiet during the lunch hour. I don't even answer the telephone when it rings. However, it looks like I'm going to have to start locking the door, since some of the boys in the office have started dropping by to ask questions. I can't really blame them for wanting an uninterrupted few minutes with their boss, but it doesn't do much good. Up to now, by the time everybody else got back from lunch, I found I had done quite a few things.

"The division manager saw me eating at my desk last week and told me I ought to get out of the office for a while during the lunch hour. He advised me to take a walk around town. He didn't tell me who would do the work I do between noon and 1:00 P.M. if I left the office to take a walk.

"The afternoons really haven't been as productive as I would like them to be. Of course, most of us are tired after a hard morning's work and then, too, lately we seem to spend a lot of time in the afternoon redoing some of the things we did in the morning. I've wondered if it was my fault that some sloppy staff work kept popping up, but I'm pretty well convinced that it is just the pressure and a lot of problems that we can't seem to solve once and for all that cause our predicament.

"There is one thing that would help us. Neither I nor any of my people go to meetings we can get out of right now. Therefore, we occasionally miss something at a meeting that we should have known that might have saved us a lot of work. But, we just can't afford the time to go to meetings the way things are now in the office!

"There is one other problem that our current pace has caused. I used to have time to talk to the people in the office about new things that were taking place but not anymore. Accordingly, when some new program or procedure comes down from higher authority, I just have to distribute it without any amplification of meaning for my people. Ordinarily, that wouldn't be too bad, but lately we have experienced a number of small incidents concerning new regulations where my interpretations and those of some of my people didn't quite coincide. We have learned to live with that situation, but it is not really the way things should be done and it has caused us a few minor problems."

Case 2–10 ————————————————————————————————

Perfect Pizzeria*

Lee Neely

Perfect Pizzeria in Southville, in deep southern Illinois, is the second largest franchise of the chain in the United States. The headquarters is located in Phoenix, Arizona. Although the business is prospering, it has employee and managerial problems.

Each operation has one manager, an assistant manager, and from two to five night managers. The managers of each pizzeria work under an area supervisor. There are no systematic criteria for being a manager or becoming a manager trainee. The franchise has no formalized training period for the manager. No college education is required. The managers for whom the case observer worked during a four-year period were relatively young (ages 24 to 27) and only one had completed college. They came from the ranks of night managers or assistant managers, or both. The night managers were chosen for their ability to perform the duties of the regular employees. The assistant managers worked a two-hour shift during the luncheon period five days a week to gain knowledge about bookkeeping and management. Those becoming managers remained at that level unless they expressed interest in investing in the business.

The employees were mostly college students, with a few high school students performing the less challenging jobs. Since Perfect Pizzeria was located in an area with few job opportunities, it had a relatively easy task of filling its employee quotas. All the employees, with the exception of the manager, were employed part time. Consequently, they worked for less than the minimum wage.

The Perfect Pizzeria system is devised so that food and beverage costs and profits are set up according to a percentage. If the percentage of food unsold or damaged in any way is very low, the manager gets a bonus. If the percentage is high, the manager does not receive a bonus; rather, he or she receives only his or her normal salary.

---

* Adapted from a course assignment prepared by Lee Neely for Professor J. G. Hunt, Southern Illinois University—Carbondale.

There are many ways in which the percentage can fluctuate. Since the manager cannot be in the store 24 hours a day, some employees make up for their paychecks by helping themselves to the food. When a friend comes in to order a pizza, extra ingredients are put on the friend's pizza. Occasional nibbles by 18 to 20 employees throughout the day at the meal table also raise the percentage figure. An occasional bucket of sauce may be spilled or a pizza accidentally burned. Sometimes the wrong size of pizza may be made.

In the event of an employee mistake or a burned pizza by the oven man, the expense is supposed to come from the individual. Because of peer pressure, the night manager seldom writes up a bill for the erring employee. Instead, the establishment takes the loss and the error goes unnoticed until the end of the month when the inventory is taken. That's when the manager finds out that the percentage is high and that there will be no bonus.

In the present instance, the manager took retaliatory measures. Previously, each employee was entitled to a free pizza, salad, and all the soft drinks he or she could drink for every 6 hours of work. The manager raised this figure from 6 to 12 hours of work. However, the employees had received these 6-hour benefits for a long time. Therefore, they simply took advantage of the situation whenever the manager or the assistant was not in the building. Though the night manager theoretically had complete control of the operation in the evenings, he did not command the respect that the manager or assistant manager did. That was because he received the same pay as the regular employees; he could not reprimand other employees; and he was basically the same age or sometimes even younger than the other employees.

Thus, apathy grew within the pizzeria. There seemed to be a further separation between the manager and his workers, who started out to be a closely knit group. The manager made no attempt to alleviate the problem, because he felt it would iron itself out. Either the employees that were dissatisfied would quit or they would be content to put up with the new regulations. As it turned out, there was a rash of employee dismissals. The manager had no problem in filling the vacancies with new workers, but the loss of key personnel was costly to the business.

With the large turnover, the manager found he had to spend more time in the building, supervising and sometimes taking the place of inexperienced workers. This was in direct violation of the franchise regulation, which stated that a manager would act as a supervisor and at no time take part in the actual food preparation. Employees were not placed under strict supervision with the manager working alongside them. The operation no longer worked smoothly because of differences between the remaining experienced workers and the manager concerning the way in which a particular function should be performed.

Within a two-month period, the manager was again free to go back to his office and leave his subordinates in charge of the entire operation. During this two-month period, the percentage had returned to the previous low level and the manager received a bonus each month. The manager felt that his problems had been resolved and that conditions would remain the same, since the new personnel had been properly trained.

It didn't take long for the new employees to become influenced by the other employees. Immediately after the manager had returned to his supervisory role, the percentage began to rise. This time the manager took a bolder step. He cut out any benefits that the employees had—no free pizzas, salads, or drinks. With the job market at an even lower ebb than usual, most employees were forced to stay. The appointment of a new area supervisor made it impossible for the manager to "work behind the counter," since the supervisor was centrally located in Southville.

The manager tried still another approach to alleviate the rising percentage problem and maintain his bonus. He placed a notice on the bulletin board, stating that if the percentage remained at a high level, a lie detector test would be given to all employees. All those found guilty of taking or purposefully wasting food or drinks would be immediately terminated. This did not have the desired effect on the employees, because they knew if they were all subjected to the test, all would be found guilty and the manager would have to dismiss all of them. This would leave him in a worse situation than ever.

Even before the following month's percentage was calculated, the manager knew it would be high. He had evidently received information from one of the night managers about the employees' feelings toward the notice. What he did not expect was that the percentage would reach an all-time high. That is the state of affairs at the present time.

Case 2–11 ————————————————————————————————
Earl Walker

Charles R. Klasson

On the evening of June 18, Earl Walker had dinner with a former business college professor who was in town on an industrial research assignment. Walker had graduated from college just six months earlier.

After dinner, Walker began to discuss his current job situation and various work experiences on this, his first major job in industry. With the professor asking an occasional question, Walker proceeded to tell the following story:

> **Earl Walker:** I've learned a lot in a very short time with this company. As you probably remember, I was very anxious to find a company in which I could build a career, and I believe I have found it. But I must admit some doubt did exist in my mind about my future in this company after the first day on the job. It did not look too bright.
>
> **Professor:** Well, let's start at the beginning. What was your first assignment?

Walker: I was hired into the company as a graduate trainee. The program lasts for two years, after which you can be assigned to any company location and position according to your abilities and interests and company needs. Training normally begins in the production department. Each trainee, and currently there are 11 in the plant, is rotated from job to job in order to learn as much as possible about all phases of plant operations.

I began there on February 1 as an engineering change coordinator in the production control department. Production control consists of three sections—material controls, material handlings, and scheduling. Getting started on my first assignment was a little embarrassing.

Professor: Why was it embarrassing?

Walker: After I had completed all the formal paper work involved in getting placed on the payroll, Mr. Snow, head of production control, took me to the office of Roger Edwards, supervisor of material controls. After a terse introduction and some small talk between Snow and Edwards, Snow said, "Mr. Edwards, we've decided to start Walker on the coordinator's job. See to it he gets started." A moment later, Snow left and there we were. Edwards did not know that I was coming into the department, nor did I know that this was to be my first assignment. Since Edwards was obviously startled at my presence, I quickly explained who I was and provided him with a little information about my background, after which he said, "Thanks for letting me know," in a somewhat perturbed voice.

Professor: Did your remarks ease the situation any?

Walker: No, not much; for Edwards immediately took me into the next office and introduced me to an hourly worker. He said, "Bill, I want you to meet your new boss—his name is Walker." After a few brief remarks, Edwards walked off much like Snow, saying, "Earl, you'll do a good job," as he left the office.

There I was not knowing anyone. It was a little embarrassing to everyone, so being nonchallant about it, I introduced myself, and then two other hourly workers came over and greeted me. It was a little awkward for the first few moments, but we all tried to make the best of the situation. For some reason, these three hourly workers were skeptical of me as though I was sent there for some ulterior reason. I assured them that I was merely a recent college graduate and that I was there to learn all I could about the engineering coordinator's job. I openly requested all their help and assistance.

The first few days on this job were difficult. I received no cooperation from these hourly workers in that they were all noncommittal about everything. I would ask direct questions and receive vague answers. I recall one incident that seemed to turn the tide. While trying to make a good impression, one morning I wore my Sunday-best suit to work and hung the jacket on a clothes rack. Just before lunch, I walked into the office and noticed an employee looking at the label in my jacket. Not noticing me, he returned to his desk as I returned to mine. I didn't say anything about it. This worker tried to look busy as he watched to see what everyone else was doing. Finally, he said, "I know exactly where you got that suit." I looked up and replied, "How do you know?" After some discussion, I got him to admit that he actually looked at the label.

With this admission, I told him we were going to get something straight and right now. By that time the other two workers had walked over to my desk and I said, "Let's everybody sit down and get something settled now. I realize that together you three men have over 45 years' service with the company, and I have less than 45 hours. I am here to learn as best I can. If you want to know something about me, you don't have to look at my jacket or ask anyone else. Ask me and I will tell you very frankly and sincerely. Now, what are your questions?"

Professor: What happened next?

Walker: I was surprised. We all talked and I answered rather direct questions for about 40 minutes. I was very fair with them and I explained everything that I could. After the question and answer session was over, I asked if everyone was satisfied. In a dead silence they looked at each other. I then said, "Now if everyone is satisfied, let me know what you want in your coffee, and I will go out and get it." So, after I came back with the coffee, I caught them in a huddle. They looked up and one fellow said, "We got this engineering change that we have to take care of here. Tomorrow morning I will show you what we are doing." I felt this was the turning point. For the rest of the week I continued to volunteer information upon request and made one last point. "Gentlemen," I said, "I don't talk in a loud voice and I would like to be treated the way I am going to be treating you fellows—with a little dignity, respect, kindness, and cooperation." They replied, "Okay, Earl." That was the first time they had called me by my first name.

Each week thereafter, the group fed me a little more information, not only about the job but about political relationships with the material control section and about the department. Innumerable times these three men tipped me off to planned pranks of other hourly workers in the section. I was told what to say and how to solve seemingly insoluble problems. Because of their help, I managed to learn and finally supervise this engineering change coordinator's job with no trouble.

Professor: You finally got off to a good start?

Walker: Yes, but it took every piece of tactful knowledge that I had at my disposal, including kindness and sternness. I let them know I was not about to be stepped on. But if it wasn't for those initial encounters with the three hourly engineer change personnel who finally accepted me, I don't know where I'd be right now. I do know this. Two of these men, I learned later, were considered troublemakers. Only 25 percent of engineering changes ever got distributed to the proper agencies on time. No joke. It was awful. There was literally no coordinating done. Since I have been on the job, these men have worked harder and are doing much more. Don't get me wrong. These men frequently bucked at my proposals and resisted change.

Let me mention one more interesting event. The people who write ECPs for me have needed a metal filing cabinet for a long time. They told me to forget about ordering one for the order would be cancelled. I talked to Edwards about it and he said to see Snow. I managed to get three old wooden bookcases that I exchanged with another section for a metal case. One morning I told the men our new cabinet should arrive at around 10:00 A.M. They all laughed and said it would never come. At exactly 10:00 A.M., in rolled the file cabinet as I had pre-planned. There was not a sound as the three men looked at each other. Finally, one asked if it would be possible to get some new binders. I opened the drawer and there were three dozen binders I had managed to squeeze out of the budget.

Professor: Looks like this job turned out fine.

Walker: This section is now drawing praise and the so-called trouble-makers in my estimation are good workers. I don't know what caused it all, but I have learned what is involved in the engineering change coordinator's job.

Professor.   How long did you work as an engineering change coordinator?

Walker: I'm still on that job, but in addition to it, at the end of March I was made a stock checker coordinator, also. This position is under the material handling section and managed by Mr. Tom Thompson. My immediate boss on the stock checker coordinator's job is Mr. Mead.

Professor: Who do you report to now?

Walker: Three people. Of course, Mr. Edwards still supervises me as an engineering change coordinator. My immediate boss is Mr. Mead. This is a ridiculous statement to make, but Mead never supervises me; however, Thompson sure does a good job of keeping me busy even though I turn all my work in to Mead. It is an unfortunate situation because Mr. Thompson gives me direct orders to do certain jobs and it consequently creates a delicate situation both up and down the line. It's fortunate that the engineering change section is now running well, for I'm spending almost all my time working for Thompson on this checker job.

Professor: What does this stock checker job entail?

Walker: I'm not exactly sure at this point. I was put on this job with no prior training or instructions. Cold. As a matter of fact this is apparently a part of the company's training program—to make you swim all by yourself on new assignments. At least this is what has happened to me on my first two assignments. While no workers report to me, I literally give orders to 12 stock checkers. These people simply count stock items received and in inventory and turn in daily stock reports. Each of three foremen (who report to Mead) have four stock checkers under their command. As a stock checker coordinator my job is to take care of unique checker problems, handle excessive or limited stock conditions, review objectives, and, of all things, give performance reviews. For this particular type work (performance reviews) the company should have a much more experienced man. You don't have somebody on the job two months giving performance reviews to fellows who have been with the company 30 years. This practice does not go over too well.

Professor: How did this job work out?

Walker: It hasn't. When a young outsider working for a general foreman gives direct orders to hourly workers who report to a foreman, you have a confusing and untenable situation. Friction—boy have I generated it! Let me give you an example of good old Tom Thompson's handy work.

One morning, after having received orders from Thompson to improve the filing procedures used by the stock checkers, I walked up to one group of four checkers who were working around one desk and said, "Good morning, gentlemen. I would like to get your opinions and ideas on rearranging your present filing system. If I'm not mistaken, by rearranging your stock cards according to card number and numerical sequence, you could improve access and counting time." Practically in unison the reply was, "Why?" After I indicated specific advantages to be gained from my suggestion, one fellow said, "Look—we have been doing it this way since time began. Why should we change now?" After further discussion, the checkers told me thanks but they were going to continue to use their old system.

Finally, I simply told the checkers we were going to do it my way, like it or not. "Well, who says?" commented one of the men. "Did our foreman tell you to change our filing system?" I replied, "I don't like to say these things, but I was told to revise the system by Mr. Thompson, our superintendent." They looked at me and said, "Who is our boss? Why are you coming down here to tell us these things?" "Because," I said, "Mr. Thompson told me to come down here. To be frank with you fellows we are going to make the change." The spokesman for the group replied, "I don't know whether we are going to do it or not. You don't know what's going on around here after one week on the job. We are making our counts—what's the complaint?"

I replied, "Let me make my position clear. I am told to do something, I do it. You are told to do something, you do it. Most of your orders come from your foreman. He is your direct boss. However, when my superior tells me to do something, I am going to do it. And when that superior of mine is superior to your foreman, *we* do it. If you don't want to do this job, you let me know right now." Nobody said a word. I commented further, "If you have any criticisms or any constructive suggestions to make, I suggest you make them through your foreman, to your general foreman, to the superintendent." After these comments, they just refused to talk to me.

Finally, one of the three foremen who supervises the stock checkers told me to stay out of his area. I requested that he complain up the chain of command, and he told me to tell Thompson myself. This I did a number of times with no satisfaction. After I mentioned my problem to Thompson and suggested that he work through the general foreman and foreman, he told me, "I don't want any advice from you, Earl, just do as I say." I told the foreman this story and asked him to stop yelling at me. Well, a couple days after this discusion, Mr. Edwards, the materials control supervisor, came over to me and suggested I lay off the pressure a little bit. He commented, "I know you're aggressive, boy—when they give you a job to do, you don't wait for anything, you just go get it done. But you can't move these checkers the way you're trying." I told Edwards, "What am I going to do? This man Thompson is over both of us. I don't know which way to turn. He is ruining my progress efficiency report as a graduate trainee. If I don't produce for him I can just see my efficiency report that goes to home office. When Thompson says now he means *now*, no if's or but's about the matter." As Mr. Edwards left, he said, "Good luck—a whole lot of it."

Professor: The checkers are not in Edwards' department?

Walker: No. Apparently, someone told Edwards to get me to lay off. I had to tell Edwards that I was acting under orders.

Professor: What did your general foreman, Mead, do while all this was going on?

Walker: Not much. After the fight he had with Thompson, they make it a practice to avoid each other. Mr. Thompson has been involved in a number of fights.

Professor: Tell me about Thompson.

Walker: He is a Harvard M.B.A., I am told. Prior to coming here with the company some nine years ago, he worked as a vice president of accounting for a small manufacturing firm. He actually got his job in this company through professional association with our controller, Mr. Jordan. After one year in our accounting department he was transferred to production control. He was made a superintendent within the production control department, but insofar as the company is concerned, he is a supervisor of equal rank with the other two section supervisors. Mr. Snow made this distinction in rank.

In terms of ability the man has it. His mind is methodical and precise. Regardless of the complexity of a problem, Thompson can work his way through it with little difficulty. Beyond analytical ability he has in my opinion a serious Achilles' heel—he just doesn't know how to handle people. Perhaps I'm generalizing, based upon all the difficult and irritating situations this man has put me into during these past few months.

Professor: How is Thompson received by other people in the organization?

Walker: Everyone dislikes him. I have never seen or experienced such intense negative feelings towards one man. He is disliked by everyone —even the operating committee, which consists of top plant management. His loud voice, rough language, and constant yelling don't help matters much. On one occasion, I told Thompson it would be appreciated if he would refrain from getting so excited. He simply said, "I am handling over 200 men. I can't afford to spend most of my time on one lousy coordinator's job. I've more important things to do." After this incident, I avoided the man purposely. I just tried to stay out of his way as others have learned to do rather effectively. My predecessor on the stock checker job finally requested to be moved due to Thompson's constant riding and harassing.

Professor: How did you finally make out on the stock checker job?

Walker: On one assignment I believe some progress was made in the right direction. A stock checker by the name of Graves was apparently in some serious trouble, for he was a labor relations case. I was instructed to observe this man in order to get some additional evidence to be used in his case. He was a fighter with a gruff voice and tough-looking face. After watching the man for a few days, the whole thing got sort of ridiculous so I talked with the general foreman about my assignment. I was told to do the best I could. So, rather than spy, I introduced myself to Mr. Graves and asked if there was anything I could do to help. "Nah," he replied while inquiring if I was another one of those guys coming down from upstairs. I said, "Another one of those guys, perhaps, but here to help you and in hopes you will help me to learn the job." Graves commented nobody had ever asked him to teach them anything. Graves finally agreed to help and we worked together all day. During that day I learned plenty about Graves, the job, and the problem that brought me to the section. That night Thompson asked me what Graves did all day. I said, "The man worked hard, as I was with him all day." "You were with him," shouted Thompson. "Yes," I said, "there's no better way to find out about a man's work than to work with him." Thompson felt Graves probably worked harder because of my presence and said so. It became evident that a large part of Graves's problem was rough treatment. Nobody trusted him. Due to personal problems, he started to drink. This in turn hurt his work—bad counts, poor work performance. When he finally straightened out, management had a poor opinion of him and really didn't give him an opportunity to earn back his self-respect.

Sensing that Graves might not maintain satisfactory performance due to increasing job pressure, I decided to have a talk with him. "Mr. Graves," I said, "You can take this for what it's worth. It is going to be a very frank, sincere, and honest statement. If you can make your weekly counts accurately, I can take a lot of pressure off your back. I don't know exactly what's going on around here. But I could back you up against any future false accusations. In other words, I'm hearing stories from both sides of the fence. From you and your co-workers and management, I'm hearing conflicting statements. Having talked and worked with you these past few days, I think you're a regular fellow and capable of not only making your count but exceeding it. Please give it a good try, Mr. Graves."

The first week following the discussion, Graves doubled his count but was still short of the job standard by five counts. I was pleased as punch. As usual, I reported Graves's performance to Thompson, who simply said, "I'll be damned. That Graves still is not producing." When I tried to defend Graves and his significant improvement in counting his stock, Thompson said, "I don't want excuses from you, Walker; that's all I get from you—conversation and no action." I said, "Yes, sir." I walked away and didn't bother to go down to see or say anything to Graves.

The next week I introduced myself to the entire checker section and worked briefly with everyone. At the end of this week, Graves exceeded his count by five. Needless to say, I was elated and happy. Thompson looked at my weekly report and said, "Well, it's not bad, but he ought to up his count." When I again tried to defend the tremendous effort of Graves, Thompson tried to convince me that this man was dragging his feet and snowing me with his performance. Ignoring Thompson's typical poor comments, I went down to see Graves and said, "Mr. Graves, I would like to buy you a coffee." After declining my offer, he said, "What do you want?" I slapped him on the back and shook his hand, saying, "Thanks for a very fine week." Graves attributed his good week and the fact that everything went well to luck.

Professor: How did Graves perform thereafter?

Walker: Just fine. He has been one of the top stock checkers ever since the week he broke his required count. Everyone was aware of his superior performance, including Thompson. In a matter-of-fact way, Thompson asked me what I had said to Graves in view of his improved performance. This was a golden opportunity to make a point. "Mr. Thompson," I replied, "I think I treated Graves as a man. I talked to him as an ordinary fellow and treated him the way I wanted to be treated. Graves still barks; he looks like he's going to chop off my head but underneath this rough appearance is a fine man. He had troubles which I recognized and together we worked them out. I think that's all it took. I'm not really sure what happened, but whatever it was it's working. This human relations business, being tactful and all, seems to have a place here. I'm not a psychologist and don't know the inner workings of people. I've tried to learn and understand the problems and working relationships of the people I work with and act and react accordingly. I've been told by some people I'm very stern, by others not too stern. But never have I been accused of being too strict or lax." Thompson nodded his head and walked off.

Professor: What seemed to be the major problem with the stock checkers?

Walker: Every Monday morning Thompson just tears me up about the poor counts. I don't mean inaccurate counts, but not enough counts. These stock checkers have a critical job, since all material purchases from vendors are purchased with a normal lead time based on up-to-date physical inventory records. If the stock checkers fail to make counts on all stock items periodically as scheduled, we can't buy correct quantities of parts or prevent excessive overages.

Anyway, what Thompson doesn't know or won't admit (and I'm not sure which) is that the amount of work downstairs generates 24 checkers' jobs based on normal work standards. We've got 12 checkers. Where are the other 12 men? They are not there. One man is presently responsible for 1,343 parts. This is a physically impossible situation. Mr. Thompson had the audacity to ask me the first week on this job why a particular man wasn't making his count. I said, "I don't know, but I'll go down and ask." "You go down and tell, not ask, that man to make his count," was the reply I received from Thompson.

I went down to the line and asked the man what was the trouble. He said, "I don't know, but I'm getting deeper in the hole all the time." "That's what I wanted to ask you about," was my reply. Mr. Kane, that's the checker, declined my offer to help in an exasperated manner while complaining that the people who used to put the stock into bin areas had been taken away by Thompson. He said, "There's nobody putting the stuff away. It's all over the floor and beginning to collect. Furthermore, there used to be two checkers on this section, now there's just me." "Mr. Kane," I commented, "Mr. Thompson believes you handle the job as is, did you know that?" To this Kane said, "Earl, I've got to explain to you a few things about what's going on around here. About four years ago when Thompson was made superintendent he called all 17 stock checkers to his office for a meeting. We were told from then on there would be just 12 checkers. But the remaining checkers would work ten rather than eight hours per day when the production line was running. This meant overtime, for which everyone was pleased. The cut stock checkers were reclassified and assigned. The remaining 12 checkers worked like dogs but managed to stay ahead. Four weeks after the reduction in checkers was made, the overtime was cut out but the checkers were not reassigned. The line ran ten hours; we worked eight and with five less men. Since this all happened, total stock parts have increased. My section is in a mess—I've no system any more. I hope nobody starts checking the accuracy of some of my counts or my low stock reports. You're not going to solve this one, Earl."

Professor: Is this stock checker another one of those situations in which Thompson placed you?

Walker: Yes, sir. While I have been badgered by this man, in all fairness to him, it stems from his inability to handle people. As an example, Thompson had me in his office one day with a door wide open that adjoined Mr. Edwards' office. The open door was all that was between Edwards' office and Thompson's office. Mr. Edwards was having a meeting with five of his analysts while Thompson was chewing me out about a minor, senseless item. A noticeable hush in conversation occurred in Edwards's office as Thompson yelled away. When Thompson finished with me, I walked, a bit bewildered, through the next office in half a daze. One of the analysts said, "Keep your chin up, Mac," as I left the room.

One of the foremen happened to see me shortly thereafter and asked me what had happened. My "nothing" reply didn't deceive the foreman as he commented, "He's really getting to you, isn't he, Earl?" My statement, "No, I've got to do a little better to satisfy Thompson," was cast off by the foreman as he said, "You'll never satisfy him—none of us satisfy him."

Next my general foreman, Mr. Mead, spotted my behavior and inquired about what the trouble was. It was funny, for he said this was the first time my walk had lost its spring. I readily admitted my problem, explaining it was beginning to discourage me that I failed to satisfy Thompson. After some discussion about the situation, Mead said, "Earl, just do the best you can. We know what you're doing. We also know Thompson and what he is like to work for. We all take it and you're taking it too. It's an unfortunate situation. You just don't know how to keep out of that man's way. You just don't know enough about the workings of this plant yet." I thanked Mr. Mead and left.

It was the strangest thing. No sooner had I finished talking to Mead when I saw Mr. Brown coming up the aisle on his electric scooter—I was in the plant. He's the director of engineering and a member of the plant operating committee. As he passed me by I heard him say, "Just keep your chin up, Earl." And I looked and said, "Okay," as he drove on by me. All of a sudden he stopped the scooter and said he'd like to talk with me. Agreeing, we then rode away to his office and sat down over some coffee. Brown's first remark was, "Earl, I've heard a few rumbles. You having any problems?" to which I replied, "No." He went on, "Earl, I've heard some stories—you can level with me."

After admitting a problem did exist and reviewing three incidents with Brown, I said, "I'm taking a badgering off of Thompson and I'm afraid he can ruin me careerwise with the company. To be frank, I want a career with the company. I'm as enthusiastic now as I was the first day I interviewed for the job. It will take a lot to dampen this energy and interest. I've got a goal. The company has a goal. I believe they are compatible and mutually advantageous. I realize it's going to take lots of training to get where I'd like to go, but I'm afraid that this man might ruin my career paperwise. I think the man is brilliant, but I also think he lacks one thing and that is the ability to handle people. He literally threatened to "get me" in some 1:00 meeting last week for permitting the checkers to spread boxes out to rest on during their lunch hour. To be perfectly frank, Mr. Brown, I am very concerned of the possibilities of this man jeopardizing my chances here. I don't know where you are getting your information from. I haven't told anyone with the exception of my general foreman earlier today."

Brown went on to say, "You have a right to be concerned. First, I attended that 1:00 meeting last week and Thompson said nothing about you. You've got to treat that fellow for what he's worth. Second, do you think for one minute the plant manager, myself, and the operating committee are idiots? We know what your progress has been to date. We read the weekly reports you prepare on each of your assignments. We talk to many people about your work—quality, quantity, willingness to learn, maturity, adaptability, and the extent to which you try to handle any and all assignments. We've watched you operate in the plant. In fact a number of people, including the plant manager, are still talking about the superb job you did down on the production line on that vacation relief assignment. Not many inexperienced people would be capable of filling an experienced man's shoes and operating a complex section at 91 percent of budgeted cost. To be perfectly frank with you, Earl, you're doing an excellent job. You just keep it up. Keep your aspirations on the goals and make proper adjustments as you proceed, always recognizing life and work represent a series of obstacles which we must learn to cope with in some acceptable and satisfactory way. Have faith. I was in the second group of trainees in this program. Your experiences bring back not-too-old memories—good and bad. There is a place for you in this company for sure."

I said, "Yes sir. Thank you very much." Mr. Brown closed his door very quietly. I was by that time on cloud nine as I walked into the plant. Oh, I was tickled pink. I really felt good. As fate would have it, Thompson descended on me about five minutes later with another insignificant item. And, you know, I actually smiled when he chewed me out. At that moment I couldn't have cared less. It seemed like I had a shot of Novocain or cocaine—I was feeling no pain. My reply was simply, "Yes, Mr. Thompson." He looked surprised and taken aback with my reply and obviously indifferent and delighted state of mind.

Professor: Did you have any kind of a performance review before Mr. Brown spoke to you?

Walker: Yes. This will top off my story for you. I had a performance review after my third month on the job. Recall that I started under Mr. Edwards as an engineering change coordinator, and after two months I received the additional assignment of stock checker coordinator under Mr. Mead. Mr. Edwards informed me that he was to give me my performance review. He indicated the engineering change coordinator's job was in fine shape and that the stock checker situation was definitely improving. Then on Friday afternoon, 30 minutes prior to quitting time, Thompson called me into his office. Rather bluntly he said, "Here's your performance review covering the first three months." I almost fell through the floor when I heard that. Without looking at the rating I asked Thompson why he had made it instead of Edwards. He didn't answer my question and only said, "I'm giving it."

The rating covered both my jobs. Under each job he had a detailed list of major weaknesses which, as he put it, "Prevented Walker from performing his job assignment successfully." A number of the items listed under stock checker coordinator were true, but represented problems I had requested help with but for which I never actually received it. The rating in total was very poor and unfair. As I attempted to inquire about each remark, Thompson cut me off and went into a long tirade concerning all my shortcomings. Finally, Thompson told me to make any comments I cared to make relative to his rating and sign it or simply accept it as is and sign it. I looked at the paper and asked, "Mr. Thompson, is this your honest evaluation of me?" After he said "yes" I asked him if he realized that anybody reading the evaluation could get nothing other than a degrading and deleterious impression of my performance. He said, "This is my evaluation of you. You've got a lot of learning to do and a lot of extra work. You just haven't been doing the job the way it is supposed to be done." "Well, Mr. Thompson," I said, "if this is way you see my job performance, and this is the way you will turn it in, I'll just sign my name. Good luck with it."

And that was my first performance review. Not only was it disappointing, it was discouraging. All it amounted to was signing my name. Edwards didn't even know about Thompson's evaluation until after I told him myself. Surprised—I guess he was. Come to find out later that Thompson requested permission to evaluate me from Mr. Snow, the production control manager.

Professor: Are you still enthusiastic about the company and your future with it?

Walker: Oh, I've got the same enthusiasm that I had earlier. Although I must confess, it was dampened a bit by Thompson simply because I was fearful that this man could destroy my career, and at 31 you can't make too many false starts. I know for a fact the overall philosophy of the company is changing. In all plants the graduate training program is in full swing. Graduates of the program will be used to fill middle and top management slots since the company failed to begin developing managerial talent when they should have. They just don't have the talent they need. It is very evident in that there is little loyalty and patriotism toward the company, in my opinion. I think employees in some cases have been so grossly mistreated that they have an "I don't care" attitude. As a matter of fact, I was startled to hear and observe that some of the older top line supervisors as well have a poor attitude. I think this attitude will change. I know this much; the only man that I have ever alienated is Thompson, and I still can't figure out why. The feeling around the office is that Thompson is afraid that he is going to be replaced, and I have been picked as the likely replacement. For the life of me I can't figure out or understand this. I don't have the experience, even though I am aggressive, hard working, and anxious to get ahead. However, I treat everything with a grain of salt in this respect when people talk about personalities on a hearsay basis.

But again, I am pleased and enthusiastic about the company and my future here. Very frankly, if I had to do it all over again, I sincerely would.

Section 3

THE ORGANIZATION

The cases in this section all use the *organization* as the level of analysis. Again, any one case may contain issues or topics which might be addressed at the level of the individual or the group, as well as the entire organization. These cases, however, are selected to illustrate organization level issues which relate to organizational behavior in several different ways.

In research work the organization has been considered as an independent, an intervening and as a dependent variable. Traditional management theorists have considered the formal organization as an independent variable, a means of introducing rationality and order into the conduct of organizational activities. Clear specification of areas of responsibility and reporting relationships is believed to reduce or eliminate overlap or confusion rising from ambiguity in task assignments, and to clarify required communication networks. The cases dealing with the formal organization should help to provide a means of examining situations where ambiguity in reporting relationships may be sources of organizational problems. Management theorists and business policy specialists consider the organization as an intervening but controlled variable, dependent upon the choice of a particular strategy and goal set, but serving as a mechanism for accomplishing organizational objectives.

The informal organization can also be viewed in several ways. The emergence of social groupings and informal communication networks is dependent upon the physical management of the workplace, the task, and the formal or planned organization relationships. The informal organization, however, also serves to provide a cohesive and coherent social fabric, with stable role relationships, rewards, and standards of conduct. Thus, while dependent to some extent on tasks, technologies, and formal requirements, the informal organization serves to shape, guide, and reward behavior in much of day-to-day work life. The cases in this section which focus on the informal organization should be of help in depicting the form and relative strength of normative influences in the informal work relationships seen in work situations. The effect of the informal organization in guiding and controlling behavior, and its system of rewards and sanctions, are topics to be explored in discussing these cases.

The topics of power and authority relate very closely to the formal and

141

informal organization. In some respects, formal authority is delineated by the formal organization. Accepted authority, however, or authority in its application, is perhaps, more readily seen as a reflection of the forces and factors found in the informal organization. The authority of person or of expertise, and the power to amend or even nullify formal authority, arise as the framework of social relationships develops and matures. Thus, one can consider these topics as dimensions of the study of formal and informal organizations, and as important indicators of the degree to which *planned* delegation to achieve *planned* objectives (that is, management) is in fact a significant element in the organization's *actual* method of operations.

The topic of organizational performance, a third subject which is dealt with at the level of the organization, encompasses both the degree to which planned goals are achieved and planned means utilized (as mentioned above), but, also, the extent to which the organization is able to maintain its resilience, its vigor, and its ability to renew itself. Any undue attention to goal accomplishment, without attention to organization renewal and responsiveness, often results in a very short range of organizational perspective, and an even shorter period of organizational effectiveness. As financial and human resources erode, the consequent imbalance in tasks results in a diminished and fatigued staff, flagging interests, and an almost inevitable dwindling of measurable performance. Thus, in examining the performance of organizations by means of goal accomplishment, it is also quite helpful to determine if objectives, either explicit or implicit, have been set to provide for the longer term ability of the organization to survive. The organization, if it is to thrive, must provide for the development of a broad range of responsiveness to changing conditions within and without the organization, and in its competitive environment. The organization's ability to attract resources under changing and adverse conditions, its ability to develop individuals capable of undertaking expanding responsibilities as the organization grows in scope and depth, and its ability to adequately deal with crises are some of the key indicators of organizational "health."

The influence of the environment on the organization is a fourth topic addressed in this section. In a sociological sense, an organization is interdependent with other organizations. The organization serves to provide certain functions to its environment, but competes with other organizations for resources—material, financial, and human. As mentioned earlier, organizations which are unable to effectively compete for resources, or which are unable to compete for functions to perform, will cease to exist. For example, as technologies change, the more responsive organizations will gain clients, or customers, at the expense of less responsive organizations. Similarly, markets may segment, permitting more responsive and better performing organizations to capture those segments which are more rewarding or more rapidly growing, or both. In the study of the cases in this section, the reader should consider a variety of environmental influences, and evaluate the organizations' responsiveness to each. Technological changes, competitive pressures, changes in consumer buying or usage patterns, social and economic factors in society at large, and a myriad of local environmental factors (political, labor market, climate, local zoning, and regulation, and the like) should all be considered as possible environmental factors.

From the works of Burns & Stalker, and Lawrence & Lorsch, the rate of change in the environment is a major factor determining the structural and operative characteristics of the organizations which are effective in that environment. Further, the characteristics of participants differ in dissimilar competitive environments, as do the demands on those persons responsible for coordinating diverse activities in achieving integrated organization-wide objectives.[1]

ADDITIONAL SELECTED READINGS

Adams, J. Stacy.   "Interorganizational Processes and Organization Boundary Activities." In Barry M. Staw and L. L. Cummings, eds., *Research in Organizational Behavior,* vol. 2. Greenwich, Conn.: JAI Press, 1980, pp. 321–55.

Berger, Chris J., and Cummings, L. L.   "Organizational Structure, Attitudes and Behaviors." In Barry M. Staw, ed., *Research in Organizational Behavior,* vol. 1. Greenwich, Conn.: JAI Press, 1979, pp. 169–208.

Dalton, Dan R., et al.   "Organization Structure and Performance: A Critical Review." *The Academy of Management Review* (January 1980), pp. 49–64.

Galbraith, J. R.   *Organization Design.* Reading, Mass.: Addison-Wesley, 1977.

Goodman, P. S., et al.   *New Perspectives on Organizational Effectiveness.* San Francisco: Jossey-Bass, 1977.

Jackson, J. H., and Morgan, C. P.   *Organization Theory: A Macro Perspective for Management.* Englewood Cliffs, N.J.: Prentice-Hall, 1978.

Magnusen, Karl O.   "A Comparative Analysis of Organizations: A Critical Review." In Nord, W. R., ed.   *Concepts and Controversy in Organizational Behavior.* Pacific Palisades, Calif.: Goodyear Publishing Co., 1976.

Pfeffer, Jeffrey   "Power and Resource Allocation in Organizations." In Staw, Barry M., and Salancik, Gerald R.   *New Directions in Organizational Behavior.* Chicago: St. Clair Press, 1977, pp. 235–65.

Steers, R. M.   *Organizational Effectiveness: A Behavioral View.* Pacific Palisades, Calif.: Goodyear Publishing Co., 1977.

Stieglitz, H.   "On Concepts of Corporate Structure." *The Conference Board Record* (February, 1974), pp. 7–13.

---

[1] P. R. Lawrence and J. W. Lorsch, *Organization and Environment,* (Cambridge, Mass.: Harvard University Press, 1967).

Case 3–1

Eastern State Psychiatric Institute

Hak-Chong Lee and Thomas J. Rybaltowski

Eastern State Psychiatric Institute (ESPI) is a facility of the Eastern State Department of Mental Hygiene located in the rural town of Birchville in Eastern State. Since its initial operation as a state mental hospital in 1920, ESPI has gradually evolved into a geographically organized in-patient facility with an increasing number of satellite programs established in individual communities of the "catchment area." This catchment area, or geographical region, served by the Institute includes all of York County, most of Warren County, and the eastern part of Duke County where ESPI is located. This area is diverse in nature, ranging from

EXHIBIT 1
Partial Organization Chart

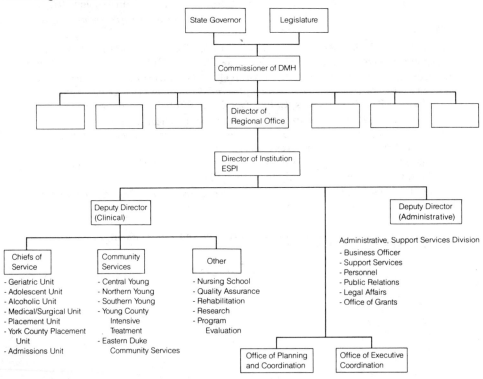

144

medium-sized cities to rural farming lands. It is currently incorporated under one of five regions in the state under the jurisdiction of the state's Department of Mental Hygiene (DMH).

MISSION AND ORGANIZATION

Eastern State's primary mission has been to offer intensive psychiatric service for those admitted to the hospital. Residential services include adolescent, mental retardation, geriatric, medical/surgical, and alcoholic units. Patients in the hospital receive around-the-clock care. Specialized programs are provided for geriatric, alcoholic, and adolescent populations. Also included is a campus school, a halfway house, and a shelter workshop which utilizes vocational programs developed through the institute's community store, food services, and Department of Industrial Maintenance.

Educational training and employment opportunities are also offered to in-patients through the active involvement in patient education of the Duke County Office for Cooperative Educational Program (OCEP) and the Office of Vocational Training and Development (OVTD) in rehabilitative activities. Programs available at the Institute comprise an important part of the overall process which prepares a resident patient for return to community life. Aside from the medical units, there are also support services including offices in personnel, public relations, program evaluation, and a business office (Exhibit 1).

As a self-contained hospital community, ESPI has been striving toward the treatment and care of mentally ill persons with a continual desire to allow patients to function effectively outside the hospital environment.

DEVELOPMENTS IN MENTAL HEALTH

Over the last decade, the patient population of the nation's mental hospitals has declined from some 490,000 to just over 215,000. Largely responsible for this decline is the growing number of community-based, out-patient mental health centers, such as community clinics, day care treatment programs, clinic drop-in centers, coffee houses, adult homes, health-related facilities, family care facilities, and mobile psychiatric centers. Such centers, or clinics, account for about 70 percent of the decline of persons in state and county mental hospitals since 1950.[1]

The move toward community-based facilities, or "de-institutionalization" of mental health patients, has been initiated by changes in mental health treatment. Dr. Richard M. Restak, a Washington, D.C., neurologist with psychiatric training, says, "For too long, psychiatry has ignored the fact that emotional disturbances are largely biochemical in nature. Recent research has proved that many, perhaps most, emotional states are determined by changes in the chemistry of the brain."[2] In recent years, it has

---

[1] "New Ways to Heal Disturbed Minds: Where Will It All Lead?" *U.S. News and World Report*, February 16, 1976, p. 2.

[2] Ibid.

been discovered that heredity and various chemicals play a role in schizo-phrenia, depression, and manic diseases. A study has shown that the em-phasis on psychiatric research, training, and treatment of mentally ill patients has begun to shift from psychology and Freudianism to chemical and biological causes of mental illness.

Dr. Roy W. Menninger, president of the world-famous Menninger Foundation in Topeka, Kansas, says, "The overwhelming majority of psychological problems are being resolved favorably when the patient gets early, appropriate, and sufficient treatment."[3] This treatment has been increasingly administered to patients on an out-patient basis through community-based mental health clinics. These community-based clinics have aided in the efficient and effective treatment of patients. It has been recognized by those in the caring professions that the mentally ill do not get better as often, or as quickly, in a hospital setting as they do in the normalizing atmosphere of the community at large.

Dr. Adams, unit chief of the adolescent unit at ESPI, also confirms the general trend in psychiatric care: "Anyone who lives long at an in-patient facility finds it much harder to return to the community. Priorities have shifted towards greater use of the out-patient facility, even though psychi-atric knowledge is not advanced far enough to completely close the in-patient hospital. A total approach is needed which develops some optimal blend between the basic in-patient services now offered and flexible out-patient services. It has been my concern for the proper placement of pa-tients into these out-patient facilities, for a reinstatement of patients back into the in-patient facility would be a crime."

Due to the apparent advantages of recent advances in mental hygiene care, a statewide trend toward de-institutionalization has been initiated in Eastern State aimed at reducing the in-patient populations of all mental hospitals in the state. The move toward de-institutionalization has been accentuated in recent years by the increasing concern of the Eastern State legislature to improve the organization and effectiveness of the state's Department of Mental Hygiene. The mental health committees of the Eastern State legislature have been developing a package of legislation to improve care of the state's mentally disabled, dilute the powers of the department's commissioner, give localities more control over planning, and mandate certain mental care standards and administrative proce-dures to ensure increased efficiency in the delivery of mental care services.

For example, one major bill in the package seeks for a creation of a mental health planning unit, taking away some of the powers now vested in the Office of the DMH Commissioner. This unit would define the authority and responsibility for state and local participation in providing mental health service. Sponsors of these legislative moves argue that there has been no statewide mental hygiene plan since 1965 and that such a plan is vitally needed at a time when the entire system is in transition from a primarily institution-based system to one that is community-based.

Due to the legislation of this kind, and as a psychiatric center responsive

---

[3] Ibid.

EXHIBIT 2
In-Patient Population Levels

Date	In-Patient Level
6/1/75	2,460
9/1/75	2,217
1/2/76	1,992
4/1/76	1,846
6/1/76	1,782
9/1/76	1,701
1/2/77	1,446
4/1/77	1,098
6/1/77	999
9/1/77	949
1/2/78	909

to current mental health needs, ESPI has been developing its services in the direction of community psychiatry and treatment and away from the centralized institution in recent years. The move away from the institutionalized hospital has been reflected at ESPI by the decline in their number of in-patients (Exhibits 2 and 3).

At the same time, the institute has been constantly expanding the range of its programs and making them as readily available and accessible to rising community needs as possible. These services, which range from prevention through intensive treatment, are designed to permit clients to

EXHIBIT 3
Placements by Facilities July–December 1977

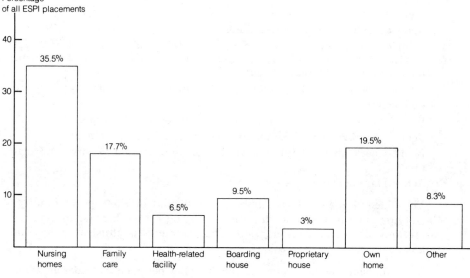

remain in their communities for treatment or assist them in returning to the community from the hospital. All treatment programs have sought to encourage growth and independence through rehabilitative activities; individual, group, and family therapy; counseling and links with services of other agencies in the helping network.

Out-patient services provided by ESPI have also been increasingly based in the communities they serve, with permanent headquarters and staff in those communities. Although the central hospital in Birchville still serves an important function for those clients who need intensive care, the institute's services are, for the most part, changing in accordance with current theories of mental health, or on a preventive, therapeutic out-patient basis.

PLACEMENT PROCESS

The effectiveness of de-institutionalization is mainly governed by the process of placing hospital patients into community-based facilities. This is a complicated process which requires close coordination among many professional, administrative and service people at the Institute as well as at the out-patient facilities (Exhibit 4).

Following is a partial list of typical activities involved in the placement process:

Meeting of placement team to assess the feasibility of releasing a patient.

Laboratory and medical tests.

Correction of medical difficulties.

Letter to patient's family explaining movement of the patient out of the hospital.

Contact county resource agent.

Application for state/county funding.

Complete forms for various state agencies including Department of Social Services, Department of Mental Hygiene, county approval forms, out-patient facility forms, and hospital forms.

Find out the availability of out-patient facilities and visit them.

Confirmation of the availability.

Wait for medical and funding approvals and doctor's signature.

Contact out-patient medical teams concerning patient movement.

Double-check financial funding, medical approvals, and facility confirmation.

Actual placement.

The placement process is further complicated by the type of facility, the city or town of residence a patient is being placed in, and individual discretions of social workers and team leaders, as illustrated by the following:

Boarding homes do not require as much money per patient as does an adult home. Therefore, funding is easier to come by. Moreover, the funding feasibility varies from one county to another.

EXHIBIT 4
Partial Organizational Structure of a Typical Clinical Service Unit

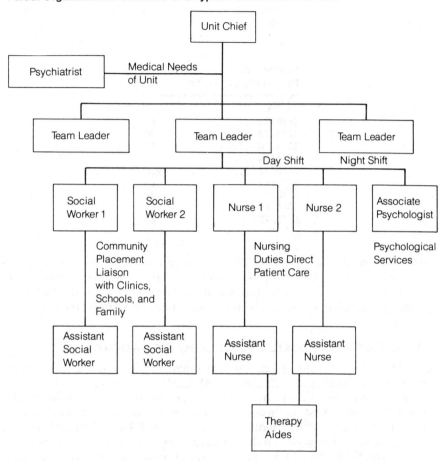

County medical approval for a patient is necessary in health-related facilities, but not in adult homes. No medical approval is necessary if a patient is returned to the care of his family, but clinical approval is needed.

It is hoped that most patients can be placed in a facility in their home county. However, it was found that approximately 55 percent of geriatric patients were being placed into a neighboring state because of a lack of facilities.

Some counties have their own out-patient mobile team or liaison office which eases the transition from the hospital to the community facility. Thus, some facilities provide transportation in transferring the patient while others require the patient to be moved by the institution.

The proprietor of a boarding house or a sponsor of a family care facility must give his approval before a patient can be transferred.

Each placement team places a patient in their own individual manner. It is left to the discretion of social workers and team leaders as to what placement activities are to take priority.

Up to now, placement of in-patients has been accomplished through informal, "in-house" directives determined by top administrators at ESPI. A typical placement process took as long as 11 weeks, but ESPI was still able to achieve a steady increase in the number of patient placements until recently (Exhibit 5). However, under the increasing pressure toward

EXHIBIT 5
Patient Placement Rate

Date	Placements
6/19/76	57
8/14/76	60
10/9/76	59
12/4/76	113
2/26/77	220
5/21/77	166
8/13/77	148
10/8/77	97
12/3/77	44

rapid de-institutionalization, ESPI could no longer continue with the lengthy and informal placement practices, but to develop a formal and efficient plan to deal with the drastic increases in patient placements which were being mandated by the Department of Mental Hygiene.

IMPACT OF ACCELERATED PLACEMENT OF PATIENTS

The increased rate of patient placement has brought a wide impact throughout the hospital. As Mrs. R. M. Link, R.N., a team leader in the geriatric unit says, "There has been great pressure within this hospital to release patients. Just last week we got a request from the director asking for a placement of 30 patients right away." Joe Pitman, director of planning at ESPI, also says, "High standards are being set by the director of this hospital; he has high expectations of what can be accomplished."

However, the implementation of the high placement goal has drawn critical reactions. S. R. Simon, chief of admissions unit, states:

> It's very hard now to place patients from ESPI. When we first started to reduce our in-patient population, the easily placeable ones had no problem in resettling. Now, we have come down to the hard-core, higher-risk patient who is extremely difficult to place. This is not only because he is the more chronic patient, but also because of a shortage of beds in community facilities. It is also very hard for someone like a social worker to coordinate all activities needed before a patient can be placed. Under such adverse conditions, we can't really expect strong commitment from placement teams.

C. Reynolds, rehabilitation department, Central Office, is concerned with current methods of placing patients under increasing placement targets:

What we need around here is some systematic procedure to transform us from our actual state to some desired one. Things are done too randomly around here. Our director, Dr. King, has asked for an additional 500 patients to be placed in the next six months. How can we do that under the present system?

Although the relocation of patients is assisted by placement teams in the placement unit, the ward social worker is primarily responsible for the coordination of all the procedures and activities leading to the eventual discharge of a patient. Social workers interact with nurses, therapy aides, doctors, and the out-patient clinic in an effort to see that a patient is properly placed. Quite often, a strong bond develops between the patient and the social worker with great sympathy toward the patient. This at times causes the social worker to be reluctant in speeding up the placement of the patient. The team leader usually oversees the activities of the social workers in the team and aids in coordinating all placement activities. However, these activities are usually quite varied and detailed with seemingly endless forms to complete for numerous agencies.

Currently, over 41 different forms are required for placement purposes. Often, one to four or more copies of many forms are also required. The excessive amount of paperwork is criticized by V. Lawrence, chairperson of DMH/DSS Liaison Coordinators Committee and social worker supervisor:

> . . . the process of resettling a patient in the community requires a great deal of paperwork, much of which is repetitive, filling out of numerous forms for referrals to community agencies for housing and financial assistance or other supportive services. Moreover, our own various community service units also require a good deal of referral information in order to accept the client for out-patient services. . . . the paperwork required is a hamper to the quality of care a patient receives. If our social workers spend all their time filling out forms, then obviously less time is left to be spent with patients who really need their services.

Mrs. R. Cusato, team leader of the geriatric unit, also says, "A lot of bottlenecks occur as all types of forms are being processed in various agencies. . . . bureaucracy is really holding us back."

However, the paperwork is not the only activity required which slows down the release of a patient. Mrs. Link says:

> The doctor's cooperation is very important. Quite often, the patient is ready to be placed and we wait around for some doctor's signature. The forms may sit on his desk for a week. We waste more time than we need to. Doctors here don't really care if a patient is released or not. They prefer to treat patients slowly and at their leisure.

Organizational changes caused by the de-institutionalization program have also produced many problems. As the in-patient population decreased, the remaining patients were consolidated into fewer and fewer wards. As the number of wards declined, entire buildings were closed and whole wards moved into remaining facilities. At one time, 30 buildings were in operation. This has been reduced to 16. The school of nursing has been on the list to be phased out as well as a halfway house. This has resulted in the reassignments of all types of workers including clinical and staff workers (Exhibit 6).

EXHIBIT 6
Number of Employees at ESPI

Date	Number of Employees
9/12/75	1,578
1/ 2 /76	1,564
4/25/76	1,578
8/14/76	1,573
10/8/76	1,553
2/26/77	1,512
8/13/77	1,524
10/8/77	1,426
11/5/77	1,362
12/3/77	1,285

C. L. Daniels, nurse administrator in medical/surgical unit, says:

> People are being laid off or moved around so much that morale is degen-enerating with all kinds of rumors. This is especially true among our older and less skilled employees. The younger and more educated workers can take a voluntary transfer to some other facility, but those who have worked here for years, when this hospital had three times the number of patients it has now, don't want to move. Job security is very important to these people.

Dr. D. J. Walker, chief of alcoholic unit, says, "With major organizational changes occurring constantly, the attitudes of employees directly affect the quality of patient care. What we need to do is not to move so fast and reassess our ultimate goals."

Other problems are also expressed. V. Lawrence states, "There are not enough community facilities to accept all patients and there may not be for a long time to come. Furthermore, I don't think that communities are ready to accept any more disturbed people in their neighborhood."

Pat Roberts, team leader in placement unit, points out another problem:

> Not only is available housing very important, but so is the need for adequate funding. Money is very tight these days and we are largely under-staffed—in fact, we've been understaffed now for a few years. This places an added burden upon those presently working. The staff shortage is particularly serious with social workers. Maybe, what we really need is more social workers and less psychologists. . . . along with the manpower shortage, funding approvals and housing are the major bottlenecks in the placement process.

Dr. King, the director of ESPI, has been meeting regularly with key professional and administrative personnel each week for several hours to discuss various programs of the institute. The problems associated with de-institutionalization have been brought up indirectly and briefly touched upon in past meetings. In May 1978, as the problems were becoming more serious, the director sent out a memorandum stating that the next staff meeting would be entirely devoted to the discussion of ESPI's programs on de-institutionalization.

Case 3–2

Project OCALA

T. Roger Manley

BACKGROUND

In the fall of 1965, IBM made an unsolicited, no-cost proposal to the U.S. Air Force, offering a general purpose IBM computer to be installed in the instrumentation room of the Titan III Vertical Integration Building at Cape Kennedy Air Force Station. The computer, the last model 7044 to be built by IBM, was to be used as part of a study designed to determine whether a general purpose computer could be used on-line to perform real-time launch control and checkout functions for a space booster and its spacecraft payload.

IBM's interest in performing such a study centered about: (1) proving that it was feasible to use a general-purpose computer for these functions; (2) gaining experience in designing and operating a large-scale system under actual launch and checkout conditions; and (3) developing healthy working relationships with Air Force and contractor personnel associated with the Titan III program. The latter interest stemmed from the fact that in about 12 to 18 months, the Air Force would be awarding contracts for its multibillion-dollar Manned Orbital Laboratory (MOL) program. MOL, which was to place teams of two military test pilots into Earth orbit for periods of 30 days, was to be launched from Vandenberg Air Force Base, California, and was to utilize the Titan III-M as its booster. The Air Force was currently defining the MOL system, and had shown a definite interest in a launch control and checkout system that would offer the speed and flexibility of a general-purpose computer. Many of the same personnel currently working on the Titan III-C program would later be working and making key decisions on the MOL program.

The Titan III facility at Cape Kennedy offered a unique opportunity to evaluate the feasibility of such a system and to compare its performance against a current state-of-the-art logic card/patch system. As proposed, the computerized system in the study would be completely passive; it would monitor what was going on, but its observations would simply be printed out rather than being fed back into Titan III decision logic circuits.

The proposed study also offered certain advantages to the Titan III contractors, especially the integrating contractor, Martin-Marietta Corporation (MMC). All would gain from the experience of working with such a system, and if it should prove successful, the possibility of more rapid data collection and more efficient analysis seemed excellent. This was a very significant consideration because, at the time of the proposal, there had been only one flight of the Titan III-C and many questions remained to be answered. From the study, MMC was hopeful of developing a single ground control and instrumentation system that could be used for the entire family of Titan III launch vehicles. Such an accomplishment would substantially lower the cost per vehicle and increase the flexibility of the system—thereby making Titan launch vehicles attractive to NASA as well as to the Air Force for future missions.

The Air Force was primarily interested in the study from the point of view of determining whether computerized ground equipment was feasible for the MOL program. Since IBM had proposed the study at no cost to the government for its equipment and personnel, and since the study would not interfere with normal Titan III checkout and launch activities, the Air Force requested a proposal from MMC for systems analysis and engineering support of the IBM effort. In requesting the proposal, the Air Force made it very clear to the MMC representatives that it had only limited funds available for such a study, and the decision to accept or reject the IBM proposal would probably rest upon the level of funding that MMC would require to support the study. Implied was the thought that MMC had better help underwrite the cost, or there would be no study.

Enthused over the possibilities of such a system, MMC responded with a bid of approximately one half of what it would cost the company to support the project. The Air Force accepted MMC's proposal, and at the first meeting held with the principals at Cape Kennedy, agreed to call the project by the acronym, OCALA (On-Line Computer And Launch Analysis).

THE TITAN III DIVISION

The Titan III program office was located at headquarters, Space Systems Division (SSD) in Los Angeles, California. Reporting functionally to the program office was the Titan III Division of 6555th Aerospace Test Wing at Cape Kennedy. Although an autonomous organization reporting directly to the commander of SSD, the Test Wing acted as on-site representatives for various program offices. Exhibit 1 is an organization chart reflecting the various relationships.

Although the Test Wing supported the program offices, its primary role was that of launch agency. Whereas the program office was responsible for defining a system, approving changes, and negotiating contracts, the Test Wing was primarily concerned with checkout and launch activities.

As shown in Exhibit 2, the Titan III Division was divided into four branches: Systems Engineering, Operations, Payloads, and Program Support. The systems branch was primarily concerned with engineering on the booster. Members of that branch functioned as test controllers for all checkout activities. It was their responsibility to insure that all technical requirements were met. The operations branch physically manned the widespread ITL facility. Its responsibilities included all forms of house-

EXHIBIT 1

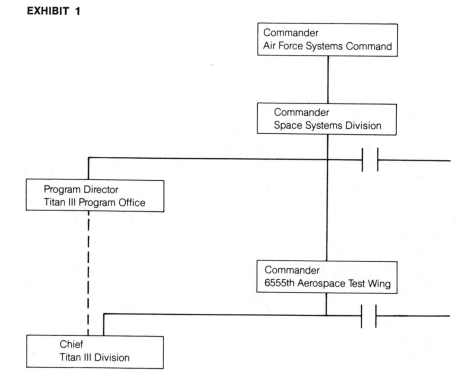

keeping, support scheduling, operation and maintenance of facility equipment. The payloads branch concerned itself solely with the various satellites and the heat shield that covered them through the early stages of flight. The program support branch, the smallest of the four, concerned itself primarily with documentation and long-range planning. At the time

EXHIBIT 2

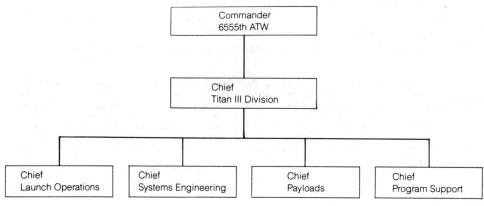

covered by this case study, the division contained approximately 180 officers, enlisted men, and civil service engineers.

Partially because of the personalities of the two branch chiefs, and partially because there was an overlap of responsibilities, a sometimes bitter rivalry had developed between the operations and systems branches. The situation was aggravated by the fact that the division chief, Colonel March, was a quiet individual with a distaste for unpleasant confrontations. Lieutenant Colonel Fredericks, chief of the systems branch, and Major Speaker, chief of the operations branch, were both highly competent and aggressive individuals. Prior to Lt. Col. Fredericks taking over Systems, Col. March had relied heavily upon Major Speaker in running the division. After Lt. Col. Frederick's arrival on the scene, however, Major Speaker had been slowly eased from the favored advisor's position.

When IBM first made its proposal on OCALA, Major Speaker, who had a Ph.D. in aeronautical engineering, came out strongly in favor of it. Lt. Col. Fredericks, partially because of the mutual antagonism and partially because he doubted that it would succeed, was cool toward the idea. As a result, when the proposal was approved, the project officer for the study was chosen from the operations branch; although the project clearly came under systems' area of interest and responsibility.

Major Speaker chose Major Ed Kroen to act as the project officer. Kroen had a graduate engineering degree, and was very interested in computers. Throughout November and December 1965, Major Kroen attended a series of meetings and conferences at SSD headquarters and at the MMC plant in Denver, Colorado. At these meetings a schedule was devised which called for the installation of the computer at the Cape in early January 1966, and for the system being operational for the launch scheduled for mid-February. OCALA would also support launches scheduled for April and June of that year.

The first hint of schedule difficulties arose when the Titan III-C vehicle C-8 launch in December 1965 failed to meet all of its objectives. On that flight, an attitude control system valve failed to close completely, and as a result the satellites remained in the transfer orbit.[1] The program director, Colonel (now Major General) David V. Miller decided that no further Titan III-C launches would occur until the source of the problem was positively identified and eliminated. A task force worked on the problem (the seriousness of which was highlighted when Neil Armstrong also experienced an attitude control system failure in his Gemini flight) and came up

---

[1] When a spacecraft is in orbit, the propellants in its main tanks are more like blobs of jelly floating around than like liquids. Because of this phenomenon caused by a lack of gravity, spacecraft were equipped with an extra, smaller propulsion system called the "attitude control system." This system differed from the primary propulsion system in that the propellants were stored inside a bladder. When the system was to be activated, pressure from a stored gas tank was applied to the bladder. The result was similar to squeezing a tube of toothpaste. The attitude control system was used for two modes: (1) for making attitude adjustments, and (2) for main tank propellant settling—the small thrust it created was sufficient to force the main propellants to the bottom of the tanks for normal operation.

with the discovery that minute glass balls which were immersed in a solvent used for cleaning the system were getting trapped in the plumbing and, under the right circumstances, could prevent a valve from closing. By the time the problem was resolved, the earliest that the next Titan III-C could be launched was in June 1966. Since OCALA was to end in that month, this meant the study would include only one launch.

While the search for the cause of the attitude control system failure was going on, and the date of the next launch a complete unknown, the first members of Project OCALA started to arrive at the Titan III Vertical Integration Building (VIB). In late January 1966, Major Kroen was transferred to the Office of Aerospace Research Detachment at Patrick Air Force Base. This left Project OCALA without a project officer.

AN ADDITIONAL DUTY

Captain Roger Toms, the officer in charge of the Titan III Operations Control Center, was vaguely aware that "some sort of a study" was going to be conducted with a computer in the instrumentation room. Because of his involvement with the launch of C–8 in December and the necessity of working on reports after the launch, he did not get the opportunity to find out much about it. He was aware, however, that Major Kroen's transfer had left the group without a project officer.

An energetic individual, he was uneasy about the prospect of facing a prolonged period of relative inactivity while waiting for testing to begin on the next vehicle. Since he had had some experience with programming while working on his master's degree, he thought that it might be interesting to work on the computer project.

Having decided that this was what he wanted to do, he approached Major Speaker after a weekly staff meeting and asked:

Toms: Ted, have you decided what you are going to do for a project officer on that computer study now that Ed Kroen has left?

Speaker: I haven't really decided . . . I guess that I'll take care of it myself.

Toms: Will you have the time?

Speaker: Not really . . .

Toms: Well, I had a chance to play around with computers some back at Rensselaer . . . if you agree, I would like to take over the project.

Speaker: I suspect you are getting into more than you realize, but I know you can handle it . . . so it's all yours. I'll put out a letter this afternoon naming you the new project officer.

Toms: Thanks a lot, Ted. I'll get on it first thing in the morning.

Speaker: Fine . . . be sure and keep me informed on how everything is going. Oh, yes . . . you might give Ed Kroen a call at Patrick and see if he can't poop you up.

Toms: Will do. I'll see you later.

* * * * *

Telephone conversation:

Toms: Hello, Ed, this is Roger Toms. How is the new job working out?

Kroen: Hi, Rog. Everything seems to be working out fine. I think that I'll enjoy it. How is everything out at the Cape?

Toms: Things were looking like they were going to be rather slow, but I just picked up your computer project.

Kroen: I gave you credit for being smarter than that.

Toms: Come on, Ed, it's not that bad . . . is it?

Kroen: Oh, boy, do you have a rude awakening coming.

Toms: What am I up against?

Kroen: Look, I left a file out at the VIB that contains all of the correspondence that has come in and gone out on OCALA. It also has copies of minutes from the various meetings that I have attended. You read them and you'll know what kind of a bucket you've inherited.

Toms: You don't sound too encouraging—what's the glitch?

Kroen: Time . . . you just don't have enough of it. Do you realize that OCALA is only supposed to last six months? And in that six months the system is supposed to be on the line for three launches? . . . When they finally find out what the problem with the attitude control system is and work out a fix, you'll be lucky to get in one launch—let alone three.

Toms: Hmm, that doesn't sound too promising.

Kroen: Not when you realize this is February, and the computer isn't even installed yet. Hell, the programmers just started coming in about the time I was leaving, and from the few words that I had with them, they sure seemed skeptical about the job ahead of them.

Toms: You sure paint a great picture.

Kroen: I wish I could tell you otherwise, but it looks pretty grim to me.

Toms: Well, okay, Ed, thanks anyway. I appreciate the file, and if you should think of anything else I ought to know, give me a call.

Kroen: Will do . . . and good luck with your new *additional* duty.

Toms: You really know how to hurt a guy . . . and to think, I volunteered for it. I'll be talking to you, Ed.

THE IBM PROJECT COORDINATOR

The Titan III Operations Control Center was located on the fourth floor of the west section of the Vertical Integration Building along with the two launch control centers, the instrumentation room, and assorted offices (see Exhibit 3). After reading Major Kroen's file the next morning, Capt. Toms left his desk in the Operations Control Center, and set about locating members of Project OCALA. The only individual with whom he was slightly familiar was Bill Downes of IBM, and at that, they had never been introduced to one another. Toms tried several offices, and then located him at a desk in the Air Force Facility Office. As he approached the desk, Downes looked up.

EXHIBIT 3
4th Floor—NW Corner—VIB

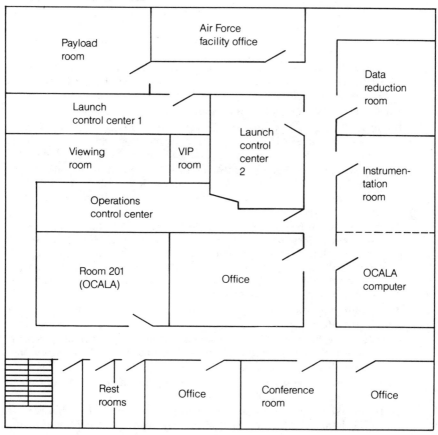

Toms: Bill Downes? I'm Roger Toms.

Downes: Hello. Welcome to Project OCALA. I was talking with Major Speaker before, and he told me that you would probably be looking me up today.

Toms: Well, I am glad that I caught you. Is this where you normally hang out?

Downes: When I am in the area, I usually make this office my base of operations. Major Kroen was kind enough to provide me with a desk.

Toms: Good, you are settled in then. How is everything else going?

Downes: Things are looking up. Would you like a briefing on where we stand?

Toms: Yes, I would. I had an opportunity to skim through a file that Ed Kroen left, and I think I have a general idea of what the program is all about . . . but the pieces aren't quite fitting together.

Downes: How's that?

Toms: Well, as I understand it from some of the schedules that I saw, if we were going to hold to the original schedule and launch C–11 this month, OCALA was supposed to be up for the test. I don't see how that could have happened when the computer isn't even installed yet.

Downes: Oh, we could have been up and gotten *some* data. Of course, we wouldn't have gotten as much as we would have on the later launches, but we would have gotten data nevertheless. The machine will come in tomorrow or the day after, but if there had been any reason, we could have had it in earlier.

Toms: How do we stand on the programming?

Downes: The programming is coming along. You understand that we are using the SPADATS routine for the monitor deck, and that all we really have to come up with are applications programs, don't you?

Toms: Well, I read that, but it seemed like a mouthful to me. I don't have a helluva lot of programming experience, but the little that I do have tells me that to write, debug, and get the programs running is going to be a whale of a job.

Downes: Wait till you see our people in action. We have some of the sharpest programmers and systems analysts in IBM assigned to this project; they really know their business. Actually, all you have to do is prod them every so often with pointed questions, and it is amazing the work that they will put out. Of course, I am more hardware ori-- ented myself . . . programming isn't my specialty.

Toms: I'm sure you know more about it than I do, so I am relieved to hear your words.

Downes: You just have to understand one thing: programmers are never happy unless they are complaining. It is just like in the military, they always balk at making a deadline.

Toms: I would like to meet them . . . and the Martin guys, too. How about taking me around and introducing me?

Downes: We'll try to run them down, but I won't guarantee that we will find them all. They are spread out all over the place. Some of our guys have taken to doing their work in their permanent offices back at Cocoa Beach.

Toms: How come you don't have one central office?

Downes: There just doesn't seem to be any room available.

Toms: I find that difficult to believe . . . how hard have you tried?

Downes: Look, if you can find us a room, we'll give you a gold-plated hero button.

Toms: How about Room 201?

Downes: We already tried that, but it belongs to UTC.[2]

Toms: They only use it on launch day. Move into it and I'll square it with Bud Franklin, the UTC manager.

Downes: Say, that is great. I'll tell the men to move in. Actually, I would rather keep my desk here. I won't be spending near as much time out here as they will.

---

[2] United Technology Center (UTC), a subsidiary of United Aircraft Corporation, manufactured the solid rocket motors.

Toms: Whatever you want . . . only, I would prefer that your people remain out here. I don't want them going back to their old offices.

Downes: Well, I didn't like the idea either, but they don't work for me . . . and they really didn't have any place to sit.

Toms: What do you mean they don't work for you? Aren't you the IBM Project Chief?

Downes: My official title is Project Coordinator. Actually, we have eight IBM personnel assigned to OCALA, and all of them work for different supervisors.

THE PROJECT OCALA "TEAM"

By the next morning, the majority of the OCALA members had established themselves at a desk in room 201. Capt. Toms had managed to meet only two members the previous afternoon—Claude Taylor, a systems analyst for MMC, and Joe Bollinger, an IBM programmer—and had made no secret of the fact that he was annoyed at not finding more of the group on the job. Word of his anger had apparently been passed on to the men, for when he entered the room, the atmosphere was painfully strained. Some of the men stopped their conversations and started scribbling notes on their programming pads or thumbing through manuals on their desks, while others talked and laughed even louder, casting defiant glances at the door.

Toms spied Taylor and Bollinger seated at adjoining desks, and walked over to them.

Toms: How is everything going this morning?

Taylor: Great, Captain . . . an office like this was just what we needed.

Toms: The name is Roger, Claude . . . not Captain.

Taylor: Good enough, Roger.

Toms: Since it looks like we have a full house, I wonder if you and Joe couldn't introduce me to the rest of the men.

Bollinger: Sure thing. Hey, you guys, come on over here and meet Captain Roger Toms. He is the man that got us this room, and is going to be the Air Force project officer for OCALA.

After the initial introductions, the atmosphere relaxed considerably. Capt. Toms made it a point to ask each man about his family, where he originally came from, and where he was living. Since the MMC personnel were temporarily assigned to OCALA from the home plant in Denver, he was particularly solicitous about their accommodations and whether their families had accompanied them. The conversation had worked itself around to what tasks the various members were working on, when the door opened and Bill Downes stuck his head into the room.

The change was immediate. Whereas everyone had formed around Toms in a semicircle joking and talking in an almost raucous manner, as soon as they saw Downes conversation ceased and most headed back toward their desks. Downes's face turned red from the obvious rebuff, but he said in a jovial tone of voice, "I stopped by the OCC to see you, and one of your sergeants told me you were in here. They are bringing in the computer, and I thought you would like to see it."

"I certainly would," said Toms walking toward the door. "I'll see you guys later," he called back to the men in the room.

As he and Downes started down the hallway toward the instrumentation room, he heard somebody say in a stage whisper loud enough to carry through the closing door, "I wonder how long that son-of-a-bitch was standing at the door?"

Downes had to have heard the comment, but gave no indication. Finally, after an awkward silence, Toms said, "It doesn't seem like you are going to win any popularity contests in that group . . . What's going on?"

"Well," said Downes in a surprisingly jovial voice, "it is just as I told you the other day: programmers aren't happy unless they are complaining. Some are mad because they feel that being on a project such as this can hurt them if it fails, but will not do them any good if it succeeds. Everyone in IBM pretty much thinks of OCALA as being my baby. They figure if it is successful, I will get the credit, but if it fizzles, they will get the blame. Then, too, they resent my pushing them. Some are fine, but there are a couple who give me nothing but grief whenever I try to find out what kind of progress they are making."

"That doesn't sound too healthy," mused Toms.

"No, it isn't," agreed Downes. "But quite frankly, after talking with you yesterday afternoon I felt optimistic."

"How's that?" asked Toms.

"Well, with you taking an active interest in the project as you apparently intend, they will have to respond to your questions without any childish displays of temper."

"What you are saying," interrupted Toms, "is now that I am on the scene, you're hoping that I will take over the prodding job."

"Essentially, that's correct," replied Downes.

By this time they had reached the door of the instrumentation room. After a pause while they watched the technicians moving the computer into place, Capt. Toms said, "You know, Bill, I am not a bit bashful about asking questions. And when I see something going on that I think is wrong, I'll not hesitate a second in sounding off. But you people are the computer experts, not me . . . so I have to take on faith many of the things I'm told. If I see someone going down a path that I know, or suspect, is wrong, I will sound off loud and clear . . . Now I don't know whether or not that's what you wanted to hear, but that's the way it is."

"That's fine," said Downes, "we both have the same interests. I realize that you haven't had any experience with large computer systems like this, but I'll tell you what questions to ask."

"Oh, no," said Toms, holding up his hand. "If you have any questions to ask, *you* ask them. If you have some information that you want to bring to my attention, that is another matter . . . but I don't believe in playing games with people."

"As you wish," said Downes, blushing once more, "but I believe you misinterpreted me."

*   *   *   *   *

For the next week, Capt. Toms devoted as much time as he could to OCALA. Fortunately, activities were relatively slow in the Operations Control Center, and Toms was blessed with having an unusually competent group of junior officers and sergeants working for him. He managed to spend some time with each individual, asking questions about their areas of responsibility, and how each part fit into the whole. By week's end, a warm relationship had started between Toms and the members of OCALA. Throughout, Toms made no pretense at having any experience with large computer systems, and emphasized that he was relying on the individual members to educate him.

Almost imperceptibly, the work habits of the project members changed. Whereas the normal working hours were from 7:30 A.M. to 3:30 P.M., Toms noted that to a man they were staying beyond quitting time. After being teased one morning about working banker's hours, Toms found himself staying later and later, and spending more and more of his time around the computer.

The OCALA group probably had two of the greatest jokers in the programming field in Larry Perkins and Fuzz Phillip of IBM. Although quiet at first, in a matter of just about two days they had reached full form and were convulsing everyone with their antics and raucous jokes. In that short time, a spirit was created that was to last the duration of the project. Normally sombre individuals found themselves taking part in the high jinks, and before long, every member of the team had a nickname. Capt. Toms became "Jolly Roger" or "Rog-Baby." It was during that same period that the official OCALA greeting came into being. Started by Gary Mayes and embellished by other members of the team, the greeting was an obscene noise made by blowing into one's palm. Certain members, such as Bugs Bellamy, could achieve astounding volume with this call.

Toms immediately perceived that the amount and noise level of the joking belied the amount of work that was being accomplished. The members seemed to derive an inordinate amount of satisfaction from being referred to as "those OCALA nuts." Although he was happy with the spirit that was developing, Toms was uneasy about the status of the project. After a week of trying to learn more about the programming effort, he still could not bring the entire effort into focus. Everyone was busy working on their individual pieces, but there was no effort to tie everything together.

At about 5:00 P.M. on Friday, Capt. Toms was in the process of clearing his desk when one of the sergeants assigned to the Operations Control Center handed him a TWX message. The message was addressed to Major Kroen, and had been sent from a Capt. Bauman at headquarters, SSD. The message requested that Major Kroen support a meeting on the following Tuesday at Cape Kennedy. The purpose of the meeting was to discuss the status of Project OCALA. Scribbled on the bottom of the message was the note: "It's your baby now. Let me know what comes up. (signed) Speaker."

Toms got up and went around to the OCALA office to see if anyone else had received a similar notification. As he entered the room, Claude Taylor was just putting the phone down. He looked up as Toms entered the room, and smiled. "I guess you just received word about the meeting, too," he said. "I just finished talking with Kent Gunderson in Denver."

"What is it all about?" asked Toms, showing the message he received to Taylor. "All this says is they want to discuss status, and you don't fly from L.A. to the Cape just to discuss status."

Taylor scratched his ear, and smiled wistfully. "Kent heard from a friend on the West Coast that somebody from the Cape had told the people at SSD that OCALA was all screwed up. Kent was afraid that it was you who was doing the talking, but I assured him that I didn't think you would do that without first raising hell with us."

"You are right, of course," puzzled Toms, "but who in the hell would be talking to the people out at SSD? And what is it that he is after?"

Taylor hesitated, then said, "I think I know who it was."

Toms looked at him intently, and then nodded. "I think I do, too . . . our jolly coordinator was out on the West Coast this week, wasn't he?"

"Yes, he was," replied Taylor.

"Well, I'll take that up with him later. The point is, he's right—OCALA is screwed up," said Toms. "I've spent better than a week now trying to get a handle on where we are and where we're going," he continued, "and I have come to the conclusion that not only do I not know the answers, but nobody else does, either."

"I think we all realize that," said Taylor. "Last week I wouldn't have given us a chance in a hundred of accomplishing anything. Now . . . with the machine finally installed, and I'm not saying this to pump you up, but your being around, asking questions, showing interest and concern— and most of all, getting us together and forcing us to talk to one another— has all made one heck of a difference. I'm sure you have noticed it, the Martin and IBM guys going out to lunch together, the joking that's going on between them . . . they're starting to pull together now—we're becoming a team."

"I've seen the change," agreed Toms, "but the best teamwork in the world won't cut it if we don't sit down and come up with a realistic plan of action."

"I agree," said Taylor, "and I think it's possible to do that now. Kent Gunderson told me to get the Martin guys together tomorrow and have an 'in-house' meeting to prepare for Tuesday's session. I asked him if it would be all right to invite you to join. Since he doesn't know you, he was kind of hesitant, but he finally agreed."

"I had a similar thought about a pre-meeting get together," said Toms, "but why exclude half the team? Let's also invite the IBM troops."

"I'll go along with that, but I would rather not have Downes there. His presence alone would be enough to ruin it. One of the big reasons that we have started to make progress is that he has been making himself scare lately."

"Okay, we'll exclude Downes," said Toms, "but the reason that we'll exclude him is because he seems to set everyone's teeth on edge—not because he is the single reason that things are fouled up."

Taylor grinned slowly. "Roger," he said, "I have never said anything negative to you or to anyone about Downes. I know that he's not to blame for everything that has gone wrong. In fact, I know—as does everyone else—that if it wasn't for him, there wouldn't be any OCALA. He's the one who conceived it, and the man who pushed it through. But after that, he should have bowed out."

"You may be right," said Toms. "He seems to know his hardware, and he is a damned fine salesman . . . but he does wear thin after a while. But you know . . . I truly believe he has the best interests of the project at heart, no matter what screwy things he does . . . and I am not going to kick him in the teeth just because he is in over his head."

"No argument," said Taylor. "As long as he keeps away, I think everything will be fine."

"Good," said Toms, "let's set up the meeting for tomorrow morning at nine. You contact the Martin guys, and I'll get in touch with the IBM troops."

"Fine, I'll see you in the morning, then," said Taylor.

"Right, Claude," said Toms, "see you tomorrow."

Case 3–3

Dumas Public Library*

Mark Hammer and Gary Whitney

PART 1

It came as a surprise when Jeff Mallet learned of the conflict between Debra Dickenson and Helen Hendricks because he knew them both personally and regarded them both as competent administrators. Debra Dickenson, 38, was the youngest mayor in the state when she was elected three years ago, and was the first female mayor in Kimball's history. She was widely recognized for her high levels of energy and dedication. Helen Hendricks, 62, had been the head librarian at Dumas Public Library for 15 years and was widely acknowledged among Kimball citizens as being primarily responsible for the high quality of the library services to the community.

Dumas Public Library serves the citizens of Kimball, New Mexico, a town of 20,000 people in rural eastern New Mexico. Kimball is dominated by the 16,000-student state university located there and this university presence creates a rather unique clientele for the public library. The library has enjoyed a history of solid citizen support and has until recently benefited from cordial relations between the library staff and the city's administration.

The library is housed in a modern, air conditioned structure with carpeted floors and attractive furnishings. Approximately 35,000 volumes are on the shelves. The 1978 budget, including payroll, acquisition of new books, and building maintenance, was $195,000.

---

* Copyright © by Mark Hammer and Gary Whitney, 1979.

The library has no formal organization. Helen Hendricks has reporting to her five full-time employees, three of whom are professional librarians. Completing the staff are 10 half-time permanent employees, 10 to 12 unpaid volunteers, and an occasional intern from the university.

The city is governed by an elected city council and mayor. Day-to-day administration is the responsibility of Ralph Riesen, the city supervisor, who is a permanent employee of the city.

Jeff Mallet, professor of management, first learned about the existence of strained relationships between the library and the city administration from Linda Turner, adult services librarian. According to Linda, feelings of distrust and animosity toward City Hall had been growing recently among the library staff. Linda was concerned about the unhealthy climate that this hostility was creating at the library.

Several weeks later Jeff had an opportunity to talk with Debra Dickenson and Ralph Riesen. Jeff said he had heard that relations between City Hall and the library were not good. Debra and Ralph confirmed that relations between the two groups had reached an intolerably low level, and they agreed something would have to be done about it. Debra and Ralph expressed bewilderment about what could be done to improve the situation. "If you have any ideas or suggestions, I'd certainly like to hear them," Debra said.

Jeff suggested that it might prove helpful to have an outsider interview members of both groups to provide some independent perspective. He volunteered his services for this purpose. Debra and Ralph readily agreed to Jeff's offer.

The next day Jeff was talking to Paul Everest, a fellow business faculty member and consultant, about the situation at the library. Jeff invited Paul to join him on the case and Paul accepted.

Next week Jeff made a series of personal visits and phone calls to the key staff members from City Hall and the library. An agreement was reached to have Jeff and Paul interview both groups and make recommendations. Appointments were made for an interview with Debras Dickenson and Ralph Riesen at City Hall, followed by one with Helen Hendricks, Linda Turner, and Maude Richardson (children's librarian) at the library.

PART 2:
The View from City Hall
As Told to Jeff Mallet and Paul Everest

Debra: I'm really concerned about the way things have developed between us here at City Hall and the library staff. There is animosity between these two groups, and the situation has been worse over the past few months. There's not nearly the level of cooperation that there should be.

I'll be eager to consider any suggestions that you *[professors]* might have for how to improve the situation. I know that something has to be done, and I'm willing to devote some time and effort to working on it.

The problem at the library is that I no longer have administrative control over their operations. In the past, the library has reported to the mayor through the city supervisor and that has worked reasonably well. Recently however, we discovered that legislation passed back in the 1930s makes it very clear that the library board of trustees has the legal authority for the conduct of the day-to-day operations of the library.

My concern is that since the library is a part of the city administration, the city is legally responsible for its operations. I'm talking specifically about legal liability for such things as personnel selection, equal employment opportunity regulations, purchasing guidelines, and budgeting procedures set down by the state. In the case of lawsuits and budget overruns, it seems clear to me that the city will be liable and hence we need to have administrative control over these matters. Also, it just makes good common sense for us to coordinate certain administrative functions from City Hall, such as personnel selection and budgeting. Basically the library staff agrees with us on this, and we have been doing many of these functions at City Hall.

One of the things that irks me most about Helen Hendricks *[head librarian]* and her staff is that they continue to insist on politicizing the budget making process, even when they know or should know that this is an extremely disruptive and unfair practice. I have made it pretty clear to all the department heads within the city that the budget making process should be one where budget requests are submitted to the city administration and to the City Council along with the implications of funding increases or decreases. Based on that input, the City Council then decides on the services that it wants in a nonemotional manner. The City Council represents the citizens and that is a perfectly democratic procedure.

Prior to the recent budget preparation period, the City Council gave budget directives to all city departments. The library board chose to ignore these directives and submitted their own budget. Subsequently, the library staff started a big political campaign to pack the council chambers at all the budget hearings with patrons of the library and other citizens who supported the library's request for more funding.

I have tried to point out to Helen how disruptive and unfair this is. The fact is that almost every city department serves some constituency and could, if they were so inclined, rally citizen support from among their clients or constituents to bring political pressure to bear on the City Council and other members of the city administration to fund their individual projects. It seems obvious to me that this is a chaotic way to try to prepare a city budget. Special interest politics has no place in the preparation of the city budget which is fair to all parties concerned. Only people who have looked at the entire city budget and have considered the total revenues available to the city and the cost and benefit tradeoffs made by each one of the city departments are in any position to judge whether any particular department is reasonably funded or not. The fact is that there are prime financial needs in all of the city departments and the library is not alone.

I support the library wholeheartedly; we all do. I'm just not one bit impressed when the librarians campaign to have a flock of citizens pack the council chambers to stand there and tell us that they support the library. That is not a helpful input to the budget making process. Everybody supports the library.

Following one occurrence of inappropriate political lobbying last fall, I expressed my annoyance to Walter Roy *[chairperson of the library board of trustees]*. Subsequently, Helen was told by the board to cease her lobbying activities. I think she got the message, but I know the lobbying did not stop. That tells me that the trustees do not have control over the library staff.

Don't get me wrong. Helen Hendricks has done a marvelous job down there at the library, but things just haven't been the same since her husband died unexpectedly two years ago. She seems to have retreated into a womb or something. I think she uses the library staff as a personal support group. I don't know who is running the library anymore, but it certainly isn't Helen. I think the staff is running the library to tell you the truth.

Ralph: I too have noticed the worsening relations between us and the library staff. Part of the problem may be the physical isolation of the library and the fact that they don't interact much with other city personnel. *[The library is three blocks from City Hall.]*

If you ask me I think there is a case of paranoia down there at the library. Some of them seem to believe that I'm out to get them. In fact, I have a definite feeling that several of the library staff members think that I'm some sort of an ogre.

I think many of the problems that the library staff think they have are more imaginary than real. I remember once I talked to Helen and she was complaining about some things. I asked her to make a list of grievances that they had, ways in which they had less money or things that weren't satisfactory. Do you know, I've never gotten any list from Helen. I really don't think they have any substantial problems that aren't of their own making.

Debra: I get the impression that the library staff feels that they are picked on and mistreated. The fact is that the library has the best working conditions of almost any other department in the city. Not only are their working conditions congenial and agreeable, but the clientele they serve are all happy and supportive of the library. It's a totally positive environment. That's quite a bit different from the city engineer's department where they have to talk to irate contractors and home owners, or the police who have to deal with drug offenders and unhappy traffic violators.

I'm still very confused about the proper roles of the library administration, the library board of trustees, and the city administration.

Ralph: Lynn King *[the city Finance Director]* is another player in this scenario. Lynn probably has more interaction with the library staff on a day-to-day basis than anybody else here in City Hall. She deals with them on matters of auditing, purchasing procedures, and employee selection procedures. There have been disagreements and friction generated over a number of these issues. Lynn really distrusts Helen as an administrator.

Debra: I really would like to hear from the library staff on their perceptions of what our problems are. I don't really know what they think.

One of the areas that Helen and I have had disagreements on has been that of Helen's classification within the city administrative system. Helen seems to think that she should be classified as a department director. The trouble is that Helen's responsibilties are simply not equivalent to those of other department directors within the city. Each of the other directors has at least two major administrative functions reporting to him or her. For example, the director of public safety has both police and fire reporting to him.

When we reorganized the city administration recently, we changed it so that Helen was reporting to the mayor through the director of public services, Jack Feldner. Helen got all bent out of shape that she wasn't reporting directly to the mayor and that she had to report through someone else. She made such a fuss about it that we finally agreed to her request and Ralph issued a memo of understanding to Helen to the effect that she still had direct access to us here at City Hall and that we would interact with her on a direct basis.

One of the City Council members introduced a proposal to classify Helen as a department head recently, but this proposal was withdrawn at my request. I'm afraid that as a result some people are getting the impression that I am not really supportive of the library. I really am, but my concern in this matter is with equity—all the other department directors have considerably more administrative responsibility than Helen does and they wouldn't consider it fair to have Helen classified as a department director.

Ralph: Helen keeps raising the issue of her salary level. I'm convinced that Helen is fairly paid in relation to other city employees. The trouble is that all city employees are underpaid compared to university salaries and we're *never* going to catch up. Dissatisfaction with pay is just one of those things that we have to accept and live with.

Despite what Helen says, I don't think salary is that big a problem. I remember from the supervision class that you *[Jeff]* taught that according to Herzberg, pay is a hygiene factor. I don't think that we're going to solve any big problems down at the library by working on hygiene factors.

Debra: An incident that happened recently will illustrate what I consider to be totally unprofessional conduct on the part of the library staff. As you know, I recently refused to reappoint Cecil Hockman to the library board of trustees after his first term expired. Now as the mayor, I have the duty and obligation to the citizens of Kimball to appoint people to boards that I think are best qualified to do the jobs. I had my reasons for not reappointing Cecil, reasons which I consider to be good. Because we are making agreements with the trustees about the administration of the library, I want trustees who will work with us to try to reach a compromise. Cecil has never agreed to any compromise action and would stop library cooperative efforts.

What happened was that somebody down at the library called a reporter and told them about my refusal to reappoint Cecil Hockman. They apparently said that I had a vendetta going against Cecil and that a reporter should look into this. The reporter did check with Mr. Hockman and got a bunch of quotes from him concerning my nonsupport for library programs. Then the reporter called me and asked me if I wanted to respond to the charges. *I was furious.* I told her, "No, I do not want to respond." I did explain my duties and responsibilities as mayor to the reporter and she subsequently decided that there was no story.

Sometimes I feel like calling Helen up here on the carpet and telling her to shape up her act or get out. It becomes clearer to me all the time that whatever else she is, Helen is not a competent administrator.

If the problems we're having with administration at the library can't be solved we are going to be forced to look at the issue of regionalization of this library; that is, of having the city library join the county system along with the library in Morton. However, it is apparent to me that the idea of regionalization is extremely threatening to everybody down at the library. This showed up recently when the Capital Expenditures Committee recommended, among other things in its report to City Council, that the feasibility of regionalization of the city's library, cemetery, and health care facilities be studied. You wouldn't believe how upset the librarians became over that recommendation. They got a City Council member to make a motion that the recommendation be deleted from the committee's report, and unfortunately it passed. The librarians clearly didn't even want the issue studied!

PART 3:
The View from the Library
As Told to Jeff Mallet and Paul Everest

Helen: I'm surprised and delighted to hear you *[professors]* report that Debra Dickenson and Ralph Riesen are really interested in improving relations with us here at the library. I feel that we have been wasting a lot of time down here because of the poor relations we have with City Hall, and I wasn't at all sure how concerned they felt about it up there.

One of the main problems that I see between us and the city administration is their general resentment toward anything involving political pressure. I sense that Debra and Ralph get upset when the community voices opinions which are contrary to their views. I sometimes get the feeling that they would like to run the city without interference from citizens. However, that's the very nature of the political process. The mayor's job is inherently a political one. You shouldn't be in that position and expect to be immune from public pressure. So, I don't think it's appropriate that Debra gets upset when the citizens rally to support a program that they want.

During the recent budget hearings we have had lots of good people come to our defense. The library board of trustees have been very supportive. The AAUW *[American Association of University Women]* has several members who have been strong supporters. These friends have been instrumental in helping us make the case to the mayor and the City Council that the community really supports a quality program here at the library.

Linda: We don't seem to have any problems of misunderstanding or non-support from either the library board of trustees or the City Council. I feel good about our relations with both of these groups. When we have gone to the City Council with our recommendations and proposals, they have been sympathetic and supportive. In the budget hearings both the library board and the City Council supported our proposed budget over the objections of Debra and Ralph. In effect, we bypassed the city administration and we came out better than if we had gone to them first, as they apparently wanted us to do.

One example of a way in which we have felt "under attack" by City Hall has been the way they have acted in regard to the appointment of members of the library board of trustees.

Helen: That's right. You probably heard that just recently Debra refused to reappoint Cecil Hockman to the board for a second term. Now Cecil has been a strong, energetic supporter of the library. He has given a great deal of his time and dedication to public service on the library board. Mr. Hockman's first term on the board has just recently expired, and for no apparent reason Debra has declined to reappoint him, even though it has been customary in the past that members serve for two terms. So, Cecil Hockman is not only eligible for reappointment, but he has demonstrated in his first term that he is a dedicated and concerned public citizen.

It seems apparent to us that Debra resents anyone who supports the library as strongly as Cecil Hockman did. You see, Cecil initiated some legal research which determined that the library board of trustees has the ulti- mate legislative authority for the administration of the library. Further- more, Cecil Hockman took the initiative to argue our budget proposals before the City Council. Debra did not appreciate either of these, I am sure, and now it seems that she is out to get him.

In the past, I have always participated with the mayor when selecting candidates for the library board. The mayor has always been glad to have my input and opinion on which citizens would be good for the library board. None of that consultation has gone on between Debra and me recently; I just find out about her board appointments by reading the newspaper.

Linda: Another way that we have felt attacked by the city administration has been the way we were treated in the recent reorganization of the city administrative hierarchy.

Helen: What they did was to demote the library by changing the reporting patterns so that instead of reporting directly to the city supervisor, I was directed to report through Jack Feldner, the director of public services.

This reassignment of the library was a serious downgrading of our status within the city. I was really upset when I learned that they expected me to report *through* Jack Feldner. Why, I have more education than Jack does, I have longer service to the City of Kimball than he does, and I supervise a *lot* of people here at the library. The very idea that the library with its staff of professionals should be considered subordinate to some- one whose main concern is parks and recreation was an appalling idea to us over here. You see, that demotes us from one of the major functional units within the city administration to merely one of the concerns of the Parks and Recreation Department. I don't have anything against Jack Feldner, but I don't think it's right to have the city library subordinate to him and his department.

I was told that in the reorganization of the city administration I was not considered an administrator *[department director level]* because I supervise so few people. However, Lynn King *[finance director]* only super- vises a few people, and she doesn't have the education I do either.

Maude: I don't think that they regard us as professionals over here, but we *are* professionals. Each one of us has had five years of college plus additional professional training, and yet we continually get treated as if we were mere clerks.

Linda: An incident which illustrates the library's diminished status was City Hall's insistance that Helen could not retain the title of "library director." The title library director is common among librarians have similar jobs to Helen's. Among the staff here at the library, it seems the logical choice of position titles. And yet the city administration insisted that Helen could not be called a "director." So they suggested that we call her the "library su- pervisor." Of course, "supervisor" denotes someone just above the clerical level; someone who is supervising a bunch of clerks. That seems natural to them, but the idea is appalling over here. We hassled back and forth over different possible titles for Helen's position and finally settled on "city librarian." This title is less descriptive than "library director" and reflects Helen's lowered status in the city.

Maude: I don't think Helen is regarded as an administrator by the city admin- istration. I don't think they really know how many people she has reporting to her, or how much leadership it takes to coordinate all the volunteer help we have. Helen has a substantial administrative job to keep this library running smoothly.

Helen: Going along with that is their resistance to paying me a salary reflecting my abilities and contribution. My salary is simply not in line with the requirements of this job, my education, and the experience I have with the City of Kimball. I know that I'm paid less than many other people in the city who have less education and less experience than I do. The city administration simply refuses to recognize the importance of my job.

Jeff: How would your salary compare, Helen, to other library directors having similar jobs around the state?

Helen: Well, I would have to say that my salary today reflects some very significant adjustments upward which were made during the 1960s. At that time the university was under heavy pressure to equalize the salaries of its female professionals, and the City of Kimball also upgraded their women's salaries at the same time. So I shared with some other women in some impressive gains during the 1960s.

If you looked just at the figures, my salary wouldn't look that far off relative to other city librarians. However, the figures don't reflect the quality of education I have received, the length of my service to the City of Kimball, and the contributions that I have made to the development of this library today.

Jeff: Could you give us an example or two of specific ways that the library's effectiveness has been impaired by the actions of members of the city administration?

Helen: Certainly. One good example would be the copier incident. That's a long story. Sometime ago we experienced an equipment failure with the copier which we had for patrons to use. Therefore, I asked permission from the board of trustees to allocate Kimball Fund [donated] money to purchase a new copier, and they approved. I went ahead with procedures to order a new copier. The next thing that I learned was that Debra had disallowed the purchase. She said that I should have checked with her first.

I was flabbergasted. I had never felt that I had to check with the mayor on decisions like that. Furthermore, I was angry because she had ruled on the decision without checking into what the reasons for it were. I felt "zapped" by Debra, like I have in several other situations.

It seems to me that I did the right thing by checking with my board of trustees on the decision I made. As you know, by legislation they have the responsibility for the administrative functions of the library. When they have approved a decision like this, what basis does the mayor have for interfering in our decision?

Another way that Debra has demonstrated her lack of support for the library is by advancing the idea that the library should be regionalized to become a part of the county system. Anybody who knows anything about the library regards this as a preposterous idea.

In the first place, to seriously consider the idea of regionalization you would have to undertake a rather comprehensive study of the consequences. That in itself would be a major, expensive undertaking, which I don't think Debra is ready to shoulder. It is clear to me if such a study were done, the result would overwhelmingly favor the present organizational arrangement. We have very little in common with the Morton Library, and nothing at all to be gained by being put in the county system.

Kimball is a unique community with citizens who have very different expectations from those in the remainder of the county, which is largely rural. The whole idea of regionalization is so preposterous that it seems to me to be irresponsible to even advance the idea.

I get the feeling that Debra is accumulating a checklist against me. I have had a fear for sometime now that Debra could at any time try to have me fired. I get the feeling in talking to them that I'm not getting straight messages from them.

At least there's one thing to be grateful for—I just passed my 62d birthday and can't be deprived of my pension if I am fired or forced to resign. I would like to stay on until I am 65, but the way things are going between Debra and me I never know.

I get to feeling sad and hopeless and despairing when I think about the way I'm regarded at City Hall. I think it's tragic when someone like me has given many dedicated years of service and has made major contributions to building a strong program, and then finds themselves spending their last few years in an atmosphere of distrust and unappreciation. I think I deserve better.

Linda: The distrust in our relationship shows itself practically every time we have an interaction. Recently I have taken on the duties of adult services librarian and have been out visiting members of other city departments discussing ways that the library could be of service to them. I have had really warm and friendly receptions from everybody I have visited, with the exception of Ralph Riesen. When I talked to him in the same way that I had the other people, I felt like I got a cold shoulder. He seemed very uninterested. What I would most like would be to talk straight to Debra and Ralph and get straight answers in return.

Helen: We shouldn't overlook the fact that there have been some positive developments recently. For example, the new personnel officer, Joyce Gardner, came down and visited us last week. She was very understanding and very sympathetic about our problems. I am rather optimistic that many of our problems concerning selection, advertising, and interviewing will be better now that Joyce is here.

Linda: The recent hiring of two part-time people with Joyce's advice and help is an example of how well things *can* be done and how we and the city administration can work together. We should find more ways to use our separate expertise cooperatively!

Helen: Also, I am encouraged by the cooperation I have been getting from Jack Feldner. He recently responded favorably to my request for a crew to come over here and help with moving books away from an area where we had a leaking roof. I haven't always felt that I've had Jack's complete support and cooperation, but lately I've been feeling better about that.

One example of an item I'll bet is on Debra's checklist against me is the fact that the library is over its budget this year. Now the reason for this is that since the budgeting processes have been centralized in City Hall, I simply haven't had access to the kind of information I need to keep track of the budget. I'm afraid that I'm going to be unjustifiably blamed for this situation. This is an example of the kind of information I should not have to ask for—they should automatically give it to me.

Linda: I *am* concerned about the way that these crises with the city affect our morale and productivity. I have observed that when these crises come up we of the staff cease to care about our work as much, we spend *much* time rehashing incidents to reassure ourselves, and we do not do as good a job because we do not feel secure or appreciated. I am amazed to see myself doing this, as I like my job, but I do find myself lowering the quality of my work when I feel threatened, and I see others doing it too. So, continued bad feelings are counterproductive and inefficient.

Maude: One indicator of the kind of relationship which Debra has with us down here in the library is the reaction she gets when she comes down here. I remember a time when she was down here recently. We were all very nervous and very alert. It was like we all suspected that she was up to no good being down here, and we had to watch her every step.

PART 4:
Meetings 1 and 2

After reviewing what they had learned in the meetings with City Hall and the library staff, Jeff and Paul decided to recommend a series of four two-hour meetings. They formulated tentative meeting agendas and sent copies to each of the five prospective participants. After informal checks had established the agreement of each of the five to the proposed meetings, the consultants sent a confirming memo to each, announcing the time and place for each of the four meetings.

Meeting 1: March 19

The agenda presented by the consultants for the first meeting included a brief introduction by the consultants, an expectations check, a sharing appreciation exercise, and a closing process check.

Following the introduction, the participants were asked to participate in an expectations check. For the first half of this exercise each person was asked to write on two separate sheets of paper (1) their hopes, and (2) their fears for the upcoming series of meetings. In the second half of the exercise these hopes and fears were shared, posted on newsprint, and discussed. This exercise activity took about 40 minutes.

The "sharing appreciations" exercise contained four steps. In the first step each of the participants was given three-by-five-inch cards and asked to write appreciation messages to the other participants. Each message was to be addressed to another person on a separate card and was to be unsigned. A format suggested was: "I appreciate _____ about you." Each person was asked to write at least one such message to each of the other four participants present.

In step two of the appreciations exercise the cards were collected and sorted and then read by one facilitator while the other wrote the appreciations on newsprint. The result was one large newsprint sheet of appreciation messages for each of the five participants.

In step three each person was instructed to add to their individual sheets other things for which they would like to be appreciated, or for which they felt they deserved appreciation.

Step four consisted of a series of one-on-one conferences where each participant met individually with each of the other four participants for five minutes. During these conferences each member of the pair was asked to *acknowledge* to the other person the appreciations which had been contributed by other participants, and further to acknowledge the appreciations which he or she had contributed or agreed with. The sharing appreciations exercise took about 30 minutes.

The final activity for Meeting 1 was a process check, where participants were invited to share their feelings about the activities of the first meeting and about the upcoming meetings.

The expectations check generated a list of hopes and fears which was posted on two large sheets of newsprint. The main themes reflected in the "hopes" list included desires to improve working relations and communications between the library and the city, to clarify reporting patterns, to know others as individuals, to develop a more relaxed atmosphere among group members, to confront differences, to reduce felt threats, and to restore library staff confidence.

The list of fears included the following: that the library would become even more committed to single-issue political activity; that the meetings would result in "unpleasant repercussions" for some; that information shared in the meetings would get out and be damaging or embarrassing; that the meetings would be a waste of time; that the library would move further away from the rest of the city and become more entrenched; and that Debra and Ralph would become too busy to attend one or more of the meetings.

The general mood during the meeting was one of caution. Jeff and Paul noted that the appreciations shared were quite general and that some uneasiness was sensed during the appreciation sharing exercise. The process check at the end of the meeting revealed mildly positive reactions. Ralph seemed cool and reserved; he said that there were no dramatic gains but that he was willing to continue. Linda seconded Ralph's sentiment. Debra and Maude seemed to be more positive and appeared to feel reassured. Helen appeared to have very positive feelings about the meeting; she expressed reduced apprehensions about the meetings and increased comfort with the other participants.

Meeting 2: March 21

The meeting began with a brief introduction to the planned activities by Paul. He also apologized for having to leave early that day. Instructions were then given for the first phase of an "image exchange" exercise. Participants were told that each group was to meet in a separate room and prepare two lists. The first list was to summarize their own group's images of the other group, including thoughts, attitudes, feelings, perceptions, and behavior. The second list was to predict what the other group's images recorded in their first list would be.

After approximately 30 minutes of list preparation time, the two groups were reconvened to share the lists. During the list-sharing period a ground rule was enforced which disallowed debate and discussion but which allowed questions for clarification.

EXHIBIT 1
Image Exchange Data From Second Meeting
of City Hall and Library Administration

A.   Library Administration views of City Hall
    1.   They are suspicious of the library.
    2.   They are well-intentioned but inept.
    3.   They are uninterested in the library program.
    4.   They are protective of their own power.
    5.   They are unfriendly.
    6.   They want the library to accept administrative changes from City Hall, but are unwilling to accept administrative changes made by the Library Board.
    7.   They don't really want public input.
    8.   They are very willing to put Library Staff (especially Helen) between power play of City Hall and the Library Board.
    9.   They are personally against Helen.

B.   City Hall views of Library Administration
    1.   They have limited or no respect for the administrative abilities of City Hall.
    2.   "Massive paranoia" exists among the Library Staff.
    3.   The librarians have been operating a propaganda organ:
        a.   Internally with Library Staff.
        b.   Externally with City Council and the public.
    4.   The Library Staff has used the Library Board as a separate political support group.
    5.   There has been a concerted program by the librarians to establish a separate political base and become invulnerable.
    6.   Library personnel operate a tight "clique."
    7.   Library personnel distrust (and dislike and despise . . .) City Hall.
    8.   Library personnel wish to do their own thing without coordination.
    9.   Library personnel don't readily accept administrative assistance.

C.   Library Administration's predictions of City Hall views of Library Administration
    1.   They think we are paranoid.
    2.   They think we are snobbish and isolated.
    3.   They think we are spreading our views of the problem among staff and public.
    4.   They think we are overprotective of the library.
    5.   They think we are inappropriately political.
    6.   They think we are encouraging the Library Board to move away from City Hall.

D.   City Hall's predictions of Library views of City Hall
    1.   They think that we believe the library is not a critical service; it is dispensable, or first to go in a crunch.
    2.   They think we are nonsupportive of the library.
    3.   They think we discriminate against the library.
    4.   They think we impose unreasonable guidelines.
    5.   They think we have a vendetta against the library.
    6.   They think we are uncaring and unhelpful.
    7.   They think that the library gets the short end of resource allocations.
    8.   They think that we are fast to control and restrict, but seldom volunteer assistance.

The librarians were invited to share their list of images of the city administration first. As they did so, Jeff (Paul had gone) summarized the entries on newsprint. Next the city administration's images of the library were shared and posted. Time was allowed for clarification questions after each list had been aired.

Next the two groups shared their predictions of the other group's list with the librarians again going first. The time required for the sharing of the four lists was approximately 40 minutes. These four lists are reproduced in Exhibit 1.

Following the image exchange periods the groups were again sent to separate rooms. This time each group was instructed to create a prioritized list of issues needing resolution. Twenty minutes was allocated for this activity.

The final activity of Meeting 2 was the sharing of the two lists of priority issues. Exhibit 2 shows the priority issues which were generated in this activity. This sharing and posting used up the remainder of the meeting time available.

EXHIBIT 2
Priority Issues for Resolution
Second Meeting, City Hall and Library Administration

A. Priorities of Library Staff
   1. Clarify the role of the Library Board of Trustees:
       a. Statewide.
       b. Citywide.
       c. Vis-á-vis the library staff.
   2. Clarify the roles of the library's staff, library administration, and City Hall.
   3. Reach agreement regarding appropriate political activity for the library.
   4. Develop mutual respect for one anothers' administrative abilities.
B. Priorities of City Hall
   1. (Debra) Inappropriate political activity.
   2. (Ralph) Resolve the perception that City Hall is doing something "bad" to Helen, i.e., perceived vendetta.
   3. Library's impression that City Hall is uninterested in the library program.
   4. Library's impression that members of City Hall are being protective of their own power.

At the conclusion of the meeting, Jeff's impression was that there was a general sense of tension relief that this long-repressed animosity was finally out in the open. Debra appeared to feel particularly good about the meeting when she left. Jeff was impressed by the casualness and informality with which Ralph engaged in musing conversation concerning the meeting with the three librarians for 15 minutes after the meeting. This was the first time that Jeff could remember Ralph's being relaxed and at ease in any of the meetings concerning the library. Jeff guessed that Ralph might have felt good that some real progress had been made during this meeting.

Two days after this meeting, Linda reported to Jeff that the librarians left the meeting feeling quite discouraged.

Consultants' Meeting: March 22

Jeff Mallet and Paul Everest met at Paul's house to compare notes on the progress of the meetings so far, and to discuss strategy for the up-coming meetings.

When Paul saw the two priority lists of issues for resolution which had been generated by the two groups, he had an immediate reaction. Paul noted that the items listed by the librarians appeared to reflect a willing-ness to compromise, collaborate, or negotiate; whereas, those items listed by Debra and Ralph appeared to reflect the expectation that it was the library which should do the changing. Jeff and Paul wondered if this was a pattern. They recalled other times when they had vague feelings that perhaps Debra or Ralph or both regarded the meetings as an opportunity to get the library to shape up. Following the meeting, Jeff had the feeling that the three librarians had seemed to take the instructions and the sessions more seriously than did Debra and Ralph. Jeff had hoped that the period for sharing the four lists would leave everyone in an introspective mood. This seemed to take place for the librarians, but not for Debra and Ralph.

After reflecting on the outcomes from Meeting 2, Jeff reported feeling overwhelmed by the pervasiveness of the issue concerning appropriate political activity. His review had led him to the conclusion that this issue was so fundamental to all the problems being experienced between the library and City Hall that it was likely to be futile to work on any specific issues before addressing this major one.

As Jeff saw it, there were two major questions which needed to be resolved. First, what is the relationship of the library board of trustees to City Hall? And second, how are the diametrically opposed views expressed by the library and City Hall concerning appropriate political activity going to be resolved? It seemed to Jeff that neither of these issues could be settled by the group which had been meeting with Jeff and Paul. Instead, it seemed more plausible that these issues needed to be referred to either the library board or to the City Council.

Paul agreed that there were no instant solutions in sight, and that the appropriate strategy for where to go with the present group was not at all apparent.

After some discussion, Paul and Jeff agreed on the prognosis that until the overriding issue of political activity was dealt with, administrative issues would probably be resistant to solution. They further agreed that it seemed unlikely that solutions to the political activity question could be generated from within the present group, and that action strategies to address this issue probably would have to come from the City Council or the Library Board.

Concerning strategy for Meeting 3, Paul and Jeff agreed to begin it by reviewing for the participants the consultants' interpretations of the outcome of Meeting 2 and to invite them to join in a problem-solving session concerning appropriate action strategies. Paul and Jeff could think of two strategies which might prove fruitful:

1. Refer the issue of appropriateness of political activity to the City Council with a request for a definitive guideline on what activities are appropriate.
2. Have Debra and Helen get together, with or without a process consultant, to work out an agreement concerning political activity.

Jeff and Paul discussed whether the issue of the newspaper reporter being called should be brought up and dealt with at the next meeting. They agreed that Debra had stored up much resentment over this issue, and that if it came out it could be a "heavy" confrontation. Jeff and Paul were very uncertain about whether the issue could be constructively dealt with in one meeting. The uncertainties concerning the outcome of such a confrontation led Paul and Jeff to agree that they should probably try to avoid confronting this issue at the next meeting.

PART 5:
MEETINGS 3 AND 4

Meeting 3: March 26

As Jeff and Paul arrived at the Savings Bank Community Room for Meeting 3, they exchanged the sentiment, "God knows what's going to happen today!"

As participants entered the meeting room, they were given a three-page handout summarizing the previous meetings' outcomes. This handout contained the data generated in Meeting 2 from the image exchange exercise and the priority issues for resolution list (Exhibits 2 and 3).

Jeff began by sharing some of his and Paul's reflections concerning the pervasiveness of the political issue. He raised the question about whether administrative concerns could be addressed while the political issue remained unsolved. He further voiced some skepticism concerning whether the present group was the appropriate one to settle the political issue, or whether it could.

At this time, Jeff spent some time reflecting on the nature of the conflict over political activities. He tried to summarize the position of each of the two parties to the conflict. In doing this Jeff emphasized his understanding that each of the parties had a position which was logically defensible, internally consistent, and supportable by others.

Jeff concluded by inviting the group members to comment on the consultants' diagnosis of the problem, and to join in a problem-solving session to identify reasonable options which could be taken. The remainder of the meeting time was used for unstructured discussion, with the exception of a brief process check at the end of the meeting.

Paul served in a process observation role during this meeting. During the time that Jeff was giving an overview of the problem situation, Paul noted the reactions of the five participants. Linda, Helen, and Ralph all seemed quite attentive. Debra and Maude were observed to be staring intently at their handouts for long periods of time. This was particularly true for Maude, who hardly shifted her gaze from her handout for almost 20 minutes. Paul noted that Maude looked dejected, and that she was avoiding eye contact with others present. Because the meeting room was chilly, Maude (along with most of the others) was feeling physically cold. Maude had also mentioned that she was coming down with a cold.

After Jeff had finished his introductory remarks, Debra abruptly initiated a discussion of political activity on the part of the library staff. Debra's remarks may be paraphrased as follows:

> Politics is a fact of life now. The library staff has started something that will be very hard to stop. They have politicized the budgeting process and it will be very hard to go back to a nonpolitical procedure. What I need to know from the library staff is whether these activities are going to continue. If they are, there are going to be unpleasant repercussions which the library staff should understand.
>
> There are two things that are really bothering me; first, the fact that someone from the library called a newspaper reporter to ask that my "vendetta" against Cecil Hockman and the library be investigated. When I got that telephone call from the reporter, I felt "angry, betrayed, and nonplussed." Second is the issue of political activity by library staff members aimed at packing the City Council chambers with citizens supporting the library. That represents a clear violation of instructions from the library board, and leads me to wonder, "Who's running the library, anyway?"

When Debra made the point that the library staff had disregarded instructions concerning political activity, Helen pointed out that the library staff did not perceive that they had received any such instructions. Following Helen's point, discussion proceeded in another direction, with no overt evidence that Helen's comment was heard or understood.

Following Debra's expression of her feelings about the telephone call, Helen and Linda expressed consternation that the telephone call had been made. Both made it very clear that they thought such a telephone call was inappropriate. Linda said, "I didn't realize we had sunk to that low a level," and Helen seconded Linda's sentiment. During this conversation Maude was noticeably quiet, and was avoiding eye contact.

Ralph said, "When I come in the library, I feel hostility all around me." When Ralph had said this, Paul intervened and asked Ralph to focus on his personal feelings when he was in this situation. Ralph's reponses generally depicted his impressions of library staff members' attitudes. Paul pursued the issue by asking Ralph two more times to focus on and report his own feelings in this situation. After Ralph's responses again did not describe his own feelings, Jeff probed him by asking if he might have been feeling hurt, or disliked, or disrespected. In response to this prompting Ralph acknowledged that some of these guesses were accurate.

At this point Paul intervened with a few observations designed to set the stage for the librarians to air some of their feelings. With a few minor exceptions, the librarians did not divulge their feelings on issues.

At one point in the conversation Debra offered "to spend a week working in the library," if that would help to resolve some of the problems. Helen responded to this offer with apparent guardedness, citing the difficulties of time scheduling and the requirements of attending the human understanding workshops currently being conducted for all city employees. Debra seemed annoyed that Helen's reaction to her offer was not totally positive. At this point Maude made a pointed observation to Debra: "I have to tell you that there are some people in the library who will be pretty hostile toward you."

The question of whether the library should regionalize by joining the Morton County system was raised. Debra expressed dismay that the library staff, the library board of trustees, and several others had reacted so vehemently to the proposal that regionalization should be studied. The librarians responded to Debra's sentiment by assertively pointing out that the proposal (which had been part of a report to the City Council by the Capital Expenditures Committee) did not call for a study but called for *implementation* which was to occur by January 1, 1980. Both Debra and Ralph replied that they were sure that the wording of the Capital Expenditures Committee report was that the January 1, 1980, date was the deadline for *completion of a study.* The librarians were equally certain that their interpretation of the report was correct. Members of both groups vowed to get a copy of the committee report to bring to the next meeting.

Discussion of the regionalization issue continued. Helen referred to a previous study concerning regionalization which had been conducted by the League of Women Voters. This study had gathered some utilization data. Helen felt that the study supported her opinion that regionalization would be most unwise. Debra said that she had not seen or heard of the league's study, and was very interested: "That's the kind of information I need to know."

At this point one of the librarians volunteered that they had prepared a "fact sheet" concerning the regionalization issue. Debra expressed surprise at hearing about the fact sheet. Paul noted that Debra seemed annoyed about learning about the fact sheet, and that Ralph gave the librarians a dirty look during this time. The librarians at this point explained that the fact sheet was prepared in response to a request by an individual City Council member.

Lively discussion of substantive issues was continuing when Jeff interrupted at a few minutes before the end of the meeting time to ask for a process check. During this check the general sentiment expressed was, "Whew! we really got into it today!" Linda said that she thought a lot had been accomplished, and nods of agreement from other participants were noted. Ralph acknowledged some real accomplishment for the first time. Paul and Jeff shared both surprise and relief that the issue concerning the reporter had been successfully dealt with and largely defused. In fact, they expressed the view that the whole issue of political activity had been defused at least somewhat.

Meeting 4: March 25

The meeting began with Paul and Jeff suggesting a review of the "Priority Issues for Resolution" list generated in Meeting 2. The consultants suggested that the group make an "action/no action" decision for each of the priority issues. This was to provide some closure for this last of four scheduled meetings.

During the last half of the meeting Paul started an action list on news-

EXHIBIT 3
City Hall and Library Administration Action List

Issue	*Action*
Calling reporter anonymously.	Announcement at staff meeting. (Helen will do. OK to break confidentiality.)
Offer by Debra to spend time in library.	Helen will schedule with staff and Debra.
Reporting relations.	Helen will draft memo to library board by May 2 asking them for direction or clarification on the following issues:
	Legal liability; errors and omissions.
	Property.
	Maintenance.
	Reporting relations.
	Political activity.
	Debra and Ralph will review memo.
	Ralph and Helen will attend May 2 meeting of Library Board.
Maintaining good relations.	Debra, Ralph, Helen, Linda, and Maude will meet for brown bag luncheons.
	First luncheon: Tuesday, April 24, 12:00 to 1:00 in Ralph's office; Linda will facilitate. Participants to begin with "check-in" concerning problem issues and good news.
	Facilitator and location will rotate for subsequent luncheons.
	Brown bag discussion item: exchanging of staff people.
Perception that City Hall is going to do something bad to Helen.	Brown bag luncheon "check-in" item.
Perception that City Hall is "inept" Perception that library staff is "incompetent."	All such evaluative stereotypes were declared inoperative by Jeff, who banned their use in thought and speech.

print, and he and Jeff pressed the participants for specific action commitments as the discussion approached agreement. The last ten minutes of the meeting was spent reviewing the list of hopes and fears generated at the beginning of Meeting 1.

The action list that Paul constructed on newsprint during the last half of the meeting is shown in Exhibit 3. The last issue on the action list, i.e., the perceptions of "ineptness" and "incompetence," still had not been discussed as the end of the meeting time approached. Jeff called attention to the issue, and shared the perception of the consultants that the range of specific behaviors which each group found upsetting in the other group seemed quite small, too small to support the "inept" or "incompetent" generalizations. He pointed out that feedback on specific behaviors had been constructively shared during the four meetings, but that feedback on broad evaluative generalizations was hard to respond to constructively. Jeff urged each participant to consciously avoid lapsing into the use of such evaluative stereotypes, and instead to concentrate on specific behaviors.

During the review of the hopes and fears lists the general feeling was that most of the hopes had been either partially or fully realized, and that most of the fears had dissipated. Concerning the fear that the meetings might prove to be a waste of time, Ralph said, "that remains to be seen." Concerning the hope that better working relations would be developed, all participants seemed to agree that this had been accomplished.

PART 6: FOLLOW-UP

A survey instrument called the Intergroup Profile was used by the consultants to measure the climate existing between City Hall and the library staff. This instrument has eight Likert-type questions concerning the climate perceived by group members, and can demonstrate differences in the perceptions of group members existing between two groups. Measurements were taken in March before the first intergroup meeting, and in May, six weeks after the last meeting. Parallel measurements were obtained from nine separate control organizations.[1]

Data analysis revealed that the library/City Hall climate prior to the meetings was considerably worse than that existing in any of the nine control organizations ($p < .0001$). Following the meeting the library/City Hall climate scores had improved substantially ($p = .001$), but were still lower than the scores of any control organization.

In early August, four months after meeting 4, a two-page written evaluation form was filled out by each of the five meeting participants. Their responses reflected general agreement that, as a result of the meetings, the climate between City Hall and the library had improved, but not dramatically.

Ralph Risen commented, "We achieved a better understanding of positions, but no real resolution of conflicts. The conflicts that exist are political rather than personal."

---

[1] Copies of the instrument and data analysis available from the case authors.

Debra Dickenson noted that the meetings had provided ". . . a good chance to share concerns," and that they resulted in ". . . better feelings for the individuals involved." She continued:

> There is a period of transition that is required—just plain time to see how we all deal with the next 'challenge to authority'. Political changes have an effect. I don't feel the library personnel understand the scope of city demands and needs any better than before. In my opinion they just feel we are being nicer to them. Their anxieties are relieved a bit so the climate is improved. There is a value to that without a doubt.

Helen Hendricks noted three specific changes which had resulted from the meetings:

1. The librarian is aware that her personal situation cannot improve but she is not threatened by further deterioration of her position.
2. The administrative reporting pattern between library administration, library board, and city supervisor has improved.
3. The library staff is more united and supportive than ever.

Additional comments made by Helen included the following:

> I believe the library's fears and concerns were substantiated by the meetings but it was good to bring them into the open. The librarian's and city supervisor's personal contacts are slightly improved.
>
> The problems at the library stemmed from the city administration decision to regroup the city program with the resultant downgrading of the library service and personal demotion of the Librarian—the view of the library. The city administration did not recognize this as the cause.

Linda Turner reported that the meetings ". . . relieved the mayor's mind by allowing her a chance to 'let off steam'. Coming from the library, I [now] feel more relaxed in talking with the mayor and city supervisor—though not totally relaxed. The city librarian and city supervisor can now talk to each other—this is by far the most important result."

Maude Richardson concurred with Linda and Helen that the relationship between the city librarian and the city supervisor was much more comfortable. She also observed that "foul-ups at City Hall are no longer seen as personally directed at the library."

Case 3–4 ————————————————————————————————

The Buzzy Company Downturn Case

Bruce D. Evans and Hugh French

THE CHALLENGE

During his regular weekly staff meeting, Mr. I. M. Topman, president of the Buzzy Company, expressed his serious concern over the report he had just received. "I have indications that there is not enough enthusiasm prevalent throughout the Buzzy plant," he stated emphatically. "We are not going to tolerate such an attitude," president Topman continued; "Buzzy people are always enthusiastic, and you, the staff members, are going to help me straighten this out!"

Most of the staff members realized that the recent business slowdown had necessitated a sizable reduction in work force, causing many key people to personally question their own job security. To avoid the stigma of being laid off, many employees often actively sought and accepted positions in other companies. Those who remained were becoming conscious of protecting their job status. Established informal communication networks were being broken as a result of people leaving. Coupled with the fact that sales were down significantly from the previous year, many staff members wondered when they could expect Buzzy's employee and financial recovery.

Mr. Topman told his staff that this trend had to be reversed. Somehow, they would have to bring about a management renewal to ensure the successful achievement of their newly established company objectives. The president charged each member of his staff to carefully consider methods for overcoming their present dilemma.

BUSINESS SITUATION

Financially, the Buzzy Company had operated profitably over the years with about 80 percent of the business defense-oriented. However, in 1969, changes in the defense market, coupled with an altered economic environment, began to reverse the trend. By 1972, consumer sales were up to 70 percent of total. Since 1978, however, an unexpected decrease in sales caused considerable alarm throughout the organization. In an effort to remain profitable in the face of declining sales, the company management found it necessary to make corresponding and significant reductions in force. In addition, wages became essentially frozen.

As viewed from top management levels, the business prospects for the future, by contrast, looked encouraging. In anticipation of improved business prospects, Mr. Topman redirected the company's business objectives toward those opportunities which would most likely yield the highest return on investment.

RECOGNITION OF PROBLEM

Mr. Topman and his immediate advisors recognized that the achievement of their newly established business objectives would require the support of an effective management organization to execute their carefully formulated plans. Unfortunately, the uncertainty that shrouded the general work force was not seen by Mr. Topman as a major obstacle to achievement of company goals. This problem was the surprisingly sticky subject which generated considerable discussion at the next few weekly staff meetings. Many staff members thought that there was an insidious decay of personal motivation eating away at the vital elements of the organization. It finally became obvious to everyone that unless the current trends were reversed, the company would be faced with the prospect of replacing key individuals.

Because of the mounting concern expressed frequently by the members of his staff, Mr. Topman appointed a special task force to investigate the problem, to evaluate various alternative solutions, and to make appropriate recommendations. The task force consisted of the director of industrial relations, Mr. O. K. Peoples; the executive assistant to the president, Mr. U. R. Helper; the director of research and development, Dr. R. N. Dees; the vice president of finance, Mr. A. C. Counter; and the director of business planning, Mr. C. N. Future. The makeup of the group was intended to represent a broad spectrum of company interests and talents.

Following the appointment of the task force, a series of meetings was held to accomplish their assigned task. It was decided that interviews with selected employees should be conducted to gather data relating to the problem. A reputable consultant firm was retained to assist in the investigation.

It was agreed that the survey data obtained from interviews throughout the company revealed at best an incomplete picture of the real problems facing the company. This was attributed to the fact that in this setting of uncertainty, people were reluctant to speak freely about their real concerns. As a consequence, the use of qualified interviewers from outside the company organization was seen by the task force as a mechanism for obtaining the data necessary for an intelligent definition of the problem.

Accordingly, the services of a reputable consulting firm, Need To Know Corporation, were obtained for the purposes of conducting confidential interviews, analyzing the data, and identifying pertinent problem areas. The results of this activity as summarized by Need To Know revealed that ". . . the central problem was communication throughout your organization—upward, downward, and laterally." This opinion expressed by the outside consultants was, of course, confirmed by the earlier reluctance of people to discuss their concern freely with company interviewers.

In addition, Need To Know interviews with many in management positions indicated a widespread desire to improve their management skills. For example, many managers indicated they would like to learn how to make better use of time in the execution of their assigned job.

Based on the findings of the consultants and their own independent investigations, the task force came to the conclusion that a management development program, specifically designed to address the identified problems and needs of the Buzzy organization, could contribute greatly toward the achievement of company objectives. Toward this end, the group then considered alternative methods of implementing such a program.

CONSIDERATION OF ALTERNATIVE SOLUTIONS

Three alternative approaches to implement the recommended management development program were considered by the task force. Identified as Plans A, B, and C, they are described briefly as follows:

Plan A—Existing In-House Talent

Adoption of this approach would involve the identification of individuals presently within the company who possess the unique talents required to implement such a program. The task force members agreed that the qualifications of the selected person (or persons) would have to include (1) an advance degree with at least a minor in education and/or psychology; (2) previous related experience in the field of management development; and (3) a keen appreciation of the unique problems and their relation to the company.

Once selected, the individual(s) would become thoroughly familiar with the problems, investigate appropriate management training objectives directed toward the specific needs, and administer the resulting management development program.

Plan B—Hiring of a Professional Management Training Director

If this approach were recommended by the task force and adopted by the company, a lengthy sequence of activities and events would occur beginning with the preparation of a fairly comprehensive description of the job to be performed, not only in terms of the immediate problems at hand, but also the longer-range requirements associated with continuing management development training. Having established such a job description, the company would then advertise for prospective applicants. The qualifications and salary requirements would be carefully screened and the best qualified would be selected. Following his employment, the new management training director would begin an extensive orientation period during which he would become familiar with the company, its people and their interrelated problems. Based on his perception of the situation and what he understood to be his assignment, the training director could select an appropriate management development program, and administer it.

Plan C—Engagement of a Professional Consulting Firm

The third alternative solution considered by the task force would involve identification of qualified professional consulting and/or management development firms. Having selected a firm whose capabilities best match the specific needs of Buzzy, the company would then contract for services including the following:

1. Confidential interviews with a representative sample of management and supervisory personnel.
2. An analysis of the results of these interviews to verify the previously identified problems.
3. Identification of other problem areas revealed by the interviews.
4. Proposal of a management development program.
5. If acceptable to the company, the execution of the program.

EVALUATION OF ALTERNATE SOLUTIONS

Having defined the alternative solutions described above, the task force then evaluated each of these in terms of advantages and disadvantages, their respective probabilities of successfully achieving the specified objectives and an analysis of required investment of resources versus the expected returns.

As seen by the task force, Plan A offered the unique advantage over the other plans that a qualified individual selected from within the company may already be well aware of the problems facing the company. Also, it was felt that such an insider would probably be more personally concerned than an outsider because of his established involvement with the company.

Several disadvantages were also recognized by the task force. It was generally conceded that it was not likely that the task force would find a man employed by the company with the required qualifications. Even if identified, making this person available for this assignment would probably require the hiring of an individual to fill the slot vacated by the man so released. Also, the reluctance on the part of potential trainees to respond openly during interviews would still exist to some degree and thereby diminish the effectiveness of the interview.

In general, it was believed by the members of the task force that Plan A had a low probability of successfully achieving the required objectives. Also, while the investment needed to implement the plan was thought to be the lowest, the expected results were similarly valued low.

Adoption of Plan B would afford the company an opportunity to more closely match the capabilities of the selected individual to the requirements of the job, thereby improving the probability of successfully achieving the objectives. Also, it was noted that this approach would have less impact on the existing operation than if an existing employee were transferred out of a critical position into the new slot.

On the minus side, the task force recognized that Plan B would require a considerable amount of time just getting to the point where the program could begin. Preparing the job description, advertising, screening applicants, selecting and hiring, orientation—all of these activities would have to precede the actual planning and execution of the program.

In considering the level of investment required for Plan B, the task force concluded that it probably would cost slightly more than Plan A and would more than likely yield a better result.

The advantages of Plan C were seen to include the following:

1. The resulting management development program would be specifically tailored to the needs of Buzzy by qualified experienced professionals trained to recognize the critical problems and needs of the company.
2. The time required to prepare and plan the selected management development program would be considerably shorter when compared with Plans A and B.

3. Probability of successfully achieving objectives would be high based on the proven performance of the particular consulting firm selected.
4. Minimal disruption of the routine company operations would occur most of the effort would be performed by the people external to the operation.

The only disadvantage seen by the task force was the somewhat higher on-going cost of conducting the program compared with what it would cost using one of the so-called in-house plans.

SELECTION OF BEST SOLUTION

Based on the foregoing evaluation of the alternative solutions considered, the task force selected Plan C, stating the following reasons orally to Mr. Topman at the next staff meeting:

1. Shortest time to implement the program.
2. Highest probability of successfully achieving program objectives.
3. Least impact on routine company operations.
4. Most reasonable investment based on expected return.

After considering several possible consulting firms for the Plan C assignment, the task force selected Need To Know Corporation based on their earlier involvement and their acknowledged reputation as a leader in their field.

IMPLEMENTATION OF SELECTED SOLUTION

Having arrived at a conclusion, the task force then wrote its report to Mr. Topman. The substance of their assignment was summarized briefly, followed by the problem definition, alternative solutions considered, their evaluation of the alternatives, and the conclusions and recommendation for subsequent action.

Mr. Topman accepted the conclusions and the recommendation of the task force, thanked them for their participation in this special assignment and relieved them of any further responsibilities. He then directed Mr. Peoples to proceed with the approach recommended by the task force.

Shortly thereafter, in response to a request from Mr. Peoples, Need To Know submitted its proposal for instituting a management development program at Buzzy. The program, to be coordinated and administered by the industrial relations department, was designed for individuals responsible for developing strategies for human effectiveness within their organization. The program addressed five major areas of interest and concern:

1. *Communication Laboratory*

A one-day session which aims at solidifying the work group into a team. The method includes both structural and nonstructural techniques. Communication barriers are to be examined and approaches to alleviating the problems are developed.

2. *Managing Management Time*

A one-day seminar which examines the content of a manager's day as opposed to the efficiency with which he carries out his activities. Special consideration to include the art of delegation, the rightful assumption of responsibility, and the use of leverage in time management.

3. *Motivation and Job Enrichment*

A one-day seminar exploring a basic philosophy of management relating to people. Consideration to be given to those needs which on the surface appear to be motivational but are not. The actual motivation needs are to be explored with an eye to immediate practical application. The application of motivation concepts to the task of job enrichment will be featured.

4. *Managerial Performance Standards*

During this one-day seminar, managers will learn the technique of writing managerial performance standards. They will study the methods of determining with their supervisor how they will be quantifiably measured before the performance takes place. Specific emphasis on effective performance review and controlling performance standards will be discussed.

5. *Development Sessions*

This series of development sessions will be conducted every fourth Friday, covering such items as problem analysis, decision-making, conference skills, managerial skills, technical skills as related to budgeting and finance, organization structures, etc. These seminars will be given by individuals having expertise in these categories.

After reading this proposal, Mr. Peoples smiled to himself and began to prepare the necessary internal papers to begin the program.

Case 3–5 ———————————————————————————————

Ambassador's Arrival

John A. Murtha

Michael Jameson is assigned to the embassy as the administrative officer; he is also the American security officer, budget and fiscal officer, and personnel officer. At the time of his arrival at the embassy, overall morale of the non-American employees was very low; they were especially disgruntled about their salary rate and were convinced that management had not been open and fair with them.

Mike held numerous meetings with the employees, had a professional position classification and salary survey team prepare a new salary schedule and, over the past two years, had built a reputation for fairness and equity in dealing with all personnel. He was fully in charge of his own section and received only general supervision from the deputy chief of mission and the ambassador. He handled all aspects of personnel with little input from his superiors. His area of authority and methods of operation were well known and accepted within the Embassy.

A new ambassador was appointed about six months ago and recently has taken a detailed personal interest in administrative affairs. He decided to interview and select all new non-American employees. When an employee who was still on probation went directly to the ambassador and threatened to leave if she did not get a three-grade promotion, he ordered a two-grade promotion, although Mike recommended against such special treatment. The ambassador's actions have become known to all employees in the embassy.

Case 3–6 ———————————————————————————————————————

Design and Delivery:
The Dilemma at Eleanor Roosevelt

Robert E. Quinn

In the often criticized field of mental health, one of the most important new developments is the concept of "de-institutionalization," a concept which represents a dramatic change in delivering services to those in need.

Since the late 19th century, the concept underlying the care of the mentally ill in state-supported facilities has been primarily custodial (what some critics have termed "warehousing"): the patient is simply locked away in an overcrowded, understaffed, depersonalized institution. Because of the growing countrywide dissatisfaction with such care, in 1955 the Mental Health Study Act was passed at the federal level, and the Joint Commission on Mental Illness and Health was established to investigate the nation's mental health problems.

In 1961 the commission published its findings and recommendations. Citing fragmented service delivery and the custodial concept itself as key problems, the commission recommended the creation of integrated and coordinated community mental health delivery systems and the de-institutionalization of antiquated public hospitals. The essence of the concept advocated by the commission is expressed by an excerpt from its report:

> The objective of modern treatment of persons with major mental illness is to enable the patient to maintain himself in the community in a normal manner. To do so, it is necessary (1) to save the patient from the debilitating effects of institutionalization . . . , (2) if the patient requires hospitalization, to return him to home and community life as soon as possible, and (3) thereafter to maintain him in the community as long as possible. Therefore, aftercare and rehabilitation are essential parts of all service to mental patients, and the various methods of achieving rehabilitation should be integrated in all forms of services, among them day hospitals, night hospitals, aftercare clinics, public health nursing services, foster family care, convalescent nursing homes, rehabilitation centers, work services, and expatient groups.[1]

---

[1] Joint Commission on Mental Illness and Health, *Action for Mental Health* (New York: Basic Books, 1961), p. 17.

Since the commission's report, various legislative acts at both the federal and state levels have elaborated the de-institutionalization concept and have provided funds for its implementation. Among the most important elements are: the establishment of a geographically defined "catchment" or service area (usually an average population of 150,000); an emphasis on "comprehensive" services that meet all the client's needs; continuity of care as the client moves through stages of development; consumer participation in decision-making; and networks of contractual arrangements between public and private service agencies in a community.

THE NEW YORK STATE DEPARTMENT OF MENTAL HYGIENE

New York State has the second largest population of any state, with a total budget now approaching $11 billion. That is not only the second largest amount spent by any state in the union but it also greater than the budgets of most countries. Although the budget supports numerous agencies and programs, by far the largest single portion of the New York State budget for state operations is allocated to the New York State Department of Mental Hygiene.

Charged with the responsibility for the care, treatment, and prevention of mental disorders, the New York State Department of Mental Hygiene has more than 69,000 employees and spends more than $1 billion per year. The New York State Executive Budget for 1974–75 provides the following official statement of the objectives and strategies of the Department:

1.   To reduce the incidence of mental disabilities through the development of unified systems of health care by state and local governments.
2.   To develop, through research, methods of treatment and prevention for all mental disabilities.
3.   To rehabilitate and support as many as possible of the mentally disabled in their communities.

While the department has a large number and a wide range of facilities scattered throughout the state, the central office of the DMH is located in the capital, Albany. Shortly after his election, Governor Hugh Carey announced the appointment—subject to approval of the state legislature—of Dr. Lawrence Kolb as the new commissioner of the DMH. Dr. Kolb, a 63-year-old psychiatrist, was formerly director of the New York Psychiatric Institute, a DMH research facility located in New York City.

As indicated in the above document, the primary objective of the DMH is "to reduce the incidence of mental disabilities through the development of unified systems of health care by state and local governments." This objective is commonly referred to as the unified services concept. It is New York's approach to de-institutionalization.

Enacted by the state legislature in 1973, the "Unified Mental Health Services Program" took effect on January 1, 1975. The program design calls for individual counties or combinations of counties to submit a five-year plan for the care of the mentally ill, mentally retarded, and alcoholics in the geographic area. Public, private, and state agencies are to be brought together in providing an integrated and coordinated program of health care, including diagnosis, out-patient and in-patient care (both short- and long-term), counseling, aftercare, and social services. If one agency cannot provide the services needed by a client, he is referred to another facility in an area equipped to handle the difficulty. In summary, the concept calls for people to be moved out of institutions and into a community where they will receive integrated rather than fragmented services.

ELEANOR ROOSEVELT DEVELOPMENTAL SERVICES

One nationally noted program within the Department of Mental Hygiene is called Eleanor Roosevelt Developmental Services. ERDS is a program for children with developmental disorders and for the retarded of all ages in a six-county area which includes Albany, Rensselaer, Columbia, Greene, Schnectady, and Schoharie counties. The organization of ERDS includes the Oswald D. Heck Developmental Center and seven "teams" or subsystems which operate in the six counties. It has a staff of over 800 and an operating budget of over $9,047,000.

The ERDS program has been directed since its establishment in 1969 by Dr. Hugh G. LaFave. Dr. LaFave, a psychiatrist nationally noted for his writings and his work in the area of community mental hygiene, is no ordinary administrator. Few of his associates feel indifferent towards him, and though he tends to be either loved or hated, both supporters and critics are in agreement that he is a near genius in conceptualizing innovative solutions to the problems of service delivery.

Dr. LaFave's past work and writings in community mental hygiene have generated a series of beliefs about the treatment of the mentally disabled which have in effect become the organizational ideology around which ERDS operates. It is called the developmental model, and can be broken down into six elements: (1) developmental perspective; (2) community-based services; (3) consumer involvement; (4) collaborative programs and services; (5) comprehensive assessment; and (6) prevention.

The ERDS Developmental Model

The *developmental perspective* is simply stated as follows: "Whereas the traditional approach labels the disability and on that basis excludes the individual from certain activities, the developmental approach assesses the individual's capacities and then seeks to develop them as fully as possible." The people at ERDS argue that the traditional approach is negative while the developmental approach is positive because it builds on the individual's strengths. The assumption is that, given a recognition of his strengths and needs and given appropriate opportunities, anyone is capable of change and growth. The model diverts professional energies from diagnostic labeling as an end in itself to the development of action programs for growth.

The idea behind *community-based services* is to maximize the individual's participation in the community. As many services as possible are provided by or through the collaboration of the family, schools, state and local hygiene units, and other agencies in the community. It is assumed that the community is responsible for its developmentally disabled, and an effort is made to strengthen the community's ability to accept and serve the individual. The approach is not only more economical than institutional care but also affords the client an opportunity to become integrated with other members of the community.

Consumer involvement ensures parent and community input to the program. Each ERDS team has a consumer board of community representatives who discuss planning, implementation, and evaluation; advise the professional staff on priorities; assist in community education; and assume various responsibilities. A representative from each consumer board is appointed to attend meetings as a nonvoting member of the board of visitors for the entire organization.

A heavy emphasis is placed on *collaboration* between two or more agencies to provide multiple services to the individual or his community. To establish such collaborative relationships, communities are encouraged to assess service needs and to develop plans for implementation. In order to maintain the patterns and rhythm of daily living, planners are encouraged to build needed services around day, evening, and overnight time periods.

Comprehensive assessment means that a child is viewed as a whole being who lives in the context of a family and community. The cooperation of family and specialists is employed to arrive at an individual prescriptive program that maintains and builds on assets and addresses the needs of both family and child.

Finally, the developmental model emphasizes *prevention*. Programs with parents, consumer groups, and various agencies operate in such areas as prenatal care and counseling for mothers considered as high risks, screening for lead levels, advocacy programs for the implementation of statutes regarding lead-free substances, genetic counseling, and a comprehensive neonatal program for high-risk newborn infants.

As indicated in Exhibit 1, the developmental model provides the organizational ideology around which ERDS operates. The advocates of the model summarize its unique features as follows: "(1) It recognizes the existence of weaknesses but makes full use of such strengths as the individual has; (2) it enlists the cooperation of a whole range of agencies through voluntary associations to government on all levels from community to state; and (3) it embraces all phases of the problem from prevention to an individualized program for the fullest possible realization of the handicapped person's potentials."

ORGANIZATIONAL STRUCTURE

ERDS is composed of seven teams and a support group. Although the teams are relatively autonomous, they follow a common set of guidelines.

EXHIBIT 1
Orbit of Community-Based Developmental Services

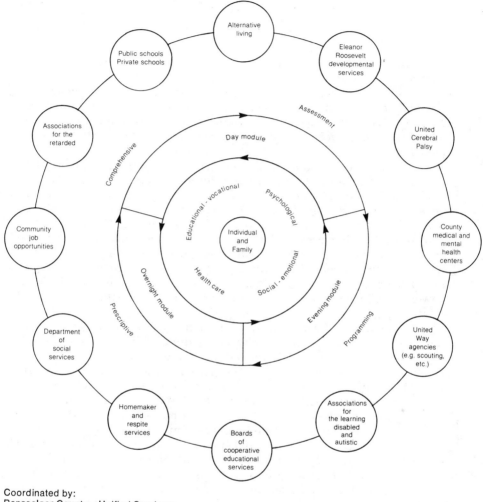

Coordinated by:
Rensselaer County—Unified Services.
Columbia County—ERDS.
Albany County—ERDS.
Green County—ERDS.
Schenectady County—ERDS.
Schoharie County—ERDS.

The leadership of the teams is characterized by a multidisciplinary orientation (social work, child psychiatry, special education, pediatrics, psychology, rehabilitation counseling, etc.) and they are staffed to maintain a balance among at least four areas: social-recreation, psychological, educational-vocational, and health care. For every professional hired, at least one person from the community (with a bachelor's degree or less) also must be hired.

The unique quality of the teams is summarized and symbolized in the use of the word "team" to refer to the organizational unit, with its connotation of a highly integrated group of people sharing the same objectives and differentiating themselves from others. The concept of team implies the existence of an opponent who must be fought through cooperative efforts.

At the team's administrative level, a high value is placed on the development of a nonbureaucratic organization to carry out the team's functions. The administrators feel that an unstructured organization is best suited to the tasks of advocacy and the achievement of the ERDS treatment model.

Further, the assumptions of the team leaders regarding the motivation of the team's members are also based on a self-actualizing, nonbureaucratic model. The team members are described as flexible individuals, desirous of working in a flexible environment and willing to experiment with both traditional and innovative ways of organizing. The team leaders take pride in what they feel is high quality work, and they also feel strongly about being associated with a pioneering effort in the delivery of mental health services. The team leaders seem very aware of their impact on other organizations, and team members place a high value on their power to influence other organizations and to spread their ideology of treatment.

In summarizing the organizational structure of ERDS, each element of the system reflects the philosophy of its director, and as a result the organization is clearly nonbureaucratic. For example, Dr. LaFave has no office but goes where he believes he is needed, establishing a temporary base of operations. Strong emphasis is placed on openness, cooperation, creativity, and innovation. While LaFave reserves a veto power over group decisions, he seldom uses it, and most major decisions are arrived at through participative decision-making techniques. The physical plants of some teams are intentionally too small, as it is felt that overcrowding will encourage members to be out in the community and not in their offices. Dress standards and strict attention to seniority are not in operation. The chain of command is not easily identifiable, and there is a heavy emphasis on face-to-face communication rather than formal written documents. (In fact, there is little emphasis on evaluation of professional performance.) The organic or ambiguous nature of the structure is reflected by the fact that despite attempts to do so, no one has been able to draw up an organizational chart that satisfactorily reflects the functioning of the organization.

GOALS AND PERFORMANCE

The objectives of the ERDS program are explicitly articulated in a series of five-year plans. These objectives are displayed in Exhibit 2.

EXHIBIT 2
Summary of the Goals of Eleanor Roosevelt Developmental Services

First Five Year Plan Jan. 1970–Jan. 1975	Results of First Five Year Plan (Jan. 1975)	Second Five Year Plan Jan. 1975–Jan. 1980	Third Five Year Plan Jan. 1980–Jan. 1985
1. Reduce admissions to institutions outside the area by development of full range of community based service choices	Zero admissions accomplished by 1973	To maintain zero admissions to facilities outside the area	To maintain zero admissions
2. Develop community based services for 2,500 clients and families through the collaborative model	2,600 persons and their families served in community program*	To serve 5,000 persons and their families in community settings through collaborative programming. (As of March 1, 1976, 3,900 persons were receiving services.)	To serve 2,500 persons and their families in community programs. Reduction in numbers due to increased prevention programs and attrition
3. Assimulate the 1,363 persons in institutions outside the catchment area equal to the capacity of O.D. Heck (744 bed capacity) . . .	745 persons assimulated back into the community	To reduce the number of persons in institutions outside the catchment area to zero by resettling remaining 575 (472 remaining as of March 1976)	—0—
4. Utilize only 10 percent of O.D. Heck 744 overnight placements while developing community programs (74.4)	75 persons using O.D. Heck for living arrangement	To utilize fewer than 300 overnight placements at O.D. Heck for living arrangements	To utilize fewer than 100 overnight placements at O.D. Heck for living arrangements

* During the month of April, 1975, 14,000 services were provided to 2,500 clients. More than half these services were provided collaboratively between Eleanor Roosevelt Developmental Services and community agencies. This includes services such as:

Day Module:
Education-Vocational.
Medical treatment.
Speech and hearing therapy.
Physical therapy.
Family therapy.
Activities for daily living.
Transportation.

Evening Module:
Social-recreational.
Adult educational programs.
Respite service for parents.

Overnight Module:
Homemaker service.
Respite.
Family care homes.
Halfway houses.
Hostels.
Nursing home care.
O.D. Heck.

As indicated in Exhibit 2, the ERDS staff claims a number of impressive accomplishments:

1. 1,373 children and adults were in state schools for the mentally retarded or in children's psychiatric units in other parts of the state in January 1970. This number has been reduced to 472.

2. Reduction in the rate of admissions to state facilities outside the area from an average of 79 people per year to 0. (At the original rate, over 450 people might have been admitted to such facilities in the six-year period.)

3. Assumption of responsibility for 200 people from other parts of the state who had been placed by other state facilities in the area prior to 1970.

4. Provision of services to over 3,900 children and adults in community settings.

5. Establishment of a range of services involving parents and other agencies that, although not yet sufficient in number or uniform in quality, provides a comprehensive coordinated system.

6. Involvement of consumers and parents in work with staff and communities at all levels of the system to develop programs and evaluate program quality.

7. Provision in community settings of services that have reached over 4,000 children and adults with developmental disabilities, or who are at high risk of being so labeled, at less cost than would be required to maintain 650 such people in institutional settings at 1975 levels of cost. At projected levels of cost for institutional care conforming to Willowbrook Consent Decree standards, as few as 300 persons might be served.[2]

8. Establishment of a system of services that makes it possible to envision a decreasing state role in favor of locally sponsored, comprehensive, community-based services. Those services would require state financial assistance, but they would cost less than a system operated and financed primarily by the state.

For further indicators of performance, see Exhibits 3, 4, 5, and 6.

In addition to the above there is still further information on the performance of the ERDS program. In spring of 1975 a team of consultants from the nearby Graduate School of Public Affairs at the State University of New York at Albany completed a three-month analysis of one of the ERDS teams. While the report is intended to describe only one of the teams, the conclusions seem to describe adequately the characteristics of the overall ERDS program.[3]

A. Organizational Strengths

1. Organizational Resources

The Team has been very successful in marshalling the energies of its own workers and those of the community to develop and provide an array of services to the retarded not available heretofore.

Both the staff and the community workers exhibited a high degree of esprit de corps and an intense dedication to the cause of the re-

---

[2] The Willowbrook Consent Decree is the result of a suit initiated by families of patients in the Willowbrook Development Center in federal district court to improve standards of care. The governor agreed to support the court's decree.

[3] This material is used with the approval of Dr. LaFave.

EXHIBIT 3
Percentage Reduction of Resident/Leave Population at State Developmental
Centers: December 1968 to September 1975

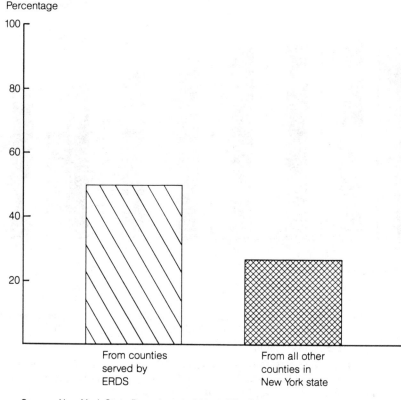

Source: New York State Department of Mental Hygiene.

tarded. It was our observation that a good deal of the community's interest was a result of the zeal of the staff of the Team.

As indicated by our survey, the members of the Team generally have a level of education that far exceeds the minimum required for their respective jobs, particularly at the worker level. The Team has been very successful in identifying and obtaining monies from various sources, including appropriations from the Department of Mental Hygiene, the Legislature, grant monies from the federal government, as well as convincing community agencies to redeploy some of their monies to services for the retarded.

A third resource is Unified Services. This concept provides a viable structure and mechanism for joint planning, development and sharing of resources between all agencies in the County. Unified Services provided the Team with a legitimate forum in which to express their philosophy about methods of treatment and it has been a major vari-

EXHIBIT 4
Percentage of People Remaining in State Developmental Centers since December 1969

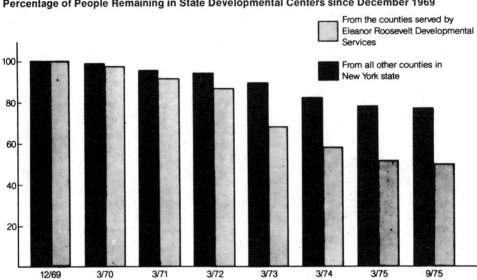

Source: New York State Department of Mental Hygiene.

able in increasing the Team's influence with other agencies and groups in the county (see DMH objectives).

2. Organizational Goals

The Team has a comprehensive and clearly defined set of goals for themselves. This is embodied in the five-year plan. The goals have considerable appeal for community organizations and groups. The goals are well understood and accepted by the administrators of the Team who, as indicated above, are highly committed to the stated goals.

3. Leadership

The Director of Eleanor Roosevelt Developmental Services is a highly charismatic, hard-driving and innovative leader. He conceptualized the goals for Eleanor Roosevelt Developmental Services, and his concepts have heavily influenced the development of team goals, as well as the organizational structure and the allocation and utilization of resources to achieve those goals. The organizational design of ERDS is unique in the Department of Mental Hygiene. The leadership of the Team is highly motivated, professional, and dedicated. They see their role as more than a job; thus they habitually spend long hours at work, work weekends, carry out multiple organizational roles, and expand or stretch their talents and influences almost beyond a point of reason. This almost missionary dedication and zeal is infectious to other staff and is a valuable tactical tool in their dealings with the community.

EXHIBIT 5
A Comparison of the Decrease in Number of People in State Developmental Centers (Three different upstate catchment areas versus area served by Eleanor Roosevelt Developmental Services)

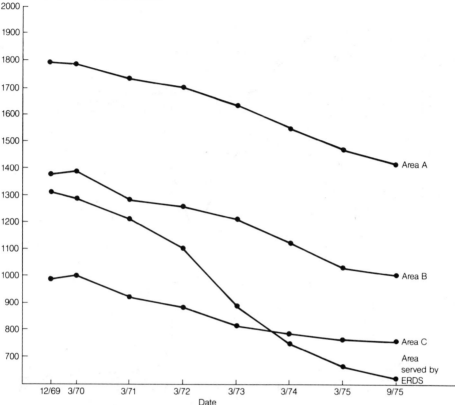

Source: New York State Department of Mental Hygiene.

4. Organizational Flexibility

The Team is a fluid, nonbureaucratic organization. It has a capacity to immediately assign and reassign staff in response to changing organizational needs. Even the use of the administrators is characterized by flexibility since they often have more than one organizational role. The organization appears to have been very successful in identifying needs and reorganizing staff and other resources to meet these needs. This style of organization has been well matched to the characteristics of the environment and the nature of the task. In general, the staff expressed satisfaction with the fluidity and informal nature of the organization and the subsequent freedom, responsibility, and room

EXHIBIT 6
Rates of Admission to State Developmental Centers

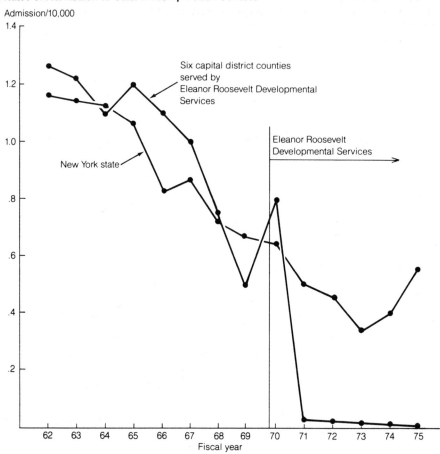

Admission/10,000

Source: New York State Department of Mental Hygiene.

for creativity which this type of organization facilitates. There appeared to be a real climate for the self-actualization.

B.   Potential Impairments

While we judged that the organization has been successful thus far, certain signals were picked up in the external environment and within the organization that revealed potential sources of organization impairment. We have divided these potential impairments into two categories, namely, short-run impairments and long-run impairments. The short-run impairments we identified fall primarily in the area of utilization of Team resources and were impairments the Team was already experiencing to some degree, and which we feel have the potential of seriously affecting staff attitude and effectiveness, if left unattended. The long-run impairments we identified pertained to the goals of the Team and its interaction with the environment and were impairments the Team did not appear to be aware of but which we perceive as potentially challenging the viability and adaptability of the Team in the next few years.

1. Short-run Impairments

    a.   Crisis Management

    The organization is characterized by an atmosphere of crisis, disorganization, and overcommitment of resources. Offices double as meeting rooms and diagnostic clinics; people carry out multiple roles and there is a constant demand for staff to work beyond the normal workday. This atmosphere affects the administrator's capacity to perform the traditional functions of supervision, coordination, and integration.

    b.   Integration and Communication

    The organization seems to lack unity. Few members have a total view of the organization. Staff members' confusion regarding their roles and their responsibilities is another area causing coordination problems. Staff do not know to whom they are accountable, to whom they are to look for guidance, socialization and rewards. This problem is particularly acute in the case of the many new employees. Since the organization does not have written job descriptions, role guidelines, or training programs, the new employee depends on informal socialization into the organization. Since lines of authority are unclear and roles are unclear, new employees experience great difficulty integrating themselves into the organization. The strongest evidence for weak integration in the organization lies in the area of communication. There are three types of communication that have to be improved within the organization: information regarding day-to-day activities; information regarding the effectiveness of the organization; and information regarding long-term goals and plans. In our study, we noted a lack of knowledge on the part of staff members of the activities, procedural changes, and personnel changes within the organization. We also noted an absence of concrete information regarding the performance of the organization and its achievements. Furthermore, especially at lower organizational levels, we found a lack of knowledge regarding broader organizational goals and philosophy.

2. Long-Run Impairments

    a.   Adaptability

    The organization's main way of dealing with its environment is through advocacy. This is a unidimensional way of dealing with the environment, in that the organization is focusing on sending messages rather than receiving them. Hence, we question their ability to realistically sense and interpret the environment. The Team came into the county with a set of goals and a philosophy of operation several years ago. We have perceived messages from other agencies in the county for a change in emphasis in the way the Team defines its relationship with the county.

    b.   Organization Direction

    The organization has had a fixed philosophy which should be reexamined. The dual pressures of changing signals from the environment and internal stress, as outlined under short-run impairments, can undermine the organization and reduce effectiveness if left unattended. It is necessary to examine the degree of fit or lack of fit, between new external and internal goals and the Team's philosophy, goals, and style of dealing with the community.

c. Leadership

The fundamental force behind the philosophy, goals and design of the Team is Dr. LaFave. The organization has been, and we think will continue to be, very dependent upon his thinking for leadership. He appears to be the main authority in the organization.

THE *ALBANY TIMES UNION*:
"WASTED DOLLARS, WASTED LIVES"

Almost simultaneously with the completion of the above report, the *Albany Times Union*, one of the two major newspapers serving the area, began to run an extensive exposé of the entire Department of Mental Hygiene.[4] Entitled "Wasted Dollars, Wasted Lives," the series included numerous devastating reports about bureaucratic inefficiency at the central office of the DMH and numerous descriptions about the bleakest aspects of the life in the institutions. Initially, ERDS and its Oswald D. Heck Developmental Center were only mentioned in summary statements criticizing programs and facilities generally. But beginning on May 9, 1975, the ERDS program became one of the primary points of focus in the series.

On May 9 the *Albany Times Union* ran a front-page article entitled "Heck, it's only (your) money," revealing that more than $6,000 in drugs and supplies were purchased by the O.D. Heck Developmental Center directly from local retail pharmacies instead of using the less-expensive state contract procedure. The article indicated that the state Department of Audit and Control was not aware of the practice. The story received coverage for several days and included a response from LaFave, who argued that ERDS wanted clients to buy their own drugs so they would have experience in the community, and that the practice was cheaper than if ERDS ran its own pharmacy.

The article foreshadowed what was to come. On May 25, six articles about the ERDS program appeared in the newspaper, raising a number of issues about the administration of ERDS. One article appeared next to a picture of Dr. Lawrence Kolb, the commissioner-designate of the Department of Mental Hygiene, quoting him as saying: "I believe that the Heck operation is one of the most innovative and encouraging developmental center operations in the state, as a matter of fact, in the country." He was further quoted as saying that he hoped the Heck operation might be a model for the whole DMH system.

Next to the above article and Dr. Kolb's picture appeared a long article

---

[4] The quotations and excerpts herein are used with permission of the *Albany Times Union*.

describing the findings of a state Department of Health report on the Oswald D. Heck Developmental Center. In response to federal regulations governing the payment of Medicaid and Medicare monies, the article cited numerous findings of "deficiencies in the area of administration, treatment programs, medical care, food services, record-keeping, pharmaceutical and dental operations, and environmental conditions." Some of the findings were:

> A table or organization indicating the major programs and administrative structure has not been made available to the center's staff;
>
> Specific job descriptions for the staff of the center have not been developed;
>
> Resident living staff for each unit does not have clearly defined job descriptions, master-staffing plans, or organizational chart stating channels of communication and delegation of responsibility and authority;
>
> Policy manuals have not been developed by the disciplines providing resident care;
>
> There is insufficient documentation to show that senior medical personnel, doctors, and psychologists perform the planning and treatment functions they are assigned;
>
> Policies are not specific for this center in the areas of admission, transfer and discharge;
>
> Policy was not available that indicated the criteria and procedure involved in resident transfer;
>
> Admission criteria was not available for review in order to determine the extent of the center's ability to provide the services required to the residents admitted.

On May 29 three articles appeared, the most potent, "Heck Center accused of neglect," arguing that the parents of many profoundly retarded children were unable to admit their children to the practically empty center. Two local assemblymen were quoted as saying that they had been unable to obtain admission for patients. The refusal to admit the profoundly retarded was an issue that was to continue throughout the summer.

On June 1 five articles appeared, the strongest arguing that there was poor accountability and control at the O.D. Heck Center, and that "some key doctors" were either ineffective or unavailable because they had "second jobs or other outside interests." The issue of second salaries was also to become a major theme in the weeks that followed.

On June 8 an article entitled "State blasts Heck Center on record-keeping" appeared, quoting parts of a state Department of Audit and Control report which indicated that record-keeping procedures in the area of payroll and personnel were extremely weak. Audit and Control, it continued:

> ... recommends a variety of changes, including verification of appointments and terminations by the business office; good record-keeping and follow-up by the personnel office; distribution of checks by a "responsible employee" of the business office "who is independent of payroll preparation;" close monitoring of employees by their supervisors so that attendance and leave records are kept "properly," and physical separation of the personnel and payroll offices.

The intense pressure on ERDS continued, and on July 19 it was reported that LaFave was asked by commissioner Kolb to take a six-week leave of absence in the midst of a DMH probe. The DMH investigations centered on administrative and personnel practices at the Heck Center and on DMH training contracts held by Albany Medical College. The contracts were a source of additional income to LaFave and other members of the staff.

The results of the probe were made public on September 7. Findings included:

> (LaFave) has not exercised administrative or managerial direction and has not provided an organizational structure which is manageable and provides direct lines of authority, responsibility, and accountability.
>
> Top level ERDS administrative and clinical staff have not provided direction, role definition, purpose, guidance, review, or control of the total operation.
>
> A lack of adherence of basic laws, rules and regulations required by the Department of Mental Hygiene and the various (State) control agencies.
>
> The staff is polarized around the issue of Dr. LaFave's continued appointment as Director, to the possible point where client services are beginning to suffer.
>
> Uncertainty of staff from the top down, as to their role and obligations and a resulting lack of accountability.
>
> In order to effect the changes we see as necessary and to tighten up the organizational structure, the responsibility and accountability that is required now that this organization has reached its present size, we have to recommend strongly that top-level administrative staff be relieved of their present duties at ERDS.

The report was met with outrage by LaFave supporters, who accused the DMH of carrying out a vendetta against LaFave. On September 10 it was reported that the governor, lieutenant governor, and several state legislators had expressed a concern to commissioner Kolb that LaFave get a "fair shake." In the meantime it was announced that commissioner Kolb would soon have a decision on the LaFave case.

Case 3–7 ───────────────────────────────

Jim Jacobson (A)

John E. Dittrich

INLAND STEEL COMPANY AND THE QUALITY CONTROL DEPARTMENT

The East Chicago plant of Inland Steel Company is one of the largest fully integrated steel plants in the world. The plant covers an area of several hundred acres, and includes operations which convert iron ore and coke into finished steel products.

THE OPEN HEARTH

The immediate environment of the work situation was the Number 2 Open Hearth Department. This department was located in one of the largest buildings in the plant. The building housed 24 basic open hearth furnaces and the equipment necessary to service them. This shop was the largest open hearth shop in the world, nearly one mile in length. The open hearth furnace resembles a shallow gravy boat, about 60 feet long. At either end of the hearth are located large burners which supply heat to the bath by burning oil, tar, or gas. Covering the front of the hearth are large water-cooled doors, with round "wicket holes" in the center. The heat of the furnaces is about 2,900 degrees Fahrenheit, and the roar of the combustion within makes normal conversation difficult, if not impossible. Most of the light in the open hearth building comes from the furnaces. At night, the glow from the furnace doors provides adequate light to read a newspaper by at the control panel—50 or more feet away.

The Open Hearth Department can be an extremely dangerous place to work. The accident rate is usually quite low; lower, in fact, than that in the average home. But, when accidents occur, they are often fatal or crippling. When "working" (making steel), furnaces often erupt in a violent slag reaction, pouring slag out of the doors and onto the floor. During the tap, when steel is drained from the furnace, furnace roofs can collapse, splashing steel and slag over the area. During tapping, the tap hole can explode, as a pocket of moisture is hit by hot steel. Slag pots erupt like volcanoes on occasion, burning anything within an area of 100 feet. At the pouring stand, full running stoppers can splash molten steel, at 2,900 degrees, horizontally for 50 feet or more as the running stream contacts the flat top of the edge of a mold. Ingots can, and do, explode, blowing plates 75 feet up through the roof. A constant awareness of possible danger is the only thing that prevents such accidents from becoming catastrophes. Men are very conscious of the possible danger, and are quick to warn each other of trouble. In addition, the company insists on protective clothing and goggles for employees in danger areas: a factor instrumental in reducing injuries from major to minor, or to none at all.

In summer, despite the Lake Michigan breezes, the temperature in the building exceeds 130 degrees. In winter, the temperature drops to well below zero in areas away from the furnaces. It is a frightening place for a new employee to work. He is constantly reminded of the dangers of the job, and can see the possibilities for serious injury or death in every direction.

Location and Function of the Metallurgical Department

Operating from the central control office located between #25 and #26 furnaces, the Open Hearth Metallurgical Division is given the responsibility of inspecting the metallurgical practices being used in the Open Hearth. From the inspector's report, the "met" (metallurgical) foreman makes a disposition of all or parts of the heat. On certain types of steel, defects can be segregated, ingot by ingot, and the defective ingots diverted to less critical specifications. On other heats, quality defects can be remedied only by diversion of the entire heat of steel. It is necessary, therefore, that the metallurgical inspector make a thorough observation and report on the processes and problems involved on each heat as it is tapped and poured.

The metallurgical department has no responsibility in making the steel. Inspectors and foremen can suggest changes in procedure, but the ultimate responsibility for the quality of the heat rests with the melter, whose men make the heat, and the pit foremen, whose men pour the heat. As is common in many inspection arrangements, considerable friction develops between the inspection and production departments over the disposition of marginal heats of steel.

The Job of Metallurgical Inspector

The metallurgical inspector is required to follow the entire steel-making process from charging the furnaces to finishing pouring at the pouring stand. Since little quality control can be accomplished during the charging process by the furnace operator, or first helper, the metallurgical inspector usually does not write up a report covering this phase of the operation. His report usually starts at the beginning of the final makeup of the heat, after the first chemical analysis is run. At that point, he records the lab analysis, taking the data from the first helper's heat card, which is kept at the furnace. The first helper is required to keep a record of the time at which tests are taken, and the time he makes various additions to the bath. The met inspector records these times, and the various additions made.

Just before tapping, the first helper takes a complete chemical analysis, or "round." The round gives the melter the needed carbon and manganese levels with which to calculate the ladle additions to be made at tap time. He calculates the amount of ferromanganese required by ascertaining the level of bath manganese, the size of the heat, the purity of the manganese additive, and its recovery factor.

During the tap, the inspector observes the process used in tapping, and observes the ladle additions. He makes visual observations of the bath during the refining process and just prior to tap. He also makes a visual observation of the ladle, after ladle additives have been made, in order to spot manganese "floaters." The melter completes the heat card, filling in the amount of ladle additions and the final tapping times.

From the furnace, the met inspector takes the card to the pit, or steel pouring area, and delivers the card to the pit foreman, who fills in pouring information after the ladle is emptied. The met inspector then proceeds to the pouring stand to inspect the molds for cleanliness before the heat is poured. If he finds dirty molds, he usually marks them off. The pit crews usually inspect the molds, but occasionally are not able to, due to time pressure.

During the pour of the heat, the met inspector makes observations about the pouring condition, and the practice used in pouring and controlling the heat at the stand. He will report the amount of aluminum pellets used in "feeding" the heat (reducing a tendency for the steel to foam), and any changes, noting the ingots affected. He will make observations on the action of the metal in the molds, indicating by mold number the specific ingots with abnormal action. He will observe the pouring of ladle tests, noting the practice used in pouring the test, and check to see that the tests are suitable for laboratory analysis. He notes the position of these tests. After the pour is completed, he notes the time, and walks down into the lower pit area to observe the ladle condition.

The ladle is dumped out, cleaning out slag which has floated on the surface of the ladle during pour. If the heat was cold, or if the ladle was cold or wet, a "skull" of solidified steel will have formed on the bottom and sides of the ladle. The inspector, together with the steel pourer, observe the skull, and make an estimate of its weight. Very thick and heavy skulls can divert the heat due to excessive segregation of impurities and generally poor ingot structure. The estimation of the ladle condition is the last step in the metallurgical inspection, after which the inspector returns to the office to complete the report.

The practices used at every step in the process differ widely from specification to specification, and the inspector must know the correct practice for each specification, and make his observations based on that knowledge. In day-to-day work, the job can be somewhat more simple, and less demanding. In actual use, the number of deviations from standard practice which can cause degrades are limited. The inspector, therefore, can "play it safe" and not report any abnormalities, and thus stay out of trouble. His report must, when reporting abnormalities, have clear and distinct reporting of the practices used, and he must be prepared to defend his report to his foreman and to the production foreman. There are several items which he must cover, even if he is not being particularly thorough. First, he must correctly report the size of the molds and the number of ingots poured. Second, he must look for floaters, since their presence is seen in the chemical analysis of the ladle tests. Finally, his report must, in general, conform to the reports written on the heat card. All of these items are purely for the inspector to "cover" for himself. If there were differences in his figures and those of the production people, he could be quite embarrassed, since this might indicate he was not on the job.

JIM'S ENTRY INTO THE DEPARTMENT
AND HIS OBSERVATIONS ON ENTRY

Past Experience with the Metallurgical Department

Jim was working in the Merchant Bar Mills as a member of the labor gang. He heard from a neighbor of his that there were openings in the met department for inspectors, and that he would qualify. He called the superintendent of the quality control department, Thomas Washburn, and inquired about the possibility of transferring to his department. He said that they would be glad to have Jim and made the transfer. The training procedure for the department at that time involved moving inspectors from the Blooming Mills into the Open Hearth after six to eight month's training as a Blooming Mills inspector. Jim developed a good working knowledge of the operations of the Blooming Mills during his training period in the mills. About five months after beginning work in quality control, he was moved to the Open Hearth for training. Jim worked about one month in the Open Hearth and then enlisted in the Air Force for a four-year hitch. By the time his four years were completed, he had forgotten what little he had learned in the Open Hearth.

Jim returned from his Air Force duty in April. The new Superintendent of Open Hearth Quality Control, Kurt Mattson, told Jim that he was now an M-1, or metallurgical inspector 1st class, due to the accumulation of seniority during his stay in the service. He told Jim, however, that he would have to pass a written test for M-1. Jim was given ten days to prepare for the test, and passed it. In order to pass the test Jim had to learn the job, and answer the questions given on an exam. He was given some instruction booklets, which were prepared for training inspectors, a list of 150 questions, of which 80 were used for testing, and was turned over to an experienced inspector for training in the Open Hearth. During his initial training period, which might rightly be called an indoctrination or familiarization period, Jim worked on the day shift with several different crews, and was trained by a number of different inspectors. Jim was reacquainted with the Open Hearth and the safety provisions and regulations, shown how to fill out the Inspector's Report Form, and taught the basic vocabulary of the report. The things Jim was shown at that time were simply the minimal requirements of the job: How to keep out of trouble . . . safetywise, and how to perform the minimal metallurgical duties.

Initial Training and Observations

Upon returning from the Air Force, Jim observed several things of interest. Prior to his Air Force hitch, no safety clothing was issued. Men working around molten metal wore old work clothes, which soon were riddled with small holes from splashes of molten steel. No goggles were issued, and the only eye protection offered was that derived from cobalt blue glasses . . . very dark to avoid burning and damaging the retina of the eye when looking at molten steel. These peculiar-looking glasses are the identifying mark worn by the old-time open hearth man. First helpers, melters, and pit gang all wear these old-type glasses. When he returned to Open Hearth, he was issued a full set of safety equipment. A green plastic safety helmet, flameproof trousers and jacket, and full goggles (half cobalt blue, half clear) for eye protection. Jim noticed that this equipment was not used by all Open Hearth personnel. Parts of the equipment were worn by some of personnel, but only the crews on the pouring stand wore the whole outfit. Floor personnel (melter, and helpers) did not wear the equipment, and continued to use only the old blue glasses.

Another item of major interest to Jim was the turnover of personnel.

When he left the company, Jim was about 33d in seniority in a staff of 35. When he returned, he was number 8. Jim's seniority position was such that he would have been the "oldest" man on at least two crews, had he been placed there. The men who trained Jim, for the most part, were men who had come to the department after he had. Furthermore, Jim had passed the test for M-1, and yet was being trained for the job as though he was a complete newcomer (as indeed he was).

Jim was issued a locker in the locker room over the central control office, and was told at the time that, as an "older" man, he was entitled to a locker to himself, whereas new employees had to share lockers with another inspector. Jim was issued the clothing, goggles, and helmet, and told to wear them at all times in Open Hearth. He was introduced to each man in the department, then turned over to an older inspector for instruction. As a rule, the older man took it upon himself to assume the responsibility for complete training of the man assigned to him. Jim was turned over to Ted McNeal, a college graduate who had come to Inland some months after Jim had left to enter the service. In addition to the job training and safety training, Ted showed Jim some of the informal rules of the department. First, the required quitting times were 3:30 P.M., 11:30 P.M., and 7:30 A.M. After that time, any inspector not relieved would go on overtime, and his relief would have his pay docked. It was customary, however, to relieve early. The typical relief time was about 20 minutes before quitting time, although some inspectors made a practice of relieving earlier than that. Also, it was a requirement that the inspector being relieved would have the met report written up—up to the time he was relieved. As a practice, however, when an inspector was relieved on the pouring stand, he would have the "card" written up . . . the portion covering the process up through the tap, and would merely verbally mention what had happened on the pouring stand. No formal lunch period was established, since heats would and did tap at all hours of the day. Lunch could be eaten any place in the shop. It was a practice, however, to eat lunch in the office. In dealing with Open Hearth production personnel, Ted indicated by his actions his position in the Open Hearth. He was cordially greeted by the melter, and by some of the first helpers. He talked to these men, usually about topics other than the job. They seemed to accept him in the job situation, but did not consult him for help of any kind. The melter would give Ted the card when he was finished with it, and little conversation ensued. In the pit, somewhat more conversation and interaction occurred. Ted knew all the steel pourers (top man on the stand) and all the pit foremen. He also seemed to know all of the permanent pit crew, but not the hookers, who performed labor or jobs on the stand. The pit crews looked to Ted for advice, on occasion, and his opinion seemed of value to them.

Ted confided in Jim some of the relations which men on the floor had with their respective foremen. There seemed a clear delineation between the foreman, a salaried man, and the men on the floor who were paid on an hourly basis. The hidden practices of many of the inspectors, and some of their peculiarities were related to Jim, with the intimation that this was "inside" information that the foremen didn't have. This delineation was noticed because of some other, more obvious, differences. First, the foremen wore white helmets, as did all the Open Hearth supervisors. Second, the office was set up with a railing which divided the office into two sections. Met inspectors rarely spent much time inside the larger section, where the desks of the foremen and the providers (production schedulers) were located, but filled out reports and ate lunches inside the smaller section. Third, the foremen and the providers drove their cars into the plant. The hourly workers had to park in parking lots located about a quarter of a mile from the gate, and nearly a mile from the locker room. Finally, the foremen rarely left the office. They seemed to spend much of their time in application of heats (assigning heat to customer orders) from met reports, and when leaving the office, often went directly to their cars and traveled to the Number One and Number Three plants to visit inspectors at those locations.

Foremen discussed heats with their men only upon receipt of the met report. If the report did not clearly explain the practices used, the foreman called on the inspector to elaborate and, if necessary, rewrite the report. As a rule, after about two weeks, a new man was left to himself. He was assigned to North Unit (the six furnaces at the north end of the building) and prepared his own reports. For the next four to five weeks, the foreman usually would go over his reports with particular care, checking very carefully the observations made, and often questioning the new inspector.

New inspectors were usually assigned to the North Unit. The floor is divided into four sections: North, North-Middle, South-Middle, and South. The South Unit had the oldest and smallest furnaces. The North Unit had the largest furnaces in the shop, and as a rule made big heats of "strip" steel (low carbon-rimmed heats, for sheet steel). Strip heats are relatively uncritical as far as metallurgical inspection is concerned. One of the norms of the department, supported by the management, is the placement of inspectors in units according to seniority. The two middle units, closest to the office, are used by Open Hearth personnel to test new furnace practices and new equipment. Also, pouring stand Number 4 is located in the middle of the pit, in back of the middle units. This stand is the only stand equipped to handle heats made with lead as an alloying element. As an informal rule, the oldest man takes the South-Middle Unit, the next oldest the North-Middle, the next oldest the South Unit, and the youngest man the North Unit. In some instances, the men had the option of selecting the unit they wished to work, but in no case was a middle unit left with an inspector unqualified to make lead heats.

In Jim's first weeks in Open Hearth, he observed that the Open Hearth personnel, for the most part, had little if anything to do with the met inspectors. They seemed to tolerate the presence of the met inspector, but rarely talked over the job. This was particularly true with new men. The older employees seemed to get along much better with Open Hearth people, but the amount of interaction was still low. The Open Hearth people worked in groups, to a large extent. The furnace crew, made up of the first helper and the second helper, formed one group. The pit gang appeared to be another group working together on each heat. Jim was also impressed with the amount of knowledge required of the inspector in working at his job. In order to converse with his foreman, with the melter foreman, and with the pit foreman, he had to have a good working knowledge of the whole process, and the alternatives presented in any situation. The number of variables in this complex process is almost incalculable, and the combination of variables further complicates the picture.

Jim was told by Ted of the tricks and stratagems used by the melters and first helpers. Ted said that melters liked to hide from the met inspector after the heat had tapped, keeping the heat card, and causing the met inspector to chase him all over the shop. Also, the melter would sometimes keep the card in his pocket, and refuse to give it to the met inspector, saying he wasn't finished with the card. They liked to act gruff and crotchety, barking at the young inspectors, and trying to intimidate them. Ted mentioned that the first helpers also liked to cause trouble. They would turn up the oil or the steam on the furnace just as the inspector approached the doors, making observations of the bath difficult, if not impossible. They also liked to indulge in horseplay, often "accidentally" soaking an inspector with a water hose or bucket. This sort of horseplay was not only directed at the met inspector, since other new or young employees got the same treatment. When questioned about the process, or problems with their particular heat, first helpers rarely were helpful. In talking with other inspectors, some discomfort was felt by the inspectors because of this constant pressure from production workers and foremen. The inspectors had the feeling that this was antagonistic, and liked to be able to "screw" someone by reporting discrepancies. There were elaborate explanations of how Brad, the oldest of the melters, had caused trouble for one of the inspectors, and how the inspector retaliated. Ted told Jim that "you just had to do the job," and "don't get smart" with the Open Hearth people, and they'd "get the message."

Ted also talked about how some of the inspectors did their work. Since the foreman rarely left the office, and since the inspector had to be in many places in the shop, inspectors often had special "hiding places" where they could sleep during slack periods when no heats were tapping. He also told how some of the men would sleep on the pouring stands, and write up the heat when it had finished . . . playing it safe, of course. Jim got the impression from Ted, however, that this was not really too acceptable, since it reflected on the ability and character of the other inspectors. "After all," he'd say, "the hardest work we have to do is carry a pad and pencil around, so why push it?" There were "legitimate" short-cuts which could be taken, however, and this involved more than anything a knowledge of the job. Knowing the job particularly well, an inspector could amble out on the floor, stroll down the line, stand on the pouring stand apparently half-asleep, and write up a complete and extremely accurate report of the practices used. Ted also mentioned how some of the men really didn't know the work very well. Their reports usually were complete, and contained enough variation in reporting from heat to heat to avoid suspicion, but rarely described a marginal heat in such a way as to place the inspector in a position of conflict with the production personnel.

Case 3–8 ───

Jim Jacobson (B)

John E. Dittrich

THE SMALL WORK GROUP

Personal Backgrounds

The group involved was composed of six persons: four floor inspectors, the senior metallurgical inspector, and the turn foreman. The other members of the complete crew were separated physically, and rarely entered the job situation. The crew worked the same shift, day and night, and during the eight months of the period in question, members did not leave the crew or change shifts.

Leo Kamradt, Foreman. Leo was, at the time, about 35 years old. He was a resident of Calumet City, Illinois, about six miles from the plant, and lived there with his wife, their two daughters, and his mother-in-law. Leo had gone to a parochial high school in the area, and served in the Air Force. Leo had been employed at Inland some 15 years or more, and had worked his way up to foreman from the met inspector ranks. He was a Catholic, and attended mass regularly. He was talkative, ebullient, and seemed, in general, to be good-natured.

George Brazinski, Senior Metallurgical Inspector. George was pretty much an enigma. He rarely said much about anything. George had about 11 years in the mill, and had more seniority than any other senior inspector. He was about 30 years old, and had served in the Army. George was married, had two or three children, and was also Catholic. George's wife, Dorothy, had worked in the department as a mill inspector, and returned to the mill recently. George often took it upon himself to maintain and make minor repairs on the optical pyrometers, instruments used by met inspectors to ascertain the temperature of the steel at the pouring stand. George had gone to high school and lived in Hammond, Indiana, five miles from the plant.

Roy Haviza, Met Inspector I. Roy had been at Inland about eight or nine years, and was an extremely competent inspector. He was about 27 years old, and the father of two children. Roy had gone to high school, and was a devout Catholic. Roy lived in the town of McCool, about 18 miles from the mill, a drive that took roughly 45 minutes each way in mill traffic. Roy was a sundowner. He owned about 20 acres of land around his house, and farmed it during his spare time. He built his own home, and all the buildings for the operation of his small farm. Roy had been a 4F during the war, due to a physical deformity. The deformity was not noticeable, but seemed to affect his heartbeat in such a manner as to cause doctors on one hand to claim he was due for a heart attack, and on the other to say he was healthy. He was very worried about his heart, and expressed the feeling that he was going to die before he got to be 40. Roy loved to talk, and could argue through an entire night shift. He was a pleasant, but argumentative person, quite sensitive to another person's feelings, and loved to probe, pick, and pry—in a gentle manner. On the job, he was difficult to argue with, because he knew his job very well, and very little could be kept from his observation.

Eddie Studniarz, Met Inspector I. Ed, or Studs, was a stocky, athletic person of about 22 or 23 years of age. He was married, and had one child. Ed had been in the service in Korea, and had seen considerable action stringing wire for the signal corps on the front lines. Ed had been to high school, and was Catholic. He enjoyed athletics, having played on service softball and basketball teams, and at the time was involved in the company softball league, as player-manager of the department team. Ordinarily, Eddie was relatively quiet, but would talk a good deal on occasion. Ed had been born and raised in Indiana Harbor, the mill town, as son of a Number 1 Open Hearth first helper. At that time, Eddie was living in an apartment house in Indiana Harbor, but was planning to buy his own home. On the job, Eddie was quiet and competent. He had been at Inland about three years.

Roderick Greig, Met Inspector I. Rod was another puzzling person. He was often loud, brash, and boorish. He also had periods where he said virtually nothing. He was about 25 years of age, married, and with one child. He had been in the Merchant Marine, and his job with Inland had been his first job after leaving shipboard. He had a high school education, but was attempting to teach himself calculus, and subscribed to *Scientific American*. He had also been at Inland about three years. He gave no indication of his religion. He lived in Gary, about eight or ten miles from the mill, in his own home. Rod seemed moderately competent in doing his work, but often seemed to take a crusading attitude about quality control, and engaged in rather violent arguments with production personnel.

Jim Jacobson, Met Inspector I. At the time, Jim was 23, married, and had one child. He was living in Gary, in a rented home, about seven or eight miles from the mill. Jim had been to high school, and had spent one year at Purdue. He worked for the department for six months, then went into the USAF. Jim returned at the end of his enlistment. During the time he was in the service, his seniority kept accumulating, since he was on service leave of absence. Jim thus had about seven years seniority. He was Protestant, and studied part of the time at work on schoolwork.

Small Group Basic Training

Jim began working with Roy for the first few days. Jim had known Roy slightly before entering the USAF, and the two soon struck up a reasonably sound friendship.

During the breaking-in period, Jim soon got to know the rest of the crew. He was sent out with Studs to follow unusual specifications which were ordered infrequently. Only once or twice did Leo send Jim out with Rod to follow heats. Without exception, Leo, George, Roy, and Studs were unfailing in answering questions about the job. All of them, prior to terminating a discussion, would strongly insist that Jim ask them any questions . . . no matter how insignificant they might seem to him. For a while Jim was reticent about asking such questions, but after asking some "feeler" questions and receiving a favorable reply, he soon began on the more basic questions. They always accepted these questions as important, and were careful in making a clear explanation of the answer. Leo would often add "you never know all there is to know in the Open Hearth" or "something new every day in the Open Hearth."

Exposure to the Job and Observations

After about one week of breaking in, Jim was told by Leo to take the North Unit. The regular man had reported off, and they would have had to put a man on overtime to fill the slot. Jim told Leo that he thought he could handle it, and he did. Jim was apprehensive and worked twice as hard as necessary, making sure that he had double-checked everything. He spent almost no time in the office, and almost panicked when two furnaces tapped at roughly the same time. He did manage to cover the job, and handed in the reports to Leo. Leo went over them with a fine-tooth comb, asking question after question, and had Jim go back to get information he had missed. After that day, however, Jim had a lot more questions to ask of Roy.

Jim learned, during the breaking-in period, that he ranked just below Roy in seniority on his crew, and had this pointed out to him on a seniority list posted on the wall near the entrance to the office. This seniority position came up later that week when, on Thursday, Leo said he was going to assign Jim to the North Unit. He said that Jim would normally work the North-Middle Unit, but that Studs was working that unit, and he didn't want to cause any hard feelings by putting a new man in and "bumping" a more experienced inspector. At the same time, he intimated that this was a temporary assignment. Jim said "fine," and told Leo he'd be glad to cover the North Unit.

Jim's assignment caused a slight stir among the inspectors, and Roy said flatly that the North-Middle Unit was rightfully Jim's. Studs, the man who could have been displaced, also mentioned to him that North-Middle was his. Jim said "No . . . I'll work North," and made no fuss over the assignment at all.

During the next several weeks Jim had his hands full trying to learn the job. He felt very much ill at ease in the three strange worlds he was in. The first, the met crew, was perhaps the least strange, and seemed like "home base." He was known there, knew the people, and talked to them a great deal. He still wasn't very well acquainted with the jargon and had only a little idea of what they were discussing at times. The second world was the Open Hearth floor, and seemed almost openly hostile. As a part of his job, Jim was required to give the providers in the central control office estimates of tapping times. These the providers recorded on the lineup which was distributed throughout the mill. When Jim walked down the floor, he was ignored almost completely. When he asked for tapping times he received several kinds of answers. The most friendly was a flat "8:30" ... nothing else. Other first helpers, when asked, turned on their heels, walked to the furnace board, and marked the estimate ... saying not a word. The last variety of reply was least welcome. Jim would ask the time of their estimate, and the first helper would blast out with a tirade ... "What the hell are you guys always bothering me about," or "you guys always press the hell out of us" (intimating that the inspectors were threatening them) and other responses equally hostile. The melter foremen were impassive. They said very little to Jim. For the most part they didn't act hostile, but they made no friendly advances toward conversation.

Jim's reaction to this was simple. First, he got angry. Next, he thought it over, and thought that this might be some kind of unconscious hazing ... thinking to himself: "I've got a job to do ... I'll do it. If this crap keeps up ... too bad. The hell with them." While this didn't ease the pressures and anxiety, it made them easier to bear. Outwardly, Jim's reaction was as follows: He asked *only* questions that he had to ask and asked politely. When the man gave him the answer, he thanked him. No familiarity, no chumminess, all business. He was always at the furnace in time to cover the heat, and did not get in the way. At the same time Jim tried to get as much information about the operations of the furnaces as he could, but from the met department.

The last, quite different world, was the pit. Here again Jim received little encouragement or help from the men. His reaction was the same. He stayed out of the way, and kept his eyes open. When a conflict appeared with the pit foreman, the foreman would insist that he was right, and imply that Jim wasn't capable of evaluating the heat. Jim's counter was this: "The hell with it—I'm not paid to argue—I'll write up the report as I see it and give it to Leo. You argue with Leo." This usually provoked another closing outburst, but seemed to handle the problem.

As time progressed, conditions became much easier. As Jim continued to work the North Unit, he began to learn the names of men. First the melter foremen, then gradually the first helpers. He began to speak to them as he saw them. Saying "Hi, Wally" while going past, but not actively seeking any friendship, and not stopping to chat. Soon, Jim began to get replies—a simple "Whaddeya say" or "Hi, Jim." His previous actions were continued—all business, and no BS *unless* they wanted to chat.

In the pit, the situation worked much the same way, but at a faster rate. Since the pit crew was the same for each heat, Jim had much more contact with the individuals in the pit, and learned names much sooner. They seemed less reticent about talking, and were more helpful. While Jim didn't learn all the names of the men in the pit, he soon learned the names of the foremen and the leadman on the pouring stand, the steel pourer.

As a result of his gradual acquaintanceship with the men in Open

Hearth, and after gradually gaining more experience with the process and his job, Jim found that the jargon seemed to be more understandable, and he began to converse more in depth with the inspectors in the department.

Status and Ranking

In Open Hearth, Jim noticed the work being done by each of the levels in the workforce. Third helpers worked together, and wore clothing of all descriptions. Little of their clothing was specialized—nor was it purchased specifically for Open Hearth work. Old dress trousers, Levis, and army fatigue pants were worn with T-shirts. Second helpers all wore long underwear, two-piece, and kept spare tops near the furnace. Their work was particularly hot. They would rinse these tops out in water after they were soaked in sweat and hang them to dry in back of the furnace, changing to a fresh, dry shirt. Second helpers almost always wore khaki work pants, either the usual suntan color or blue-grey. In general, their clothing was more uniform than the third helpers. Rarely did they wear an outside shirt. All their clothing was purchased, specialized work clothing. Second helpers kept track of the wheelbarrow for the furnace, and other hand tools used in working on the furnace.

First helpers also wore a sort of uniform. They wore the same long underwear as the second helpers. As a rule, they wore an outside shirt, and all clothing was clean, but worn. First helpers stayed near the front of the furnace, and tended the coffee pot. The first helpers had lockers in back of the furnace panel where they kept extra shirts, coffee and cups, and the coffee pot.

Melters wore a work uniform of purchased work clothing. Khaki shirt and pants topped off with a white helmet were their uniform. Melter's names were neatly lettered on the side of their white safety helmets.

Differences could be seen in the work activities of the men. Third helders did a great deal of physical work (shovelling lime and dolomite, lifting and carrying heavy materials). Their work, however, depended on the activity of the unit of six furnaces, and was usually sporadic. The second helper had virtually continuous physical hard work. His work was skilled, and required experience and knowledge in addition to physical strength.

The first helper had little physical work to do. His job was manning the control board and operating the furnace. Often he would use his shovel to make an addition to the bath or work on the front wall, but this activity was at his discretion.

The melter did almost no physical work. He supervised the unit, and observed and directed the activities of others.

Within the met inspection department, Jim also began to notice status differentiation and symbols. The older employees wore ragged but clean clothing, had dirty helmets and goggles flecked by blobs of solidified steel. The new employees had stiff, new work clothes with shiny work shoes. There was a studied air of nonchalance about the older employees. They always seemed to know what was going on, were never surprised, and, in general, were quite a casual bunch. The newer employees rushed about and spent much of their time out on the floor. Finally, the older employees seemed to assume a much higher degree of personal responsibility for activities in their unit. If a marginal heat was made, they made their appraisal and would argue their points strongly with pit foremen, melter foremen, and their own foreman. On one occasion, a heat of specialty steel was made with insufficient aluminum added at the furnace. The inspector on the heat, one of the most experienced in the department, made the decision to add aluminum at the pouring stand. He then directed the pit crew to add the required amount of aluminum. This was *not* his responsibility, and involved not only the money in the steel, but a direct violation of the job requirements and descriptions. As it turned out, he saved the heat. The incident was discussed at length in the department, not just between inspectors, but among foremen. Jim had the feeling that this was regarded as a risky maneuver, but highly commendable.

Other inspectors, perhaps slightly less experienced, also took it upon themselves to direct the activities of pit personnel, and assumed the responsibility for assisting in the production of a good heat.

Another symbol of status, mentioned earlier, was the lead heat. Since this heat was given only to experienced men, any man with lead heats in his unit enjoyed a position of somewhat higher status. External factors seemed important determinants of status. In the technical work involved, education seemed to be important. College men started out in the department as M-4 rather than M-5. College-trained men were often asked for opinions on technical matters by other members of the department. In being introduced to this group, Jim had several characteristics quite different from those possessed by the normal new employee. First, he wasn't completely new. Second, he had formal recognition of this experience— the M-1 rating. Third, Jim had some college training. Fourth, his earlier training was the same as those who were now the oldest men on the crew (Leo, George, and Roy).

When Jim was introduced to the group, all of the four factors above were made known to all the group members. George made a point of identifying him with his former experience. Leo, in talking to Jim in the presence of other members, referred to experiences they had had in the Blooming Mills prior to Jim's Air Force hitch. The seniority list was posted in the office, on the wall facing the entrance door. Within one week after Jim joined the group, a new list was made up with his name in the proper chronological position. On the weekly work schedule was listed the turn, the date, and each inspector's name and rating (M-5, M-4, M-3, M-2, and M-1). Finally, Jim's experience level was immediately obvious to all the members of the crew since nearly all of them participated in his training. The entire crew participated wholeheartedly, but quietly, in Jim's training. They worked hard at explaining the processes involved, and did not embarrass him by ridiculing his questions or inexperience. Also, Jim concentrated most of his questions on members of the group with higher status: Roy, George, and Leo. He did not attempt to violate the tradition of experienced men working in the North-Middle Unit, even when it was clearly pointed out to him that he had that alternative. When Roy and Studs mentioned to Jim that this was his prerogative, he did not use the status factors to obtain a high-ranking job.

Case 3–9 ——————————————————————————————————

Jim Jacobson (C)

John E. Dittrich

After several months in the North Unit, and after learning a great deal about the Open Hearth and its personnel, Jim began to converse more freely with the members of the group. By this time he had developed enough experience to discriminate between various practices, and had learned the language of the shop. It was near the end of the period in the North Unit that the group began to knit together.

Until this time, the group seemed to be a rather loose organization. Formal requirements were met, and the job was accomplished, but the group seemed quite loose. The men spent more time in the office, but usually discussed off-the-job topics, and did not appear to work closely with Leo. During Jim's training, the group began to focus its attention on him—they seemed to cooperate in training him, and when one member was making an explanation, the others would chime in with useful additional bits of information. Also, during this period they began to have joint experiences on the job. Roy and Jim were on several heats which had severe ladle reactions (chemical action taking place in the ladle, causing marked changes in chemical content and subsequent downgrade). Studs and Jim were on a heat which had extremely bad pouring conditions due to a complete power failure in the pit. Leo, on several occasions had Jim accompany him on his visits to the Blooming Mills. What developed out of these joint experiences was a certain rapport—sharing of on-the-job situations and a consequent closer tie between individuals, and a stronger bonding of the group. Men began spending more time in the office, ate lunch together, would go to the canteen for each other, and job topics began to be discussed more frequently.

Jim's activities were much different by this time. Jim knew the men much better and could concentrate more on the job. His notebook was full of specifications, and he had fewer and fewer questions to ask. He could not only handle two heats at the same time, but on occasion handled three at once.

The Lead Heat

Leo, sensing this development of competence, began asking Jim to accompany the other men on specialized heats, particularly the leaded heats. He had intimated when first assigning Jim to the North Unit that the assignment would be temporary. He then said that, after two or three months had passed, Jim would have to learn the lead heats to really be an M-1, and be able to handle the two middle units. To teach Jim the lead process, he began an intensified program of training, and had Jim observe every lead heat possible.

Leaded steel is used by the screw machine trade. It can be machined easily into nuts, bolts, spark plugs, and other machined products, and does not lose the basic strength of its molecular structure. (Resulphurized and rephosphorized high-machinability steels are brittle when hot and cold respectively.) Due to the peculiar characteristics of molten lead at high temperatures, it is necessary to add the lead to the molten steel in the pit. In adding lead to ingots, distribution is particularly significant. If added too soon, the lead settles to the bottom of the ingot. If it is not added steadily, it forms lumps and loses strength. The correct quantity of lead must be added to avoid loss of either machinability or strength.

To solve all of these problems, the engineers rigged an air-powered gun that blew fine shot lead into the stream of steel coming from the ladle. In order to control the distribution of lead in the ingot, a valve was arranged to quickly open and close the gun. To control the quantity of lead blown out, the operator timed the period that was required to blow out a given weight of lead, in seconds, at a given pounds per square inch (psi) air pressure.

Operational authority for the lead gun was given to the inspector. He made all calculations, adjusted air pressure on the lead gun, and directed the activities of the man operating the lead gun air valve. In addition, he made an ingot-by-ingot report of the timing, lead additions, distribution, and top-off procedure. (Topping off is the slow filling of the top one eighth of the ingot to assure adequate compensation for shrinkage.) In addition, he was required to record the scale readings and calculate the actual pounds of lead used.

The lead heat was an important assignment for the met inspector. Leaded steel has peculiar chemical properties which make it unusable in unleaded form, and thus, unsalable. The alloying elements were extremely expensive, as was the whole pouring process. Extra stand personnel, special nozzle liners, and a special ventilation system for drawing off poisonous lead fumes were all used exclusively on leaded heats. A downgraded leaded steel heat, therefore, represented very high costs and very low salvage value.

Personal Observations

Jim's impression of leaded heats during his first visits on the lead stand were confused. First, the stand was extremely crowded. Ventilation hoods extended well into the narrow stand and made the walkway quite narrow. Also, the lead gun and its trailing air hose seemed quite obstructive. Normally, only 4 or 5 men would work a given heat. On lead heats twice that number were used, and since lead heats often drew spectators, 15 or 20 men on the stand was not unusual. He also became aware of the intense concentration required of the met inspector. The inspector was equipped with a stopwatch and clipboard, and rarely if ever indulged in casual conversation during the pour of the heat. Studs told him, "Don't ask me anything on a lead heat till it's over." Later, Jim found out the reason for this. The job of adding lead required an extreme degree of carefully calculated judgment in order to achieve both distribution and weight.

Lead Heat Training

In training for lead heats, Jim had little to do. The job was so complex that many of the variables were difficult to explain. Studs worked before and after each heat explaining what he had done and why, but little of the explanation meant anything to Jim. He observed two or three heats with Studs, and about the same number with Roy. After this brief training, he "took" a lead heat, with Studs leaning over his shoulder.

Jim was startled at the difference between observing and running the heat. He was also disturbed by the pressures exerted on the inspector and by the amount of judgment required. For the first few heats he had trouble keeping up with recording information, and his weight averages were highly variable.

Group Development and Analysis

Working on the lead heats seemed to provide the tie which finally drew the group into an integrated unit. Until this time, relations had been more or less perfunctory. Group members had been doing their jobs, writing reports, and following the formal job requirements without much interaction. Any additional contact seemed concentrated to a high degree on Jim's training. Training Jim, while providing an opportunity for additional conversation, seemed more a duty than a voluntary and agreeable job. Jim's temporary slot in the North Unit, and the realization that he would soon end up in the North-Middle Unit, placed an air of expediency or artificiality on the training. Jim was expected by all to learn the job quickly. He was given new jobs much more rapidly than other new inspectors. More important, he was talked to as an equal by Roy and Studs. The impression he received was that they felt that he had just forgotten the job during the last four years, and would soon remember and relearn it. On Jim's part, the pressure to do well was intense. They expected it of him, and he felt that he would lose face or betray their confidence in him if he didn't do well. By the time Jim had worked several lead heats, the training period was over. He was able to handle the job, not just that of met inspector but that of M-1.

The character of group interaction changed during this time. During training, Leo spent a good deal of time in personal supervision of Jim's reporting. His requests for additional information came less often, and he began to ask questions of a less formal and more confidential nature. Leo began to seek specialized information from Jim as he did the other M-1s. Jim continued to ask questions about steelmaking. Leo was always interested, and didn't mind spending the time necessary to explain the problem.

Jim also began to address Leo with less formality, and joined in the joking and light conversation in the office to a greater extent. Jim had the feeling that he could handle the job, and felt less insecure in the group. He felt much more at ease, both on the job, and in the social atmosphere of the office. Leo, in his infrequent trips to the pit would "bet" what the ladle condition would be, before the heat had finished pouring. If the ladle condition fell in between their estimates, a loud, joking argument would ensue. When he would also guess the production in ingots from a heat, similar arguments would arise. Roy, Studs, and Jim began to joke agressively with Leo about aspects of the job. Leo would reply by making playful threats about catching them loafing on the pouring stand. Leo accompanied Jim on a lead heat on which considerable trouble was encountered (something he had not done before). The lead addition and the met report had his complete approval. He complimented Jim on the stand, and later in the office for the way the heat was handled.

Group activities increased: Locker room chatter, eating lunch together, riding to work together, and trips together to the Blooming Mills and the canteen. Leo, Roy, and Jim were perhaps the most active members of the group. They did more joking and talking, and initiated more cooperative activities. George, who had been virtually silent the preceding two or three months, began joining in. Rod continued much as he had in the past. He rarely entered into the conversation, but would explode into the office with a startling statement, such as "The crooked politicians are at it again" (referring to a tabloid he was waving). He would eat in the office, reading the paper, and remain silent. Completing his lunch, he would belch deliberately and loudly, laugh at the group's expression of discomfiture, and leave. At other times he would bring a calculus book to work and study during his spare time. When the shift change occurred, he would ask Ted how to solve particular calculus problems. Rod also brought copies of *Scientific American* to work and read them for hours. He seemed pleased when any of the group would shake their heads at the technicality of the editorial content of his magazine.

In group conversation, Rod had little to say. When asked to comment on a job topic, he usually blustered and introduced an emotionally involved situation which he had encountered in the past. George, on the other hand, would contribute, but in a dry, matter-of-fact way. His reference point was also past experience, and rarely involved the solution of new problems.

Off-the-job activities were relatively limited. Leo made it a point to invite all the crew members out on payday night to a local tavern for beer and hot dogs. When any demurred, Leo would wheedle and plead, usually succeeding in his efforts. These outings fell on 4 P.M. to 12 A.M. shifts, and rarely lasted over an hour. They usually had only one or two beers, and left the tavern by 12:15. The only member of the group who didn't attend nearly all the time was Rod.

Productivity of the Group

During the following five or six months some additional changes took place. These changes, while not as striking perhaps as some of the earlier ones, to Jim had great significance. The first area of change involved the productivity of the met-inspector group. Jim had the feeling that the group did a much more thorough job of inspection, and delineated more clearly the abnormalities which occurred. Jim also observed and partici- pated in a great deal more constructive quality control efforts than he had noticed in the early months. The group not only observed and recorded information about the heats which they followed, but assisted the produc- tion personnel in a variety of ways. When really troublesome heats were made, they actively engaged in troubleshooting and corrective activities. Their performance on the critical and difficult lead heats improved greatly, and they were actively engaged in problem solving on the leaded steel program.

In observing and assisting Roy and Studs, and in handling his own lead heats, the variations in the lead gun's performance were particularly vexing to Jim. In coffee-klatch discussions, the group would try to solve this problem, and would advance various hypotheses as to the cause of the trouble. Then, on the next lead heat, they would go down on the stand and check their theory out in practice. They managed to uncover some hitherto undiscovered peculiarities about the lead gun, and gained a great deal of knowledge about the gun and its effective operation. Their per- formance improved considerably, and it soon became uncommon for any of the entire group to vary significantly from the unofficial standard set by the "exceptional" inspectors.

After Jim had been broken in on the lead heats, he continued to work for some time in the North Unit. When lead heats came up in the North- Middle, he was usually either free or on a heat of his own in the pit. In either case, he would go down on the lead stand and help Studs on the heat. Studs certainly didn't *need* the help, since he had broken Jim in on the lead heats, but Jim went down anyway. On these trips Jim would monitor the air pressure (the pressure valve had a habit of creeping), assist Studs in obtaining scale readings, and stand by to assist in the event of trouble. More than anything, these were social visits, but on several occasions the help was needed and was appreciated. Jim did the same thing with Roy, and continued this practice long after he was broken in.

After about five or six months, Studs took a vacation, and Jim was told by Leo to take his unit. This was a real pleasure to Jim for several reasons. First, he liked the more complex heats made in the middle units. They offered a much wider variety of specifications, and were more challenging. Second, he began working lead heats regularly. Third, he was close to the office and could spend more time in the office talking to Leo, George, and Roy than he had been able to while working the North Unit. Finally, the unit being close to the office reduced the amount of walking involved, and made the job physically less tiring.

Jim had no trouble handling the North-Middle Unit. He didn't know the floor personnel, but by this time he had quite well established group rela- tionships within the met group, and the hostility presented by the Open Hearth group was much easier to handle. Also, by this time he had developed personal confidence in his ability, and felt that he had risen in the rank ladder. The floor personnel knew that the met department put only experienced men in the middle units, and seemed to accept him much more readily than had the men in the North Unit.

While working in the North-Middle Unit, Jim noticed some rather interesting things happening on the lead heats. On his first few heats, Leo sent George down to "help out." George balked, saying "Aw, he can handle it," but accompanied Jim according to directions. After three or four more heats, this time by himself, Jim noticed Roy dropping down to visit. He usually didn't bother Jim, but talked to the pit foreman or steel pourer, and was available if needed. His visits were social and in no way meant to Jim that he was incapable of handling the heat. On these social visits Roy was at his beck and call, and would quickly answer Jim's request for assistance. The assistance was usually in the form of some essentially menial task which Jim could have handled by himself, but which could have been handled very easily by another man. They compared notes on the lead heats, and would question each other about heats on which they had not had the opportunity of helping out.

When Studs came back, Leo placed him in the North Unit, and left Jim in North-Middle. Jim was concerned about Studs's feelings, and made mention of it to him. Studs said, "No, it's your unit. You should have it" in a perfectly straightforward manner, acting not the least put out. He began coming down on lead heats with both Roy and Jim as Jim had done when he had worked the North Unit.

During the last few months of this group experience, group cohesion was very high. The group did not engage in many outside activities as a group, but continued to work together very actively within the mill. Helping out began to occur on other special heats as well as the lead heats, and active discussion of critical metallurgical problems continued. Jim observed that no group member missed a day of work during that period. The beer and hot dog outings continued regularly during that period. The group also began to discuss their crew as a crew, and Leo said several times that "this is the best crew I've ever had." They talked about the competence of the crew, and mentioned the fact that this was the only crew with four M-1's on it.

Section 4

MANAGEMENT INTERVENTIONS

The cases and incidents in this section address topics under the general headings of (1) organization development and planned change; (2) management development; (3) joint goal-setting and management by objectives (MBO); (4) punishment and discipline; (5) performance appraisal; (6) behavior modification; and (7) job design and redesign. This section is designed to help the students of management and organization behavior further develop their human skills by actually applying them in real work situations through several avenues of management action.

When analyzing the following cases, the reader may find the model of Professor Robert Kahn, from the University of Michigan, helpful. Kahn sees the work of managers in organizations consisting of technical, human, and conceptual skills (see Figure 4–1).

Technical skills are defined as those advanced techniques required to produce the product of the organization. For example, in a manufacturing firm, such as TRW, engineering is one of the technical skills required to produce space communications. The counseling skills needed by a counselor in a state social service agency is another example.

FIGURE 4–1

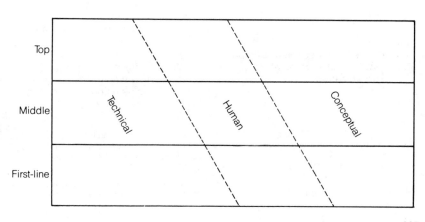

Conceptual skills are management's abilities to see the complete or whole picture and analyze how the organization relates to its larger environment and society. Conceptual skills relate to long-range goal-setting and planning. Typical conceptual questions that managers attempt to answer are:

1. What will our product mix be in five years?
2. What will our marketing strategy be for that mix?
3. What types of people will we need in five years to produce that product? Can we hire them from universities or must we design an internal training program?

Human skills are the capabilities for interpersonal and group interaction that are needed by managers to produce more effective work teams. About 80 to 90 percent of a manager's problems in complex organizations are human problems, yet first-line managers are normally selected on their technical skills (the best technician is promoted) and soon discover that they need human skills. Recently, a poll of new supervisors indicated

FIGURE 4–2
Typology of Interventions Based on the Size and Complexity of the Work Group

Target	Types of Interventions
Interventions designed to improve the effectiveness of individuals	Life and career planning Management development* Punishment and discipline* Performance appraisal* Behavior modification* Sensitivity training
Interventions designed to improve the effectiveness of dyads/triads	Third-party peacemaking Process consultation Joint goal-setting and MBO*
Interventions designed to improve the effectiveness of teams and groups	Family T-group Survey feedback Job design/redesign* Team building Education in decision making and problem solving
Interventions designed to improve the effectiveness of the total organization	Survey feedback Organization development and planned change* Strategic planning Corporation meetings Sensing

  * Cases on these interventions are included within this section. For a description and review of all interventions see Wendell L. French, Cecil H. Bell, Jr., and Robert A. Zawacki, *Organization Development: Theory, Practice, and Research* (Dallas: Business Publications, Inc., 1978), pp. 113–316.

  Source: This is a modification from W. L. French, C. H. Bell, Jr., and Robert A. Zawacki, *Organization Development: Theory, Practice, and Research* (Dallas: Business Publications, 1978), p. 115.

that 89 percent of those surveyed desired more knowledge of how to work with people.[1]

Thus, the cases in this section were selected to highlight human and conceptual problems and the application of management techniques toward their solution.

Another typology of management techniques (interventions) that we have found helpful is a classification that is based upon the size and complexity of the work group (see Figure 4–2).

As can be noted above, the cases and incidents in the final section of this book have been selected to highlight individual, group, and organizational level interventions. The objective is to place the reader in an ongoing real-life organization with the purpose of refining the understanding and application of various management tools and techniques. We believe that the reader can benefit from practicing helping skills rather than only reading about them, and recommend the adoption of a helping role as a mental set in case analysis and preparation. It is our belief that a conceptual understanding of a particular management intervention and an understanding of its level of application (see Figure 4–2) can have maximum impact only when situations are described in a form which permits the student to fully understand its impact, and to recognize the behavioral "fallout" from that intervention—a recognition that may require exploration at any one or all of the levels of analysis used in the earlier sections.

ADDITIONAL SELECTED READINGS

Arvey, Richard D., and Ivancevich, John M. "Punishment in Organizations: A Review, Propositions, and Research Suggestions." *Academy of Management Review* (January 1980), pp. 123–32.

Burke, W. Warner, and Schmidt, Warren H. "Management and Organization: What Is the Target Group?" *Personnel Administration* (March-April 1971), pp. 44–57.

Davis, Louis E., and Taylor, James C. *Design of Jobs.* Pacific Palisades, Calif.: Goodyear Publishing Co., 1979.

Fisher, Robert W. "When Workers are Discharged: An Overview." *Monthly Labor Review* (June 1973), pp. 4–17.

French, Wendell L., and Bell, Cecil H. *Organization Development.* Englewood Cliffs, N.J.: Prentice-Hall, 1978.

French, Wendell L., Bell, Cecil H., and Zawacki, Robert A. *Organization Development: Theory, Practice, and Research.* Dallas: Business Publications, 1978).

Hackman, J. R., et al. "A New Strategy for Job Enrichment." *California Management Review* (1975), pp. 57–71.

Hollmann, Robert W. "Applying MBO Research to Practice." *Human Resource Management* (Winter 1976), pp. 28–36.

Kane, Jeffrey S., and Lawler, Edward E. III,. "Performance Appraisal Effectiveness: Its Assessment and Determinants." In Barry M. Staw, ed., *Re-*

---

[1] Quoted by Lester Bittel, *What Every Supervisor Should Know,* 3d ed. (New York: McGraw-Hill, 1974), p. 18.

search in Organizational Behavior, vol. 7. Greenwich, Conn.: JAI Press, 1979, pp. 425–78.

Locke, Edwin A.   "The Myths of Behavior Mod in Organizations." *Academy of Management Review,* Oct. 1977, pp. 543–53.

Luthans, Fred, and Martinko, Mark J.   *The Practice of Supervision and Management.* New York: McGraw-Hill, 1979, pp. 412–22.

Oldham, Greg R., and Hackman, J. Richard.   "Work Design in the Organizational Context." In Barry M. Staw and L. L. Cummings, eds., *Research in Organizational Behavior,* vol. 2. Greenwich, Conn.: JAI Press, 1980, pp. 247–78.

Rosenbach, William E., Zawacki, Robert A., and Morgan, Cycil P.   "Research Round-up." *Personnel Administration* (October 1977), pp. 51–61.

Taylor, Robert L., and Zawacki, Robert A.   "Collaborative Goal Setting in Performance Appraisal: A Field Experiment." *Public Personnel Management* (May-June 1978), pp. 162–70.

Wiard, Harry.   "Why Manage Behavior?—A Case for Positive Reinforcement." *Human Resources Management* (Summer 1972), pp. 15–20.

Case 4–1 ───

Detroit Ranger District (A)

Craig C. Lundberg

The snow was falling heavily, slanting into the headlights of Dr. Eric Lund's car as he drove through the corridors of forest up the mountain pass on his way home from the retreat session of the Detroit Development Team (DDT). There was no other traffic and the rhythmic noise of the windshield wipers prompted reflection. Dr. Lund wondered whether the purposes of the session had really been accomplished and, in puzzling over this matter, recalled his first knowledge that there would be such a session.

It had been in the early part of the second week of March 1975, when Professor Lund received a call from Bill Devoe, the regional training officer for the United States Forest Service. Professor Lund and Mr. Devoe had been acquainted for several years, the latter on several occasions inviting Professor Lund to act as consultant in several parts of the region and to conduct several management development sessions for regional managers. Mr. Devoe knew that Dr. Lund was a business professor at the state university and was active as a behavioral consultant to management, particularly with regards to organizational change. In the telephone conversation, Mr. Devoe explained the purpose of his call:

> In the Cascade National Forest, which you're familiar with, there's this district up to the east of Salem called Detroit.[1] These people have undertaken a really ambitious project of self-studying their district in an

EXHIBIT 1
Detroit District Organization, 1975

Regional Forester

Forest Supervisor, Cascade National Forest

District Ranger

Siviculture Department	Timber Sale Plans	Timber Sales Department	Fire Department	Recreation Resources and Other Departments	Business Management Department
-Reforestation	-Logging System Specialist	-Timber Sales Officers	-Helicopter		-Personnel Specialist
-Timber Sale Inspection		-Small Sales	-Suppression		-Purchasing
-Fuels Specialist		-Appraisal Specialist	-Preventional Detection		-Shop
		-Resale	-Spotter		-Public Information
			-Support		

---

[1] See Exhibit 1 for the Detroit Ranger District Organization. Presented at a Case Workshop and distributed by the Intercollegiate Case Clearing House, Soldiers Field, Boston, MA 02163. All rights reserved to the contributors. Printed in the USA.

attempt to change it for the better. They've done this by creating an internal team, a kind of cross section of the district, to do the tough study job. This team just isn't getting its act together, they seem to have trouble getting together and working as a real team. Recently, the ranger got himself onto this team, and he called me up and asked if I could help them do something to get the team functioning. This is kind of short notice. They have, at the end of the month, set aside a weekend for the team to go away to a retreat-type session. I'd like to ask you and several other people to go on the weekend and see what you can do to help this team get on with its task.

After some conversation about the exact dates and the fee, Professor Lund agreed to act as a consultant to the retreat session, although he asked Mr. Devoe if he might have more information about the ranger, the DDT and the district, and who else might show up as consultants. Mr. Devoe responded that he was really pressed for time at that moment, that in fact there were several long-distance calls waiting for him. He said that he would dictate this information on cassette and send it to Professor Lund within the next few days. Excerpts from this cassette appear below.

The Detroit District is the furthest from the forest supervisor's office and often feels out in left field, so to speak. They've been through all kinds of changes, most of them under the guise of more productivity and efficiency. Detroit sits on a large reservoir way up in the mountains. Previously, Detroit had been split into two districts, one Detroit and one Mill City, and a number of the presently employed personnel still live the 20 or 25 miles down the highway in Mill City. As I say, the split and the subsequent merger of the districts was supposed to result in all kinds of better economics, greater amount of productivity, and so forth. But, in fact a lot of things went the other way. For example, there were two engineers and one of the engineers one morning found himself leaving and to this date doesn't know why. There was a guy that was "A" ranked for promotion who was at that time in place as a ranger's assistant, and there were some new people brought in from other districts, most of them promotable candidates, many of them no longer there, too. One of those people brought in at that time was in the timber function, but is now promoted to a different kind of job, in fire, I think. His name is Baldy Burns. He underwent open heart surgery some time ago, but now is back on the job and looks great.

At the time of all this merger and unmerger of districts, the forest was under Jim Disney as the forest supervisor, and the forest was normally referred to as Region 13 or Disneyland.[2] I should point out that the Cascade is one of the three largest forests in the region and probably the greatest timber harvesting unit we have. Anyhow, all the changes on the Detroit resulted in all kinds of things—one of which is that they felt they were a pretty culturally deprived group. They produced a lot of timber and had some slack in the old days which was fast disappearing, but really felt too far from the forest headquarters. Now, after the remerger of districts, there was a big emphasis in the region on job enrichment. I can remember going down to the Detroit with a couple of other people at that

---

[2] There are 12 regions in the U.S.F.S. See Exhibit 2 for the relevant organization.

EXHIBIT 2
Organization of the U.S.F.S.

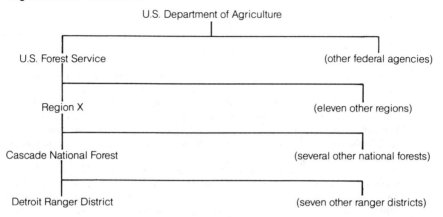

U.S. Department of Agriculture

U.S. Forest Service — (other federal agencies)

Region X — (eleven other regions)

Cascade National Forest — (several other national forests)

Detroit Ranger District — (seven other ranger districts)

time and discovering that their job enrichment really hasn't been oc-curring. Actually, instead of being job enrichment, there was job de-en-richment. Actually, when Disney retired, a new supervisor came in, Jones, who was like second or third generation forest service—real charismatic—anyhow he moved in and reorganized the entire forest again and a lot of outsiders came in and did a lot of acts with these people. For instance, Jim and Maggie Craton came in and did some development sessions and are now known all over the forest as the Maggie and Jiggs Act. Also, my neuropsychologist friend, Donald Silver, did some lectures about stress and things. These are really great if you want to do something with them, you know as pump priming, but nothing ever ensued or followed. People on the forest now refer to sort of having gone to church with Silver. Other changes—this engineer came in from another region and he reorganized engineering on the district and centralized it very much under Jones's bidding. A lot of people really got turned off on the district. Anyhow, after about a year and a half they had to turn it into a zone so that now Detroit shares some engineering services with other districts and don't have any of their own. Anyhow, just like with the engineers or engineering types on the district, people are really getting up tight. The ranger at that time, Rickbagel, was excommunicated. Everybody at the district level thought of him as being Jones's puppet.

So, we have a first-class, second-class citizen thing going on. People on the district see themselves as being used and as the stepping-stones of other folks. Secondly, there is a heck of a clash between technicians and professionals within the same unit on the district. Of course, this isn't just restricted to Detroit. Anyhow, there's a whole bunch of stress going on, and as we know, one of the ways to relieve stress is to become much more defined in terms of your own technical area, hence hoping to get stability in your work life.

And then this other new ingredient came and that was a new district ranger moving down from the north of the region. Donald Dew moved down there and was told that, in a sense, he would become the model dis-trict. That is, he was to reorganize it and based on all that, the other districts on the forest would follow whatever model he came up with. Shortly after that he also found that this was one of the selected districts to move up to GS-13. In the meantime, just about the time Donald moved, his wife up and left. I believe there is a trial separation going on. His wife, I believe, is over in the Rockies somewhere. Don't believe a formal divorce yet, but at least a trial separation is going on.

Donald told the new supervisor, Dave Webber, who is very much cut off the old Forest Service block, so to speak, a younger guy moving in from back east, to stick it. Eventually, though, they negotiated and Donald got some concessions in that the districts would not all necessarily follow after his district and I guess there were some good feelings about this. Donald then formed a work group and said, "You know that your task is to do this and I want a cross section representation." So every department elected someone onto the DDT.

And the team did have a meeting with the forest supervisor and other rangers on the supervisor's staff and got a go-ahead. Donald did take his own folks over to a couple of the forests to the east to look at the different kinds of organizations to see if they were working. The day they came back and reported to the other district employees I was there and heard their presentation. It was not the smoothest or most easily received report you've ever heard. In fact, one of the outgrowths of that was the kind of thing we're going to be doing hopefully for a few days over at Trail Creek.

While listening, Dr. Lund thought to himself that perhaps there was going to be a lot of challenge in the Trail Creek meeting. There seem to be a lot of factors impinging on the DDT as well as their difficulties internally. The cassette continued:

I know several of the people over on the district, I've been working with Baldy Burns, and Elton White, who I think is with the recreation gang. Another guy I've worked with is Lou Moss, who works in the fire shop. I guess Baldy is in the timber shop. Elton is really competent but quiet, Baldy is an old timer and I think not too eager for change. Lou is a newer guy to the Forest Service and full of piss and vinegar.

Anyhow, Donald called me, as you know, and asked if I could help them design something to get their team together. We're going to have a whole clutch of consultants, Rich Maitland from Montana and Ralph Simmons from Portland you know. We're also going to have Helen Fox from Portland. She's been interested in the public involvement and environmental stuff. Also we're going to have David Milton who's back from the Rocky Mountains and has done a number of management things for us in the region. I'll be there, of course, and yourself. I don't have a really clear plan of how we might operate. As you can see, we're going to have all kinds of expertise amongst the consultants.

At this point Dr. Lund had some uneasy feelings. He wondered if he could work with the DDT and coordinate enough with the other consultants. Getting the consultants' act together probably was going to be very important. Mr. Devoe's voice continued:

Recognize that the DDT group is really a diagonal slice of the district and secondly that they have very little exposure to the variety of things that other forests do. We're going to have to devise a framework for the entry of these people into the team building work, for these people are pretty darn gun-shy. They're talking about think tanks and are very, very uptight. I brought up the issue of spouses being invited and that just about freaked them out. In contrast, it would just about be mandatory if it were on other units someplace else in the region. So, all in all, there's a sense of really covering your fanny.

On late Saturday afternoon the several consultants met together at Summit Lodge on their way to the retreat site. Over coffee and pie, Bill Devoe once again outlined his understanding of the DDT's need. Most of this short meeting was spent in casual, get-acquainted endeavors by the consultants who didn't know one another. Devoe emphasized that the retreat would probably need some structure but that they ought to go really slow and not force too fast a pace in the retreat. The consultants then, in their individual cars, proceeded as a convoy over the pass and down on the eastern side of the mountain, finding their way to Trail Creek Lodge just about dusk. The DDT had proceeded them and the lodge had a fire crackling in the main fireplace and the dinner had been started. (Exhibit 3 provides information about who was at Trail Creek Lodge.)

Soon after the consultants arrived and sleeping space had been apportioned in the several cabins surrounding the lodge, everyone met in the

EXHIBIT 3
Participants at the Trail Creek Retreat

Name	Title
Mr. Bill Devoe	Regional Training Officer
Dr. Eric Lund	Professor of Behavioral Science and Administration, State University
Dr. Rich Maitland	Professor of Forestry, University of the Rocky Mountains
Dr. Ralph Simmons	Professor of Systems Analysis, City University of the West
Ms. Helen Fox	Free-lance consultant, City of the West
Mr. David Milton	Free-lance consultant, Salt Lake City
Mr. Donald Dew	Ranger, Detroit District
Ms. Mary Jo Miller	Administrative Assistant, Head of the Business Management Department
Mr. Baldy Burns	Professional Forester, V. Tinker Sales Department, Timber Sale Officer
Mr. Elton White	Professional Forester, Recreation and Other Resources Department
Mr. Lou Moss	Technician, Fire Suppression Unit
Ms. Jane Vernell	Clerk-Secretary, assigned to Timber Sale Inspection Unit, Silviculture Department
Mr. Gary Dunbar	Technician, Timber Appraiser, Presale Unit, Timber Sales Department
Mr. Ed Wilson	Professional Forester, Reforestation Unit, Silviculture Department

main lodge for dinner, prepared and served by Lou Moss with help from some of the women on the DDT. Dinner was casual, people gently inquiring about who one another were, what they did, and where they came from. Retiring with coffee to the living room with its roaring fire, rustic interior, and several large comfortable couches, people continued to socialize for another hour or more before turning into bed.

Sunday morning broke with the sun shining brightly on the snowfields around the lodge and with snow beginning to drop off the large fir trees surrounding the lodge. Breakfast was again served by Lou Moss and by 9:00 A.M. the dishes had been taken care of and people had once more assembled in the living room with its fire. At this point, Bill Devoe spoke briefly by way of introduction saying in general terms why they were all together. In the gentlest terms possible, he pointed out that the consultants had been invited primarily by him, but at the DDT's initiation, to do what they could to help the DDT get a better handle on their work and to become more effective as a team. He then turned to members of the DDT and asked if they would tell something about the district and about what the DDT had been doing as a way of bringing the consultants up-to-date.

Until lunchtime there was a free-flowing conversation about the district, its activities, personnel, and some of the issues that members of the DDT thought that the district faced. Increasing variety and amount of work was mentioned, minorities, more pressure from external organizations, that the subcultural difference between professionals and technicians was an issue, that a good part of the district was in a wait-and-see stance, very skeptical about the DDT.

After a casual lunch when everyone was reassembled back in the living room, the consultants began to ask questions—some of them technical about Forest Service matters as perceived or experienced on the district. These questions came largely from Rich and David. Other questions had to do with the general management of the district. These questions coming from Ralph, Eric, and Helen. Bill Devoe had retreated very much to an observer role at this time. As the consultants warmed up to their questioning, subconversations occurred over and over again.

By coffee break, around 2:45 that afternoon, a number of interesting observations had been shared. One was that the DDT was not in very much contact with other members of the district; second, that the DDT really had very little idea of what it was about; third was the unmistakable conclusion that the DDT was not very unified, that there were, in fact, coalitions there, largely in terms of age, functions, and gender. Mary Jo, during the past several hours, had been one of the most talkative members of the DDT. Lou and Donald also had been very talkative. Gary, Jane, and Elton, however, had been relatively quiet. During the coffee break Eric took Elton and Lou off to chat. Eric asked Lou and Elton what their impressions were of what had gone on so far, and he was told it "seemed ok" although it "wasn't clear what was happening." Eric then asked how strong various members of the DDT were as persons, particularly Donald. The clear and immediate answer to this question was that Donald was perceived by these two men as being very strong, as well as very bright.

On reassembling after the coffee break Eric began to ask Donald about his views of being on the district and its ranger. Donald began to speak slowly and carefully, actually repeating much of what had been learned before. Eventually, with continued questioning by Eric, he began to slowly talk about his own thoughts and feelings regarding being a ranger at that time:

> You know being a ranger isn't what people think it's cracked up to be. Everyone thinks, "Here's this new guy with the reputation. Let's see what he can do." I feel like everyone expects me to be a super ranger! Somehow I'm supposed to leap over tall mountains in one jump, to stamp out forest fires magically, to have the forest super and the other big boys eating out of my hand. Everyone at the district stands around with their hands in their pockets waiting for me to somehow bring about enthusiasm and change in the district singlehandedly.

As he spoke about living up to this image of a super ranger, Donald began to speak quieter and quieter. After a pause, he began to sob and went on haltingly:

> Nothing is clearer to me than that I'm not a super ranger. I'm probably a pretty good ranger, but I'm human, too. God, I feel alone here. I can't do it alone. I feel so damn isolated. I sure need help. Help from everybody. Otherwise nothing will get done.

Donald put his head in his hands and sobbed some more. After a pause, Mary Jo got out of her chair and moved over to Donald and put an arm around his shoulder. The rest of the room sat in shocked silence, but as the ranger finished, others began to murmur such things as "we didn't know," "I never looked at it that way before," "Gee, we're really sorry, Don, 'cause we think you're really a good guy," and so on.

Dr. Lund then suggested that everybody ought to "take a short break, get more coffee, and catch our breath," a suggestion quickly accepted by all. During the break, Eric and Rich went with Donald onto the porch and chatted. Donald said that he was very relieved to say what he had, that he had it building up in him for a long time, and that he was a little apprehensive about the way people might respond to it, but he certainly felt better for it. Rich and Eric both commented that it was a big risk for him to say what he had, but that it was probably useful that people began to see their ranger as a human being.

Reassembling in the living room, the consultants were at the outside of the circle formed by the DDT. The conversation that picked up continued that which had been occurring just before the break. Even the previously quiet members of the DDT, Gary and Elton and Jane, spoke up saying that basically they felt their ranger was a good one, that the DDT probably had talent, that the district certainly needed their efforts, and so forth. The remainder of the afternoon was spent in a couple of exercises suggested by Helen and Eric. One of them had the DDT physically arrange themselves in terms of the amount of contact they had with one another on the job. Another was to physically align themselves in terms of how close they felt to one another with the amount of distance indicating experienced social distance. By the time dinner preparations had to be started, there was a general sense of exhaustion on the one hand, and a growing sense of excitement among members of the retreat on the other.

As dinner preparations were started, everyone seemed to be pitching in, consultants and DDT, helping to prepare salads, setting the table, peeling potatoes, finding pans, and so forth. Dr. Lund, who had to leave the retreat at this time, went around and talked to a few people. He said goodbye to his fellow consultants and Bill Devoe, suggesting to them that in the evening session and tomorrow morning (which were also scheduled), they do some more skill building on clarifying communications, but eventually get the DDT into a work session. He suggested that the topic might be how and what to report to the district on their retreat. He strongly urged that this be held as a regular work session of the DDT, and that it be interrupted as appropriate by the consultants to process the group and to offer suggestions of how to proceed more effectively. With that, Dr. Lund went to the ranger, "Donald, I hope our paths cross again in the future. You showed a lot of guts in there today, and as you can see, your team is starting to come alive." He then suggested to Donald his ideas about a little more skill building, that the DDT should have a work session getting ready for going home, and reporting to the district on this retreat. As he and Don walked to Eric's car, Dr. Lund finished his remarks. "Anyhow, if there's anything I can ever do in the future, please call on me. You have my office phone. I've really appreciated being here and getting to know you."

With that, Dr. Lund started his car and began the trip home.

Case 4–2 ————————————————————————————————

Detroit Ranger District (B)

Craig C. Lundberg

In August 1975, Mr. Donald Dew, ranger of the Detroit Ranger District, began a search for an external consultant. This search was at the wish of the Detroit Development Team (DDT), which, since the beginning of the year, had been involved in a major self-study project for the district.[1] Mr. Dew contacted the regional training officer, Mr. Devoe, about possible consultants, and was reminded that Dean Peter Burke of the State University School of Business was someone that might help. Mr. Dew remembered

---

[1] See Case 4–1 for information about the District organization and the Detroit Ranger District. Presented at a Case Workshop and distributed by the Intercollegiate Case Clearing House, Soldiers Field, Boston, MA 02163. All rights reserved to the contributors. Printed in the USA.

that he had heard Dean Burke give a presentation on management by objectives (MBO) to regional Forest Service managers previously and this led to his calling the Dean in late August. Mr. Dew was aware that the school of business at State University had been involved with the Forest Service in several ways in recent years, either by putting on executive and supervisory training programs of various kinds or by its faculty consulting with national forests and districts throughout the region.

On calling Dean Burke, Mr. Dew explained his need and an appointment was set up. Following that phone conversation, Dean Burke, in turn, called Professor Lund and in that conversation discovered that Professor Lund knew Mr. Dew and had had some acquaintanceship with the DDT (see Case A preceding). On the day that Mr. Dew visited the school of business, Professor Lund sat in on the meeting with the dean. It quickly came out that Mr. Dew thought he needed a wide variety of help. He knew that, because of various changes in Forest Service management practices, some technical help with computers and management systems might be necessary, as well as some organizational management expertise. The dean quickly excused himself and suggested that Mr. Dew and Professor Lund might want to continue chatting, he also mentioned Professor McTavit, a professor of management science, as being someone who might help. Professor McTavit was contacted, and Mr. Dew and Professors Lund and McTavit met in Dr. Lund's office to continue talking. Mr. Dew pointed out that the DDT only had until the end of the year to come up with a diagnostic report, including recommendations for change. He shared his opinion that the team had recently started to bog down after having a summer in which a lot of good problems had been identified. Professors Lund and McTavit indicated they were generally interested and had time available to consult with the district, and the three men discussed the probable number of contact days required and their fee. At the end of this conversation, the professors said that they would write up a rough proposal which Mr. Dew would need to obtain money from the National Forest Service. The contract would state that they would help the DDT prepare its report but that it would be understood that the two business professors would have two tasks. One was to facilitate the development team and its work, the second was to provide expertise on management systems, organizational structure, and similar management topics, as such expertise was not readily available within the district. A couple of days later the two professors met to talk about the contract and rough it out, as per their agreement with Mr. Dew. Professor Lund then called the ranger, said that they had a draft of the contract, and that it would be sent. Mr. Dew said that he would be going through the university town in the next week and that he would stop and pick it up. He further agreed to have a meeting with the consultants in which they could interview the ranger to get a better feel for the district and what they might do to help it.

In the third week of September, Mr. Dew showed up at Professor Lund's office at the appointed time. Professor McTavit had been called out of town and so Professor Lund and Mr. Dew held an approximately two-hour conversation without him. The conversation was largely a question and answer period; Professor Lund asking about the current organization of the district (see Case A) and details of personnel and activities. He learned that the district was involved in a wide range of activities. As he had some contact with the DDT in March at their Trail Creek meeting, he also asked Mr. Dew what had happened as a result of the Trail Creek session. The ranger said that the DDT had gone back to the district immediately after the retreat, had called a meeting of all district personnel, and had reported on their work to date and what had happened at the retreat. Dew said that it was a little embarrassing because the DDT didn't feel that they could report that the ranger had cried and that people had mostly sat around and talked for a couple of days. But, nevertheless, he reported that the other district personnel had seemed very interested and appreciative of being informed. A lot of questions had been asked at the meeting, and coffee break discussions for days had focused on what the DDT was doing. Mr. Dew also said that in April the DDT had invested quite a lot of energy in surveying the problems in the district by soliciting lists from all district personnel. They had then consolidated the lists and circulated it within the district (see Exhibit 1). In addition, the DDT and the ranger at the end of April had taken their list of problems to a meeting in Portland with the regional training officer, Mr. Devoe, and other members of the region's intensive semester participants.[2] At this meeting in Portland they had found confirmation from these other experienced Forest Service managers on the reality of the problems listed.

Mr. Dew reported that in July, Baldy, one member of the DDT, had been replaced by him and that this had caused quite a lot of strong feelings in the district since Baldy was an "old timer." The DDT had also solicited from the forest supervisor constraints to their work and they had received some. They had also listed a set of desired characteristics of a ranger district. It was in the later part of July and early August, however, that the DDT had decided to intensively examine alternative organization structures and, as these discussions began to happen, the notion was expressed that external assistance might become necessary to identify criteria for choosing among alternative organizational structures as well as providing a source of other ideas and experience. As the discussion of alternative structure and examination of possible problem solutions continued, the enormity of the organization study was experienced once again by the DDT, and this had then led to the search for an external consultant. Mr. Dew said that in the past few weeks the DDT had not seemed very productive—they'd spent almost all their time drawing alternative charts and arguing about them. It seemed like everybody had a favorite structure and wasn't very open to hearing about others. Professor Lund and Mr. Dew then talked about the schedule of visits. It was quickly identified that the DDT had a meeting later in September, and it was agreed that that might

---

[2] An in-house management training program attended by 14 staff members from national forests in the region.

EXHIBIT 1
DDT Consolidated List of District Problems

1. "Instances when staff, individually or collectively, does not coordinate due to poor communications causing lack of direction and productions fall down."

2. "Manpower leveling not being planned between sections, resulting in some sections being busy and others slack, cross training is poor, poor utilization of talent."

3. "Lack of coordination in planning and development of timber sales projects."

4. "Minority employees have not been integrated into the district."

5. "Lack of involvement at all levels results in poor management, lack of trust, lack of accomplishment, individual dissatisfaction, poor efficiency, etc."

6. "Poor individual career and life planning, job enrichment, performance evaluation, and counseling."

7. "Supervision:
   a. Supervisors not selected on a rational basis.
   b. People not prepared when they step into the role of a supervisor.
   c. Inconsistency in supervisors.
   d. Lack of proper delegation and lack of followup after delegation is made.
   e. Lack of concern for sub employees.
   f. Too many employees to supervise at one time.
   g. Lack of firmness at proper times (and fairness).
   h. Roles and responsibilities not always clear to supervisors and others.
   i. Not enough credit given for work.
   j. Supervisors expected to do it all—supervisors should expect completed work."

be a good time for the consultants to initiate their visits. It was planned that the consultants would use the first meeting to get acquainted with the DDT, to get the DDT's version of what they had been doing and what yet needed to be done, and to then play it by ear.

On September 28, Professors McTavit and Lund met at 7:45 A.M. at Professor Lund's house to team up to drive to the district. Because of the impending semester and other events, they had not really had a chance to talk much before. During the drive up into the mountains, well supplied with a thermos of coffee, Professor Lund shared the above information about his interview with the ranger and they talked about the task ahead of them.

Case 4–3 ——
Attitude Survey at Artisan
Frank C. Barnes

In early summer 1976, 29-year-old Bill Meister was a little surprised at his "superstar" status. One year ago, in a crisis situation, he had taken over as president of the $10 million-a-year, family-run company and successfully halted Artisan Industries' slide into bankruptcy. Outsiders, such as the banks and suppliers, had renewed confidence in the company and the employees now looked toward a chance at higher wages and job security.

Bill had looked forward to shaping up and heading an exciting, highly competent organization. He was greatly interested in the newest concepts of management, frequently commenting on the latest book or sending a copy of an article to his managers. The behavioral writings made a lot of sense to him and he was, himself, quite perceptive of behavioral processes in meetings or situations. The participative management systems and cooperative team environments were ones Bill wanted very much for Artisan.

However, in his first year he had slowly begun to doubt that his managers and the work force were ready. On a number of occasions he had observed his managers manipulating rather than cooperating, and the workers appeared neither skilled nor productive. The first-line supervisors lacked any current management training and had been of little use so far in his efforts. For example, when he discussed the workers' desires with the supervisors he was told they wanted a retirement program and higher pay, nothing else. Bill felt, however, this was really only what the supervisors themselves wanted.

Bill was ready to scale back his expectations, if necessary, and view improvement in the personnel systems as a very long-term project. Rather than guess at what the employees saw and wanted, it made sense to carry out an attitude survey. From this he could sharpen his understanding of the employees and choose his actions more wisely.

BACKGROUND

Artisan had been founded by Bill's father, a classical entrepreneur, in the early fifties. His father had done well against many setbacks to bring the company to its current size, but things had not gone well in recent years. He had fought against Bill's replacing him as president and several tense months resulted. Only outside pressure from the lenders resulted in Bill's ascension to the presidency.

In May 1975, when Bill Meister became president, Artisan was in critical condition. Sales had fallen off dramatically, there had been little profit for three years, the number of employees had fallen from 600 to

370, modern management systems existed in no area of the company, and there were few qualified managers. "When I took over, sales were running 50 percent off and we could not get a line of credit through our suppliers, we were on a cash basis only, inventory was still relatively high, accounts receivable were running over 120 days, manufacturing was without anyone in charge, and the company was sustaining a loss of approximately $10,000 a week. The general situation looked pretty hopeless."

But Bill had managed to turn things back around and 1975 had ended with the best profit in several years, $390,000. His major accomplishments had been improving the product line for salability and implementing a price increase.

The company was one of four making up the wooden decorative products industry. Sales were seasonal, peaking with the Christmas period. Artisan's customers were some 13,000 retail shops which were serviced by outside sales representatives, and regional market shows were an important part of the marketing activity. The product line consisted of over 1,400 items and included almost anything for the consumer, from a tea cart, which was the largest item, to a clothes pin-type desk paper clip, which was the smallest.

Production was accomplished in two similar rural plants employing a total of about 300 people. Kiln-dry lumber entered at the back and progressed through six departments before finishing with stains, packing, and warehousing. Most jobs did not require high skill levels and wage rates were relatively low. Visitors to the plant considered the work pace quite slow; the supervisors, however, did not. Orders were small, usually under 200 items, and made up of seven parts on the average. Thus runs were small, not at all like mass production.

Bill felt production efficiency was a major problem. In talks with machinery salesmen and other visitors to the plant over recent months, he had come to feel that the machinery was generally appropriate; but based on guesses about his competitors, he felt his labor costs had to be reduced. Early attempts to work with the plant superintendent and the various supervisors to systematically improve output had met with no success. The supervisors had been unable to identify the needs for change in the plant or to develop the programs for bringing about improvement. To help the supervisors begin to improve their operations, a weekly production meeting had begun in June of 1975. At the meeting the supervisors were to examine the total dollar output and total labor cost for each plant for the past week, compare it to the labor percent goal set by Bill, and think about what could be done to improve operations for the coming week. Data on departmental performance was not available. During the first several meetings, a visiting consultant had to provide direction and ideas; the plant superintendent and his supervisors volunteered no ideas about what specifically limited the prior week's output. It was Bill's opinion that this kind of thinking and planning was not required under his father's management. The supervisors, in general, felt nothing was wrong in the plant, and really seemed puzzled at the thought of doing anything except continuing what they had always done.

Recently, an engineer from a competitor visited Artisan and dropped the following comments. He stated that Artisan's workers were, on average, two thirds as good as his. He added that this was the least directed operation he had ever seen, with the slowest pace and the lowest level of knowledge of this type of work. He noted they knew only the simple way of doing the job. Only one man in the company, for example, was able to count the board feet of lumber, a skill possessed by the smallest cabinet shop and essential for any kind of usage control.

THE STUDY

In May, a business professor from a nearby university organized the study with Bill. It was based on a written questionnaire administered to all employees. The questionnaire was designed (1) to find out what employees wanted—for example, more pay, retirement plans, more or less direction, etc.; (2) to gain insight into the probable impact of participative management moves; (3) to establish benchmarks of employee satisfaction so that changes over time could be monitored; (4) to develop an objective profile of the workers; and (5) to look for significant differences in attitudes between the various stratifications possible.

The survey included questions developed specifically for this situation as well as a highly regarded attitude instrument, the Job Description Index (JDI). Although the wording was considered simple, many of the workers did not understand such words as "stimulating," "ambitious," or "fascinating," and it became necessary to read the entire questionnaire to them in small groups during an hour break period. The final page of the seven-page instrument contained open-ended questions, such as "what do you like most about the company?" The employees answered the questions very cooperatively and in good spirits.

The study provided some basic data, such as that minorities accounted for 80 percent of the 300 employees; white females were the largest group at 40 percent. The work force was 58 percent female, 57 percent white, and 39 percent over 45 years old. And as many people had been with the company under two years as had been with the company over ten years—24 percent. The study also provided information about employee age.

The four-page JDI was summarized into attitudes toward five dimensions—pay, promotion, supervision, work, and co-worker. The two pages of special questions were reported by frequency of response and mean response on the original questionnaire form. The open-ended responses were discussed generally.

On the JDI tables, the "Overall" score was created by combining questions 37 (reversed), 44, 50, 53, and 57 from the special questionnaire. The fifth of employees with the highest scores were labeled "satisfied" and compared with the fifth with lowest score, i.e., "dissatisfied."

All of this data could be grouped and summarized by any of the heading descriptions—department, sex, race, age, and years with company. Exhibits 1 through 6 show part of the data presented.

EXHIBIT 1
Special Questions for the Total Group

DEPARTMENT_____   TOTAL GROUP_____

SEX:	42.2% Male 57.4%	57.7% Female 42.5%	WH FEM = 38.7% BLK MAL = 23.5% BLK FEM = 19.0% WH MAL = 18.7%	
RACE:	White 19.8%	Negro 19.8%	Other 21.4%	39.0%
AGE:	Under 25 23.2%	26-35 34.8%	36-45 18.5%	Over 45 23.5%
YEARS WITH COMPANY:	Under 2	2-5	6-10	Over 10

% of ANS

HOW IMPORTANT WOULD IMPROVEMENT IN
THE FOLLOWING THINGS BE TO YOU?

	RANK	Very little or not at all	A little	Fairly important	Very important	Extremely important	Mean	St. Dev.
Longer coffee breaks	15	33.7	20.0	16.5	18.1 (←3)	11.7 (0→)	2.54	1.41
More holidays	8	19.0	19.0	23.0	23.6 (4)	15.4 (9)	2.97	1.34
Guaranteed work	2	9.7	3.9	8.7	25.8 (7)	51.9 (8)	4.06	1.28
Flexibility in hours or days off	10	29.7	11.2	18.2	21.8 (4)	19.1 (0)	2.89	1.51
More overtime opportunity	17	40.8	14.1	12.4	17.3 (3)	15.4 (3)	2.52	1.53
Better insurance	6	26.0	8.9	16.1	21.7 (4)	27.3 (9)	3.15	1.55
Better working conditions	1\4	14.1	10.3	13.8	27.0 (6)	34.7 (2)	3.58	1.41
Retirement plan	3	12.0	6.5	9.7	18.5 (7)	53.2 (2)	3.94	1.40
Higher pay	1	3.2	5.4	8.0	19.2 (8)	64.1 (3)	4.36	1.05
Education refund	16	40.8	14.0	14.4	14.7 (3)	16.1 (1)	2.51	1.52
Treated more as an individual	7	29.6	8.1	18.2	21.5 (4)	22.5 (4)	2.99	1.54
Better way to get complaints heard	5	22.3	11.0	13.6	23.3 (5)	29.9 (3)	3.28	1.53
Better equipment	2\4	16.4	12.1	14.8	23.6 (5)	33.1 (7)	3.45	1.46
More direction from supervisor	14	33.8	20.0	12.5	18.4 (3)	15.4 (4)	2.62	1.48
More opportunity to learn and improve self	3\4	14.8	9.8	14.1	26.9 (6)	34.4 (1)	3.56	1.42
More say in how my department does things	13	37.1	14.5	13.2	18.7 (3)	16.5 (5)	2.63	1.53
More opportunity to contribute to company success	9	24.5	14.9	18.9	24.2 (4)	17.5 (2)	2.95	1.44
Better decisions by top management	12	29.8	21.4	14.9	16.2 (3)	17.8 (4)	2.71	1.48
More information on what's going on	4\4	16.1	9.7	12.3	29.4 (6)	32.6 (4)	3.53	1.44
Be more in charge of own self	11	33.3	10.7	16.8	19.7 (3)	19.4 (9)	2.81	1.54

Other:

EXHIBIT 1 *(continued)*

WHAT IS YOUR OPINION ON THE FOLLOWING
STATEMENTS? DO YOU AGREE OR DISAGREE?
Please mark the appropriate box.

	Strongly disagree	Disagree	No opinion	Agree	Strongly agree	Mean	St. Dev.
I enjoy taking this test.	3.2	3.8	17.3	44.4	31.3	3.97	.96
My pay is fair for this kind of job.	34.4	35.3	5.4	19.9	5.0	2.26	1.26
My coworkers are good to work with.	2.9	3.5	7.3	49.4	36.9	4.14	.91
My complaints or concerns are heard by management.	12.2	18.4	17.1	39.5	12.8	3.22	1.24
Things are getting better here.	8.3	12.1	23.2	38.9	17.5	3.45	1.16
The supervisors do a poor job.	25.3	39.9	17.2	9.1	8.4	2.35	1.19
I am fortunate to have this job.	3.2	3.8	15.7	48.7	28.5	3.95	.94
Working conditions are bad here.	17.3	41.7	16.3	17.9	6.7	2.55	1.16
I benefit when the company succeeds.	12.4	24.8	16.9	31.3	14.7	3.11	1.28
I have all the chance I wish to improve myself.	11.8	21.4	19.2	31.3	16.3	3.19	1.27
The company is well run.	6.1	18.2	28.1	36.1	11.5	3.29	1.08
Communications are poor.	13.4	27.8	25.2	21.6	12.1	2.91	1.23
I don't get enough direction from my supervisor.	19.6	37.5	20.2	13.1	9.6	2.56	1.22
I enjoy my work.	2.8	2.5	10.1	47.5	37.0	4.13	.90
I look for ways to improve the work I do.	1.0	2.6	8.0	51.4	37.1	4.21	.77
I need more of a chance to manage myself.	8.3	25.2	26.5	26.5	13.4	3.11	1.17
I don't expect to be with the company long.	28.9	30.8	23.6	9.5	7.2	2.35	1.19
Morale is good here.	6.2	15.0	18.0	39.5	21.2	3.55	1.16
We all do only what it takes to get by.	32.2	39.7	10.1	12.7	5.2	2.19	1.17
I am concerned about layoffs and losing my job.	9.9	16.9	13.1	32.8	27.4	3.51	1.31
I like the way my supervisor treats me.	4.2	5.1	11.9	42.4	36.3	4.02	1.03
We need a suggestion system.	3.0	7.9	25.6	38.4	25.2	3.75	1.01
I want more opportunity for advancement.	4.02	8.7	17.4	36.1	33.5	3.86	1.10
My supervisor knows me and what I want.	5.1	15.4	18.3	40.5	20.6	3.56	1.13
We are not expected to do a very good job here.	48.2	29.1	4.2	10.2	8.3	2.01	1.30
There are too many rules.	18.1	38.2	21.0	12.6	10.0	2.58	1.21
I feel like part of a team at work.	5.7	6.7	12.4	50.3	24.8	3.82	1.06
The company and my supervisor seek my ideas.	14.2	19.4	24.6	29.1	12.6	3.06	1.25
I can influence depth goals, methods and activities.	9.5	22.0	34.8	25.2	8.5	3.01	1.09
There is too much "family" here.	20.7	24.6	25.2	15.9	13.6	2.77	1.31
This company is good for the community.	2.2	3.5	11.1	36.3	46.8	4.22	.93

EXHIBIT 2
Special Questions for "Years with Company" Groupings

DEPARTMENT_____   YEARS WITH CO.

SEX:	Male	Female	
RACE:	White	Negro	Other
AGE:	Under 25	26-35	36-45	Over 45
	23.2%	34.8%	18.5%	23.5%
YEARS WITH COMPANY:	Under 2	2-5	6-10	Over 10

HOW IMPORTANT WOULD IMPROVEMENT IN
THE FOLLOWING THINGS BE TO YOU?

UN 2 x———— 2-5
OV 10 ◄———┘ 6-10

Scale headings (diagonal): Very little or not at all | A little | Fairly important | Very important | Extremely important | INCR.

Question	Very little or not at all		A little		Fairly important		Very important		Extremely important		INCR			
Longer coffee breaks	26	26	23	26	16	19	20	14	15	15	2.7	2.7	2.5	2.2
	51	36	11	18	14	15	17	22	7	9	1.4	1.4	1.4	1.4
More holidays	15	19	19	14	30	22	21	30	15	16	3.0	3.1	3.1	2.7
	26	15	23	24	23	19	15	24	13	19	1.3	1.3	1.3	1.3
Guaranteed work	13	10	6		15	10	19	26	46	56	3.8	4.2	4.1	4.2
	7	7	6	7	6	5	27	34	54	46	1.4	1.2	1.2	1.2
Flexibility in hours or days off	22	32	19	8	19	20	21	22	18	18	2.9	2.9	3.0	2.9
	34	26	6	17	18	15	19	20	22	22	1.4	1.5	1.5	1.6
More overtime opportunity	24	37	18	12	13	18	28	13	16	21	2.9	2.7	2.6	1.9
	40		15		8		21		17		1.4	1.6	1.6	1.3
Better insurance	26	31	11	10	17	13	21	21	26	26	3.1	3.0	3.3	3.3
	60	17	14	13	9	21	11	19	6	30	1.5	1.6	1.5	1.5
Better working conditions	15	9	13	13	7	17	29	21	36	41	3.6	3.7	3.7	3.3
	24	7	4	13	14	17	31	32	26	32	1.4	1.3	1.2	1.5
Retirement plan	17	9	9	9	19	6	20	25	35	52	3.5	4.0	4.0	4.2
	10	13	4	4	6	9	11	15	69	59	1.5	1.3	1.4	1.3
Higher pay		3	4	4	4	7	27	15	65	71	4.5	4.5	4.2	4.1
	7	4	7	9	13	7	17	22	56	57	0.8	1.0	1.1	1.3
Education refund	23	46	12	16	18	15	24	10	23	14	3.1	2.3	2.7	2.0
	59	33	12	16	9	16	10	14	10	22	1.5	1.5	1.6	1.4
Treated more as an individual	29	28	4	11	24	14	22	21	21	28	3.0	3.1	3.2	2.8
	40	19	2	15	19	20	21	22	19	24	1.5	1.6	1.4	1.6
Better way to get complaints heard	22	25	15	11	13	14	27	18	24	33	3.1	3.2	3.5	3.4
	24	12	6	16	12	14	22	30	36	28	1.5	1.6	1.4	1.6
Better equipment	13	13	12	14	19	6	24	27	31	41	3.5	3.7	3.3	3.3
	22	18	7	16	20	16	19	24	32	28	1.4	1.4	1.5	1.5
More direction from supervisor	31	37	29	20	15	8	14	20	11	15	2.4	2.6	2.9	2.6
	40	21	6	29	19	12	21	17	15	21	1.3	1.5	1.5	1.5
More opportunity to learn and improve self	12	16	12	9	9	15	33	19	34	41	3.7	3.6	3.7	3.4
	17	8	9	14	20	12	27	35	27	33	1.4	1.5	1.3	1.4
More say in how my department does things	38	40	13	15	17	14	15	16	17	14	2.6	2.5	3.0	2.6
	41	23	10	16	19	12	17	29	20	19	1.4	1.5	1.5	1.6
More opportunity to contribute to company success	32	24	15	16	19	17	24	23	10	20	2.6	3.0	3.3	2.9
	28	16	10	16	24	14	22	30	16	24	1.4	1.5	1.4	1.4
Better decisions by top management	27	26	22	25	21	14	15	18	16	18	2.7	2.7	3.0	2.6
	40	23	16	21	11	15	11	19	21	21	1.4	1.5	1.5	1.6
More information on what's going on	19	15	12	14	12	10	38	27	20	35	3.3	3.5	3.6	3.6
	15	15	6	8	17	13	29	26	33	38	1.4	1.4	1.4	1.4
Be more in charge of own self	29	35	10	13	16	15	28	20	16	18	2.9	2.7	3.0	2.7
	40	25	6	14	21	19	13	19	21	23	1.5	1.5	1.5	1.6

Other:_____

EXHIBIT 2 (continued)

WHAT IS YOUR OPINION ON THE FOLLOWING
STATEMENTS? DO YOU AGREE OR DISAGREE?
Please mark the appropriate box.

Statement	Strongly disagree	Disagree	No opinion	Agree	Strongly agree	INCR.
I enjoy taking this test.	6 2	5	17 17	44 44	33 32	4.0 4.0 3.9 4.0
	3 2	4 8	16 21	46 38	31 32	1.0 0.9 1.0 0.9
My pay is fair for this kind of job.	30 44	42 38	4 3	16 11	7 4	2.3 1.9 2.3 2.7
	27 32	25 34	9 7	34 23	6 4	1.2 1.1 1.2 1.3
My coworkers are good to work with.	4 3	4 3	10 5	43 54	38 36	4.1 4.1 4.1 4.3
	1 4	3 5	4 9	52 46	39 36	1.0 0.9 1.0 0.8
My complaints or concerns are heard by management.	10 12	16 21	32 16	33 43	9 8	3.1 3.1 3.3 3.3
	16 14	18 17	9 14	40 40	18 15	1.1 1.2 1.3 1.4
Things are getting better here.	6 11	10 14	33 22	38 45	13 9	3.4 3.3 3.5 3.6
	9 9	10 14	19 29	40 29	23 29	1.0 1.1 1.3 1.2
The supervisors do a poor job.	23 25	46 44	17 16	7 8	6 8	2.3 2.3 2.1 2.6
	29 30	24 44	18 18	15 2	15 7	1.1 1.2 1.1 1.4
I am fortunate to have this job.	6 3	1 4	20 19	46 48	26 26	3.9 3.9 3.9 4.2
	4 3	3 7	10 13	52 46	35 31	1.0 0.9 1.0 0.7
Working conditions are bad here.	16 18	44 42	15 18	22 17	4 3 7	2.6 2.5 2.6 2.5
	21 16	39 40	17 18	14 22	9 4	1.1 1.2 1.2 1.2
I benefit when the company succeeds.	14 12	21 31	23 16	30 29	11 12	3.0 3.0 3.1 3.3
	9 13	24 24	16 15	31 35	21 13	1.2 1.2 1.3 1.3
I have all the chance I wish to improve myself.	18 9	24 22	21 19	27 34	12 17	2.9 3.3 3.2 3.3
	11 13	21 20	16 23	34 25	18 20	1.3 1.2 1.3 1.3
The company is well run.	6 6	13 16	33 22	40 38	9 9	3.3 3.3 3.2 3.3
	1 11	27 20	24 22	31 35	16 13	1.0 1.0 1.3 1.1
Communications are poor.	12 12	33 29	26 23	20 26	9 11	2.8 3.0 3.1 2.8
	18 13	28 23	25 25	16 25	13 15	1.1 1.2 1.3 1.3
I don't get enough direction from my supervisor.	16 25	46 35	20 16	14 14	4 11	2.5 2.5 2.5 2.7
	19 17	30 42	26 21	10 13	15 8	1.1 1.3 1.1 1.3
I enjoy my work.	7 2	1 2	11 9	49 51	31 36	4.0 4.2 4.2 4.2
	1	1 6	13 7	41 46	43 42	1.1 0.8 0.8 0.8
I look for ways to improve the work I do.	1 1	3 2	13 6	56 59	27 33	4.0 4.2 4.3 4.4
		1 4	4 9	47 38	47 49	0.8 0.7 0.8 0.6
I need more of a chance to manage myself.	7 7	33 27	28 26	23 31	9 10	2.9 3.1 3.2 3.2
	12 11	16 26	30 18	29 22	13 24	1.0 1.1 1.3 1.2
I don't expect to be with the company long.	18 28	27 32	37 21	12 11	7 9	2.6 2.4 2.2 2.1
	37 35	30 33	21 17	6 10	6 6	1.1 1.2 1.2 1.1
Morale is good here.	5 5	17 9	21 19	46 47	12 20	3.4 3.7 3.6 3.4
	13 4	20 22	13 13	25 39	30 24	1.0 1.0 1.2 1.4
We all do only what it takes to get by.	30 34	40 33	15 12	12 14	3 8	2.2 2.3 2.2 1.9
	38 30	44 42	6 8	9 17	3 4	1.1 1.3 1.2 1.0
I am concerned about layoffs and losing my job.	4 8	26 16	15 14	29 35	26 28	3.5 3.6 3.5 3.3
	16 14	15 13	15 11	33 34	22 29	1.2 1.3 1.4 1.4
I like the way my supervisor treats me.	4 4	7 2	15 10	34 43	40 42	4.0 4.2 4.1 3.8
	4 4	11 2	11 13	44 48	30 33	1.1 1.0 0.9 1.1
We need a suggestion system.	2 3	12 7	25 28	41 32	21 31	3.7 3.8 3.7 3.8
	4 2	6 10	24 24	40 45	27 20	1.0 1.0 1.0 1.0
I want more opportunity for advancement.	3 5	4 11	17 12	36 30	40 42	4.1 3.9 3.9 3.7
	4 4	10 8	23 14	41 44	21 30	1.0 1.2 1.1 1.1
My supervisor knows me and what I want.	7 4	27 10	19 18	28 46	19 23	3.3 3.7 3.6 3.6
	3 6	19 12	13 19	46 44	20 19	1.2 1.0 1.1 1.1
We are not expected to do a very good job here.	54 55	29 29	3 2	9 7	6 7	1.8 1.8 2.4 2.1
	45 38	31 26	6 6	10 20	9 11	1.2 1.2 1.4 1.3
There are too many rules.	10 18	54 36	19 19	10 18	7 10	2.5 2.7 2.8 2.3
	29 17	29 32	29 23	9 13	6 15	1.0 1.2 1.3 1.1
I feel like part of a team at work.	7 6	4 7	16 10	46 55	26 23	3.8 3.8 3.7 3.9
	3 7	9	10 15	55 43	24 26	1.1 1.0 1.2 1.0
The company and my supervisor seek my ideas.	19 19	21 22	29 20	24 29	7 10	2.8 2.9 3.2 3.4
	7 8	16 24	24 24	31 30	23 14	1.2 1.3 1.2 1.2
I can influence depth goals, methods and activities.	7 12	31 26	35 37	22 18	4 8	2.9 2.8 3.1 3.3
	9 8	10 23	36 29	35 29	10 12	1.0 1.1 1.1 1.1
There is too much "family" here.	28 16	25 25	33 25	10 18	4 17	2.4 2.9 2.7 3.1
	19 23	16 30	23 21	24 11	19 15	1.1 1.3 1.3 1.4
This company is good for the community.	4 4	6 2	17 14	34 41	39 39	4.4 4.1 4.3 4.5
		9 6	7	30 24	51 50	1.1 1.0 1.0 0.6

EXHIBIT 3
Special Questions for "Sex and Race" Combinations

DEPARTMENT _____   SEX AND RACE _____

SEX:	42% Male / 57%	58% Female / 43%	WH FEM = 39% / BLK MAL = 24% / BLK FEM = 19% / WH MAL = 19%

RACE: White   Negro   Other

AGE: Under 25   26-35   36-45   Over 45

YEARS WITH COMPANY: Under 2   2-5   6-10   Over 10

HOW IMPORTANT WOULD IMPROVEMENT IN THE FOLLOWING THINGS BE TO YOU?

W.M. x ——— W.F.
B.M. ◄——— B.F.

Question	Very little or not at all	A little	Fairly important	Very important	Extremely important	?
Longer coffee breaks	67 33 / 16 23	7 25 / 21 23	7 20 / 18 18	12 16 / 29 16	7 7 / 16 21	1.9 2.4 2.9 3.1 / 1.4 1.3 1.5 1.3
More holidays	28 21 / 14 14	19 23 / 16 14	25 21 / 26 23	21 21 / 25 29	8 14 / 19 20	2.6 2.8 3.3 3.2 / 1.3 1.3 1.3 1.3
Guaranteed work	9 9 / 5 16	5 4 / 2 4	5 11 / 7 6	30 21 / 24 32	51 54 / 62 42	4.1 4.0 3.8 4.4 / 1.2 1.3 1.4 1.0
Flexibility in hours or days off	41 27 / 33 24	9 13 / 8 13	20 20 / 10 21	17 23 / 31 17	13 17 / 19 26	2.5 2.9 3.1 3.0 / 1.5 1.5 1.5 1.6
More overtime opportunity	48 52 / 35 23	16 16 / 15 10	14 11 / 11 16	16 11 / 18 26	5 9 / 22 26	2.1 2.1 3.2 2.8 / 1.3 1.4 1.5 1.6
Better insurance	25 26 / 28 27	9 10 / 4 13	19 20 / 11 11	18 22 / 25 21	30 22 / 32 27	3.2 3.0 3.1 3.3 / 1.6 1.5 1.6 1.6
Better working conditions	26 9 / 12 16	9 10 / 10 14	14 22 / 9 7	21 28 / 29 26	30 32 / 40 37	3.2 3.7 3.5 3.7 / 1.6 1.3 1.5 1.4
Retirement plan	16 14 / 7 10	2 9 / 9 6	11 9 / 7 14	18 16 / 27 15	54 53 / 49 56	3.9 3.9 4.0 4.0 / 1.5 1.5 1.3 1.3
Higher pay	4 3 / 2 4	12 2 / 2 10	19 8 / 2 4	26 19 / 11 22	39 69 / 84 60	3.8 4.5 4.2 4.7 / 1.2 1.0 1.2 0.8
Education refund	46 52 / 38 24	17 17 / 11 9	13 11 / 15 21	11 10 / 19 22	13 10 / 17 25	2.3 2.1 3.2 2.7 / 1.5 1.4 1.5 1.5
Treated more as an individual	36 32 / 28 25	11 7 / 9 7	16 24 / 7 21	23 21 / 20 21	14 17 / 35 26	2.7 2.8 3.2 3.3 / 1.5 1.5 1.5 1.7
Better way to get complaints heard	32 14 / 31 24	6 11 / 10 15	15 15 / 14 11	26 25 / 19 19	22 35 / 27 31	3.0 3.6 3.2 3.0 / 1.6 1.4 1.6 1.6
Better equipment	22 15 / 13 18	11 13 / 15 10	20 15 / 13 12	18 26 / 35 16	29 31 / 24 44	3.2 3.5 3.6 3.4 / 1.5 1.4 1.5 1.3
More direction from supervisor	47 31 / 30 33	15 19 / 29 20	11 15 / 5 16	18 22 / 16 15	9 14 / 20 16	2.3 2.7 2.6 2.7 / 1.4 1.4 1.5 1.5
More opportunity to learn and improve self	16 16 / 13 16	11 6 / 13 13	19 21 / 6 7	32 27 / 28 21	23 31 / 40 44	3.4 3.5 3.6 3.7 / 1.4 1.4 1.5 1.4
More say in how my department does things	40 39 / 30 36	14 14 / 21 13	11 14 / 16 11	16 24 / 18 14	19 10 / 14 26	2.6 2.5 2.8 2.6 / 1.6 1.5 1.7 1.4
More opportunity to contribute to company success	18 26 / 29 22	11 13 / 15 21	18 20 / 22 17	30 24 / 24 19	24 17 / 11 21	3.3 2.9 3.0 2.7 / 1.4 1.4 1.5 1.4
Better decisions by top management	26 25 / 32 38	21 17 / 32 23	19 17 / 11 11	14 20 / 14 13	19 21 / 12 16	2.8 2.9 2.5 2.4 / 1.5 1.5 1.5 1.4
More information on what's going on	16 17 / 11 20	13 12 / 5 9	16 11 / 11 14	25 28 / 33 30	30 33 / 40 28	3.4 3.5 3.4 3.9 / 1.4 1.5 1.5 1.3
Be more in charge of own self	47 34 / 24 31	9 13 / 7 10	18 20 / 16 11	11 18 / 33 21	15 15 / 20 28	2.4 2.7 3.1 3.2 / 1.5 1.5 1.6 1.5

Other:_____

EXHIBIT 3 (continued)

WHAT IS YOUR OPINION ON THE FOLLOWING STATEMENTS? DO YOU AGREE OR DISAGREE? Please mark the appropriate box.

Statement	Strongly disagree	Disagree	No opinion	Agree	Strongly agree	Means / (S.D.)
I enjoy taking this test.	3 5	5	24 13	41 52	29 28	3.9 4.0 3.9 4.1
	5 4	3	14 23	42 39	39 31	0.9 0.9 1.0 1.0
My pay is fair for this kind of job.	10 41	35 33	7 8	41 17	7 2	3.0 2.1 2.3 2.0
	46 32	36 39	6	10 17	9 7	1.2 1.1 1.3 1.3
My coworkers are good to work with.	2 3		3 2 8	66 52	30 35	4.2 4.1 4.1 4.2
	4 1	4 8	4 14	51 32	39 45	0.7 0.9 1.0 0.9
My complaints or concerns are heard by management.	13 16	9 21	15 16	49 40	15 8	3.4 3.0 3.3 3.4
	7 10	24 18	13 25	38 32	18 16	1.2 1.2 1.3 1.2
Things are getting better here.	4 11	12 12	19 29	46 37	19 12	3.6 3.1 3.5 3.5
	9 7	11 14	18 23	44 33	19 23	1.0 1.2 1.2 1.2
The supervisors do a poor job.	11 27	44 42	15 21	20 6	11 5	2.8 2.2 2.4 2.1
	31 32	47 27	6 23	9 6	7 12	1.2 1.1 1.3 1.2
I am fortunate to have this job.	1	2 3	16 21	58 56	25 20	4.1 3.9 3.8 4.2
	2 10	2 7	7 14	50 31	40 39	0.7 0.8 1.3 0.8
Working conditions are bad here.	24 12	47 34	12 27	14 25	3 2	2.3 2.7 2.6 2.4
	12 23	60 37	7 11	14 14	7 16	1.1 1.0 1.4 1.1
I benefit when the company succeeds.	9 10	13 34	13 18	45 28	21 10	3.6 2.9 2.9 3.2
	11 21	24 22	19 17	30 25	17 15	1.2 1.2 1.4 1.3
I have all the chance I wish to improve myself.	7 14	14 22	24 27	41 27	14 11	3.4 3.0 3.2 3.4
	7 17	24 25	10 10	43 22	16 26	1.1 1.2 1.5 1.2
The company is well run.	2 6	24 24	28 31	38 31	9 6	3.3 3.1 3.4 3.6
	5 11	7 14	22 27	57 25	11 23	1.0 1.0 1.3 1.2
Communications are poor.	7 14	30 22	30 24	20 27	13 13	3.0 3.1 2.8 2.7
	16 15	29 35	27 21	18 17	9 13	1.1 1.3 1.3 1.2
I don't get enough direction from my supervisor.	19 14	32 43	25 26	12 10	12 6	2.7 2.5 2.5 2.6
	21 29	37 35	12 11	23 10	7 15	1.3 1.0 1.4 1.2
I enjoy my work.	2 1		3 7 13	55 48	36 36	4.2 4.1 4.0 4.3
	8 3		3 2 15	56 33	39 41	0.7 0.8 1.2 0.7
I look for ways to improve the work I do.	2		7 7	46 61	46 33	4.4 4.3 4.1 4.1
	4 1	8	7 13	58 35	32 43	0.7 0.6 1.0 0.8
I need more of a chance to manage myself.	11 6	26 25	28 33	21 28	14 9	3.1 3.1 3.2 3.2
	3 15	29 19	24 18	26 29	17 18	1.2 1.0 1.3 1.1
I don't expect to be with the company long.	30 31	37 32	19 27	5 5	9 5	2.3 2.2 2.5 2.4
	32 25	27 27	18 28	20 10	4 10	1.2 1.1 1.2 1.2
Morale is good here.	9 4	21 19	17 20	38 39	16 18	3.3 3.5 3.7 3.8
	7 6	40 13	13 20	52 30	24 31	1.2 1.1 1.2 1.1
We all do only what it takes to get by.	20 33	50 46	16 9	13 10	2 3	2.3 2.0 2.3 2.3
	35 41	32 27	9 7	19 13	5 12	1.0 1.0 1.4 1.3
I am concerned about layoffs and losing my job.	11 7	19 19	18 11	35 35	18 29	3.3 3.6 3.3 3.6
	12 14	10 19	12 14	34 25	32 28	1.3 1.3 1.4 1.3
I like the way my supervisor treats me.	7 2	2 8	17 12	50 45	24 34	3.9 4.0 4.0 4.3
	4 7		9 9	38 34	50 42	1.0 1.0 1.2 0.9
We need a suggestion system.	2	7 7	30 22	38 43	25 26	3.8 3.9 3.7 3.6
	2 7	9 7	36 21	32 36	21 29	0.9 0.9 1.2 1.0
I want more opportunity for advancement.	2 1	7 12	25 22	46 33	21 33	3.8 3.8 4.0 3.9
	6 10	6 7	16 6	40 31	33 47	0.9 1.0 1.3 1.1
My supervisor knows me and what I want.	2 3	13 14	25 18	45 43	16 22	3.6 3.7 3.4 3.6
	4 10	14 21	18 14	47 31	18 25	1.0 1.0 1.3 1.0
We are not expected to do a very good job here.	42 51	33 34	9 3	9 8	7 4	2.1 1.8 2.3 2.0
	54 45	21 22	4 4	11 14	11 15	1.2 1.1 1.5 1.4
There are too many rules.	17 21	41 34	29 33	10 11	2 7	2.4 2.5 2.7 2.9
	15 17	38 37	15 16	11 18	22 13	0.9 1.1 1.3 1.4
I feel like part of a team at work.	7 3	7 4	14 15	56 57	16 20	3.7 3.9 3.9 3.8
	5 8	14 6	9 10	41 40	31 37	1.0 0.9 1.2 1.2
The company and my supervisor seek my ideas.	9 17	12 23	22 27	40 26	17 7	3.4 2.8 3.2 3.1
	11 16	21 15	28 21	30 27	9 21	1.2 1.2 1.4 1.2
I can influence depth goals, methods and activities.	5 10	14 26	30 44	42 18	9 5	3.4 2.8 3.1 3.1
	7 13	24 16	35 31	22 27	11 13	1.0 1.1 1.2 1.1
There is too much ''family'' here.	19 12	19 20	21 28	24 24	17 17	3.0 3.1 2.4 2.3
	30 29	32 30	26 26	4 6	9 10	1.4 1.3 1.2 1.2
This company is good for the community.	2 3		3 9 7	43 38	47 50	4.3 4.3 4.0 4.3
	3	2 7	17 16	29 34	52 41	0.8 0.9 1.0 0.8

EXHIBIT 4
Special Questions for "Satisfied versus Unsatisfied"

DEPARTMENT_____ SATISFIED VS UNSATISFIED _____

SEX:	Male	Female		
RACE:	White	Negro	Other	
AGE:	Under 25	26-35	36-45	Over 45
YEARS WITH COMPANY:	Under 2	2-5	6-10	Over 10

HOW IMPORTANT WOULD IMPROVEMENT IN THE FOLLOWING THINGS BE TO YOU?

SATIS.
UNSATIS.

Each grid cell shows the SATIS. percentage (top) and the UNSATIS. percentage (bottom). The two right-hand columns show SATIS. and UNSATIS. values.

	UNSATIS.–SATIS.	Very little or not at all	A little	Fairly important	Very important	Extremely important	←SATIS.	←UNSATIS.
Longer coffee breaks	−.6	45 / 27	19 / 23	6 / 6	14 / 28	16 / 16	3.4 / 1.5	2.8 / 1.5
More holidays	.8	21 / 7	24 / 18	19 / 18	23 / 34	13 / 23	2.8 / 1.3	3.6 / 1.3
Guaranteed work	.3	11 / 5	5 / 6	11 / 5	19 / 24	55 / 60	4.0 / 1.4	4.3 / 1.1
Flexibility in hours or days off	.8	38 / 18	11 / 7	18 / 18	13 / 24	21 / 34	2.7 / 1.6	3.5 / 1.5
More overtime opportunity	−.3	34 / 48	16 / 13	13 / 8	23 / 13	15 / 19	2.7 / 1.5	2.4 / 1.6
Better insurance	.5	29 / 20	11 / 8	16 / 15	19 / 18	25 / 39	3.0 / 1.6	3.5 / 1.5
Better working conditions	.9	22 / 6	16 / 3	13 / 14	18 / 29	32 / 48	3.2 / 1.6	4.1 / 1.1
Retirement plan	−.5	2 / 14	8 / 2	11 / 17	10 / 14	69 / 53	4.4 / 1.1	3.9 / 1.4
Higher pay	.5	8 / 5	9 / 5	9 / 8	16 / 11	58 / 77	4.1 / 1.3	4.6 / 0.8
Education refund	.3	53 / 40	15 / 18	12 / 12	5 / 13	15 / 17	2.2 / 1.5	2.5 / 1.5
Treated more as an individual	1.0	39 / 14	14 / 6	9 / 16	17 / 22	20 / 41	2.7 / 1.6	3.7 / 1.4
Better way to get complaints heard	1.3	38 / 8	10 / 8	10 / 11	19 / 14	24 / 59	2.8 / 1.7	4.1 / 1.3
Better equipment	.6	20 / 11	14 / 5	11 / 14	25 / 22	30 / 48	3.3 / 1.5	3.9 / 1.3
More direction from supervisor	.8	45 / 24	15 / 8	8 / 24	16 / 18	16 / 27	2.4 / 1.6	3.2 / 1.5
More opportunity to learn and improve self	.5	17 / 8	17 / 3	6 / 13	19 / 32	41 / 44	3.5 / 1.6	4.0 / 1.2
More say in how my department does things	1.4	52 / 19	18 / 3	10 / 19	10 / 27	11 / 33	2.1 / 1.4	3.5 / 1.4
More opportunity to contribute to company success	.6	18 / 13	22 / 5	16 / 23	24 / 23	21 / 36	3.1 / 1.4	3.7 / 1.3
Better decisions by top management	3.2	76 / 2	21 / 6	3 / 27	/	/ 66	1.3 / 0.5	4.5 / 0.7
More information on what's going on	1.2	30 / 9	9 / 5	14 / 8	28 / 14	19 / 64	3.0 / 1.5	4.2 / 1.3
Be more in charge of own self	1.2	50 / 16	9 / 8	8 / 19	14 / 19	19 / 39	2.4 / 1.6	3.6 / 1.5

Other:_____

EXHIBIT 4 *(continued)*

WHAT IS YOUR OPINION ON THE FOLLOWING
STATEMENTS? DO YOU AGREE OR DISAGREE?
Please mark the appropriate box.

Statement	UNSATIS.–SATIS.	Group	Strongly disagree	Disagree	No opinion	Agree	Strongly agree	Mean	S.D.
I enjoy taking this test.	0	←SATIS.	5	6	13	36	41	4.0	1.0
		←UNSATIS.	2	5	13	52	29	4.0	0.9
My pay is fair for this kind of job.	–.7		30	30		31	9	2.6	1.4
			53	33	5	8	2	1.9	1.0
My coworkers are good to work with.	–1.2		2	2	3	24	70	4.6	0.8
			2	6	14	52	27	3.4	0.9
My complaints or concerns are heard by management.	–1.1		10	10	6	51	24	3.7	1.2
			27	28	9	27	9	2.6	1.4
Things are getting better here.	–2.2				5	41	55	4.5	0.6
			28	38	13	16	6	2.3	1.2
The supervisors do a poor job.	.5		55	21		8	16	2.1	1.5
			14	40	22	16	8	2.6	1.1
I am fortunate to have this job.	–1.2					41	59	4.6	0.5
			12	8	28	36	16	3.4	1.2
Working conditions are bad here.	–.8		48	34	7	3	8	1.9	1.2
			8	28	19	33	13	1.1	1.2
I benefit when the company succeeds.	–1.0		13	15	7	39	27	3.5	1.4
			20	34	22	20	3	2.5	1.1
I have all the chance I wish to improve myself.	–1.7		3	11	6	36	44	4.1	1.1
			27	29	22	19	3	2.4	1.2
The company is well run.	–2.2				2	59	39	4.4	0.5
			19	48	30	3		2.2	0.8
Communications are poor.	.5		21	38	12	16	13	2.6	1.3
			19	19	16	23	23	3.1	1.4
I don't get enough direction from my supervisor.	.3		38	29	6	10	18	2.4	1.5
			17	31	27	17	8	2.7	1.2
I enjoy my work.	–1.4					19	81	4.8	0.4
			13	5	27	41	16	3.4	1.2
I look for ways to improve the work I do.	–.7		2		2	20	77	4.7	0.7
			2	6	10	52	30	4.0	0.9
I need more of a chance to manage myself.	.5		22	22	13	19	24	3.0	1.5
			8	11	28	33	20	3.5	1.2
I don't expect to be with the company long.	.3		51	16	5	10	18	2.3	1.6
			25	28	22	14	11	2.6	1.3
Morale is good here.	–2.0			2	5	36	58	4.5	0.7
			19	36	22	20	3	2.5	1.1
We all do only what it takes to get by.	.4		48	36	8	2	7	1.8	1.1
			30	43	10	13	5	2.2	1.1
I am concerned about layoffs and losing my job.	.2		21	19	2	16	43	3.4	1.6
			9	14	13	38	27	3.6	1.3
I like the way my supervisor treats me.	–1.0		3	2	5	32	59	4.4	0.9
			11	11	22	38	18	3.4	1.2
We need a suggestion system.	0		5	8	23	35	28	3.8	1.1
			5	6	21	37	32	3.8	1.1
I want more opportunity for advancement.	.1		10	11	8	31	40	3.8	1.3
			5	5	21	33	37	3.9	1.1
My supervisor knows me and what I want.	–1.2		7		7	44	44	4.2	1.0
			11	30	22	21	16	3.0	1.3
We are not expected to do a very good job here.	–.1		59	14		9	17	2.1	1.6
			49	27	8	10	6	2.0	1.2
There are too many rules.	.7		37	36	8	7	12	2.2	1.3
			18	27	22	18	16	2.9	1.3
I feel like part of a team at work.	–1.2		3	2	3	44	48	4.3	0.9
			19	11	19	37	13	3.1	1.3
The company and my supervisor seek my ideas.	–1.2		9	13	18	33	28	3.6	1.3
			33	24	21	14	8	2.4	1.3
I can influence depth goals, methods and activities.	–.6		9	19	19	38	16	3.3	1.2
			16	27	32	16	8	2.7	1.1
There is too much "family" here.			44	19	18	8	11	2.2	1.4
			16	17	17	23	27		
This company is good for the community.	–.7		2	2	3	24	70	4.6	0.8
			3	8	25	25	38	3.9	1.1

EXHIBIT 5
JDI Scores for "Year with Company" and "Sex and Race" Combinations

YEARS WITH COMPANY

UNDER 2												
16.7	13.0*	1.6	6.3	23.8	52.4	15.9						
40.4	10.0		2.9		8.6	7.1	5.7	18.6	21.4	21.4	14.3	
31.4	10.7	1.4	5.7	5.7	2.9	7.1	14.3	15.7	32.9	10.0	4.3	
41.4	9.0			1.4	1.4	1.4	8.6	10.0	17.1	25.7	15.7	18.6
11.9	7.6	30.0	17.1	18.6	15.7	17.1	1.4					
7.4	4.9	40.0	44.3	8.6	2.9	4.3						
2 TO 5 YEARS												
17.4	12.5*	1.1	3.2	24.2	50.5	21.1						
41.9	9.8	1.0	1.0	1.9	1.9	7.6	7.6	16.2	19.0	25.7	18.1	
31.2	9.3		1.9	3.8	5.7	16.2	19.0	18.1	19.0	11.4	3.8	1.0
40.3	10.5		1.0	2.9	1.9	4.8	7.6	7.6	15.2	24.8	17.1	17.1
9.9	6.9	36.2	25.7	15.2	11.4	10.5	1.0					
5.6	3.9	63.8	23.8	9.5	2.9							
6 TO 10 YEARS												
17.6	12.2*		2.0	33.3	35.3	29.4						
39.9	11.4		3.6		12.5	7.1	5.4	10.7	23.2	19.6	17.9	
32.4	9.4	1.8		3.6	1.8	17.9	19.6	7.1	25.0	21.4	1.8	
40.6	10.9	1.8			5.4	1.8	12.5	1.8	14.3	23.2	23.2	16.1
11.5	6.8	26.8	17.9	28.6	12.5	14.3						
7.6	5.1	44.6	28.6	21.4	1.8	3.6						
OVER 10												
17.6	9.3*		7.4	23.5	38.2	30.8						
42.7	8.9				5.6	7.0	5.6	19.7	18.3	18.3	25.4	
34.3	8.6		1.4	2.8		8.5	21.1	16.9	22.5	21.1	4.2	1.4
40.5	11.9		1.4	7.0		4.2	5.6	7.0	14.1	19.7	18.3	22.5
11.5	8.0	31.0	23.9	15.5	7.0	18.3	4.2					
8.2	5.2	38.0	31.0	22.5	5.6	2.8						

EXHIBIT 5 *(continued)*

RACE & SEX

WHITE MALES												
17.4	8.6*	1.8	1.8	26.8	46.4	23.2						
42.1	10.6		1.7	1.7	6.9	8.6	3.4	15.5	13.8	20.7	27.6	
36.2	8.1	1.7			8.6	15.5	12.1	27.6	27.6	5.2	1.7	
41.5	11.7		5.2	3.4	1.7	8.6	8.6	6.9	20.7	13.8	31.0	
13.7	7.6	15.5	25.9	20.7	8.6	25.9	3.4					
9.9	5.8	25.9	32.8	25.9	8.6	6.9						
WHITE FEMALES												
16.8	12.5*		5.5	31.2	45.0	18.4						
41.3	10.2	1.7			0.8	6.7	8.3	6.7	15.0	20.0	20.0	20.8
32.1	9.6	0.8	1.7	5.0	3.3	10.8	18.3	19.2	21.7	14.2	4.2	0.8
39.6	12.0		2.5	4.2	2.5	5.8	6.7	5.0	16.7	18.3	20.0	18.3
7.9	6.2	48.3	27.5	10.0	7.5	5.8	0.8					
5.7	3.8	60.0	27.5	10.8	1.7							
BLACK MALES												
17.6	11.4*	1.5	10.3	19.1	33.8	35.3						
38.9	11.4	1.4	2.7	2.7		6.8	5.5	5.5	20.5	26.5	17.8	11.0
29.9	10.3	1.4	5.5	4.1	4.1	15.1	21.9	9.6	24.7	11.0	2.7	
39.3	10.3	1.4		1.4	1.4	5.5	11.0	9.6	16.4			
12.5	7.5	26.0	13.7	26.0	15.1	16.4	2.7					
7.6	4.8	39.7	37.0	17.8	2.7	2.7						
BLACK FEMALES												
18.5	14.5*			16.0	58.0	26.0						
44.1	7.5					1.7	5.1	6.8	13.6	23.7	27.1	22.0
31.9	8.2			3.4	5.1	16.9	15.3	18.6	27.1	11.9	1.7	
42.6	6.6						5.1	8.5	22.0	32.2	18.6	13.6
13.3	6.6	15.3	18.6	30.5	15.3	20.3						
6.0	4.0	55.9	32.2	10.2	1.7							

EXHIBIT 6
JDI Scores on Eight Major Organizational Groups

JDI

Area of Satisfact.	Score Obs	% tile	S T D	D E U	3	8	13	18	23	28	33	38	43	48	53+
TOTAL COMPANY															
Overall	17.4		0.7			4.8	25.1	44.5	24.8						
Coworker	41.2	40	10.3		0.3	1.3	0.9	0.6	6.0	7.5	6.3	16.0	20.4	21.1	19.5
Work	32.2	35	9.5		0.6	2.2	3.8	3.1	12.9	18.2	16.0	23.9	15.1	3.5	0.6
Supervsn.	40.4	40	10.7		0.3	0.9	2.8	1.9	3.8	7.9	7.2	16.4	22.6	18.6	17.6
Promotion	11.1	70	7.3		30.5	22.0	19.2	12.3	14.5	1.6					
Pay	7.1	20	4.8		47.8	32.1	14.8	3.1	2.2						
PLANT ONE															
Overall	17.1		0.8			5.8	28.1	41.3	24.0						
Coworker	40.4		11.3		0.7	2.1	2.1		7.1	6.4	6.4	17.0	19.9	18.4	19.9
Work	31.6		9.1		0.7	1.4	4.3	3.5	14.9	17.0	19.9	21.3	14.9	2.1	
Supervsn.	38.4		11.3		0.7		5.7	2.8	5.7	8.5	7.1	17.7	23.4	15.6	12.8
Promotion	11.7		6.8		23.4	22.7	24.8	15.6	12.1	1.4					
Pay	6.6		3.9		47.5	36.2	14.2	2.1							
PLANT TWO															
Overall	18.1		1.0			4.2	18.8	44.8	31.3						
Coworker	39.8		9.5			1.0		1.0	5.9	12.9	8.9	15.8	21.8	20.8	11.9
Work	31.3		9.3			4.0	2.0	5.0	13.9	20.8	15.8	25.7	8.9	3.0	1.0
Supervsn.	42.6		8.0				1.0		2.0	5.0	9.9	16.8	24.8	24.8	15.8
Promotion	11.0		7.5		32.7	22.8	15.8	11.9	14.9	2.0					
Pay	5.9		4.5		61.4	24.8	10.9		3.0						
SATISFIED															
Overall	23.0		0.0						100.0						
Coworker	43.8		7.8						1.6	7.8	4.7	15.6	23.4	23.4	23.4
Work	35.9		6.9						7.8	17.2	18.8	28.1	23.4	3.1	1.6
Supervsn.	43.9		7.9						4.7	1.6	4.7	20.3	21.9	21.9	25.0
Promotion	15.0		7.3		15.6	7.8	31.3	15.6	25.0	4.7					
Pay	8.7		5.9		39.1	25.0	25.0	4.7	6.3						
UNSATISFIED															
Overall	11.6		2.6		3.1	21.9	75.0								
Coworker	35.6		13.2		1.6	3.1	4.7		17.2	12.5	4.7	15.6	7.8	20.3	12.5
Work	25.7		9.7			7.8	10.9	7.8	18.8	26.6	12.5	7.8	6.3	1.6	
Supervsn.	34.5		13.0			1.6	12.5	3.1	7.8	15.6	6.3	10.9	18.8	12.5	10.9
Promotion	8.2		6.2		46.9	25.0	12.5	9.4	6.3						
Pay	5.6		3.9		64.1	21.9	12.5	1.6							

Note: Columns 3 through 53+ represent "% of Answers by Interval."

EXHIBIT 6 *(continued)*

					JDI							
MANAGEMENT & STAFF												
15.9	2.5			42.9	57.1							
38.0	9.3					14.3	14.3			28.6	28.6	14.3
39.4	3.5							14.3		42.9	42.9	
48.0	7.1							14.3		14.3	14.3	57.1
18.7	6.8	28.6				71.4						
15.9	5.9	28.6		14.3	28.6	28.6						
OFFICE												
16.6	3.7		5.6	27.8	55.6	11.1						
45.8	6.5						5.6	5.6		27.8	38.9	22.2
36.6	9.8			5.6		11.1	5.6	16.7	22.2	22.2	11.1	5.6
47.4	7.8						5.6	5.6	11.1	5.6	16.7	55.6
6.9	6.5	66.7	11.1	11.1		11.1						
7.7	5.1											
SUPERVISION												
19.7				16.7	33.3	50.0						
46.8	8.6					7.7		15.4				
39.2	6.8						23.1	23.1	38.5	15.4		
46.1	6.9					7.7		7.7	23.1	30.8		30.8
16.1	8.2	15.4	15.4	15.4	7.7	38.5	7.7					
12.2	5.5	15.4	15.4	46.2	15.4	7.7						

Case 4–4 ———————————————————————————————

Peoples Trust Company

Hrach Bedrosian

The Peoples Trust Company first opened its doors to the public on June 1, 1875, with a total salaried staff of eight members: a treasurer; a secretary; and six assistants (three of whom held the positions of day watchman, night watchman, and messenger). Located in a large, midwestern city, the original company had occupied the basement floor of a new five-story office building with an electric-bell system, steam heat, and steam-driven elevator.

During its early years, the trust company had concentrated its activities on providing vault services to its customers for the safekeeping of tangible items and securities. Management had been able to develop the reputation of being a highly conservative trust company that concentrated on a relatively small and select market of wealthy individuals from the local area. In the years following, the vault service had been retained as an accommodation to its customers, but the company's emphasis had slowly shifted from vault service to a wider range of banking and trust services.

Until the early 1900s, banking services had overshadowed trust services in terms of asset volume. Following the turn of the century, trust assets had begun to grow at an increasing rate. Over the years, the company had been able to achieve an impressive record of sound and steady growth. According to a story often told in banking circles: "Peoples Trust was so conservative that they prospered even during the Depression!"

In 1953, with the appointment of a new president, a new era began for Peoples Trust Company. Between 1953 and 1968, trust assets under supervision rose by $145 million, while deposits increased by more than $20 million. The company entered 1975 with about $2 billion in trust assets and $90 million in savings deposits.

Accompanying this recent growth has been the company's desire to fashion a new image for itself. In 1969, Mr. Robert Toller assumed the presidency of Peoples Trust. In 1972, he remarked: ". . . it should be said that the old concept of a trust involving merely the regular payment of income and preservation of capital is largely obsolete." Accordingly, the investment division of the company had been expanded and strengthened. Similar changes had been effected in the trust and estate administrative group and other customer services. Among these were the improvement of accounting methods and procedures, the installation of electronic data processing systems, and complete renovation of the company's eight-floor building and facilities. Most recently, the company had extended its services into the field of management consulting. This had been acknowledged as a "pioneer" step for a banking institution. The president recently characterized the company as "an organization in the fiduciary business."

At the time these data were gathered, the company had a total of 602 employees. Of this number, 109 were in what is considered the "officer-group"[1] positions of the company. The company's relations with its employees over the years have been satisfactory, and Peoples Trust is generally recognized by city residents and those in suburban areas as a good place to work. The company hires most of its employees from the local area.

In the period before 1970, Peoples Trust had provided satisfactory advancement opportunities for its employees, and it had been possible for a young high school graduate who showed promise on the job to work his way up gradually to officer status. Graduates of banking institutions were also sought for employment with the company. Ordinarily a man was considered eligible for promotion to the job above him after he had thoroughly mastered the details of his present position.

Prior to 1970, the total staff of the company was small enough so that there was no need to prepare official organization charts or job descriptions. Virtually all of the employees knew each other on a first-name basis, and they were generally familiar with each other's area of job responsibility. New employees were rapidly able to learn "whom you had to go to for what."

---

[1] Membership in the officer group is determined by an employee's being legally empowered to represent the company in a transaction.

In 1970, the company management called in an outside consultant to appraise its organizational structure and operations and to confer on the rapid expansion and diversification of banking services that the company had planned. The presence of the consultants and the subsequent preparation of organization charts and job descriptions reportedly "shook up a lot of people"—many feared loss of their jobs or, at least, substantial changes in the nature of work and assignments. However, there was little overt reaction among the officer-level employees in terms of turnover and/or other indices of unrest.

Over the years it had been the policy of the company to pay wages that were at least average or a little above the average paid by comparable banking organizations in the area. This, combined with favorable employee relations and the stable and prestigious nature of the work, resulted in a low turnover of personnel. The bulk of employee turnover occurred among the young female employees who filled clerical positions throughout the company's various departments.

Since 1970, the personnel picture of Peoples Trust has been shifting. Several changes have taken place in the top management of the company. By adding several new customer services, the company has altered the very nature of its business. This has resulted in a trend toward "professionalization" of many of the officer-level positions, in that these positions now require individuals with higher levels of education and broader abilities. The impact of these changes on current employees has been a matter of concern to several executives in the company, particularly to Mr. John Moore, manager of the organization planning and personnel department. Mr. Moore described his picture of the situation to the researcher as follows:

> Our problem here is one of a changing image and along with it the changing of people. As a trust company, we had no other ties with a man's financial needs . . . we could only talk in terms of death. We wanted to be able to talk in terms of life, so we got active in the investment-advisory business.
>
> The old wealth around here is pretty well locked up, so we wanted to provide services to new and growing organizations and to individuals who are accumulating wealth. Our problem is one of reorientation. We used to provide one service for one customer. We now want to enter new ventures, offer new services, attract new customers. The problem has become one of how to make the change . . . do we have the talent and the people to make the change?
>
> We have a "band" of people (see Exhibit 1) in our organization . . . in the 35 to 50 age group who came in under the old hiring practices and ground rules.[2] Given the new directions in which our company is moving and the changing job requirements, it's clear that, considering their current qualifications and capabilities, these individuals have nowhere to go. Some have been able to accept this; and this acceptance includes watching others move past them. Others have difficulty accepting it . . . a

---

[2] Mr. Moore drew from his files a list of ten individuals who he felt were representative of the group whose lack of appropriate experience or qualifications created a road block to their future development and advancement with the company. These men are described in Exhibit 1.

few have left . . . and we haven't discouraged anyone from leaving. For those who can't accept it, there is the problem of integrating their career strategy with ours. We've articulated our objectives clearly; now the individual needs clarification of his own strategy.

EXHIBIT 1

Name	Age	Education	Date of Hire	Positions Held
Gerald Horn	37	Two-year technical institute of business administration	1965	Messenger Clearance Clerk Accounting Clerk Unit Head (working supervisor) Section Head (supervisor)
Richard Gaul*	30	Two-year junior college program in business administration	1967	Business Machines Operator Section Head (supervisor) Operations Officer
Fred James	35	B.A. degree local university American Institute of Banking	1966	Loan Clerk Teller Accounting Unit Head (working supervisor) Section Head (supervisor)
Harold Wilson*	35	One year at local university	1971	Methods Analyst Operations Unit Head (working supervisor) Systems Programmer Property Accounting Dept. Head
Martin Pfieffer*	32	Prep school	1967	Messenger Accounting Clerk Section Head (supervisor) Department Head
James Klinger	38	B.A. degree from local university	1962	Messenger Accounting Clerk Records Clerk Unit Head (working supervisor) Administrative Specialist
Ralph Kissler*	35	B.A. degree from local university co-op. program	1964	Messenger Real Property Specialist Assistant Estate Officer
Charles Ferris	42	Two-year junior college program in business administration American Institute of Banking	1952	Messenger Deposit accounting Section Head (supervisor) Unit Head (working supervisor)
William Jagger	54	High school	1939	Messenger Trust Liaison Clerk Accounting Clerk Bookkeeping Section Head
Thomas Geoghigan*	42	Two-year junior college program in business administration	1959	Messenger Securities accountant Property custodian Office Manager Assistant Operations Officer

* = Officer

As I see it, change caught up with these individuals. They had on-the-job training in their own areas, but that doesn't help them much to cope with the new demands. New functional areas are being melded on top of old ones (see Exhibit 2). For example, marketing is new; so is electronic data processing. They both require qualities that our existing employee staff didn't have.

To date, we have not approached any of these people in an individual way to discuss their problems with them. Our objectives are to further develop these people, but we'll first have to get the support of the department managers who supervise them.

We want to find ways to further develop personnel of the kind represented by this group through a variety of approaches. I am thinking here not only of formal job training in management development, but also of management techniques that would help individuals identify new kinds of qualifications or possible new standards of performance they must take into consideration in planning their own personal growth.

We have to change the conditioning of old times throughout the company. A recently hired MBA is now an officer. Years ago that couldn't have happened so rapidly. And not everyone here is in agreement that the appointment I just mentioned *should* have happened the way it did. We have to develop support in our company for the new recruiting image.

There are two things which really concern me most about this whole problem: (1) We have a problem in under-utilization of resources, and (2) there is a problem which is presented to the growth and development of the company in having some of the individuals I have been discussing settled into key spots. The company really bears the responsibility for the current situation as I described it. In addition, what this all means to me is that our personnel function may change considerably over the coming year.

After this interview with Mr. Moore, the researcher talked with other company executives to learn their views of the problems outlined by Mr. Moore. The findings from these interviews are presented below.

INTERVIEW WITH FRED BELLOWS—MANPOWER PLANNING

Historically we have been conservatively managed . . . you might say "ultraconservatively." But now we want to change that image. Several years ago there was a revolution in top management. In 1969, Mr. Toller took over and brought in young people, many not from the banking field but from other types of business and consulting organizations. Our employment philosophy may be stated as follows: "We want above average people . . . for above average pay . . . and we want to give them a chance to learn and grow and move with the organization." This applies mainly to those in whom we see management-level potential.

They are told in their employment interview that if they don't see opportunity with us, then they should leave. This is in contrast to the old philosophy that this is a secure place to work, that you can stay here by keeping your nose clean, and that you can sit and wait for pot luck to become a trust officer.

Many people are caught in this changing philosophy. A case in the trust administration division is a good example. There we have a man in a Grade-10 job who has been with the bank eight years. We just hired a new man out of college and put him in that same Grade 10. Now they're both at the same level, but they're entirely different people in terms of education, social background, etc.

Now the head of our trust division bucks this sort of thing. He argues that we don't need all "stars" in the company. Yet, the president wants young, dynamic men who can develop and be developed. So I'm trying to get the trust division to define: what does the job really require?

We have a number of people with two years of accounting training who have been with the company anywhere from six to nine years. Under our old system they'd be okay, but under the new system they're not. They're not realistic about their future. Our problem is that we're being honest, but few are getting the message.

We bring in a new man . . . ask others to train him . . . and then promote him over their heads. We have people whose jobs we could get done for a lot less money. When, if ever, do we tell them to go elsewhere?

INTERVIEW WITH LARRY ANDREWS—CONTROLLER

There is no question but that there has been a complete revolution around here. In the past, we were in business to serve the community, to handle small accounts, to help the little old lady who needed investment service. Our motto was: "Help anyone who needs help." Our employees were geared to this kind of work orientation and felt at home with it. They could easily identify themselves with this sort of approach to doing business. Most people were quite comfortable; their personal goals coincided with the company goal.

But we found that we couldn't make any money conducting this kind of business. So, we've had to extend our services to attract people who have money and can afford our service. Now the company goal has changed. For example, the trust department is now concerned with the management of property in general. The "dead man's bank" has become the "live people's service organization." So we've had to create a kind of snob appeal that too many of our people can't identify with or don't believe in.

Many problems have emerged from these changes. Before, a man's knowledge of the detail of his job was his greatest asset. He worked to develop that knowledge and protected it. Now—and I'm speaking of supervisory jobs—the important factor is to have some familiarity with the work but to be able to work with people; to get others to do the detail. Too many of our people still don't understand this. . . .

The route to the top is no longer clear. Over a five-year period this organization has changed. There have been reorganizations, new functions created, and some realignment of existing functions. Many who felt they had a clear line to something higher in the organization now find that that "something" isn't there anymore.

We've had lots of hiring-in at higher levels. Many old-timers have been bypassed. In some cases, the new, outside hirees came into jobs that never existed before, or were hired into a job that had previously existed but which is now a "cut" above what it was before. What used to be a top job is now a second or third spot.

What we need now are people who are "professional managers"—by that I mean a supervisor versus a technical specialist. Years ago supervision could be concentrated in a few key men . . . but in the past five years we've grown 20 percent to 30 percent and have a management hierarchy. A man used to be able to grow up as a technical specialist and develop his managerial skills secondarily.

To a small extent it's a matter of personality, too. We have a new president, and what is acceptable to him differs from what was acceptable to his predecessor. There's a new mix of personal favoritism that goes along with the new vogue. Technical specialists are "low need" as far as the company is concerned. I estimate we now have about 30 people in this category in officer-level jobs.

INTERVIEW WITH TOM MARTIN—MARKETING DIVISION HEAD

There have been many changes over the past six years. Mr. Toller took a look at the entire organization . . . and then hired a consultant to do an organizational study. It was sort of an outside stamp of approval.

His hope was to move some of the deadwood . . . the senior people who were past their peak and didn't represent what the company wanted anymore in its managerial and officer staff. Few of these individuals have the capacity to change, and for others it may already be too late to change. Many had leveled off in their development long before these changes came about, and the changes just made it more apparent. Early retirement has been given to some of those over 60. Others remained as titular head of their departments, but in essence report to a younger man who is really running the department.

Banking used to be a soft industry . . . you were hired and never fired. If you were a poor performer, you were given a lousy job that you could stay at. No one was ever called in and told to shape up. The pay was so poor it attracted people who wanted to work in a sheltered area, and they were satisfied to try and build a career in that area. So it was a job with low pay, high prestige, and some opportunity.

Our biggest problem is to convince people that they are not technicians anymore, that they are to *supervise* their subordinates and work to develop them. Apparently for many older individuals . . . , and younger ones, too, this is an impossible assignment. They can do the jobs themselves, but having anyone else do it in any other way runs against their grain.

If our rate of personnel growth over the next ten years is as fast as the previous ten years, I'm afraid we can only absorb about 50 percent of our most promising people.

INTERVIEW WITH JAMES FARREN—
TRUST ADMINISTRATION DIVISION HEAD

We have several people for whom there is very little opportunity anymore. We just don't see any potential in these people. There are about 15 of them who are in their forties and are really not capable of making any independent decisions. We're trying to get them to see other opportunities . . . both inside and outside the company. For example, our real estate group was big in the 1950s and 1960s. We're trying to make it important again, and there may be some opportunities in that area.

To give you an idea of the problem we're faced with: One man is really a personality problem. He's an attorney but he can't get along with others. He wants people to come to him; he focuses on detail too much; and he has great difficulty in telling others what to do and how to do it. He has to do the job all by himself.

EXHIBIT 2
Peoples Trust Company Organization Chart, June 1975

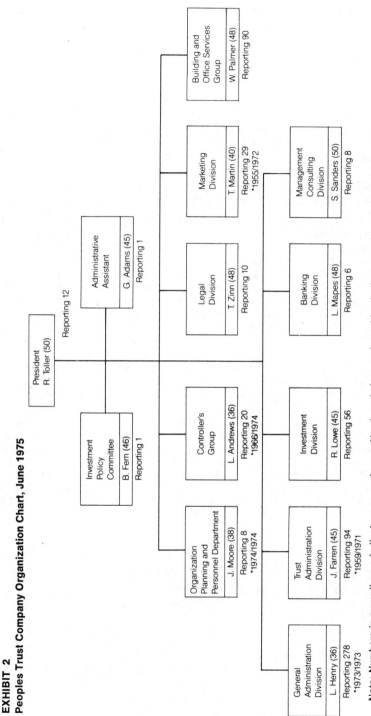

Note: Numbers in parentheses indicate manager's age. Numbers below each position indicate number of subordinates.
* Indicates year in which manager joined the company and year in which he assumed current position. For example, Mr. Larry Andrews joined Peoples Trust Company in 1966, and became Controller in 1974.

Another man: We gave him a section to supervise but he really hasn't measured up. But, he was the president's pet. I suppose we'll let him continue on—he's 57 . . . and then retire him early.

Another case: A female; she really has ability, and continually asks where she can go in the organization. I had to tell her that we're just not at the point where we can take a female into a higher job, and honestly suggested that she might explore opportunities outside the company. Well, she did, and apparently came to the conclusion that she's not so bad off here, after all. She's got so much invested time here that it's difficult to make the break.

INTERVIEW WITH MR. L. HENRY—
GENERAL ADMINISTRATION DIVISION

The company has been undergoing basic change. In the past, if a man demonstrated technical competence he was promoted, and that was fine while the company was a small, stable group, and everyone knew what the other was thinking. But then, many in the senior group began to retire. With this "changing of the guard" and the growth of the company, many of us have lost communication with our counterparts. Many of us are new in this field, new to this company, and, of course, new to each other. But we recognize this, so half the communication problem is solved. In a sense, we're not constrained by "how it was done before."

My people have reacted to all this change by sitting back and waiting, seeing which way things are going to go, then, I guess, deciding whether they are going to join you or not. Most of my people are relatively recent employees—as a matter of fact, of the 278 people in my division, only 11 have been with the company more than ten years. Conversion to EDP will really create a lot of changes in my area. Out of my officer group, there is only one man—he's 58—who is a problem to me in terms of his current and future usefulness. I'm concerned about him but haven't come to any conclusions about what to do. He doesn't report to me directly, he reports to one of my immediate subordinates, which maybe lessens the irritation. I don't think it was the company's policy at any time in the past to retain a man they felt they could do without. I don't think that policy is any different today, and I certainly hope it doesn't change in the future.

Case 4–5 ————————————————————————————————

Safety First (or, Whatever Happened to Equal Opportunity?)

Gopal Pati and Darold Barnum

Middle West Metal Fabricators, a large manufacturer of steel parts, began an active affirmative action and equal opportunity program about four years ago. They went far beyond the legal requirements, not only making special efforts to hire and promote qualified women and racial minorities, but also conducting supervisory education programs considered among the best in the industry. Thus, all supervisors were explicitly

EXHIBIT 1
Partial Organization Chart

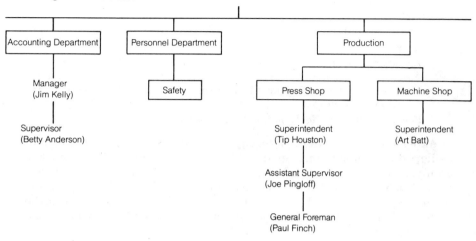

informed of top management's strong commitment to equal opportunity, received extensive training in the legal and human aspects of discrimination, and discussed and rediscussed what it all meant for their own jobs and for the organization.

Mrs. Betty Anderson was one of the program's success stories. She was hired three years ago as a management trainee, and successfully completed a demanding training program which developed her supervisory skills as well as her ability to perform many jobs on the shop floor and in the office. By early 1977 she had been promoted to a supervisor in the general accounting department (see Exhibit 1). Although she was one of a small number of female supervisors, and initially had to put up with some male resentment, she was reasonably content with her progress and felt that she had a good opportunity for continued advancement with the company.

In mid-1977 a labor dispute resulted in the union's refusal to work overtime, and it was decided to use the plant's management on the production line on weekends to perform necessary overtime work. (In this plant it was not unusual for managers and supervisors, including those from the office, to work on the floor when such disputes occurred.)

The first weekend's management work force was chosen from those working on Friday. Anderson was sick on Friday, so she did not work that weekend. When she came to work on Monday, a few people made remarks such as "Weren't there any soft jobs for you?" "Well, I guess when you have connections . . ." Because Anderson did want to pull her own weight, she specifically asked Jim Kelly, the accounting department manager, to be sure she was scheduled for the following weekend. Later in the week Kelly informed her that she would be working on the weekend, and she was very pleased. On Friday afternoon the following conversation took place:

Kelly: Betty, you still plan to work tomorrow, don't you?

Anderson: I sure do! Where will I be?

Kelly: Right here in the accounting office.

Anderson: But all the other supervisors will be working down on the floor!

Kelly: *[Turning and scratching his head]* Well, well.

Anderson: Look, there are lots of jobs in the press shop I can do very well. I worked there for 15 months when I was a trainee, and I know the equipment. Frankly, I know more about it than many of the floor supervisors.

Kelly: *[Smiles but looks puzzled]* Well, we will see.

Anderson went to work Saturday morning and found a number of assignments that she considered "make-work" on her desk. She spent the entire day in the accounting office completing these tasks. During the day several people asked her if she was working on Sunday also. She told them she did not know. The more she thought about the vagueness of the entire situation, the more annoyed she became. Late Saturday afternoon Kelly stopped by to see her.

Anderson: What happened, Jim? Why didn't I work on the floor?

Kelly: They don't want any women out there at all. A lot of equipment is dangerous and they're afraid a woman would get hurt.

Anderson: Are you kidding? There are women material handlers working down there!

Kelly: Yes, but they are doing "soft jobs."

Anderson: I don't want a "soft job." I want to work like everybody else. Why did you train me on those jobs during my training period anyway?

Kelly: Don't you like to preserve your femininity? *[Becomes very defensive]* If you want to work that badly, come in tomorrow anyway. *[Silence.]*

Anderson really did not want to work on Sunday. However, she felt that the opportunity for women to advance in the company was being hurt by such differential treatment, and she had to assert herself in the organization if she and others were ever to be treated equally. That evening she received a call from Kelly.

Kelly: Hey, you are coming to work tomorrow, aren't you?

Anderson: Oh, sure. Is there any problem?

Kelly: *[Hesitating and apologizing tone]* Oh, no. I gave some thought to our conversation this afternoon when I was riding home. You know, you were right. You are entitled to work in the shop.

Anderson: Oh, thank you, Jim. Good night.

Anderson reported to work on Sunday morning to No. 6 press line in the press shop. Just before the job start-up time, Anderson talked to the superintendent of the press shop, Tip Houston.

Anderson: Are you sure my being here is not going to create any problem?

Houston: Oh, no, not at all. Bulk of my supervisors like the idea, although they felt that women were not very well prepared for this kind of job. *[Smile]*

Anderson: How about all of those months I spent as a trainee in this department? You mean to say that the things that you guys taught me aren't any good?

Houston: *[Smile, no response.]*

The line ran well. Anderson, well equipped with proper clothing, gloves, and goggles had no trouble and contributed as much as any other supervisor. During the late morning hours the line broke down and the whole crew, including Anderson, were assigned to the 12th line. Anderson asked the press shop's general foreman, Paul Finch, about her assignment in this new line. While Finch was thinking about what to do with her, one of Anderson's fellow supervisors asked her to work with him. Finch was relieved because he didn't have to make a decision which might turn out to be the wrong one. Everything went smoothly, with the 12th line getting good quality production and Anderson demonstrating that she could handle the job. Around 11 o'clock, however, Finch showed up at the 12th line and approached Anderson.

Finch: I have been told to take you off the press.

Anderson: Why?

Finch: They don't want you to work on the press. They don't want you to get hurt.

Anderson: Who are "they"?

Finch: The superintendent of the machine shop does not want you to be there. He went to Pingloff *[assistant superintendent of the press shop and Finch's immediate superior]* and Pingloff told me to take you off.

Anderson: But I'm working in the press shop. What business does the superintendent of the machine shop have to tell me that I can't work here? What's going on?

Finch Well . . .

[Anderson immediately went to see Tip Houston, the press shop superintendent, and told him what had happened.]

Houston: *[After hearing what Anderson had to say]* Isn't this stupid? I don't believe this . . . Well, it's about lunch time anyway. After lunch you go back to work on the 12th line.

During lunch hour Houston told Pingloff to put Anderson back on the 12th line after lunch. He also told Anderson about this instruction. Anderson went back to the 12th line after lunch and work was again going on smoothly. Around 1:00 P.M. the safety man suddenly appeared, to talk to Anderson.

Safety Man: Come with me. I'll find somebody else to do this job for you. I don't want you to get hurt.

Anderson: *[Irritated]* Hey, look. I'm doing my job. I'm qualified. There's no problem here. I've my safety things on. I'm trained. What's the big deal?

Safety Man: If something happened to you, I'd kill myself.

Anderson: Would you do the same thing if someone else got hurt?

Safety Man: *[Angry]* No, because that's different.

Anderson: How come?

Safety Man: Look, if I can't talk you out of it, I'll have you taken out of the line.

He left the area immediately, but after a few minutes, he came back with assistant superintendent Pingloff and a man who had been pulled from another department to replace Anderson.

Pingloff: Mrs. Anderson, Tom is going to replace you. I know the risk—I don't want you to get hurt.

Then he put his arm around her and said, "Come on. Let's clean the No. 6 line."

Anderson: *[Blowing up]* What's going on around here?

Pingloff: *[Yelling]* Nobody wants the women to get hurt. You can't change this place in a week. If someday we have ten women supervisors, things will be different.

Anderson: What's the difference between one and ten?

Pingloff did not respond. The safety man faded away. Anderson stood there and started reflecting. She recalled how Pingloff had not wanted her to work in the shop from her very first day as a trainee. She recalled what Pingloff said to one of the other employees three years ago: "We don't want any 'broads' in the press shop because there are no beds and kitchens."

Anderson left the line, went to her accounting office, and sat down at her desk. She felt empty, frustrated, and robbed of her dignity. She went to the ladies' room and burst into tears. Around 2:00 P.M. she went home exhausted after working about 70 hours that week. Sadness and a feeling of defeat enveloped her. She thought of many options, including quitting or filing a sex discrimination charge.

Case 4–6 ——————————————————————————————

MBO in Action

Leon C. Megginson and Terrell F. Pike

The Quality Paper Corporation began a new managerial approach to training, developing, and utilizing its personnel in the early 1960s. It adopted a practical philosophy which evolved into an integrated management system of five subsystems, including organizational planning, human resources planning, work planning, education and training planning, and achievement reinforcement.

It was emphasized that all of these activities comprised the broad range of priority of duties of each and every manager. At the time of this case, this integrated system provided a conscious, deliberate, and structured way of performing each of the normal management leadership functions in achieving performance at "a cost effective" level.

The total system included writing job descriptions, setting up job qualification requirements, preparing organization charts, developing a series of supervisory and management development programs, having each employee develop his or her own job descriptions, establishing standards in an effort to have each manager of the organization involved in an active, ongoing, and positive system of work planning, based on the concepts of management by objectives (MBO).

By 1967, a formal system was instituted to have all managers develop their own job improvement objectives. These job improvement objectives were then made a part of the managers' annual career reports.

However, the formal program could only be as effective as its implementation by specific personnel, in a given location. The program was instituted at the River City Mill in 1968.

BACKGROUND INFORMATION ON THE RIVER CITY MILL

The River City Mill was the most versatile mill of its type in the world, having a diversified range of product lines with a corresponding complexity of operations. The mill employed 200 supervisory employees, of which over 100 were first-line supervisors. There were 1,600 hourly and production employees and 100 to 125 clerical employees. The mill operated 24 hours a day, 362 days a year, closing only for Christmas, Labor Day, and the Fourth of July. "The rest of the time, economic conditions permitting, we run flat out," said one manager.

River City Mill produced four different kinds of pulp and utilized six paper-making machines in production. Between 500 and 1,000 different end products were manufactured and sold to approximately 1,200 buyers. Most of these products were shipped to U.S. buyers, with a small proportion being exported to the Caribbean.

According to John Hogan, director of management development, it had been company policy, regarding supervisory positions, to develop a balance between supervisors with technical backgrounds and supervisors with practical experience in paper making. The people with practical backgrounds came up through the ranks of operators and had progressed into supervision. The technically oriented personnel were primarily college graduates in the fields of chemical, mechanical, civil, or electrical engineering. The purpose of this policy was to insure that the mill would have among its supervisory personnel a good balance between practical experience and advanced paper-making technology.

When the River City Mill attempted to implement an MBO program, it encountered problems with the personnel in objective-setting. Hogan said that the supervisors with the practical backgrounds did not have the disciplined thinking processes instilled in them that one could obtain from a college curriculum, and that many of these supervisors could not understand or accept the concept of setting objectives. A number of them felt that setting objectives was nothing more than a paper exercise.

One of the first things that was tried at River City Mill with regard to objective-setting, was what was called a "grass roots" approach. The first-line supervisors set objectives for themselves. Then, the departmental managers consolidated those objectives into the departmental objective. Finally, the mill manager consolidated the departmental objectives into the overall mill objectives. However, this process did not work very well. There were always some objectives which people in other areas did not personally feel like supporting. For example, one manager might have certain industrial relations objectives which would be supported by the Industrial Relations Department, but not by the maintenance people or by other workers. The managers and supervisors did not accept these objectives voluntarily. Instead, the objectives had to be forced upon them. Another example was environmental objectives which some production employees would not accept. There were also problems with efforts to implement Equal Employment Opportunities Commission (EEOC) objectives.

For a couple of years, the grass roots approach was tried, and River City Mill obtained some improvements from the approach. Supervisors set their own objectives, which were then discussed with the department manager who would either modify them, approve them, or make substitutions. The department manager would then submit his objectives to his supervisor who would do the same. This process would go on all the way up the chain of command to the mill manager.

One of the difficulties encountered was that the supervisor and superintendents could only see a limited part of the mill operations. Although lower-level managers could comprehend their own jobs, many were unable to understand how their jobs fit into the overall mill operations. For example, a shift foreman with 75 people to supervise, worked on a rotating shift basis. The foreman worked the 7:00 A.M. to 3:00 P.M. shift one week, the 3:00 P.M. to 11:00 P.M. shift the next week, and the "graveyard" shift from 11:00 P.M. to 7:00 A.M. the following week. This rotation was on a staggered basis so that sometimes the foreman worked weekends, and at other times he could be off on the weekends. Only when the foremen worked on the day shift did they have an opportunity to talk with their own supervisors. Therefore, these shift foremen were not in a position to establish any meaningful objectives which tied into the overall mill objectives.

In one instance, a foreman set as his objectives reducing waste on the shift and increasing production on a given machine by "X" percent over the historical figure. In order to achieve these objectives, a new pump would be necessary because one of the existing ones could not have handled the volume to be produced. However, the foreman himself did not have the authority to purchase the pump. The decision to buy the pump had to be approved by an individual in a position three levels higher than his. The foreman was trying to meet his objectives and improve his performance when someone three levels higher in the chain of command refused to buy the pump. Mr. Hogan said:

> We kind of floundered around when the "grass roots" approach was first initiated. But by the end of 1969, in December, the mill management had enough direction to know what was being expected of them and to get ready for 1970 when the MBO program actually went into effect.

EXPERIENCE WITH MBO IN 1968–1970

The MBO program actually began in 1968 and 1969 with extensive training of managers and hourly workers in problem-solving skills. More than 100 managerial employees and over 200 top-rated hourly operators and mechanics completed this type of training.

In the fall of 1969, the mill had a problem with an excessive amount of lost production time on the paper machines. Through an extensive study and through informal discussions with the mill staff, department heads, foremen, and top-rated hourly people, the causes of "down time" were found, and efforts were made to correct them.

By December 1969, most of the facts concerning down time and its causes had been accumulated. The employees and supervisors had been trained in problem-solving techniques, the other new managerial techniques were in operation, and the mill was ready to attempt the MBO program.

Gus Robert, the mill manager, tried out the new approach being advocated by the company, with certain modifications. He began by asking departmental managers to make commitments to reduce down time as part of their objectives.

The departmental managers were called together for a meeting after each of them had already done a considerable amount of investigation concerning conditions in their own areas of responsibility. The performance of each area was reviewed on a team-approach basis, and each department manager was shown how production was a reflection of his own performance. Suggestions for reducing down time and increasing production were made. These suggestions indicated that some paper grades could be run more productively by changing refining procedures, eliminating size press applications, allowing increased speeds, and so forth.

Mr. Robert first set the overall mill objective, based upon the early discussion, at a 3.7 percent production increase, independent of capital spending. This mill objective was then translated by Mr. Robert and his department heads into a list of priorities that the mill was to attempt to achieve. The MBO effort was to coincide with another program to reduce down time and increase profits.

Bob Jones, assistant to the mill manager, took the list of mill priorities for the year, and, working with departmental supervision, helped develop departmental priorities to support the mill priorities. For example:

If you are going to reduce "down time" on machine No. 1 by "X" percent, you will be running that machine "X" percent more and will be producing more tonnage. Then top mill management said to the pulp mill, "You have been producing a certain number of tons of pulp per day and now you will have to produce that amount plus 'X' percent more." The power plant was then told, "You have been generating this much power and electricity, and now more is needed. Here are your targets for the year."

Then, the finishing and shipping department was told, "You have been shipping a certain number of tons each day, but now you are going to have to gear up your materials and your materials handling equipment, get your boxcar supply in order, get your suppliers alerted that they are going to have increased rates and will be handling 'X' percent more shipping during the year. Therefore, each of them can be ready to handle the increased production when it comes."

The entire mill, with the exception of the administrative area, was given an outline for each facet of the operation which was needed to support the increased operations and productive time on the paper machines. Said Mr. Hogan:

> We wrote it down for them, handed it to them, and said, "OK, now go to it." It wasn't very democratic, and we may have not used all of the participative management we should have, but it seemed to do the job. We increased productivity 6.2 percent, which far exceeded our goal of 3.7 percent.

In February and March 1970, eight hours of work improvement training was conducted for approximately 100 managerial employees and 250 hourly employees. When this training was added to the previous training in problem solving, a set of tools was provided to not only accomplish the objectives, but to surpass them.

EXPERIENCE FROM 1971–1976

While overall productivity increased 6.2 percent, there were some people who resisted the imposition of objectives. It "teed off" some of the people involved. They resented being told what they had to do, and what objectives they had to reach. At the same time, a new manager was assigned as mill manager. He was a more participative leader who wanted the managers and the hourly employees to have greater input in setting their own goals and objectives and in determining how they would achieve their targets.

In 1971, the level of economic activity declined. This had important effects on new orders to River City Mill because the paper-making industry varied directly with the level of economic activity of the general economy. Economic activity declined in 1971, recovered in 1972–73, and then decreased during the second half of 1974. River City Mill did not have sufficient orders during 1971–72, and production went down. Although management still set "key work objectives," it was impossible for the mill to reach the goals that had been achieved in 1970. The mill did achieve results from using key work objectives, but even into 1975, 1976, and early 1977 it could not achieve the results it had obtained earlier. The mill did not have the "totally organized approach" that it had in 1970 and, consequently, did not obtain the same results. Mr. Hogan stated:

> Productivity went way down during 1971 and the following period. One of the difficulties in adjusting to changes in the environment is you're operating everything that you can, and selling it. Then, you have a situation where part of your mill is shut down for lack of orders, there is an eight-week backlog of product to be sold, and you're operating "off the teletype machine." When an order comes in, you grab it off the teletype machine, rush it out to one of the machines, get them to produce it, send it to the shipping department, and have it sent out as soon as possible. It is almost impossible to determine then what actually causes productivity, or whether a given group of people or machines is productive. The usual standards don't work and do not apply in such a situation.
>
> We have standards set for our operations, but it is difficult to measure whether a given unit is doing what it is supposed to do or not. The standards are generally based upon running at a fairly high level of operations. If you do not have that level of operation, you cannot have long production runs so that you can obtain the efficiencies of large-scale production.
>
> With shorter production runs, inefficiencies creep in. You have to set up your equipment to produce different kinds of products and different weights of paper. These adjustments and changes result in more machine "down time" and cause you to lose production. Your production standards just don't cover these contingencies.

The mill manager was replaced as a result of the experiences that occurred during this period of time. Yet, according to one official, "He was partially the victim of business conditions."

EXPERIENCE FROM 1977 ON

Mr. Hogan outlined the experience of the mill from 1977.

> As of July 1977, River City Mill went back into an integrated program. A new round of setting priorities and objectives was begun. It started with the manager and his staff who set the overall mill priorities. These priorities were passed down to the department heads who held meetings with their supervisors and told them what the departmental objectives were. Meetings were held with the management development staff to help them translate the mill objectives and departmental objectives into specific objectives for each unit.
>
> The current round of improvements were not only designed to implement the management by objectives program and set key work objectives, but to improve communications among the employees. All supervisors and foremen were told to hold crew meetings with their hourly employees. They were to help the workers understand what the mill was all about, what the mill was trying to do, what the current concerns were, and to pass to them information that they needed in their work, and to solicit their support and commitment toward helping achieve mill objectives.

Case 4–7 ————————————————————————————————

Problems on the Night-Shift Cleaning Crew

Donald J. Petersen

St. James Hospital is a 200-bed facility located in a large midwestern city. It is owned and operated by a Catholic order. Two nuns administer the hospital: Sister Joan, the president, and a vice president. The remaining sisters have managerial control over all major areas of the hospital, including nursing services, X-ray, nuclear medicine, emergency, and building services. These sisters all have degrees in management and have prior experience in their respective specialty areas.

On a Tuesday night the hospital's emergency room received a call from an incoming ambulance reporting a patient's arrival. The preliminary diagnosis was internal bleeding caused by unknown sources, a finding which called for immediate exploratory surgery—nurses and doctors were called.

At 8:30 P.M., 15 minutes after the patient entered Surgery, Sister Joan was informed of the emergency. She learned that the patient was an old and close friend and immediately left her office for the operating room, a very rare occurrence for her at any time of day.

Upon entering the operating room area, Sister Joan discovered three clean-up women sitting in the doctors' lounge watching TV. She immediately inquired what they were doing and why they were not working. One of the women replied, "Sister, we're on our break." Sister Joan responded, "Don't let me catch you watching the doctors' TV at break, lunch, or any other time of the day!" With that, Sister Joan continued through the operating area, put on a surgical coat, and proceeded to check on her friend.

At the time she kept thinking that the women weren't telling her the truth about the break.

The next morning, at breakfast, Sister Joan questioned Sister Ruth, the manager of the operating room, about the three women and their jobs. She asked her if these women would be on their break at that time of night. Hesitating, Sister Ruth replied, "Yes, they would most likely be taking their break about that time." To that, Sister Joan replied, "Well, just keep them out of the doctors' lounge."

After breakfast, Sister Ruth thought about the situation. She knew that the women had been finished with their work but were not on break when Sister Joan saw them. The women usually worked no longer than five or six hours on any given night. Their function was to clean the surgical instruments used during the day as well as the equipment in the nine surgical rooms and surrounding areas. She also knew that Sister Joan would not know the routine for this shift because Sister Joan had just become president last month, arriving from another hospital in the East. The biggest consideration was the relationship Sister Ruth had with these women. Fifteen years ago there were two women working the shift. The third one was added ten years ago. In these years, Sister Ruth had developed a real friendship with them.

Sister Joan, after learning this, was still not satisfied with the situation. Being new, she wanted to get a better understanding of the operating room jobs. She asked Sister Norma, manager of personnel, to come to her office with the job duties list for all operating room personnel. When Sister Joan examined them she found none for the clean-up women. When asked why there were none for the clean-up women, Sister Norma explained, "It is one of those jobs that is so diversified in nature that it is impossible to formulate a list of duties. Many different jobs in the hospital fall into that category." To this Sister Joan replied, "You can take the lists back—I'll get back to you later."

Sister Joan decided to have the clean-up women watched during their shift. However, she knew she had to get someone up to Surgery who could view the women without being suspected of checking on them. Sister Joan also realized if she were to send someone to the operating room area, or went there herself, the women would become suspicious and would manage to keep busy at the "right times."

Earlier, Sister Joan had noticed that a request had been made for a new sterilizer by the operating room staff. It would take one man at least three nights to install it. She decided to order the machine and brief the maintenance man who would install it.

After the maintenance man had finished installing the machine, he reported his findings to Sister Joan. He explained that the women started work at 2:30 P.M. each day. At 3:30 P.M. they took their lunch break. When they returned at 5:00, instead of continuing their work they would watch the news on the television in the doctors' lounge. They then proceeded to work, from 5:30 until anywhere from 7:00 P.M. to 9:00 P.M., depending on how busy the day had been. After that, they would sit and watch television until their quitting time at 11:00 P.M.

Upon receiving this information, Sister Joan was very upset. With all the complaints about hospital costs being so high, she couldn't understand why anyone could let this happen. With that thought in mind she called Sister Ruth to her office for an immediate conference.

Case 4–8

Gibson Bank and Trust Company

Geraldine Byrne Ellerbrock

Gibson Bank and Trust Company is located in Acre, Arizona, which is a small city and serves an agricultural community extending beyond a radius of some 50 miles. Harry Boke came to work at the bank upon graduation from college. A native of Chicago, he had spent most of his life there before going to study at a university in the Southwest. His training at Gibson Bank consisted of being in each department for two months—it was on-the-job training with periodic attendance at seminars given by the banking association. After this year-long training program, Harry was to be given the title of assistant manager and be in charge of all small loans.

For the first two months he was a cashier. The head cashier, Joan Milles, reported at the end of the period that his work was accurate, that he was well accepted by the other cashiers, and that the customers remarked upon his pleasant, accommodating manner. When Harry was asked about his job, he replied, "I enjoy living in a small town where people call me by name. It's great here. Since I was a kid, I've wanted to work in a bank. Now they are paying me for something I have always wanted to do."

Then Harry was transferred to the accounting department. When his supervisor, Sidney Dedson, was asked about his work, Dedson said, "Harry needs to be shown only once a procedure we use. He has even devised some methods to check his own accuracy with complicated procedures. He is a bright young fellow." Peggy and Richard, Harry's coworkers, were also complimentary. Peggy said to Richard, "Harry fits into our group very well. If I need any information, he stops what he is doing and gets it for me." Richard replied, "I hated getting involved in that lawsuit, but not only did Harry supply all the information he offered to testify if someone from the bank was forced to do so." In his evaluation at the end of the first month in the department, Mr. Dedson praised Harry's attention to detail and the accuracy of his work. Another coworker, Sue, said she heard Harry tell someone in the coffee shop in the building, "Gibson is a great place to work. I enjoy my job. It's interesting. People say banks are cold and calculating. I haven't found that to be so. Everyone has been friendly and helpful. There is a great deal of warmth shown a newcomer."

During the second month in a routine check, Mr. Dedson discovered some errors in Harry's accounts. Mr. Dedson thought, "This is strange. Those mistakes would have been obvious when he reconciled his other accounts. I had better check his work more carefully for awhile." He observed him closely for a day or two and was surprised to find that another employee, Pam Riggs, also was checking his work surreptitiously.

During a coffee break later, Mr. Dedson remembered that he had neglected to ask the garage to check his clutch pedal. It wasn't springing back and it might be serious. He told Will, "I had better call the garage from the pay phone. I just sent a memo out to every one in our department saying, 'The phones are to be used for business only.' I feel I must do as I say." When he was looking up the number in the phone booth, he could not help overhearing the conversation at a nearby table. Pam Riggs was talking to a young man and woman: "Harry is a nice guy. I feel he. . . . but I don't want him to get hurt."

The following week a lawyer representing Mrs. Smithe in regard to her estate came storming into the bank. Mr. Dedson was summoned. He did not tell the vice president, George Johnson, that Harry had been doing work on this account. He told Mr. Johnson, "I will personally look into the matter, and see that every statement is accurate before it leaves here. We pride ourselves on our customer relationships, and it is rare that we ever make a mistake."

Case 4–9

Ed Jackson's Rules Problems

John E. Dittrich

Ed Jackson is plant manager of the Pueblo plant of ZBG Industries, a large corporation involved in the design and manufacture of components used in the refrigeration and air conditioning field.

In recent months, a number of severe injuries have occurred to employees resulting from hazardous action on the part of the injured employee. While no two accidents involved violation of the same safety rule or rules, all appeared to be the result of knowledgeable violation of a clearly posted rule; a rule which had been included in either the safety orientation for all new employees (i.e., employees must wear goggles when operating welding, brazing, or spot welding equipment), or in the instructions for performing a specific job (i.e., maintenance work must never be performed on equipment until *after* the electrical control box switch has been locked by padlock into the *off* position).

In addition to the human suffering and man-hour loss caused by these accidents, workmen's compensation costs have risen very sharply. Ed has repeatedly instructed his managers to (1) assure themselves that employees have been given safety orientation training; (2) observe at all times for safe performance; (3) demonstrate safe practice to workers by the managers' own safe practice.

To employees, Ed has warned that unsafe practices must be stopped, and that he intends to severely discipline persons observed violating safety rules. Following that warning, several employees were severely reprimanded, and received suspension without pay for periods ranging from one week to 30 days.

Last night, in an unoccupied section of the plant, Ed observed Charles Sommerfield, an experienced and highly skilled supervisor, as Charlie made his way through the machines. Ed noted that as Charlie progressed through the area to reach a location where several of his workers were at work, he crossed three roller conveyor lines by "skating" across them on foot, then ducked beneath a moving belt conveyor, ignoring a sign which stated "Cross at Catwalk Only" and the catwalk itself, which was located about 75 feet from his crossing. Ed could not determine whether the workers noticed Charlie's approach.

Case 4–10 ——————————————————————————————————————

Is There a Better Way?

W. D. Heier

Mike Miller was not very fond of personnel rating systems. He had always felt, too keenly perhaps, that the evaluations he made of an individual's performance could dramatically, and sometimes drastically, affect the man's entire career. This was a little too close to omnipotence to suit Mike. Still, it was that time again and, since there wasn't any use in delaying the unpleasant chore past Friday's deadline, Mike got out the 15 rating sheets and started to work.

He had barely gotten started when Pat Parsons, one of the new managers from another department, knocked on his door and asked for a few minutes of time. Noting that Mike was working on the evaluation forms, Pat commented upon the coincidence since this was why he had come to talk. It developed that Pat had no previous experience in rating people and was seeking advice how to proceed.

Mike found himself in a quandary. He knew what he did and how he went about the task, but he was not at all sure that his approach was the best possible. He wanted to help Pat but was reluctant to give advice about a matter in which he truly lacked confidence in his own actions.

As might be expected, Mike temporized, while he gathered his thoughts, by talking about the company's policy statements concerning evaluations. Those written statements expressed the philosophical bases for having personnel evaluations, gave some general guidance regarding completion of the rating forms, and established the reporting and reviewing dates.

Pat listened quietly until Mike finished and then stated that, while this was all well and good, he needed to know specifically how Mike really approached the actual rating of each of his men. Seeing that there was no avoiding the issue, Mike briefly described his procedure as:

1. Comparing the individual's output in terms of what is expected of him.
2. Evaluating the individual's knowledge of his job.
3. Ascertaining how the person relates to his fellow workers and his superior.
4. Estimating his future potential.

Mike stated that this framework permitted him to establish an overall impression of the worker's value to the organization and, from that, he proceeded to record the individual markings required on the form. Mike said that he rarely made any extra written remarks, although it was permissible to do so. Mike concluded his remarks by saying that he mentally ranked his subordinates in an order-of-precedence list and then checked to see that the evaluation ratings came out correctly. If not, he made some adjustments in the ratings.

In response to Pat's question as to whether Mike kept a running record of his subordinates' performance during the rating period, Mike stated that he used to do so but had not found it helped too much, so he stopped. Mike explained that he considered progress, which was best shown by recent performance, to be a better rating basis than trying to "average-out" a full rating period's activity.

The next question was really a difficult one for Mike to answer. Specifically, Pat wanted to know whether Mike gave much thought to morale factors in making his markings. After talking about the matter for some minutes, Mike finally admitted that he did consider morale to a great extent.

Mike also was asked if he knew how other supervisors marked, and if he tried to keep in line with the other raters. Mike admitted he had some general idea, but no specific knowledge, of how other people rated their subordinates. Mike expressed the hope that he rated as highly as others did, since he didn't want his good men to suffer because of a difference in raters. Mike admitted that he leaned a little toward the "high side" of the sheet just to be sure of this but defended this action by saying he had some top-notch people in his branch. Mike gave as an example the fact that one of his subordinates, who was the fastest man with figures Mike had ever seen, always received an outstanding rating. After all, as Mike noted, if he was the best "figures man" in the division, no one should be able to get a better rating.

The next question was concerned with the factors Mike considered in assessing a subordinate's potential. Mike said that he considered, basically, the promotability of the employee. If a man was qualified to be promoted— i.e., trained, had sufficient time in grade, and was a good man—then his potential was good. If he wasn't ready for promotion for some reason, then his potential was obviously limited, at this time. Mike stated that he had found it necessary to use this approach in order to be consistent in his rating. He explained that he found it impossible to say that a man had good potential but that he wasn't good enough to be promoted.

Pat's final question was to ask Mike how he handled the counseling interview sessions required by agency policy. Mike said that he had encountered no real problems. You simply told the outstanding employees they were doing a fine job, which they already knew, and advised them to keep up the good work. The few average subordinates were advised that they had done a good job and to keep on improving their performance. Mike did admit that, on two occasions, he had given marginal ratings to employees. In both cases, he told the employees that their work was passable but not as good as they could do if they applied themselves. Both men left the company for other jobs within a few months of the counseling session. Mike was of the opinion that their performance potential was so poor that they and the company were better off for their departure.

Pat thanked Mike for his assistance and advice and returned to his office.

Case 4–11 ——

Virginia Employment Commission

J. David Hunger and Thomas L. Wheelen

On April 23, 1975, a meeting was held at the central office of the Virginia Employment Commission. In attendance were Bill Jolly, director of personnel and training; Jack Richardson, director of training (Bill's immediate subordinate); and two faculty members from the McIntire School of Commerce of the University of Virginia. Bill Jolly, who arranged the meeting, began the discussion by stating that "we have to do something about our performance appraisal system. The state's service rating program is inadequate and needs to be changed at least insofar as the VEC is concerned. Our present system of appraisal has been damned by almost everyone I talk with. After checking with my superiors, I have received permission to develop a more appropriate rating system. The only requirement given me by the state Department of Personnel is that the rating forms sent to them for their files must have a P–9 format. In other words, instead of using the elements given, such as 'Habits of Work' or 'Intelligence', we can put in our own titles. Of course, we can use additional forms for our own use inside the VEC if we want" (see Exhibit 1).

Bill went on to say: "We have done a lot of thinking and work on this question and have developed a new kind of appraisal program. It's called PACE—Performance Analysis and Counseling of Employees. I think it's

EXHIBIT 1

G.O. Form P-9 (Rev. 12-70)
(Submit one copy of this form to the Division of Personnel)

COMMONWEALTH OF VIRGINIA

SERVICE RATING

AGENCY TITLE		AGENCY	POSITION	TRAN	EFFEC DATE	SOCIAL SECURITY NO	SERVICE RATING	CLASS CODE

EMPLOYEE NAME	LAST	FIRST	INIT	APPR	ACTIV	S-ACTIV	PER CENT	CLASS TITLE

CHECK APPLICABLE ADJECTIVE UNDER EACH ELEMENT					
HABITS OF WORK	AMOUNT OF WORK	QUALITY OF WORK	COOPERATION	INTELLIGENCE	INITIATIVE
POOR 0 ☐	POOR 0 ☐	POOR 0 ☐	POOR 0 ☐	POOR 0 ☐	POOR 0 ☐
FAIR 2 ☐	FAIR 2 ☐	FAIR 2 ☐	FAIR 2 ☐	FAIR 2 ☐	FAIR 2 ☐
GOOD 3 ☐	GOOD 3 ☐	GOOD 3 ☐	GOOD 3 ☐	GOOD 3 ☐	GOOD 3 ☐
VERY GOOD 4 ☐	VERY GOOD 4 ☐	VERY GOOD 4 ☐	VERY GOOD 4 ☐	VERY GOOD 4 ☐	VERY GOOD 4 ☐
EXCELLENT 6 ☐	EXCELLENT 6 ☐	EXCELLENT 6 ☐	EXCELLENT 6 ☐	EXCELLENT 6 ☐	EXCELLENT 6 ☐

Was this rating discussed with the employee?   Yes ☐   No ☐

Rated By _____   _____
              NAME   CLASS TITLE

Approved _____   _____
              NAME   CLASS TITLE

NOTE
• BEFORE RATING THIS EMPLOYEE BE SURE THAT YOU UNDERSTAND THE ELEMENTS AS EXPLAINED IN THE PRINTED INSTRUCTIONS.
• IF EITHER 'POOR' OR 'EXCELLENT' IS CHECKED IN THREE OR MORE ELEMENTS, ON THE OTHER SIDE OF THIS REPORT DESCRIBE THE BASIS FOR THE EXCEPTIONAL RATING.
Where an explanation is required on the reverse side, carbon paper will be necessary.

a worthwhile program—at least it's a change from our present system! I have sent copies to the commissioner and to division heads and local office managers. Responses, especially from the local offices, have been mixed. The main complaint has been that PACE includes a lot of paperwork and will take too much time. They have a valid point. As you may know, with the present recession, our people have a huge workload trying to process unemployment benefits as well as find people jobs."

"As a result, I am hesitant to go ahead with the proposed program until I am sure that it makes sense for us," continued Bill. "I'd like you university types to read my proposal, evaluate it, and provide me, if necessary, with some recommendations for improvement. If you like it, I would like to start planning the implementation as soon as possible."

BACKGROUND

The Virginia Employment Commission (VEC) is an agency of the State of Virginia with programs funded by the federal government. The organization was created December 18, 1936, by the Virginia legislature when it passed the Virginia Employment Compensation Act. The original name of the organization was the Unemployment Compensation Commission of Virginia. The commission was entrusted with two major programs of public service: (1) insurance protection for many workers involuntarily unemployed, and (2) placement help for job seekers. In 1960, the name of the agency was changed to the Virginia Employment Commission. This was done to emphasize the many employment services the organization offers, such as special programs of manpower research, as well as cooperative manpower projects of skills training before and after employment for youth, veterans, older workers, handicapped, and agricultural workers. Examples of such services are the Work Incentive Program (WIN) for women; the Job Bank, a computerized system of job listings; and special Veterans Job Fairs, and outreach services for handicapped veterans. The commission, through its Manpower Research department, prepares numerous booklets and reports dealing with occupations, wages, employment and unemployment levels, potential labor supply, and many other facets of current and projected labor market conditions needed by industrial developers, educators, and manpower planners.

The VEC functions as a state agency through an administrative office staff and a chain of local offices. The broad, statewide services rendered by the commission require a close relationship with other state agencies, such as Department of Welfare, and the cooperation of civic groups, labor, schools, and private industry. Much of the work conducted by the VEC has been initiated by various state and federal laws as well as by Presidential Executive Orders and requests by the governor. Examples of these are: (1) the Virginia Unemployment Compensation Act which sets coverage and benefit limits; (2) Virginia House Joint Resolution No. 26 directing the VEC to "actively seek out and locate employment for welfare recipients"; and (3) Public Law 92–540 dated October 1972 which superseded the President's Executive Order 11598 (Jobs for Veterans Program) and required all prime contractors and first tier subcontractors doing business with the federal government whose contracts were in excess of $2,500 to list their job vacancies (excepting union contract hire agreements and jobs exceeding $18,000 a year) with the state Employment Security Agency. As a result of these laws and orders, the VEC is involved in many diverse areas and its employees are often quite constrained by rules and regulations in their everyday activities.

The Virginia Employment Commission is directed by a commissioner appointed by the governor. As shown in the following organization chart, three associate commissioners are responsible for the work of the various departments and local offices. For example, the director of employment services has under him an assistant director for employment services and one for manpower programs. Reporting to these managers are various supervisors and assistant supervisors. Insofar as the local offices are concerned, field supervisors report to an associate commissioner for field operations. Each field supervisor oversees local offices in his area. A local office manager runs each office. Depending upon the size of the office, the manager may have reporting to him an assistant office manager and some general supervisors. There may be anywhere from 3 to 15 nonmanagement workers in a local office (see Exhibit 2).

PRESENT APPRAISAL SYSTEM

The Virginia Employment Commission is one of the several state agencies which function under state merit system rules governing certification of qualified persons for employment, promotion, and transfer. As stated in the booklet *Service Rating of State Employees*, revised July 1, 1949, "Merit or efficiency rating, in accordance with the terms of the Virginia Personnel Act and the provisions of the rules for the administration of the Virginia Personnel Act, is designed for positive development of employees within the various classes of positions, and for promotion from class to class." This booklet is provided to each rater and is supposed to be read before completing the P–9 form. The following quotations are taken from the booklet:

> It is desirable in the large agencies that each employee be rated by at least two scorers; one, the person in immediate charge of the group, and the second, the immediate supervisor of the person. The scorer doing the initial rating will be in close contact with the employees and will understand their habits and quality of work. The next in authority will be generally acquainted with the work being done, if not in intimate touch with the employees. Where there are variations in the two ratings compiled, discussion should be held in order to harmonize the differences or otherwise the ratings should be referred to the department head.
>
> The score sheet provides that if an employee be rated "Poor" or "Excellent" on as many as three elements, a special letter should be sent in giving definite reasons for the rating. It is realized, of course, that the adjectives used after each element may be subject to different interpretations, but, on the whole, the common acceptance of the meanings of these

EXHIBIT 2

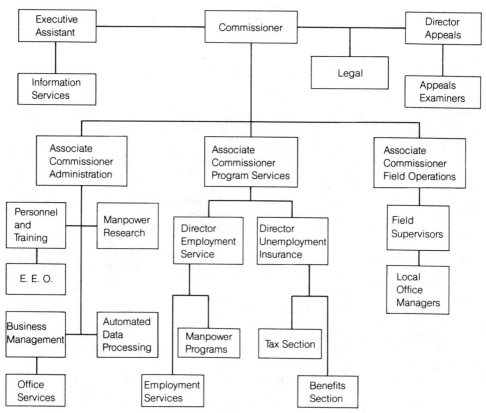

adjectives, particularly as interpreted by the five groups under each element in the direction for scoring, will invite reasonable uniformity.

The booklet goes on to provide some assistance to the raters in terms of what behavior is considered "poor," "fair," "good," "very good," or "excellent":

Habits of Work

If the employee to be graded may be

Described by these: Is frequently late in getting started to work.

Appears indifferent to his work and responsibilities.

Wastes time in visiting and talking.

Takes too much time with outside matters.

Check "Poor"   Seeks easy or avoids difficult tasks.

Is not industrious and does not concentrate on work.

Described by these: Is usually regular in getting started to work.

Shows interest in work and some appreciation of
responsibilities.

Attempts assigned tasks willingly.

	Does not loiter around the office or otherwise waste time.
Check "Fair"	Shows evidence of some industry and determination.
	Gives reasonable proof of capacity to improve in habits of work.
Described by these:	Is prompt in getting started to work.
	Shows appreciation of the job and its responsibilities.
	Performs assigned tasks in acceptable manner.
	Is primarily industrious and only occasionally and incidentally seems to waste time.
Check "Good"	Is a reasonably steady worker and keeps work up to date.
	Performs work with tolerable speed.
Described by these:	Is diligent in beginning his work and in its performance.
	Completes readily the tasks assigned.
	Does work with reasonable speed.
Check "Very Good"	Applies self to job with industry and in such manner as to raise no question about waste of time.
	Not only keeps abreast of the work assigned, but shows willingness and capacity to make contribution to other work in the office.
Described by these:	Is a most diligent worker.
	Excels in the amount of work turned out and in the type of work done.
Check "Excellent"	Demonstrates those habits of work which would make the highest contribution to office performance.
	Handles office or field work with highest facility.

The element "Intelligence," which has been the subject of considerable criticism by raters is described as follows for "poor":

Intelligence

Described by these:	Appears to be dull and confused.
	Does not seem to grasp the meaning of instruction or directions.
Check "Poor"	Shows little ability to learn new work.
	Shows slow mental reaction to any office procedure.
	Is easily rattled and unstable in thinking.

PROPOSED PROGRAM (PACE)

Following are excerpts from the PACE proposal:

Objectives of the Program

The major objectives of the PACE program are:

1. To uncover exceptional talent and identify promotable personnel.
2. To improve performance.
3. To establish a uniform and valid basis for effecting personnel changes.
4. To discover training needs.
5. To stimulate self-improvement.
6. To provide the employee with an understanding of how he is doing.

Procedure

Phase I—Agreeing on Specific Tasks Required to Do the Job

The employee must establish short-term performance goals for himself. The supervisor enters the process only after the employee has (a) done a good deal of thinking about his job; (b) made a careful assessment of his own strengths and weaknesses; and (c) formulated some specific plans to accomplish his goals. The supervisor's role is to help the employee relate his self-appraisal, his "targets," and his plans for the ensuing period to the realities of the Commission.

The first step in this process is to arrive at a clear statement of the major features of the job. Rather than a formal job description this is a worksheet drawn up by the employee. It defines the broad areas of his responsibility as they actually work out in practice. The supervisor and employee discuss the worksheet jointly and modify it as may be necessary until both of them agree that it is adequate.

(See Exhibit 3, Worksheet for Performance Analysis, for an explanation of task analysis.)

Phase II—Establishing Standards of Performance for Each Task

Using the worksheet the employee then establishes his goals which become performance standards for the next six months to one year. They are stated explicitly and detailed as to the proposed action which will accomplish the goal. This in turn, is discussed with the supervisor and modified until both are satisfied with it. Changes can occur when the supervisor and the employee see problems in the same way and agree on the means of solving them. Agreement on mutual goals will set standards for performance.

(Exhibit 3, Worksheet for Performance Analysis, offers an explanation of performance standards.)

Phase III—Appraisal by the Employee

At this point, specific benchmarks have been set for analyzing performance. Responsibilities have been established, performance standards have been agreed upon. At the end of the performance period the employee makes his own appraisal of what he has accomplished, measured against the targets he had set earlier. Factual data is used wherever possible.

The employee is examining himself in order to define his strength and potential and to inspect any weakness which may be overcome or reduced. Specific accomplishment may be detailed on the performance worksheet.

Phase IV—The Evaluation Interview

The "interview" is an examination by supervisor and employee together of the employee's self-appraisal, and it culminates in a resetting of targets for the next period of time.

The evaluation interview may take place at intervals spanning the performance period. It is not necessary to wait until the end of the performance period and may be very beneficial to the employee to have several intermediate evaluation steps along the way.

It is important that by the conclusion of the interview the employee realizes the extent of his performance. It is the supervisor's responsibility to advise, coach, and guide the employee, using the performance data at hand, to a correct interpretation of the value of his performance. There should be a meeting of the minds on this so that the completion of the Service Rating form will reflect the evaluation of both the employee and the supervisor.

Phase V—Performance Rating

The supervisor utilizes the service rating form to transmit an evaluation of the employee's performance to management.

The employee should have complete knowledge of the completed service rating. In any case where "fair" or "poor" characterizes a performance element the employee is required to initial or sign the form indicating he has seen the service rating.

The Commonwealth of Virginia, GO Form P–9 (Rev. 12–70), Service Rating (Exhibit 4) has been revised to incorporate rating elements for task analysis and work relationships. Changes have been kept to a minimum to reduce administrative problems with the submittal of service rating forms to the state.

Phase VI—Reinforcement

The field supervisor or division head conducts an informal interview with the manager or supervisor, using a copy of the individual's worksheet as a guide to supplemental analysis and planning. The field supervisor or division head asks the supervisor for his overall opinion of each employee's performance and specific reasons to substantiate it; what plans the supervisor has or what plans he might make to improve each employee's performance; whether he is performing effectively or ineffectively.

The information developed from this contact is noted in writing on the worksheet and provides a basis for personnel status changes, training and

EXHIBIT 3

Pace Worksheet for Performance Analysis

NAME _____ LOCATION _____

CLASSIFICATION _____ SUPERVISOR _____

PURPOSE OR OBJECTIVE OF PRESENT POSITION: _____

Task Analysis

Major Work Assignments	*Tasks Involved*
[Task analysis involves breaking major work assignments down into specific tasks which describe what the employee does. An example for a clerical position is outlined below.]	
Types all correspondence for the office.	Composes and types routine letters. Types letters from handwritten draft. Types memoranda.
Prepares six office reports.	Assembles data from incoming studies. Tabulates data into standard form. Types office reports.
Handles incoming and outgoing mail.	Opens and distributes mail. Prepares outgoing material for mailing. Places outgoing mail in pickup area.
Maintains filing system.	Separates material for filing. Decides which material should be filed. Cross indexes material for ready reference. Files material in proper location.
Acts as office receptionist.	Greets visitors to the office. Gives information. Hands out literature. Directs visitors to desired offices.

EXHIBIT 3 *(continued)*

Standards for Performance	Evaluation					Dates	Results Supporting Performance
	0	2	3	4	6		
Standards of Performance are precise descriptions of what a job incumbent must do under existing work conditions to perform in a manner satisfactory to the supervisor. *Evaluation Numbers* relate to a rating of 6–Excellent; 4–Very Good; 3–Good; 2–Fair; 0–Poor. Excellent–Standards have been exceeded for the most part. Very Good–Standards have been met with minor exceptions and some have been exceeded. Good–Standards have been met with minor exceptions. Fair–Standards have been barely met. Poor–Standards for the most part have not been met.							*Results Supporting Performance* are defined by pure output measures (time, quality or quantity) or an analysis of events that occur while the job is in progress. (See Exhibit 4.)

COMMENTS

Strength Areas: _____

_____

_____

Areas Needing Improvement: _____

_____

_____

Recommendations: _____

_____

_____

staffing. This is, in effect, a plan of action for each employee worked out between the supervisor and higher management. Appropriate notes are maintained by both parties; the worksheet should remain with the employee's supervisor.

EXHIBIT 4
Proposed Revision of P–9 Form

G.O. Form P-9 (Rev. 12-70)
(Submit one copy of this form to the Division of Personnel)

COMMONWEALTH OF VIRGINIA
SERVICE RATING

AGENCY TITLE			AGENCY	POSITION	TRAN	EFFEC. DATE	SOCIAL SECURITY NO	SERVICE RATING	CLASS CODE

EMPLOYEE NAME	LAST	FIRST	INIT	APPR	ACTIV	S-ACTIV	PER CENT	CLASS TITLE	

CHECK APPLICABLE ADJECTIVE UNDER EACH ELEMENT

TASK ANALYSIS		WORK RELATIONSHIPS			OSI ELEMENT*
QUALITATIVE	QUANTITATIVE	ASSOCIATES	SUPERVISOR	SUBORDINATE	
POOR 0 ☐	POOR 0 ☐	POOR 0 ☐	POOR 0 ☐	POOR 0 ☐	POOR 0 ☐
FAIR 2 ☐	FAIR 2 ☐	FAIR 2 ☐	FAIR 2 ☐	FAIR 2 ☐	FAIR 2 ☐
GOOD 3 ☐	GOOD 3 ☐	GOOD 3 ☐	GOOD 3 ☐	GOOD 3 ☐	GOOD 3 ☐
VERY GOOD 4 ☐	VERY GOOD 4 ☐	VERY GOOD 4 ☐	VERY GOOD 4 ☐	VERY GOOD 4 ☐	VERY GOOD 4 ☐
EXCELLENT 6 ☐	EXCELLENT 6 ☐	EXCELLENT 6 ☐	EXCELLENT 6 ☐	EXCELLENT 6 ☐	EXCELLENT 6 ☐

Was this rating discussed with the employee?   Yes ☐   No ☐

*Identify Other Significant Influencing Element _____

Rated By _____
                        NAME   CLASS TITLE

Approved _____
                        NAME   CLASS TITLE

NOTE
• BEFORE RATING THIS EMPLOYEE BE SURE THAT YOU UNDERSTAND THE ELEMENTS AS EXPLAINED IN THE PRINTED INSTRUCTIONS.
• IF EITHER 'POOR' OR 'EXCELLENT' IS CHECKED IN THREE OR MORE ELEMENTS, ON THE OTHER SIDE OF THIS REPORT DESCRIBE THE BASIS FOR THE EXCEPTIONAL RATING.
Where an explanation is required on the reverse side, carbon paper will be necessary.

Explanation of Elements on Service Rating Form

Task Analysis—Breaking the job down into specific tasks which describe what the employee does.

Qualitative—A measure of how well the employee performs, the adequacy of performance, expressed by degrees of performance towards a known standard. May be measured by thoroughness, accuracy, errors, omission, and other expressions of quality.

Quantitative—Measures what the employee has accomplished and expressed by the amonut of work towards a known standard. May be measured by output data, numbers, volume, percentages, and other expressions of quantity.

Work Relationships—Relationships established with work associates, the supervisor, and subordinates (if a supervisory position), and the impact of the relationship upon the employee's work. Consider the effect on the associates in performing their jobs, and the effect on the supervisor in performing his job, and on the employee himself in performing the job.

OSI (Other Significant Influencing Element)—Aspects of performance considered apart from measuring work against specific standards. These are behavior events significant enough to influence performance or work relationships. Based on observable behavior, the rating which should be explained, pinpoints critical incidents affecting performance, effect on associates, supervision, subordinates, the public, or the employee himself.

The OSI element permits the rater some freedom of evaluation without restriction to a limited number of categories involving tasks or relationships

EXHIBIT 4 *(continued)*

and takes into consideration that there are other factors affecting performance besides the elements named.

Training

There must be an understanding of task analysis, performance standards, rating elements, form usage, and procedure to have a standard approach to PACE with as many communication barriers removed as possible. Training will involve an examination of problems in performance evaluation, practice in writing performance standards, practice in evaluation procedure, preparation of reports, and on-the-job coaching.

Securing acceptance of the program by supervision is an important part of the training process. Responses by commission supervision in 1970 to a survey on employee performance revealed widely differing ideas on an appropriate performance evaluation system, but there has been a continuous interest for an improvement in performance rating and this should assist in gaining acceptance of PACE.

Arrangements will have to be made to train new supervisors as they are appointed or the program will deteriorate.

Aer Lingus—Irish (B)*
Case 4–12 ————————————————————————————

Stephen A. Allen

SELF-MONITORING OF PERFORMANCE IN PASSENGER RESERVATIONS UNITS

In January 1975, executives of Aer Lingus's sales organization met to review and discuss recent experiences with the Call Management Program, an experiment in self-monitoring of performance by personnel in two of the passenger reservations units. Present at the meeting were Mr. Martin Dully, general sales manager; Mr. Michael Delaney, head of field sales; Mr. John Russell, sales offices manager; and Mr. John Ryan, an internal consultant from the staff development department. (See Exhibit 1 for organization of the sales department at Aer Lingus.) The meeting had been requested by Messrs. Russell and Ryan in order to update management on their experiences with using the Call Management Program on an experimental basis and to request management's approval for extending usage of the system to all sections within the passenger reservations unit as well as offering the system to other Aer Lingus regional reservations offices in Ireland and continental Europe.

———————

EXHIBIT 1
Partial Management Organization—General Sales Department

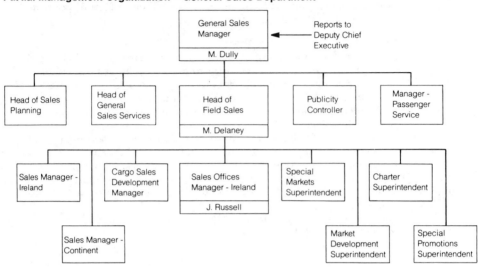

BACKGROUND INFORMATION

Mr. John Russell, who had initiated the Call Management Program, was responsible for all Aer Lingus reservations and ticket offices in Ireland and continental Europe.[1] Reporting to him were a central passenger reservations unit, the Dublin Airport ticket operations, two ticket offices in Dublin, and several smaller regional offices located in Ireland and on the continent (see Exhibit 2).

The passenger reservations unit, located at Aer Lingus headquarters adjacent to Dublin Airport, employed between 70 and 80 telephone reservations clerks who were responsible for completing passenger reservations initiated via the company's main Dublin number. The unit was divided into three sections:

1. A *Short-Haul Section* handling all services within Ireland and cross-channel. This section handled a large volume of calls but was not faced with complicated computations for the reservations.
2. A *Long-Haul Section* handling reservations for trans-Atlantic flights, continental Europe, and connections through Europe to other areas not served by Aer Lingus. This section often encountered rather complex situations in quoting fares and arranging reservations.
3. An *Agency Section* handling all bookings initiated by travel agents. This section dealt with both long- and short-haul reservations.

---

[1] Aer Lingus activities in North America and Great Britain were carried out by separate organizational units which had their own sales groups and reservations and ticket offices.

EXHIBIT 2
Sales Offices Organization

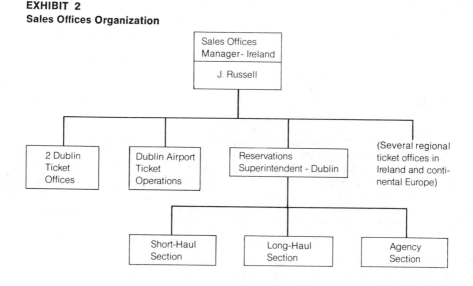

Each clerk worked at a desk which was equipped with a terminal[2] linked to the company's ASTRAL computerized reservations system, a telephone, and various fare and route manuals. The basic task involved answering queries concerning particular travel arrangements from prospective passengers; offering the appropriate services; quoting fares; and checking and making reservations via the computer.

A majority of the reservations clerks were young women. The typical clerk would have graduated from high school at age 18, and the telephone reservations position would have been her first job. New recruits started in the short-haul section and, after one or two years, could move to the long-haul or agency sections and from there to one of the ticket offices. By 1974, the difficult economic climate and an increasing tendency for the women to continue working after marriage, had reduced annual turnover in the passenger reservations unit substantially below the 20 to 25 percent experienced during most of the 1960s.

The purposes of the Call Management Program were to encourage the reservations clerks to become involved in evaluating their own performance, to set goals for themselves, and to establish a built-in system of feedback. Mr. Russell's interest in this program had grown out of several discussions he had had in early 1972 with John Ryan, a member of the staff development department.[3] As part of his work in the training area,

---

[2] The terminal consisted of a keyboard and a CRT (cathode ray tube) display.

[3] The staff development department at Aer Lingus was a service department which conducted training programs and provided consulting in the organization development area. It was a free resource for "internal clients" and became involved in projects only at a client's request. John Ryan had joined staff development in 1965. Prior to that he had occupied management positions at Aer Lingus in research and planning and in commercial negotiations.

EXHIBIT 3
Summary of 1971 Job Enrichment Experiment in Long-Haul Reservations Section

The Major Changes:

1. Staff would themselves deal with requests for special handling from passengers booked in by them. Requests for special handling, such as for stretcher treatment or kosher food, were formerly passed to a supervisor for action.
2. The group would in future arrange their own roster, provided that manning requirements were met.
3. Staff would be encouraged to compute and quote complex fares to passengers. Previously, these had been automatically passed to a special section.
4. Staff would play a more active market research and selling role. For example, they would pass on information on potential cargo sales arising from passenger bookings; also, they were given authority to initiate canvassing calls to major business accounts.
5. On a group basis they would monitor the performance of the section against the agreed telephone answering standards.
6. Staff would be consulted on the periodic modifications to the computerised reservations system.
7. Staff would participate in the training of juniors and new entrants.
8. Each staff member would be responsible for maintaining tariff manuals and a personal file of travel information.

Results Four Months After Implementation

1. There was an increase of almost 50 percent in the number of bookings which were transferred to the airline in question here from airlines with which the bookings had originally been made. These transfers occurred as a result of passengers' contacts with the telephone reservations staff.
2. The staff whose jobs were enriched were considered by their managers and supervisors to be showing far more initiative, generally, in seeking out new business through telephone contacts with, for instance, business houses and various types of associations.
3. Morale was generally considered to be very high by the supervisors in the area. To quote one supervisor: "People take a more active rather than a passive approach to their work. Such procedures as are required to be followed are followed voluntarily."

Source: L. Gorman and E. Molloy, *People, Jobs, and Organizations* (Irish Productivity Center, 1972), pp. 130–31.

Mr. Ryan had been exposed to a technique developed by Mr. Neil Rackham, a British behavioral scientist, for categorizing and recording interaction patterns in meetings. This technique involved recording the frequency of occurrence of various types of behavior (e.g., giving information, supporting, interrupting) by trained observers and then providing feedback through quantified profiles of the group and its individual members. It was used to improve group membership skills through an analysis —goal-setting—feedback cycle which included (1) discussion of the quantified profiles; (2) having each individual set improvement goals by increasing (or decreasing) his use of one of the measured behaviors; (3) giving each individual an opportunity to practice his "improvement plan"; and (4) repeating the entire cycle along with development of additional improvement goals. Although the behavioral scientists had initially used this approach as a team-building technique for management groups, their clients in an airline had become interested in its possible application for improvement of telephone contacts with customers. The behavioral scientists had gone on to develop a simplified version of the original technique as an on-the-job training and self-development package for telephone reservations clerks in several airlines. John Ryan had described this approach to Mr. Russell and questioned whether he might be interested in pursuing something similar for his personnel.

Mr. Russell had found the concept intriguing for several reasons. Aer Lingus was facing increasing competition from other airlines, and Mr. Russell believed that the key differentiating factor among airlines was not fares, equipment, or speed, but the quality of service the customer received —including high quality service in arranging reservations. He reasoned that any technique that offered a possibility for monitoring and improving customer service was worth considering. Also, although morale was good in his units, he believed a secondary benefit of such an approach might be additional improvements in motivation and job satisfaction. An additional reason for Mr. Russell's interest was that in 1971 he had obtained very good results from a job-enrichment experiment in the long-haul section (see Exhibit 3 for a brief summary of the experiment and its results).

DEVELOPMENT OF THE CALL MANAGEMENT PROGRAM

The first step in developing the program was to decide on a set of behavioral categories which would provide appropriate measures of the telephone conversations of the reservations clerks. Messrs. Russell and Ryan met with Mr. Rackham to learn the details of the approach he was using with other airlines. With his help, they analyzed a small sample of tape-recorded telephone contacts of Aer Lingus clerks. They then discussed the results of their sample analysis with the supervisors in the passenger reservations unit and eventually agreed upon a modified set of measurement categories (shown in Exhibit 4).

The second stage in developing the program was to generate a larger sample of recorded telephone contacts and to train the supervisors in accurate analysis of these data. It was decided to concentrate on the 30 clerks who worked in the long-haul and agency sections. The clerks were informed that participation in this experimental program was voluntary and that they would later receive feedback on the results. This initial "selling" of the program was conducted by Mr. Rackham. All of the clerks volunteered to participate.

During the next few weeks a sample of 20 calls per clerk was tape recorded (for a total of 600 observations). These calls ranged in duration from less than one minute to up to 40 minutes, depending on the customer requirements involved. The recording device was located in another area so that the clerks did not know precisely when they were being recorded. They were, however, given the option of requesting to be recorded (or not

EXHIBIT 4
Behavior Categories in Call Management Program

1. *Giving Schedule/Tariff Information:*
   Giving information on flights, fares, times, or any matter contained in the published flight schedules.

2. *Giving Other Information:*
   Giving any information which is not contained in the flight schedules, e.g., information about hotel reservations, car hire, taxi hire, public transport, weather.

3. *Seeking Additional Information:*
   Any other information which assists the agent in making a booking, i.e., "What is passenger's name? When and where passenger can collect tickets, etc."

4. *Establishing and Clarifying Needs:*
   Eliciting information about the passenger's travelling needs, i.e., "When does he want to go," "Where does he want to go," time of day/week/year. Short stay/long stay. Fare/Status—e.g., child, family, student. In general, any information which enables the agent to select the most appropriate flight schedule and fare for each passenger.

5. *Building on Needs:*
   We define a building on needs behavior as one which extends or develops an expressed need of the passenger's in a way which makes Aer Lingus better able to fill that need. This behavior is particularly important where the existing service offered by Aer Lingus does not correspond directly with the passenger's expressed need. The following fragment of conversation illustrates this and shows how building on needs acts as a link between establishing and clarifying needs behaviors and proposing a sale.

   Passenger: I bought a ticket in Amsterdam from BEA/BA and I am booked to travel back through London arriving in Schiphol at 12:30. This is too late for a meeting I have in Leyden.

   Agent: What time do you want to be in Schiphol, Mr. Smit?   *(Establishing and Clarifying Needs)*

   Passenger: I want to be there by 11:30 at the latest.

   Agent: Did you know that on that day we have a direct flight to Amsterdam which arrives there at 10:50?   *(Building on Needs)*

   Passenger: No, I didn't. It sounds perfect for me.

   Agent: Well, then, shall I book you on that flight, Mr. Smit?   *(Proposing a Sale)*

   Passenger: Please do.

6. *Offering Alternatives:*
   Proposing two or more alternatives for consideration, i.e., alternative flights or alternative routes.

7. *Proposing A Sale:*
   We include in this category any behavior by an agent which made/makes a bid to book passenger on an Aer Lingus (or other) flight, whether or not the booking was tentative.

8. *Supporting:*
   Any behaviors which show agreement, support, or encouragement for anything which passenger has said.

EXHIBIT 4 *(continued)*

9. *Checking Understanding:*
   Checking that passenger is sure of information given to him, i.e., he understands which aeroplane he is going on, its route, and times of departure, etc. Also, checking that the agent has the message correctly, e.g., repeating a name or a timing after it has been given by the caller or summarising the transaction.

10. *Indicating Delay:*
    Explaining to passenger that there will be a delay in call, and indicating its likely duration and reason for it.

11. *Using Caller's Name:*
    Using the caller's name during the conversation where appropriate.

12. *Interrupting:*
    When the agent speaks before the passenger has finished speaking.

13. *Expressing Disagreement/Irritation:*
    When the agent disagrees with or is angry with the passenger.

14. *Other Behavior:*
    Any behavior by the agent which the analyst is unable to classify under any of the preceding categories.

recorded) at specific times. No one exercised this option. At this point in the experiment the clerks did not know the specific measurement categories.

Analysis of each recorded conversation was carried out separately by the supervisors and by the staff development department. Each analyst completed a worksheet for each call (see Exhibit 5) in which he/she simply checked the number of times the clerk engaged in each behavioral category during the conversations. Whenever six calls had been coded for a clerk the results were rank-ordered by category, and a correlation of the rankings by the two independent analysts was computed in order to check the reliability of the measures. These correlations for the 600 call sample had averaged 0.98. The worksheets also provided the raw data for computing individual and section profiles showing the relative frequency with which each behavior category was used (Exhibit 6 shows the format for an individual profile).

When the profiles were completed, the clerks were brought together in groups of six or seven to discuss the results and begin the first round of goal setting. The first part of these meetings was devoted to explaining the behavioral categories and analyzing the group profile of another airline. A typical set of reactions by the clerks to this group profile was as follows:

Clerk A: Proposing a sale accounts for only 0.3 percent of the total. That looks awfully small. What does that mean?

Clerk B: There are some calls where proposing a sale isn't appropriate. The customer may simply be saying book me on flight "X."

Clerk C. That's true for some calls, but with 0.3 percent for the whole section, I suspect they're missing some opportunities to propose a sale.

EXHIBIT 5
Worksheet for Coding Recorded Calls

Agent's Name _____   Supervisor's Name _____

Behavior Category	1	2	3	4	5	6	Total	Rank Order
Giving Schedule/Tariff Information								
Giving Other Information								
Seeking Additional Information								
Establishing & Clarifying Needs								
Building on Needs								
Offering Choice of Alternatives								
Proposing a Sale								
Supporting								
Checking Understanding								
Indicating Delay								
Using Caller's Name								
Interrupting								
Expressing Disagreement/Irritation								
Other Behavior								
Total								

They also noted that "good profiles" would differ between public and agency calls because the agents usually knew precisely what they wanted and were on first-name terms with most of the reservations clerks.

After developing some rough criteria for an effective profile, the clerks were shown the group profile for their own section and asked to critique it. They then met individually with their supervisors and a member of the staff development department to discuss their own profile and to set improvement goals. In this meeting the supervisor highlighted those areas where she thought the clerk was doing very well. The clerk was then asked to consider the rest of the profile and identify any categories where she would like to change (e.g., to do more or less of category "Y"). She was told not to try to change the whole profile but to concentrate on one or two categories. Finally, the clerk was told that when she felt she had achieved her improvement goals, she should request her supervisor to monitor a

EXHIBIT 6
Individual Feedback Sheet

Agent's Name _____   Total No. of Calls Analyzed _____

Behavior Category	Total Behaviors No. %		Agency No. %		Long-Haul No. %		Short-Haul No. %	
Giving Schedule/Tariff Information								
Giving Other Information								
Seeking Additional Information								
Establishing & Clarifying Needs								
Building on Needs								
Offering Alternatives								
Proposing a Sale								
Supporting								
Checking Understanding								
Indicating Delay								
Using Caller's Name								
Interrupting								
Expressing Disagreement/Irritation								
Other Behavior								
Total								

small sample of calls.[4] The supervisor would monitor the calls live, give the clerk direct feedback, and retain the data for eventual recomputation of the section profile.

INITIAL RESULTS OF THE PROGRAM

In May 1972, three months after introduction of the program, a new group profile was computed (see Exhibit 7). Mr. Ryan and the section supervisors believed that it represented a substantial improvement in call behavior. Some of their reasons were as follows:

---

[4] The supervisor was able to monitor calls live by simply plugging into a telephone jack at the clerk's desk. It was anticipated that tape recording would be used only for occasional reliability checks as the program matured.

EXHIBIT 7
Group Profiles for Long-Haul Section, 1972

Category	Aer Lingus Office	
	Initial	*After 3 Months*
Giving Schedule/Tariff Information	21.9	14.7
Giving Other Information	9.7	6.0
Seeking Additional Information	11.1	7.1
Establishing & Clarifying Needs	7.6	9.4
Building on Needs	0.3	0.1
Offering Alternatives	0.3	0.1
Proposing a Sale	0.5	1.6
Supporting	18.9	25.7
Checking Understanding	7.1	11.0
Indicating Delay	7.3	8.7
Using Caller's Name	2.4	4.5
Interrupting	0.6	–
Expressing Disagreement/Irritation	–	–
Other Behavior	12.3	11.1
Total	100.0	100.0

Reduction in *giving schedule/fare information*—Previously, some clerks had been overloading the customer with too much technical information rather than helping him specify his needs. They were now avoiding this by spending more time on *establishing and clarifying needs* and *supporting.*

Increases in *proposing a sale, checking understanding,* and *using caller's name.*

The reservations clerks reacted quite favorably to the program, indicating that it

1.   Helped them achieve better control over the call.
2.   Made them more aware of their own behavior. As one clerk put it, "When asked previously whether I used the customer's name I would have said—and believed—'Of course, we were trained to do that'. I was really surprised when I saw objective evidence on how little I was actually doing it."
3.   Provided richer and more objective feedback.
4.   Allowed them to develop and work on goals which they personally believed were meaningful rather than simply having uniform, imposed standards.

By June 1972, the staff development department had handed over full responsibility for the program to the supervisors and clerks. The timing of additional feedback and review sessions was left to their discretion, and in most instances the reservations clerks continued to request new performance samples when they felt they would be useful. The basic methodology of the Call Management Program was also incorporated into the job training practices for new reservations clerks.[5]

---

[5] Previously, training had consisted of a short technical course on use of the computer terminal and fare structures plus lectures and role playing exercises on how to handle customer contacts. Mr. Ryan felt that use of the Call Management method

THE BROADER ISSUE OF QUALITY

Mr. Russell had been satisfied with the initial results of the experiment and had become interested in its wider implications for the whole idea of "quality control" of customer contacts. The basic measure of quality prior to the Call Management Program had been the number of incoming calls not answered within 20 seconds. The telephone system in the passenger reservations unit was linked to a central control panel at the supervisor's desk which flashed a light when an incoming call was not switched to a clerk and answered within 20 seconds. The supervisor then picked up the call, apologized to the customer, and asked whether he wished to wait for another connection or call back. Each delay of this type was automatically recorded on a meter. Management had set a service standard of 80 to 90 percent undelayed answers (depending on the staffing level). The supervisors had also monitored calls to check their quality, but this had been done sporadically and was totally subjective. The clerks had often complained that they received conflicting signals from different supervisors.

SUBSEQUENT DEVELOPMENTS

Over the next year the staff development department had secured local management permission to set up similar experiments in the New York and London reservations offices. In New York the overall effect proved to be much less marked than that in Dublin, and by early 1975 the experiment was allowed to lapse. In London the program received few initial volunteers and did not move beyond the first feedback stage. Mr. Ryan felt that the disappointing results in these two offices could be explained by two factors. First, although local management had shown initial support for the program, it later appeared that the participative requirements of the experiment had not fit with the leadership styles of many of the first-line supervisors in these offices. The second factor was that at the time of introduction both offices were beginning to feel the pressures of having to maintain traditional workloads with fewer staff because of declining Aer Lingus revenues.

By 1974, the Dublin office was encountering similar pressures in the area of workload versus staffing. Although its level of bookings had been falling, it still encountered the previous levels of telephone activity. With staff reductions occurring through attrition, supervisors were forced increasingly to fill in for clerks, and by June 1974 the Call Management Program had fallen into disrepair.

PROPOSAL TO EXTEND THE PROGRAM

In summarizing their experiences with the Call Management Program, Messrs. Ryan and Russell indicated that they had learned at least three things with regard to implementing this technique:

---

offered a much more potent, on-the-job approach for developing customer contact skills of new clerks.

1. That it was essential to develop positive commitment from first-line supervisors at the earliest possible date. Without such commitment the program could not be sustained and probably should not even be introduced.
2. That a realistic schedule had to be firmly agreed to for all steps in introducing the program and for periodic follow-ups after the first cycle.
3. That management would have to be prepared to place as much emphasis on the Call Management measures as it placed on the traditional call delay measures.

Based on these experiences, Messrs. Ryan and Russell stated that they felt the Call Management Program should be reinstituted on a voluntary and permanent basis at Aer Lingus. They noted that supervisory and management support still existed at the Dublin passenger reservations unit and that the program could be implemented in all sections with minimum costs in terms of supervisors' time. Mr. Ryan had also contacted several of the smaller regional offices and had secured support for possible introduction of the technique in Manchester, Glasgow, and Cork. Mr. Ryan noted: "In contrast to their larger New York and London counterparts, these are small, compact (maximum of 12 people) offices with a family atmosphere. I can see the system working informally but well in these settings."

Case 4–13

Roger Smothers' Bubble Bottle

Yohannan T. Abraham and Earl Burk

A Midwest company employing some 15,000 workers is in the business of manufacturing both consumer and industrial products. The company's production workers in its various plants are organized by one of the largest AFL–CIO affiliates.

Its research and development unit, organizationally arranged within the die-cut products section, is headed by Dan Sample, who six months ago assumed that position when his predecessor, Jim Smart, was promoted to corporate vice president. The R&D unit has some 90 employees who are assigned to one of the 12 responsibility centers. Each group leader reports to director Dan Sample.

For the past 2 years or so Roger Smothers, who had a total of 15 years with the company, headed the specification group, one of the 12 responsibility centers in the R&D unit. Smothers knew his job well; he also was instrumental in designing and implementing a computerized system of issuing product specifications that has resulted in reducing the time needed for specification issuance from three weeks to 48 hours, with 24-hour capability. Roger, however, had a personal problem which interfered with his work more than once. During his long tenure with the firm, Roger suffered from alcoholism for at least half the time. This has resulted in chronic and extended absenteeism and frequent slips in his performance. His supervisor, Jim Smart, counseled him several times and warned him about the consequence of such behavior. In fact, once Jim gave Roger an ultimatum, but did not follow through when Roger later committed the infraction.

Now that Jim's position as supervisor has been assumed by Dan Sample, the problem of Roger Smothers fell upon Dan. Roger was no different, having been absent twice because of the drinking problem since Dan assumed his new position. Dan warned Roger that he would lose his job if he were to miss work again due to his personal problem. Three weeks passed and Roger was gone again—this time for several days. Upon his return, even though Roger attempted to soothe the distraught Dan by letting him give him a "piece of his mind," Dan followed through with his warning and dismissed Roger effective the same day. Later, Sober Smiles, a specification group member, was placed in the position vacated by Roger.

Nothing eventful happened for two weeks when, much to Dan's surprise, Roger was rehired as a member of the specification group. Upon inquiry, Dan was told that insufficient evidence of Roger's drinking problem had been documented in his personnel file.

Case 4–14 ————————————————————————————————————

Uris Hall Dormitory Kitchen*

Charles I. Cash

PART 1

The history of the dormitory began in 1947. The building was built to house 30 men, provide food service to these men, and contain the needed room for office space. At that time the cafeteria staff included 11 women and 1 male student worker. The organization of work was as follows: one lady worked during the morning and early afternoons as cashier; 5 of the remaining 10 worked from 5.00 A.M. until 1:00 P.M.; and the other 5 worked from 1:00 P.M. until 8:00 P.M.

The male student worked in the evenings as a cashier and dishwasher. Two of the ladies, Mrs. A and Mrs. B, served as the head cooks. One worked in the morning, the other worked in the evening. Their duties were limited to preparing food according to the menus, and assigning work. Each of the ladies under the head cook had a specialty, such as baking, salad making, or dishwashing, and each ordered her own supplies in light of the scheduled menus.

---

* Adapted from a course assignment prepared by Charles I. Cash for Professor J. G. Hunt, Southern Illinois University–Carbondale.

Because of the relatively small number of people served, the women were not pressured to prepare large quantities of food. The student cashier was looked upon as an outsider, but generally he was accepted, especially if some strenuous task was necessary. The cooks prepared 20 meals a week (Sunday night being the exception).

The menu was known because it repeated itself weekly, with only occasional variations. With but two exceptions, the workers had had ten or more years of duty in the dormitory when the case observer first came upon the scene. He was impressed with the quality of the food which, although repetitious, was very good, as everyone agreed.

The organization of work was as follows. The head cooks supervised the other cooks, the dishwasher, and the cashier. The setup was identical with each of the two crews. The student worker was treated well by the ladies because he was helpful when they needed him; he also happened to be the dormitory director's son. The ladies were all in their middle or late sixties, except the cashier who was about 50 years old. They were all either married or widowed, and all had one or more children who were no longer living at home.

The women were all skilled in their work, as evidenced by the good food. All but one of them, the eldest who did the baking, had completed grade school, although only five had finished high school, and none had attended college. They were all of Protestant background, and all lived in the city or just outside it. The ladies got along together extremely well and were always willing to help each other. They took turns serving at meal time so everyone had a chance to eat, and they frequently rode to and from work together. When any of them became sick, the others would always give everyone a day-by-day account of the stricken individual's condition.

Several of the women attended the same church in town. They all conversed freely and at length at meal time or any other time, and in the case observer's two years at that dorm, he never knew of any hard feelings among them.

The head cook pretty much let the other cooks carry out their assignments as they wished. Troubles encountered in the job were typically blamed on the dorm director. Working conditions were adequate although not modern. Much of the equipment installed in 1947 was still being used at the time of the case. Many time-saving devices, such as electric can openers and electric dishwashers, were not available. The cafeteria was not air conditioned although two large fans were utilized in the summer, and the cafeteria was always warm in winter.

In spite of these less than ideal conditions, the ladies rarely complained. They seemed to be accustomed to the old equipment and were comfortable using it. As for the activities of the people, all of the cooks did part of the buying, and all took turns serving.

The other activities will be described for each group. At 5:00 A.M. when the morning crew arrived, all turned their attention to getting breakfast ready by 7:00 o'clock. The ladies were assigned typical breakfast preparation duties. After breakfast, and after eating and helping the dishwasher get started, each lady began preparing her own part of the noon meal. One lady had sole responsibility for making the various salads, two others prepared the vegetables, one cooked the meat, and the fifth made the desserts. This routine was strictly followed unless someone was ill. In this case, one of the ladies in the evening group worked all day, or all of the ladies of the morning crew shared their stricken comrade's duties.

The activities of the evening crew were similar. They did specialized jobs, much like the morning crew, in preparing the evening meal. However, after the meal was over at 7:00 P.M., they all helped clean the kitchen for the next day. In the cleaning process the ladies assumed the job of cleaning the area in which they worked in preparing their specialty. There were some strong sentiments among the ladies about their work and their relationship to each other. These women had worked together for a long time, and had built strong and lasting friendships. Although each jealously protected her individual independence in her specialty, there were strong feelings that each owed it to the others to make sure her part was done well and on time. During the few times when someone did not have her part of the meal ready when it was time to begin serving, the sanctions of the other ladies were overt, verbal, and sharp.

Production was satisfactory in every way. There were very few people who did not like the food. The ladies appeared to be satisfied. They did not seek other employment, which was plentiful.

PART 2

The dorm was recently purchased by State University and then rebuilt and considerably enlarged. Some two years later, it emerged from the expansion with facilities for 278 men and women, a recreation hall, a large dining hall, a library, and a chapel.

All of the old crew was invited to work in the new kitchen, and they all accepted the invitation. To accommodate the increased volume, additional people were required, as were clearer lines of organization. Initially, all of the old crew were put together in one group along with one new person. This group worked in the morning. In addition, ten more women were hired to work the evening shift. Six male students were hired to operate the new automatic dishwasher and to take out garbage during the rush periods. A new organizational structure was developed for the growing organization.

A cafeteria supervisor was hired to head the entire cafeteria operation. This lady had a number of years of experience in running large food service facilities. She was given the responsibility for planning all menus, buying the food, assigning jobs, and scheduling workers. The only authority she was not given was the right to hire and fire workers and to make her own budget. These two functions were assumed by the dormitory director. The work remained divided on a functional basis. The only change was that more ladies were assigned to each specialty. The work was divided among the following categories: meats, vegetables, salads, desserts, and dishwashing. The morning crew moved its working schedule back an hour. They started at 4:00 A.M., and worked until 1:00 P.M. The evening crew worked from 1:00 P.M. until 9:00 P.M. A head cook was chosen in each group. She was responsible for seeing that things were done when the supervisor was not present.

The kitchen duties now called for the combined efforts of more than one woman. The interactions were very limited because the ladies rarely saw each other, and the two groups prepared their own meals. Thus, the evening crew started making the evening meal from scratch rather than serving what was prepared in the morning. The only exception was that the desserts were all made in the morning.

Brand-new equipment was placed in the cafeteria. An emphasis was placed on obtaining equipment capable of preparing large quantities of food in the most efficient manner. The building was air conditioned, well lighted, and carpeted.

The workers were no longer allowed to order their own supplies. The new supervisor assumed this function entirely. It was necessary to order different kinds and different quantities of food now that 300 were being fed instead of 30. The old crew was accustomed to cooking rather small roasts, for instance, but in the new building they were asked to cook very large roasts. Soon a lot of trouble was evident concerning the kinds of food being ordered. The old crew felt that the supervisor was not doing a creditable job. They made their sentiments well known in verbal discussions with the supervisor and in written statements to the director. They claimed the food was impossible to cook, of inferior quality, and a waste of money.

Their second gripe concerned the hiring of a lady to work in the morning who was not of the old group. The ladies objected to her presence for two reasons. First, she was loud. She was not belligerent or profane, but she had a husky, bellowing voice. She was also given to lengthy seizures of singing at the top of her booming voice. None of the other women possessed these characteristics and objected rather strongly to the noise.

This was not their most serious objection, however. This lady, whom we shall call Mrs. Loud, also frequently extolled her own great skill in large kitchens though she had had only one year of experience. Not only did Mrs. Loud boast of her own abilities, she also tried to instruct the other ladies in the proper method of cooking. Mrs. Loud felt that her supposed expertise qualified her to boss the other ladies. A long succession of incidents followed in which Mrs. Loud became an increasingly bad influence on the morning crew. Finally, two of the ladies went to the supervisor and explained that they could no longer tolerate Mrs. Loud and would quit if she was not replaced.

There also was a problem concerning the dishwasher. One lady was assigned the entire job of washing dishes at the old dormitory and the old crew accepted this as proper procedure. However, the volume of business and the mechanics of the automatic dishwasher at the new cafeteria necessitated that the ladies sometimes help the lady assigned to the dishwasher. This was especially true when the student helpers were not available.

Many of the women did not like or accept this situation and were rather upset about it.

They first objected because they felt that the woman assigned to the job was not doing her job properly. It soon became evident that this was not the case. Rather, at times the volume of dishes simply was too much for one woman to handle. The student workers alleviated the problem to a great extent, but there were still times when the cooks were required to help. Scraping and washing dishes is not the most desirable or satisfying job in a kitchen, or anywhere else for that matter. Each lady was assigned a specialty and took pride in her work, so broadening these duties to include this kind of activity did not go over well. Long and sad grumbling was often voiced by the cooks who had to wash dishes.

The evening crew was also plagued by some problems. First, there was the problem of adjustment for the new employees. As previously stated, all the old employees were put on the morning shift, so all the evening crew was new. Three of the ladies had no previous experience working in a large cafeteria, so they had much to learn. The part of the job involving the cleaning of the cafeteria each night also became a problem. The ladies felt that they were being imposed upon because the morning crew had no such duties. Several of the women had expressed displeasure at the cleaning chore and had said that they would quit "if the opportunity arose for another job."

A more serious problem involved the head cook of the evening crew, who was black. Mrs. Jones was an extremely hard worker and a very good cook. She also possessed a pleasing personality. She was hesitant to take the job as head cook because she felt the other ladies, who were all white, would object to the assignment. The dorm director indicated to the case observer that he was afraid that trouble would result from the arrangement, but that Mrs. Jones was best qualified for the job, and he needed her in the position. Mrs. Jones finally took the job after much persuasion.

The reaction of the other ladies was quick and quite strong. The resentment grew almost visibly while Mrs. Jones tried to ignore it. The displeasure displayed itself in such things as tardiness, slovenly work, and frequent bad meals. The situation worsened with time. Finally, the circumstances became so desperate that the director felt some action had to be taken. The last straw came when Mrs. Smith, an avid segregationist, was asked to clean up a mess made by Mrs. Jones, and promptly left the job.

The third group of people working in the new dormitory was the student workers. At the old dormitory, only one student was working, but the new dormitory required the part-time help of six students. These workers were all young men who lived in the dorm. They worked mainly at the noon and evening meals when as many as 325 people were served. Their work was done almost entirely on the automatic dishwasher, which was used to capacity during these peak hours. They also did some cleaning chores and stocking, but were generally limited to washing dishes.

Although these students were generally aware of the problems in the cafeteria, they did not take sides or engage in any way in the squabbling. Their consensus seemed to be to come in, do the work, and get out as fast as possible. The cooks and other staff considered these students as welcome help. As one put it, "I don't know what we'd do without them."

The output of the cafeteria during this period was not desirable. The production of food was adequate, although it was frequently not on schedule or in proper quantities. Morale was not high, and many of the women, both old and new employees, expressed dissatisfaction in their jobs. This dissatisfaction was mainly centered on the assignment of duties, the personalities of fellow workers, and the lack of consideration that the workers felt they were receiving from the management. As a consequence, the director felt that some changes were necessary, and he made plans for some reorganization to take place as soon as possible.

PART 3

The following changes were made. First, Mrs. Loud was transferred to the evening shift to replace Mrs. Smith. Second, another lady was hired to help run the dishwasher. Third, a greater effort was made to see that student workers were available at the busiest times during the day. The evening crew's problems were largely righted as time passed. The ladies came to accept Mrs. Jones when they realized how fair she was and how she tried to get the work done well.

As for the cleanup chores, the director finally called a meeting with the ladies and explained to them that he realized the work was not enjoyable, but that it had to be done, and the morning crew could not do it because it would be impossible to expect them to come any earlier than 4:00 A.M. The ladies were strongly opposed to continuing the cleaning process but became less ardent in their views when the director explained the situation. They finally agreed to continue cleaning up at night in return for not having to work on any Sundays. The morning crew had been handling the Sunday duties but had requested that some of the night crew occasionally substitute so that the entire morning crew would not have to work every Sunday. The new arrangement was acceptable to the morning crew after a 15-cent per hour raise was offered for Sunday work.

With the passage of time, the evening crew solidified into a more coordinated force and ironed out many of its own troubles by simply getting better acquainted. Mrs. Loud integrated well into the evening crew. She was somewhat quieter. Six months after the reorganization, the output of the cafeteria had made several turns for the better. Quality and promptness of production was more satisfying than it had been the previous fall. Satisfaction seemed to increase almost daily. No one left the job after the reorganization.

The ladies in the evening crew formed friendships, and the morning crew became noticeably more content following the exit of Mrs. Loud.

Case 4–15 ——————————————————————————————————

Deep River Insurance Company

Paul J. Champagne

In recent years job enrichment has been heralded as a cure for many of the problems of the workplace. The question, however, is just how much can such a program be expected to achieve. The following case presents a typical job enrichment program which, in the eyes of management, was a failure.

Jim Anderson, the director of the Deep River office of a large insurance company, had for some time been concerned with problems of absenteeism, turnover, and generally poor morale. Job enrichment was suggested as a possible solution and he decided to pursue this course of action.

THE PROGRAM

Originally, Anderson proposed to conduct a program in the home office data input departments and possibly Deep River keypunch, but as of June 1972, he was actively promoting the possibilities of a much broader project encompassing all Deep River operations. While top management gave this proposal serious consideration, by the end of 1972 it was decided that a more limited program should be conducted in the Deep River office. To that end, an attitude survey was administered in the spring of 1973 to all Deep River clerical employees. The survey was designed to measure employees' attitudes toward ten major aspects of their jobs: (1) advancement; (2) responsibility; (3) workload; (4) job content; (5) salary; (6) supervision; (7) communication; (8) working conditions; (9) training; and (10) management. The results identified three problem areas: job content, responsibility, and communication. It was decided that a job enrichment program would effectively address itself to these issues.

The coding services department was chosen to participate in the program for several reasons. Attitude survey scores from this department were decidedly negative on all three problem areas. Moreover, in coding services no other major problems were identified through the survey, and there were enough task functions to make enrichment possible. After discussions with local area administrators and the superintendent of the department, a final "go" decision was made.

Early in May 1973, a four-day off-site workshop was conducted to provide a better understanding of the principles of job enrichment. Participants included all first-line supervisors and their assistants, Deep River management, organizational development personnel, and an outside, hired consultant. Upon the recommendation of the consultant, worker participation was rejected on the basis that (1) it was management's prerogative to restructure jobs; (2) it would be awkward for supervisors and subordinates to jointly plan changes in subordinates' jobs; and (3) the expectations of the subordinates might be unrealistic and the actual changes, therefore, disappointing. Workshop members began to apply the principles of Herzberg's motivation-hygiene theory, working out ways of translating responsibility, achievement, recognition, and growth into work-related items. During "greenlighting" or brainstorming sessions, supervisors contributed ideas for improvement of subordinates' jobs without criticism or comment. During "redlighting" sessions, priority items based on what had to be done first were listed, including possible barriers within management's control and possible steps to overcome them. Subgroups composed of pairs of supervisors and assistant supervisors then selected those items they wished to implement in their units.

At the conclusion of the redlighting and implementation sessions, five items were recommended: (1) coders would take turns handing out work; (2) individual coders would begin requisitioning materials directly from filing units; (3) coders were to become experts in their own areas of responsibility; (4) branch offices would be assigned to coders; and (5) coders would begin reviewing their own error sheets returned by the branch offices. Following the workshop, the supervisory teams met with internal and external consultants every two weeks through the early summer of 1973 to plan the implementation.

Early on, the problem of possible loss of earnings under the company's existing wage incentive plan was discussed by management. Under wage incentive, every job was studied, using time and motion techniques, to determine efficient work cycle times. When an employee produced at a rate equal to 70 percent of maximum possible efficiency a bonus was added to the employee's base salary. For some this amounted to $40 or more per week.

The basic problem was that enrichment training time would not count toward the weekly bonus. Therefore, employees participating in a job enrichment program involving extensive retraining would be penalized. A number of possible solutions were suggested, including dropping the wage incentive and increasing base salary. It was finally decided to deal with the problem by (1) lengthening the overall training time to minimize time off measurement, and (2) giving participating employees a bonus equal to the amount lost under the wage incentive during training. Each trainee was compensated for the time off measurement with a single payment of $20 to $40. While this amount was small it was sufficient to induce 55 percent of the coding services employees to participate in the program. Until this solution was proposed, only 28 percent of the eligible employees had volunteered for the program.

Once retraining was completed, jobs were retimed so that each participating employee's weekly wage incentive bonus would remain at about the same level as it had been prior to retraining. No attempt was made to reclassify the "larger" jobs (i.e., increase the weekly base pay) since management did not perceive the issue of money as a possible source of trouble.

Most job enrichment programs involve some anticipated changes in the job time cycle; not so here. Under enrichment, coders were expected to handle an entire unit of work, including correction of errors, but no change was made in the wage incentive time standards. For example, if an auto-liability coder performed all the 44 separate tasks required on one unit of work, the time standard for 100 percent efficiency was 33.42 minutes. During the enrichment program this did not change; 100 percent efficiency was still 33.42 minutes. The only difference was that participating coders were required to know and (if necessary) perform each and every task in a unit of work while nonparticipating coders were not. Participating coders were also accountable for errors made by the branch office or keypunch. If an error was detected in incoming work, the coders would contact the branch office by telephone, teletype, or memo. When an error was detected by the company computer, the coder was expected to pull the file, reconcile the error, and see that it was processed correctly by the keypunch operators. All of this took time and required that the coders work harder and faster than before in order to stay within the wage incentive time standards. Management did not seem to realize the negative effect of this on coders' attitudes toward enriched work.

On October 1, 1973, the program was officially launched using the training schedule devised during the workshop. Membership was strictly voluntary but everyone was encouraged to participate. The program was presented by management as a method for increasing employee interest and job satisfaction. All those who participated in the program were female high school graduates (average age, 22).

Coding services were composed of three basic units, special multi-peril (SMP), Loss, and auto and liability coding (ALC), with each responsible for coding premium or loss evidence on all types of casualty insurance, i.e., marine, fire, auto, personal liability, etc. The coded information related to the billing, accounting, and statistical experience of the branch offices. This information was then forwarded to the keypunch department for input into the company's computer system.

Prior to job enrichment, work was distributed to individuals without regard to the branch office that initiated it. Under the program, task modules were established, providing complexity, completeness, discretion, and feedback for a unit of work. After employees had been retrained, all work forwarded from branch offices was assigned to specific individuals, requiring them to perform all tasks and functions necessary to process the work. This created continuing individual accountability for a whole unit of work, and clearly associated individual workers with particular branch offices.

At about the same time that job enrichment was getting under way, a number of other changes were being implemented which affected the entire Deep River staff. Late in 1973 and early in 1974 a number of steps were taken in an effort to deal with a variety of other problems identified by the 1973 attitude survey. For example, carpeting was installed, employees were given better explanations of the company bonus plan, job classifications in a number of departments were revised, improved vending machines were installed in the lunchrooms, rest room facilities were improved, open posting of jobs was begun, greater effort was made to open

EXHIBIT 1
Employees Who Opted to Retain Enriched Jobs after Completion of the Trial Program

Unit	Number eligible for program	Number opting for and participating in program	Number opting to remain in program three months after end of program	Number opting to remain in program one year and three months after end of program	Percent remaining in program one year and three months after end of program
Auto-Liability Coding	31	23	9	3	13%
Loss Coding	31	5	2	1	20%
Special Multi-Peril Coding*	13	13	13	13	100%
Total	75	41	24	17†	41%

* Special multi-peril coders decided as a group to retain enriched jobs.
† The attrition from the program was not the result of turnover; two employees initially in the program quit the company in the spring of 1975, while two others quit in the spring of 1976. All had opted not to retain the enriched jobs before quitting.

communication channels between supervisors and subordinates, and a modified flexi-time program was instituted. Since management was attempting to deal with several pervasive problems, no incongruity was seen between these changes and the ongoing job enrichment program.

By the early part of 1974, 41 out of 75 eligible employees were performing enriched jobs. In March 1974, a follow-up attitude survey was conducted focusing on the same issues as its predecessor. To management's surprise and dismay, there was little or no change in employee attitudes. Responsibility, job content, and communication were still reacted to negatively. The results were particularly disappointing in view of the ongoing job enrichment program. Management had expected that enrichment would improve employee attitudes and when it did not, faith began to wane in its ability to produce the desired outcomes.

The final evaluation at the end of one year's operation of the program indicated some reduction in turnover and absenteeism. The productivity figures were less conclusive, however. While the situation in coding services had improved, the rest of the Deep River staff showed even greater gains. Based on these findings, management labeled the program a failure and decided to discontinue all job enrichment activity. They felt that the results of the program were not sufficiently impressive to justify the expense of job enrichment.

Anderson and his staff decided not to expand the program to other units in the Deep River office. But even though future job enrichment programs were shelved, branch coders were allowed to choose whether or not to retain their enriched jobs. Among the three units, SMP chose as a group to continue under the program; in ALC and Loss, only 4 of the 28 participating employees chose to remain and were still in the program one year and three months later (see Exhibit 1).

THE RESULTS OF JOB ENRICHMENT

Absenteeism

During the program absenteeism among participating employees showed marked improvement, as shown in Exhibit 2.

From October 1, 1974, average absenteeism in the enriched group dropped 2.2 days per year while among nonparticipating personnel it increased 2.9 days. During this same period the overall Deep River staff also experienced some improvement, but only 0.6 of a day.

According to the three unit supervisors in coding services, job enrichment had its most noticeable impact on absenteeism. When an enriched employee was absent for any period of time, the person's work was distributed to other members of the unit. This had an impact on the absent employee since errors made by someone else could interfere with the ongoing relationship established between the coder and the branch offices. Errors or delays, though made by someone else, were nevertheless the responsibility of the employee assigned to the branch. Rather than have to deal with problems created by others, employees apparently made a greater effort to be present.

EXHIBIT 2
Annual Absenteeism*

Coding Services	October 1, 1972 through October 1, 1973 (before Enrichment)	October 1, 1973 through October 1, 1974 (during Enrichment)
Enriched Job Participants .... (n = 41)	5.6	3.4
Nonenriched Job Participants .... (n = 34)	7.0	9.9
Deep River Clerical Staff (Exclusive of Coding Services) .... (n = 400)	7.8	7.2

* The average number of days absent per employee: the total number of absences in a year among the employees in a department divided by the average number of employees in that department.

Turnover

Turnover among participating employees was also reduced (see Exhibit 3). Turnover in the enriched group was reduced by 50 percent from the previous year. In addition, among employees on enriched tasks turnover was 10 percent less than among other personnel in coding services. However, this gain was overshadowed by the overall improvement in the Deep River office where turnover was 3 percent less than among the enriched group. To management it appeared that better results had been obtained without job enrichment.

Even though absenteeism had improved dramatically, turnover made a stronger impression on management. It was apparently viewed as much more important in terms of the company's operations.

EXHIBIT 3
Annual Turnover*

Coding Services	October 1, 1972 through October 1, 1973 (before Enrichment)	October 1, 1973 through October 1, 1974 (during Enrichment)
Enriched Job Participants .... (n = 41)	72.4%	32.6%
Nonenriched Job Participants .... (n = 34)	72.4%	43.1%
Deep River Clerical Staff (exclusive of Coding Services) .... (n = 400)	67.1%	29.6%

* The percentage of employee turnover per year: the total number of quits in a year divided by the total number of employees in the appropriate units.

Productivity

Management expected job enrichment to have a dramatic impact on productivity, but as Exhibit 4 indicates, the results of the program were inconclusive. Productivity through the third quarter of 1974 among enriched employees was 14.8 percent higher than the nonenriched group, but the overall trend in coding services was downward. From January 1, 1974, through October 1, 1974, productivity in the enriched group had dropped 2 percent (97.3 to 95.3). During the fourth quarter of 1974 this

EXHIBIT 4
Productive Efficiency in 1974 by Unit*

Unit		1st Quarter 1974	2nd Quarter 1974	3rd Quarter 1974	4th Quarter 1974
Loss Coding	Enriched (n = 5)	94.8%	89.8%	94.0%	100.8%
	Nonenriched (n = 26 to 28)	98.8	90.0	92.5	89.0
Auto-Liability Coding	Enriched (n = 23 to 24)	97.7	97.0	91.7	94.0
	Nonenriched (n = 7 to 8)	95.8	86.8	69.7	73.6
Special Multi-Peril Coding	Enriched (n = 13 to 18)	99.4	95.5	100.1	97.8
	Nonenriched (n = 0)	—	—	—	—
Total Coding Services	Enriched (n = 41 to 48)	97.3	94.1	95.3	97.5
	Nonenriched (n = 33 to 34)	88.0	88.5	81.1	80.0
Total Deep River Clerical Staff (exclusive of Coding Services (n = 400)		94.0	96.0	93.0	unknown†

* Productivity was measured by how effectively a unit of employees utilized its time: the unit's average efficiency (i.e., how much work it processed in a given period of time) multiplied by the average percentage of time on measurement (i.e., the amount of time the employees engaged in measured work. This excludes lunch breaks, rest breaks, training time, etc.).

† The utilization for the fourth quarter of 1974 was not computed for the total Deep River clerical staff by the company.

trend was reversed slightly. The enriched group increased to 97.5 percent by the end of 1974. During the first three quarters of 1974 productivity among the nonenriched employees declined from 88 percent to 81 percent, a drop of 7 percent, and the fourth quarter of 1974 showed a further decline to 80 percent.

Even though the overall experience of the enriched group was better than that of the nonenriched employees in coding services, the lack of a clear trend was disturbing to management. It was particularly so in comparison with the rest of the Deep River staff where productivity through the third quarter of 1974 had been almost stable.

When third quarter productivity for enriched employees was examined by unit only SMP showed any improvement. Loss was down slightly, as was ALC. Even though productivity among nonenriched employees in Loss and ALC was also down this offered management little solace. The productivity trends further reinforced management's growing skepticism about the utility of job enrichment.

Exit Interviews

Shortly after the formal end of the program on October 1, 1974, company organizational development personnel conducted interviews with 28 employees, selected at random from among those involved in job enrichment. The results showed that 82 percent of those interviewed felt the enriched tasks to be more interesting, but a large majority (79 percent) also felt participants should be paid more. Bonus making ability during enrichment was a major problem for 71 percent of these employees (see Exhibit 5).

EXHIBIT 5
Follow-up Interviews with Randomly Selected Participants in the Enrichment Program*

	Response	Percentage Agreeing (Total n = 28)
1.	The job was more interesting and enjoyable.	82
2.	Should be paid more.	79
	a. Job classification should be raised.	29
	b. Bonus making ability was a major problem.	71
	c. The job should be retimed.	54

* Content analysis of interviews with 28 of the 59 participants in job enrichment.
Source: Interviews conducted by home office organizational development personnel.

While these data reveal the basic problem encountered by management, comments made by the employees interviewed indicated even more forcefully the primary reason for their continuing discontent. The one item of greatest concern to the coders performing enriched tasks was the problem of lost bonus money during the program.

Comments as the following were common:

> "I like the idea of branch coding, but thank goodness I don't depend on the bonus money."

"I like branch coding but because you get such a variety of work it is very hard to make your efficiency. I think the rates [basic job classification] should be raised."

"I don't like branch coding, because without my bonus money my base pay is nothing. I find myself becoming very disgusted and not even caring about my work. You work harder now and have nothing to show for it."

"I like branch coding because of the variety of work, but I find I have nowhere near the efficiency I used to. If someone offered me a job that paid about the same as my base pay right now, I'd take it. Before, I never would because of my great bonus money. But now, I'd jump at the chance."

"I like branch coding because I like the variety of work . . . [but] I also think we do a lot of work for our pay—I mean I really work harder now than I did when I was a regular coder."

Within the individual units, employee reaction to job enrichment was much the same. For example, SMP branch coders felt the training was good, but the training payment was too low to adequately compensate for lost bonus earnings.

In response to the question: "How do you feel about the changes?" all four people interviewed in SMP responded that they were generally more satisfied with the enriched job. They liked having responsibility for particular clients. Most (three of four) felt they had more control over the work. All mentioned the increased task variety of the enriched job as a favorable feature. Their major gripes centered around the loss of bonus money which accompanied job redesign. They felt they should be paid a higher base salary since it was definitely harder to earn the same bonus on the new job.

ALC branch coders felt that their training payments had been inadequate when compared to the bonus they could have made on the old job during the same time period. Four of the coders interviewed in this unit were making significantly less bonus money than they had on the old job. The problem was not due to the intrusion of extra jobs into their work by the supervisors, but rather was seen as the need for adequate retiming of work standards to allow for the numerous new tasks involved. As one of the employees put it, "They (management) didn't look at the whole picture before putting it in (job enrichment)." Or as another stated, "It's more mental work for less money."

The comments from Loss were much the same. One coder, for example, said that her bonus had slipped from approximately $40 to $13 per week. This eventually caused her to drop out of the program, since, as she put it, "I'm working here for money."

Case 4–16 ————————————————————————————————
Job Enrichment Reconsidered— A Trial among Keypunch Operators

Paul J. Champagne

INTRODUCTION

When a job enrichment program succeeds, the explanation often given is that improved performance is the result of employee reactions to more interesting, exciting, challenging work. A recent article by Parke and Tausky (1975) suggests that this interpretation is erroneous. A better rationale may be found by examining the tangible consequences employees face as a result of their performance; attention should be focused on feedback, accountability, rewards, and penalties embedded in the organizational control structures. Which of these positions offers the best approach? The case reported here, implemented in the keypunch department of a major insurance company,[1] attempts to provide support for the latter.

THE THEORY OF JOB ENRICHMENT

The theoretical justification for most job enrichment programs is Herzberg's two-factor theory of motivation (1966), which in turn is based on Maslow's hierarchy of needs (1954). Herzberg's primary contribution is the hypothesis that job satisfaction and dissatisfaction, rather than being opposite points on a continuum, are two separate dimensions affected by different sets of variables. Satisfaction (and motivation) is the result of job content factors, such as achievement, responsibility, and growth in competence. Factors affecting the job environment (hygienes), such as pay, promotion, and fringe benefits, only lead to reduced dissatisfaction. Therefore, if jobs can be redesigned to allow for increased discretion, variety, and responsibility, workers will respond with improved work behavior.

In conjunction with Herzberg's theory, most job enrichment programs utilize several implementing concepts in order to evaluate and design jobs. The following action steps were part of this insurance company's program (Janson 1975):

1. *Natural Units of Work.* This is the process of grouping work items according to any logical system for the purpose of carving an individual responsibility out of a random group of work items. This can then become the basis for client identification and continuing accountability. Some logical grouping of work items are: parts of the alphabet or numerical systems, geographic areas, functions, types of business, single companies, groups of companies. Many others are possible as well.
2. *Client Relationships.* This is the process of establishing continuing ac-

—————————————
[1] The identity of the company is confidential.

countability for a unit of work and delineating all of the responsibilities and functions associated with that client.

3. *Job Module Design.* This involves assembling all the tasks and functions that can form one full process job assignment. Module Design is done by analysis of three dimensions of the job content:

    a. *Task Combination.* This requires analyzing all the tasks before, after, and around the job in lateral directions. Those that add meaningful growth opportunities are removed and reassigned or discontinued.

    b. *Vertical Analysis.* This is the process of loading into the job meaningful added responsibilities from the job above and deloading undesirable tasks which may be automated or discarded.

    c. *Diagonal Analysis.* This analysis requires examination of those tasks above the job being enriched which are currently being performed in another unit, division, or department. These responsibilities are loaded into the job when they are highly related to the core job and will complete the modular design of that job.

4. *Feedback Systems.* This refers to the usual supervisory feedback or performance data and also the more potent direct feedback which the employee receives himself directly from the job process. The intent is, of course, to provide the worker with continuous data with which to determine and correct his own errors, to build a "score card" on his performance, and be able to answer, continuously, the question "How am I doing?"

5. *Task Advancement.* This includes not only establishing paths for promotion but also the establishment of proficiency levels within the present job market by blocks of increasing responsibility enabling workers to mark their own growth on the way to promotion.

THE EVOLUTION OF THE PROGRAM

The program was an outgrowth of an ongoing Operations Improvement Program (OIP) concerned mainly with productivity and efficiency. Operating statistics revealed that in many areas the company was not meeting performance criteria deemed desirable. The personnel responsible for the OIP were aware of "quality of working life" developments, especially of the use of job enrichment to improve efficiency and, since the company was experiencing trouble with absenteeism, it seemed reasonable that the shortcomings of performance might be based in motivational problems. With this assumption, efforts were begun to institute a job enrichment trial program (Janson, 1975).

The program began July 1, 1970, and ended one year later. Its purpose was to alleviate problems of absenteeism, work quality, and work quantity. The employees who participated were members of two different keypunch units; one group served as a control, the other the test or achieving group. Several specific criteria were used in the selection of these participants. A group was sought which exhibited four major characteristics: (1) problems related to motivation; (2) boring tasks which would offer a real challenge to the effectiveness of job enrichment; (3) at least two units or sections performing the same work; and (4) a management team receptive to job enrichment.

The keypunch units satisfied all of these requirements and more.

IMPLEMENTING THE PROGRAM

Prior to July 1, 1970, a job reaction or attitude survey was administered to all keypunch operators and unit leaders. It attempted to measure nine areas felt to be related to work motivation. Specifically:

1. Is the work itself interesting?
2. Is the job wasteful of time and effort?
3. Is there freedom in planning the work?
4. Does the worker have a say in how the work is done?
5. Does the job provide opportunity to advance?
6. Is there job feedback?
7. Is the job too closely supervised?
8. Is the job worth putting effort into?
9. Is feedback from superiors awkward or tense?

In addition to the survey, a sample of keypunch operators from both control and test groups were interviewed in order to further determine their reactions to work. At the same time, work was begun to develop a system for measuring absenteeism, quantity of work, and quality of work.

MANAGEMENT SEMINAR

Early in July 1970, a three-day seminar was conducted for the operations director, management, and assistant manager of the data input division and the supervisor of the keypunch area designated as the achieving group. This three-day session took place in a location away from the office and possible work interruptions. The format for the material covered at this seminar was structured and controlled, but the atmosphere was informal in order to encourage a free exchange of views. Reading materials germane to the seminar were distributed prior to the actual sessions.

The contents of this initial seminar included the following:

1. A review of the research on job attitudes and behavior.
2. An opportunity for the attendees to examine their personal attitudes toward people and work.
3. An orientation to Herzberg's motivation-hygiene theory and its relation to the job enrichment program.
4. A practical examination of job enrichment implementation techniques and their problems.
5. Discussions concerning the role of the management team in creating meaningful work.

JOB ENRICHMENT WORKSHOP

Following the management seminar, a three-day Job Enrichment Workshop was conducted during August 1970 for the unit leaders, supervisor, and assistant supervisor of the achieving group. This group was also given reading material in advance, and the techniques used to introduce job enrichment concepts were similar to those utilized the previous month for the middle and first level management personnel.

The first day of this workshop was devoted to a review of the major concepts and ideas of job enrichment. Following that, the second and third days were concerned with greenlighting/redlighting sessions. The greenlighting session was without restrictions and participants were encouraged to suggest ideas free from any discussion of their feasibility. Once the first few ideas were coaxed from the group, the rest followed in swift succession with little or no resistance.

By the time the workshop ended, a total of 73 possible job change items had been introduced. It was then necessary to establish an action plan whereby each greenlight item could be researched for feasibility and methods of implementation. It was agreed by the group to hold weekly meetings, following the workshop to redlight or weed out impossible or impractical greenlight items, and by the end of 1970, the original list of 73 items had been reduced to 25 for implementation.

For purposes of analysis, four items were most important: First, keypunch operators would become responsible for their own work. Included in their enriched job was responsibility for scheduling—and for meeting those schedules.

Second, operators would correct obvious coding errors. Prior to the job enrichment trial, they were told to punch information as they saw it. Since they know coding well, it was frustrating for them to punch the wrong codes.

Third, each operator would correct her own errors. Previously, the errors came back from the computer and were given to any operator to correct. The new system provided feedback and aided in training.

Fourth, operators would deal directly with clients. Before the trial, work from unidentified sources was given to them in one hour batches. After enrichment, an operator had her own customers with full responsibility for those clients' jobs. If there was a problem, the operator, not the supervisor, would discuss it with the client. (This approach brought in an aspect of entrepreneurship and accountability.)

Throughout the entire implementation process, unit leaders were encouraged to continue the greenlighting process on their own in order to reinforce the feeling that job enrichment was more a continuing style of leadership than a one-time program. In addition, each leader maintained a chart for the people in her unit. Whenever a new responsibility was given to a keypunch operator, that fact was recorded and dated on the implementation chart.

RESULTS OF THE PROGRAM

The results of the project were even more favorable than management had originally expected. Turnover was the only area that did not show improvement but this was never a real problem anyway. According to management the improvements in work behavior resulted in actual cost savings of $65,000 annually, with potential savings of $90,000 annually.

QUANTITY OF WORK

Two measures of productivity were kept in the keypunch group: the Throughput Rate and Effectiveness Ratio results.

The Throughput Rate was a measure of the average number of computer cards keypunched per hour of work, including verifying for accuracy. As Exhibit 1 illustrates, both control and achieving groups were fairly similar in throughput at the start of job enrichment. After nine months, the achieving group increased its throughput by 39.6 percent, while the control group increased only 8.1 percent. Stated another way, the achieving group had increased its capacity to process work by nearly 40 percent.

EXHIBIT 1
Throughput Percentage Increase or Decrease: Control Group versus Achieving Group (job enrichment implementation period compared with base period [January 1970–July 1970] average)

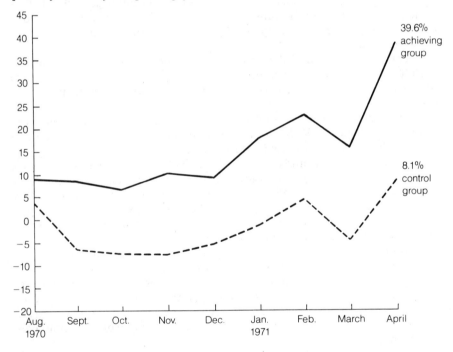

The Effectiveness Ratio indicated the number of hours required to complete a given number of computer cards as compared with the number of hours that should be required as determined by work measurement standards. At the start of job enrichment the achieving group was at 78 percent of standard. At the conclusion of the program they were operating at 104 percent, an increase of 26 percent.

ATTITUDES TOWARD WORK

Attitude surveys were administered both before and after job enrichment. Nine categories of job attitudes noted above were measured and in all cases the post job enrichment survey showed an improvement for the achieving group. The results for the control group were essentially static. The achieving group's score on all nine items rose 16.5 percent (see Exhibit 2). Management considered this to be a significant upturn considering the type of job involved.

EXHIBIT 2
Job Reaction

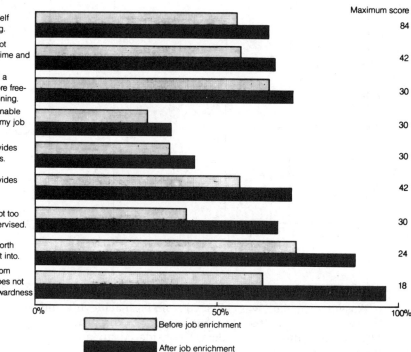

	Maximum score
1 The work itself is interesting.	84
2 The job is not wasteful of time and effort.	42
3 I do not feel a need for more freedom in planning.	30
4 I have reasonable say on how my job is done.	30
5 The job provides opportunities.	30
6 The job provides feedback.	42
7 The job is not too closely supervised.	30
8 The job is worth putting effort into.	24
9 Feedback from superiors does not involve awkwardness or tension.	18

Before job enrichment
After job enrichment

QUALITY OF WORK

Data was collected for approximately 40 achieving group keypunch operators. Prior to job enrichment, 40 percent of these operators were punching work of outstanding quality. Outstanding was considered to be an error rate of 0.5 of 1 percent or less. At the conclusion of the program 55 percent of the operators had achieved an outstanding rating while operators in the "poor" group decreased 50 percent (see Exhibit 3). Poor work was considered to be anything over a 4 percent error ratio.

For the two months prior to the study, the 40 operators had a collective error rate of 1.53 percent. For two months toward the end of the study the collective rate was reduced to 0.99 percent.

EXHIBIT 3
Quality of Work

Percentage of achieving group

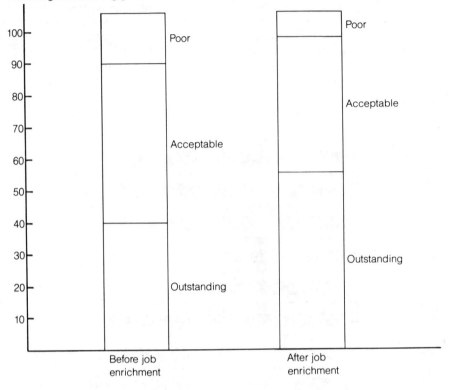

Before job
enrichment

After job
enrichment

ABSENTEEISM

Absenteeism data was collected from both achieving and control groups for two periods of time, 11 months prior to the program and 11 months after its initiation. Management considered an absence to be any sick time and any unpaid personal time.

As Exhibit 4 illustrates, the absenteeism rate for the achieving group, prior to job enrichment, was approximately ten days per employee per year. This compared to 8.5 days in the control group. After the program, absenteeism in the achieving group went down to slightly more than 7 days, while the control group increased to just over 11 days. These figures represented an improvement of 24 percent for the achieving group and a decline of 29 percent for the control group.

REACTIONS OF EMPLOYEES

In addition to the hard data, taped interviews were held with operators before and after job enrichment. The comments listed below were typical.

EXHIBIT 4
Absenteeism

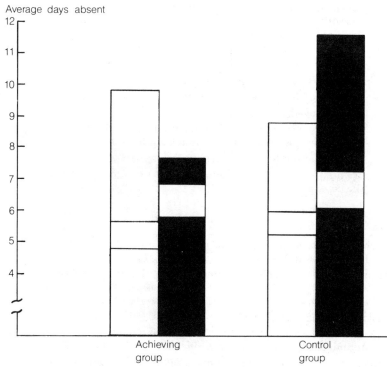

While these did not give a quantitative picture of changing response to the job, management felt that they represented an accurate change in the attitudes of employees. This was further evidence for the success of the program. Responses were as follows:

Before Job Enrichment

> "I do the same job all day long. Time drags and I end up watching the clock. If I thought I was going to do this same thing for even six more months, I wouldn't do it."
>
> "I'd like a job with more responsibility."
>
> "They don't care if the work is right or wrong, just send it through. You can't take any pride in that."
>
> "The job is more aggravating than enjoyable."
>
> "Nobody likes to do junky work."
>
> "They don't seem to know you're around."
>
> "It's not the money. You can't really be happy if that's all you're working for."
>
> "If I was called upon to do more than just sit there and get the work out it would be better. I'd feel more into things."

After Job Enrichment

Question: Do you talk about your job much at home?
Answer: Once in a while I tell my husband little things.
Question: What was the last thing you told him?
Answer: I said, "Hey, they're letting some of us have our work go un-
verified. Pretty good, huh?"

"I feel good because the responsibility rests with me."

"Everyone knows their job. We work as a team."

"Now I have a complete job."

"I know our supervisor will make the right decision for the people in the
Department. He has grown so much in the past year."

"We're allowed to make decisions."

"I know why we're here doing what we're doing. We can make money for
the company."

CASE REFERENCES

Herzberg, Frederick. *Work and the Nature of Man.* Cleveland: World Publishing Co., 1966.

Janson, Robert. "A Job Enrichment Trial in Data Processing—in an Insurance Company." In Louis E. Davis and Albert B. Cherns, eds., *The Quality
of Working Life.* New York: The Free Press, 1975.

Maslow, Abraham H. *Motivation and Personality.* New York: Harper, 1954.

Park, E. Lauck, and Tausky, Curt. "The Mythology of Job Enrichment: Self-
Actualization Revisited." *Personnel* 52 (1975), pp. 12–21.

Skinner, B. F. *Beyond Freedom and Dignity.* New York: Vintage Books, 1971.